Inflation, Depression and Economic Policy in the West

Inflation, Depression and Economic Policy in the West

edited by
Anthony S. Courakis

1981
MANSELL, London
ALEXANDRINE PRESS, Oxford

ISBN 0 7201 0915 9 (Mansell Publishing)
0 906661 00 5 (Alexandrine Press)

Mansell Publishing, a part of Bemrose U.K. Limited,
3 Bloomsbury Place, London WC1A 2QA

Alexandrine Press, P.O. Box 15, 51 Cornmarket Street,
Oxford OX1 3EB

First published 1981

British Library Cataloguing in Publication Data

Inflation, depression and economic policy in the West

   1.   Economic history – 1945–
   I.   Courakis, A S
   330.9'181'2   HC59

   ISBN 0–7201–0915–9 (Mansell Publishing)
   ISBN 0–906661–00–5 (Alexandrine Press)

Printed in Great Britain by Henry Ling Ltd, at the Dorset Press, Dorchester Dorset and bound by Mansell (Bookbinders) Ltd, Witham, Essex.

Contents

The Contributors

MICHAEL ARTIS, Professor of Economics, University of Manchester.

HORST BOCKELMANN, Director, the Deutsche Bundesbank.

JEAN-CLAUDE CHOURAQUI, Head, Monetary and Fiscal Policy Division, OECD and Lecturer at the Institut d'Etudes Politiques de Paris.

ANTHONY S. COURAKIS, Fellow, Brasenose College, Oxford.

EMILE DEN DUNNEN, Economic Adviser, the Nederlandsche Bank, N.V.

WALTER ELTIS, Fellow, Exeter College, Oxford.

CHARLES GOODHART, Chief Adviser, Bank of England.

ROBERT J. GORDON, Professor of Economics, Northwestern University and Research Associate, U.S. National Bureau of Economic Research.

JOHN A. KAY, Research Director, Institute of Fiscal Studies and Fellow, St John's College, Oxford.

ROBERT MABRO, Fellow, St Anthony's College, Oxford.

RAINER MASERA, Head, International Monetary and Fiscal Problems Section, Banca d'Italia.

MARIO MONTI, Chief Economic Adviser, Banca Commerciale d'Italia and Professor, Universities of Milan and Turin.

TOMMASO PADOA-SCHIOPPA, Head, Banking and Financial Markets Section, Banca d'Italia.

PETER SINCLAIR, Fellow, Brasenose College, Oxford.

Preface

'The ultimate goal of a positive science', Friedman once remarked, 'is the development of a theory that yields valid and meaningful predictions about phenomena not yet observed. Such a theory is in general a complex intermixture of two elements. In part it is a language designed to promote systematic and organized methods of reasoning. In part it is a body of substantive hypotheses designed to abstract essential features of complex reality.' From this standpoint the experience of the last ten years has posed and, as recent developments suggest, continues to pose many challenges to the profession. Inflation, unemployment, wage behaviour, falling profits, company liquidity, falling investment, rising savings ratios and erosion in the real value of personal sector assets, the share of government in total income and expenditure, the size and means of financing budget deficits, the rate of growth of monetary aggregates, the structure of financial markets, the impact of oil prices and more generally behaviour in commodity markets, the role of exchange rate variations, the role of incomes policy, the role of demand management policies, the nature of expectations, spring easily to mind as pieces in the puzzle of interrelationships that policymakers and academic economists have had to rethink and which, with varying degrees of emphasis and coverage as between countries, comprise the subject of this volume.

Most of the papers included in this volume were presented to a conference organized with the financial support of Fox-Pitt Kelton Inc. To them and to Bridget Rosewell who helped with the organization of the conference, to the authors for revisions to their papers for publication, and to Nicholas Weinreb for help in compiling the index, I wish to express my thanks.

Anthony S. Courakis

2 riders :- — monetary expansion, not fiscal
— open economy, taking into a/c fixed/floating ex- r
not closed economy.

International Monetarism, Wage Push, and Monetary Accommodation[1]

Robert J. Gordon

The 'monetarist' view of . . . the acceleration of inflation since 1965 [is] that it has been the ultimate consequence of an increase in the rate of world monetary expansion, an increase attributable primarily to the excessively expansionary monetary policy pursued by the United States in recent years.

Harry G. Johnson[2]

I find the alternative explanation . . . which regards the basic cause as increased trade-union militancy . . . more plausible.

Nicholas Kaldor[3]

There is little doubt, then, that the wage-inflation idea does not apply to the inflationary experiences we have seen in the real world . . . Only when the macroeconomic implications of the wage-inflation hypothesis are traced through and confronted with the facts does it become apparent that it cannot be sustained.

Arnold C. Harberger[4]

1. Introduction

While 'supply shocks' in oil and food are widely agreed to have aggravated the inflation problem in many countries in 1973–75, no consensus has yet emerged to explain the earlier acceleration of inflation between the mid–1960s and 1970–72 in the major industrialized nations outside of North America. Instead, two major schools of thought, 'international monetarist' and 'wage push', have developed alternative explanations having radically different policy implications. The first group views inflation within a conventional macroeconomic framework as an 'international monetary phenomenon' and identifies its fundamental cause as an excess demand for commodities generated by government actions. Any attempt to bring in other factors, particularly those of the wage-push variety, is dismissed as a resort to 'amateur sociology and politics' which can play 'no part whatsoever in the problem'[5]. The wage-push or 'sociological' school of thought disagrees, pointing to the spontaneous wage explosions which occurred in a number of European countries in 1968 and 1970 as evidence of the special non-economic character of the recent inflation. Wage claims are viewed as part of a continuing conflict over income shares among competing social groups, and the events of the 1968–70 period reflected labour's 'long-smouldering resentment and dissatisfaction'[6].

2. Aims of the Paper

The sources of inflation in the main industrialized nations in the period of fixed exchange rates have not yet been adequately established. Both the international-monetarist and wage-push arguments are unsatisfactory and incomplete. The acceleration of wages and prices in 1969–70 in the major nations outside of the United States followed a continuing *deceleration* of their rates of monetary growth between 1963 and 1969. For the 'world'—the United States plus seven other important industrial nations[7]—the 1969–70 acceleration of wage rates preceded by almost a year the 1971 explosion of money and international reserves, in apparent conflict with the international-monetarist explanation. Wage-push proponents have not made their case either, because autonomous wage increases do not automatically pass into the price level.

This paper accepts from the outset the proposition that world inflation must in the long run be a world monetary phenomenon. Confirmation of a connection between the rates of growth of world money and prices, as in several recent studies, is viewed as only the first step in the development of a fuller understanding of the inflation process, because the sources of changes in world money are left unexplained[8]. A correlation between world prices and money does not rule out wage push as a source of world monetary growth. Instead of viewing international-monetary and wage-push factors as competitive explanations of inflation, a more comprehensive theoretical framework is presented which incorporates these two ingredients as possible explanations of the behaviour of the monetary authorities, together with fiscal deficits, supply shocks, and a countercyclical monetary reaction function.

Since a time-series correlation between inflation and monetary growth is consistent with several sources of monetary growth, a more discriminating empirical methodology is required. An empirical study of the United States and seven other major industrial nations attempts to determine whether the data are consistent with an effect of any or all of the possible sources of monetary accommodation.

Among the major questions to be answered are the following: If U.S. monetary growth is to be blamed for the acceleration of inflation in other countries, by what channels was this impulse transmitted? Did patterns of causation differ among countries? Were some countries better able than others to pursue countercyclical rather than procyclical monetary policies? Did differences across countries in the degree of accommodation to supply shocks in 1974 correspond with the degree of accommodation to wage push or reserve inflows in the earlier period? Do episodes of wage push identified by others appear to have been genuinely exogenous or were they preceded by episodes of monetary accommodation? Can the breakdown of the Bretton Woods system be treated ultimately as another casualty of the Vietnam War, or did domestic events in other countries play a role?

Answers to these questions are useful not only for an understanding of history, but for future policymaking: Is control of the money supply either necessary or sufficient for a nation to control its inflation rate? Is it likely that monetary authorities will be able in the future to insulate the inflation rate from the tendencies to wage push, or are incomes policies required as a cure?

Finally, the paper raises a methodological question of interest to many economists caught in the middle without any particular allegiance to an international-monetarist or wage-push view of the world: Can econometric techniques uncover *systematic* tendencies toward procyclical accommodation or countercyclical activism on the part of central banks, or do shifting targets and priorities defy statistical generalizations and call instead for a more descriptive and anecdotal approach to monetary history?

3. International-Monetarist Approach

The international-monetarist approach begins from the proposition that under fixed exchange rates the world inflation rate is determined primarily by previous changes in the rate of growth of the world money supply. This follows from two basic propositions which previously had been emphasized by U.S. monetarists addressing issues of a closed economy: the stability of the demand-for-money function, and the lack of any long-run tradeoff between inflation and unemployment. Both of these elements have been tested by international-monetarist economists who have estimated structural equations describing the behaviour of the demand-for-money function and the expectational Phillips curve for the 'world' (usually the Group of Ten)[9]. Further, reduced-form tests have found that changes in the world rate of monetary growth have preceded changes in the world inflation rate[10].

The behaviour of individual countries is characterized not only by stable national demand-for-money functions and vertical long-run Phillips curves, but by two additional features. First, capital is mobile among nations, so that international reserves tend to flow in or out as necessary to set a nation's money supply equal to its demand for money, which depends primarily on its price level, real output, and interest rate[11]. Second, commodity arbitrage maintains the tradable-goods portion of the domestic price level fairly close to the world price level of tradable goods, while labour mobility communicates changes in prices of tradable goods to the nontradables sector[12]. Thus any event that raises the foreign price level tends to push up both the domestic price level and the domestic money supply, irrespective of the reaction of the domestic monetary authorities.

The international-monetarist approach traces the acceleration of inflation outside the United States in the late 1960s back to U.S. fiscal deficits incurred to pay for Vietnam expenditures, which induced an acceleration in the growth rate of the U.S. money supply and price level. Inflation then spread from the United States to other countries by four main channels of transmission[13]. First, the 'direct price influence' working through commodity arbitrage raised the prices of tradable goods everywhere. This then pushed up the marginal value product of labour and of other factors of production and hence domestic costs, raising the prices of nontradable goods[14]. Second, the trade surpluses of other nations induced by the fact that U.S. income growth was higher than their own, as well as by deteriorating U.S. price competitiveness, boosted foreign levels of production and income through the conventional 'Keynesian demand-pressure mechanism'. Third, the 'Bretton Woods monetization channel' allowed U.S. balance-of-payments deficits to be paid for by the creation of U.S. dollar liabilities which expanded the monetary base of many nations and further fueled their own domestic inflation rates. Fourth, an acceleration of U.S. inflation could have raised domestic expectations of inflation directly, leading to higher wage and price increases. The channels were connected, since the direct effects of higher prices for tradable goods, higher real output, and higher expected prices for nontradable goods, all raised a nation's transaction demand for money and, with freely mobile capital, attracted the international reserves needed to bring the domestic money supply into equality with higher money demand.

In the long run under fixed exchange rates, then, policymakers in small countries should regard inflation as part of the external environment rather than under their own control. Domestic 'wage push' by unions cannot contribute to domestic inflation; worker groups that achieve a higher nominal wage when the price level is determined abroad can raise their own incomes only at the expense of unemployment and lower profits, particularly in the tradable-goods sector. Incomes policies designed to control wage push may be able to influence the unemployment rate or the distribution of income, but not the inflation rate.

But the international monetarist's denial of a role for an autonomous wage push in the world inflation process is not totally convincing, because the symmetry between tradable-goods prices and domestic wages is ignored. Both are determinants of domestic prices and the transaction demand for money. An autonomous wage push could raise the demand for money and, with perfect capital mobility, suck in the reserves needed to provide the base for a higher domestic money supply. If commodity arbitrage is perfect, the profits of firms in the tradable-goods sector will be squeezed, but there is some evidence that commodity arbitrage is not perfect, at least in the short run[15]. The increase in domestic monetary growth would contribute to an acceleration in world monetary growth and in the world rate of inflation, particularly if an autonomous wage push were to occur in several countries simultaneously.

4. The Wage-Push, or 'Sociological', Explanation

In its most extreme form, proponents of the wage-push view argue that the inflation rate depends entirely on the aggressiveness of labour unions in pressing wage demands. Peter Wiles has claimed, for instance, that 'we have moved from wage claims based on the actual situation in the trade . . . to claims picked out of the air. . . .'[16]. The underlying source of wage push is viewed variously as a conflict over the fairness of the income distribution and wage structure; as the result of the rise of the tactics of the New Left and the decline of authority; and as a consequence of a communications revolution that increased awareness of foreign wage claims. The independent influence of money and aggregate demand is often viewed as negligible[17].

While money is sometimes rejected as a *cause* of wage behaviour, changes in money are viewed as a *consequence* of wage push in many discussions. Sooner or later the central bank will have to raise the money supply in order to accommodate the higher transaction demand for money created by higher wages. Richard Cooper has made this point succinctly:

> The wage level in the modern economy is indeterminant because in the final analysis the monetary authorities must—for political reasons—provide a money supply adequate to ratify any given level of money wages, no matter how it was reached, in order to avoid excessive unemployment[18].

Some British commentators admit the monetary connection[19]. But this acknowledgment is by no means universal[20].

Several investigators have found that wage equations for major European countries require the use of dummy variables to explain particular episodes of sudden acceleration in the rate of wage change[21]. While a significant positive coefficient on a dummy variable indicates only that something is happening that cannot be otherwise explained, the timing of the wage accelerations correspond to widely recognized incidents of aggressive labour behaviour, particularly the French general strike of May 1968, and the Italian 'hot autumn' of 1969.

The wage-push explanation has been universally condemned by proponents of the international-monetarist view, but empirical critiques by international monetarists have involved tests of unnecessarily restrictive versions of the sociological approach. For instance, any influence on wages of excess commodity or labour demand or proxies for inflationary expectations is cited as negative evidence, implicitly ruling out a more eclectic framework in which both the aggressiveness of workers and conventional economic variables might be influential. Further, tests by international monetarists have measured wage-push effects by including variables representing time lost in strikes rather than the dummy variables cited earlier. To the extent that workers achieve their wage aims by threats of strikes that are not actually carried out, wage push could exist but nevertheless be uncorrelated with strike variables[22]. Unfortunately, this problem makes it difficult to link puzzling episodes identified by significant coefficients on dummy variables to any quantifiable proxy for labour militancy.

5. The Demand for and Supply of Monetary Accommodation

International monetary effects and wage push are only two of the possible sources of inflation. A useful framework for analysis of the sources of inflation is to distinguish factors which create pressure on the central bank to 'accommodate', that is to react by raising the money supply, and those factors which help to explain why the central bank reacts as it does to these sources of pressure. A 'demand for monetary accommodation' is created by domestic demand shifts, domestic cost push, and demand and supply shocks from abroad. The 'supply of monetary accommodation' by the central bank depends on the weights in its countercyclical reaction function, its own degree of political independence from the government, and the extent of the government's attempts to influence its chances for re-election by manipulating the economy[23].

DOMESTIC DEMAND SHIFTS

When the real money supply is held constant, an increase in domestic expenditures will tend to alter interest rates, whether its source is a change in consumer attitudes, business expectations, government spending, or tax rates. An increase in spending shifts the 'IS curve' of intermediate macroeconomic theory to the right up a fixed 'LM curve', and the central bank is forced to raise the money supply if it desires to offset part or all of the in-

crease in interest rates which would otherwise occur. Thus part of the blame
for the 1963–66 acceleration of the rate of monetary growth in the United
States can be attributed to the boom in automobile spending and fixed investment, not just to the tax cuts of 1964–65 and the acceleration of defence
spending which began in 1965.

The classic source of pressure for monetary accommodation is the need
by governments to finance higher expenditures, particularly in episodes of
war and post-war reconstruction, when taxes are costly or impossible to
collect. The optimum inflation rate occurs when the marginal costs imposed
by inflation on holders of money balances are equated to the marginal
administrative and allocative costs imposed by conventional taxes[24]. In
general it will be optimal for the government budget to be financed partially
by money creation, and the rate of money creation will depend positively on
the share of government spending in income, and negatively on the costs imposed by taxes.

Thus money creation tends to accelerate during wartime both because the
government spends more and because taxes are harder to collect, and tends
to be higher in countries where tax evasion raises the cost of collecting direct
taxes. A temporary acceleration of government spending during wartime is
more likely to be financed by money creation than a permanent acceleration
during peacetime which justifies additional facilities and personnel for the
collection of conventional taxes. Taxpayers stand to gain from inflation at
the expense of holders of nominal-fixed assets, so that money creation is
likely when the political position of the latter group is weak, as during the
Russian Civil War hyperinflation of 1918–21. In countries with thin or
underdeveloped capital markets, fiscal deficits cannot be financed by sales of
interest-bearing bonds, also tending to lead to money creation. This last
factor may be unimportant in an open economy with freely mobile capital
and widespread investor confidence, since the national debt can be sold to
foreigners rather than to the central bank.

COST PUSH

Central banks may be under pressure not only from autonomous demand
shifts, but also from autonomous wage and price increases negotiated in the
private sector. The chain of causation between cost push and monetary
accommodation is likely not to be unidirectional but to operate both ways,
since workers will be more likely to make large wage demands and firms will
be more likely to accede to them when there is a widespread expectation
based on past behaviour that the central bank will provide the money
needed to pay the bill[25]. At first glance the motivation for wage push may
seem elusive, at least in a closed economy, since prices are likely to be
marked up over any autonomous wage increases achieved by workers,
leaving real wages unchanged. Further, workers who 'push' thereby take

the risk that the monetary authority will not accommodate, in which case they will have created unemployment for themselves, although this direct connection between money, wage claims, and unemployment may not be an important constraint on union leaders in countries with decentralized bargaining, e.g. the United States.

In the long run with centralized bargaining an autonomous wage push, if accommodated, raises the inflation rate and redistributes income away from holders of money toward taxpayers, including the workers who initiate the process. In the short run more varied patterns of redistribution are possible. For instance, the workers initiating the push may gain at the expense of other workers who have less market power or who are tied to existing contracts. Even if a push causes unemployment, the first fired will be the last hired, possibly leaving the older and more senior workers who control union politics with a net gain[26].

Finally, an additional channel for redistribution is present in an open economy with fixed exchange rates, where the prices of tradable goods are linked to prices in the rest of the world. A domestic wage push may achieve a restribution by squeezing profits in tradable-goods industries, at least during a transition period before devaluation occurs.

Perry and other commentators have cited a 'contagion' hypothesis to explain the simultaneous emergence of wage push in several countries in 1968 and 1970. An explanation is also needed for differences among countries in the 'propensity to push'. The extent of nationalized industry is cited by some writers as a source of wage push and for the intemperance of British and Italian unions as contrasted with those in Germany, Sweden, and the United States. Nationalized industries are weaker opponents for unions than are private firms who fear that they may be bankrupted if monetary accommodation fails to occur. First, the demand for the products of nationalized industries is relatively inelastic; second, there is no particular pressure to raise prices if the government stands ready to subsidize increased industry losses; and third, those losses (like any fiscal deficit) add to the pressure for monetary accommodation.

An interesting distinction can be made between countries whose 'common-interest organizations' (unions, cartels) were destroyed during or after World War II, and those whose institutions have become rigidified by inertia and the passage of time[27]. Another source of conflict over the income distribution in the form of wage push may be a cultural aversion to rational negotiation:

> ... Various groups maintain and prize an attitude and phraseology of unbending opposition and hostility ... The Chilean situation appears to be weighted more heavily with the avoidance of agreement, with the maintenance of a militant stance as the desired benefit and inflation as its cost[28].

The ideological orientation of the British and Italian labour movements may make nationalization and wage push indirectly the result of the same inbred cultural trait in those two countries.

Supply shocks, e.g. crop failures or the formation of commodity cartels, are like any other type of cost push in creating problems for the monetary authorities. Failure to accommodate will create unemployment, but accommodation may unleash an inflationary spiral if workers attempt to maintain their original real wage level intact. In this sense escalator contracts which rigidify the real wage structure raise the chances for hyperinflation and thus reduce the likelihood that the authorities will take the risk of accommodation[29]. In the same way, the reaction of authorities to a wage push depends on a guess whether workers will push again after mark-up price increases by firms have eroded initial real wage gains.

DEMAND AND SUPPLY SHOCKS IN AN OPEN ECONOMY

An increase in foreign demand is communicated to the domestic economy through an increase in the price of tradable goods, both imports and exports, and through an increase in the trade surplus, which raises real GNP. The trade surplus directly creates added foreign exchange reserves, and this effect is reinforced if the monetary authorities maintain the initial level of the domestic component of the monetary base ('domestic credit'), since higher prices and output raise the demand for money and pull in the extra reserves needed to support a higher money supply. Thus in the case of a 'demand shock' from abroad, there is an unambiguous expansionary effect transmitted through the three channels of price, income, and monetary effects.

Monetary accommodation is automatic under fixed exchange rates when capital is mobile, and the domestic money supply depends on the determinants of domestic money demand, prices, output, and the world interest rate. Domestic initiatives in monetary policy are impossible with perfect capital mobility. An open-market purchase which expands domestic credit is offset by an equivalent decline in international reserves, and an open-market sale designed to counteract the inflationary effects of a domestic cost push will be futile as well[30]. In this sense capital mobility provides an incentive to workers and others considering an autonomous push, since their own actions can directly induce a rise in the money supply by pulling in international reserves. Only when capital is less than perfectly mobile can the central bank attempt to sterilize part of the reserve inflow by open-market sales of its domestic assets, restrictive rediscount policy, or an increase in the reserve requirements of commercial banks.

THE SUPPLY OF MONETARY ACCOMMODATION AND
THE MONETARY REACTION FUNCTION

The mere existence of pressure on the central bank does not imply that it will act either to accommodate or to resist. A central bank following

Friedman's constant growth-rate rule for the money supply would ignore such pressures entirely[31]. More likely is a central bank which attempts to vary the growth of the money supply, or some other monetary instrument over which it believes it has more direct control, with the aim of maximizing a social-welfare function. Higher unemployment and inflation, and lower foreign exchange reserves, are all evils which may be resisted by counter-vailing shifts in monetary policy. There is a large literature in the United States and Canada on 'monetary reaction functions' which estimate the response of the central bank to changes in the target variables[32].

Two sets of conflicts constrain the reaction of policymakers. First, even an idealistic attempt to maximize society's welfare collides with the in-compatibility of achieving short-run improvements in both unemployment and inflation, or both unemployment and the foreign balance. In those rare situations when the economy is initially at optimum inflation and un-employment rates, idealistic motives would lead to monetary restriction in response to a higher domestic fiscal deficit or an expansionary foreign demand shock. But wage push and supply shocks allow no easy solutions, for a central bank must choose whether to resist their stimulus to inflation by contracting or, alternatively, to resist unemployment by expanding.

Second, 'idealistic' weights on target variables derived from economic theory may conflict with 'popularity' weights motivated by political expediency. Evidence of a substantial lag of inflation behind changes in un-employment introduces a distinction between short-run targets which maxi-mize votes for an incumbent government's re-election, and long-run targets which maximize economic welfare. Lindbeck has stressed the distinction between long-run 'idealistic' weights on alternative policy targets and short-run 'popularity' weights influenced by the possibility of exploiting lags for electoral advantage[33]. And Nordhaus has examined an extreme case where myopic voters learn nothing from past elections and provide an incentive to policymakers who manage to create a roaring output expansion sufficiently close to election day so that the lagged inflationary consequences occur after the incumbents are safely re-elected[34].

The most important implication of the political inflation literature is that the link between the sources of pressure for monetary accommodation and the monetary reaction which emerges may be highly variable. Fiscal deficits or wage push may induce a more expansive reaction during the year pre-ceding election day than during other periods of an incumbent's term, leaving the relation between these factors and inflation too loose to identify by the simple econometric techniques used heretofore.

Other than papers on the timing of elections, little has been written on political factors which favour inflation. Hibbs presents evidence that inflation rates in postwar Europe have been proportional to the extent of participation of socialist/labour parties in government[35]. Michael Parkin argues in the British context that inflation has been encouraged by the political power of young debt-ridden 'swing voters' who shift their fickle support to the party which appears most likely to inflate away the real value of their debts[36]. Finally, in those countries where the central bank is institutionally relatively insulated from the political process (United States, West Germany), one is less likely to observe a disparity between the idealistic and popularity weights on economic targets[37].

6. A Framework for Empirical Testing

The general framework developed in the preceding section identifies a large number of variables upon which the behaviour of the domestic money supply may depend—private and government expenditures, wage push, foreign prices, international reserves, domestic unemployment, and elections. The aim of the empirical section is to determine whether any of the component hypotheses can be confirmed or denied, for the United States, for the 'Other Seven' (the aggregate of seven major industrial countries besides the United States), or for any of the seven countries individually.

CHAINS OF CAUSATION

The central task of the empirical work is to estimate an equation in which the growth rate of the money supply is the dependent variable, and the set of independent variables includes those claimed above to be possible determinants of central-bank behaviour. In addition to the money equation, equations with the growth rates of wages and prices as alternative dependent variables are estimated, in order to assess the role of autonomous wage push as a source of inflation. Table 1 lays out the expected pattern of signs on coefficients in equations explaining the behaviour of the money supply and domestic wages, according to the various subhypotheses.

For instance, the first column lists the pattern of signs in the money equation predicted by the international-monetarist view. Consider the response of the economy to a foreign demand shock, the type of event that the international-monetarist approach blames for the worldwide acceleration of inflation in the late 1960s and early 1970s. Higher foreign demand stimulates both higher domestic output and higher tradable-goods prices. The simultaneous increase in reserves is partly a direct result of the trade surplus, and partly an indirect result of the higher demand for money induced by both the price and output effects. A money-supply equation should exhibit positive signs on current or lagged determinants of money demand, particularly domestic prices and output. Because of the focus here on the after-effects of autonomous wage movements, the domestic price index is

Table 1. Pattern of coefficients in money and wage equations predicted by five subhypotheses.

	Money equation					Wage equation		
	International monetarist	Wage push		Deficit financing	Counter-cyclical reaction function	International monetarist	Wage push	
		With monetary accommodation	Without monetary accommodation				With monetary accommodation	Without monetary accommodation
Independent variable	(1)	(2)	(3)	(4)	(5)	(6)	(7)	(8)
1. Money	...	...	...	...	...	+	+	+
2. Wage rate	+	+	0	...	<1.0	...	...	...
3. Domestic output	+	...	...	...	−	+	+	±
4. Traded-goods prices	+	(+)	(0)	...	<1.0	+	+	+
5. Full-employment fiscal deficit	...	...	...	+	...	...	...	...
6. International reserves	+	...	...	...	+	+	...	...
7. Autonomous wage-push dummy variables	...	...	...	...	...	0	+	+

Sources: See text discussion. The parentheses on traded-goods prices for the wage-push subhypotheses in the money equation indicate that consistency is not a necessary feature of those approaches.

proxied in table 1 by the combination of tradable-goods prices and domestic wages. The role of international reserves is to identify the effect on money-supply growth of shifts in the demand for money caused by factors other than tradable-goods prices and domestic output and wages. The absence of a positive sign on international reserves in the money equation suggests the possibility that central banks succeed in varying their domestic assets to off-set reserve flows and thus manage to sterilize some shifts in the demand for money. This would tend to deny that the supply of money is determined exclusively by the demand for money.

A positive sign on international reserves is consistent not only with the international-monetarist approach, but also with the countercyclical-activist view that an inflow of reserves allows a central bank to pursue its domestic price and output objectives in a more expansionary direction than would be possible if reserves were being lost. The countercyclical activists (column 5) would also expect that an increase in the growth rate of real out-put should lead to a reduction in the growth rate of the money supply. As for the variables reflecting nominal wages and tradable-goods prices, the coefficient in the money-growth equation can be positive but should be significantly smaller than unity (so that a wage or price acceleration is allowed to cut the level of real balances).

Some interpreters, particularly those identified with the international-monetarist camp, have tested a restrictive version of the wage-push approach which requires wage behaviour to be entirely independent of any macroeconomic variables. A broader view is that autonomous forces are capable of shifting the rate of wage change, *given* domestic and world prices, domestic output, and monetary growth. Two versions of this broader wage-push approach are listed in separate columns in table 1: a wage push that is subsequently accommodated by the central bank (column 7), and a wage push that is not accommodated (column 8). The positive signs on line 7 in columns 7 and 8 represent the crucial autonomous wage-push effect. Since this autonomous influence is denied by most adherents to the international-monetarist view, a zero coefficient is entered in column 6 on line 7.

But evidence of an autonomous wage push, in the form of significant positive coefficients on appropriate dummy variables in the wage equation, is not sufficient to validate the wage-push approach *as a theory of inflation.* First, the higher level of wage rates may cause a squeeze on profits rather than an increase in prices. This possibility may be greatest for a small, open economy and may result if the central bank does not provide the money to accommodate the wage increase. It is treated as a separate subhypothesis regarding the money equation in table 1 in the column reflecting wage push without monetary accommodation (compare columns 2 and 3). Not only is the coefficient on wage rates in the money equation equal to zero (line 2), but for consistency the money supply should not respond to increases in tradable-goods prices either (line 4)[38].

Shifts in domestic demand may lead to monetary accommodation if the central bank is attempting to stabilize interest rates. While private shifts in the IS curve are difficult to measure empirically, it is possible to include an estimate of the full-employment fiscal deficit as an additional variable in the money equation, with a sign expected to be positive if deficit financing has contributed to episodes of monetary acceleration, as in column 4.

The overview in table 1 suggests that distinguishing the international-monetarist view from the subhypothesis of wage push with monetary accommodation may be rather difficult. Joint feedback between money and wage rates is admissible under either approach, as indicated by the positive coefficients on wages in the money equation and money in the wage equation. Nevertheless, the signs on coefficients in table 1 indicate that the framework can still yield interesting conclusions:

1. Zero coefficients on international reserves in the money equation would tend to raise the probability that central banks were able to sterilize changes in the demand for money that attracted reserves, suggesting exceptions to the international-monetarist assumption that the domestic money supply is determined exclusively by the demand for money.

2. Zero coefficients on dummy variables in wage equations in periods when wage push is alleged to have occurred would tend to deny the relevance of the wage-push hypothesis and to confirm the negative verdict of previous empirical tests of that view produced by the international-monetarist camp.

3. Nonpositive coefficients on wage rates in the money equation, together with positive wage-push dummy coefficients, would tend to indicate that any episodes of wage push were not accommodated, a view that is consistent with columns 3 and 8 of table 1.

4. Negative coefficients in the money equation on domestic output, or positive coefficients below unity on wages and tradable-goods prices, would tend to confirm the countercyclical-reaction approach and provide evidence against destabilizing accommodation.

5. Positive coefficients on the full-employment deficit would tend to confirm the deficit-finance subhypothesis without denying any of the others.

The pattern of signs in table 1 can be viewed from a broader perspective. First, the money equation provides a test of whether changes in the money supply are truly exogenous, dependent only on the fixed aims of the central bank, or whether the central bank reacts systematically to events in the economy (in which case econometric equations that treat the money supply as exogenous yield biased coefficients). Both international monetarists and wage-push proponents expect that the monetary authorities will behave passively, allowing an acceleration in monetary growth in response to a higher demand for money, whereas those who view the authorities as a central component of an activist stabilization policy hope that negative coefficients will emerge on the output ratio and zero or small positive coefficients will be attached to changes in nominal wages and tradable-goods prices.

TESTS FOR EXOGENEITY AND FEEDBACK

Empirical testing requires attention both to the signs of coefficients and to timing relationships. In an influential article Christopher Sims proposed testing for patterns of feedback between a pair of variables by running two regressions, with each as dependent variable and both leading and lagged values of the other as independent variables[39]. Significant coefficients on the leading values of a right-hand variable indicate that it is endogenous, influenced by feedback from the left-hand variable.

A second method, which was originally proposed by Granger and which Sims has recently implemented for the United States and West Germany, also involves estimation of a separate equation for each endogenous variable but substitutes lagged values of the dependent variable for leading values of the independent variables[40]. Now a dependent variable is identified as exogenous if the coefficients on all the current and lagged values of the independent variables in its equation are zero. A separate equation is estimated for each variable of interest. For instance, the hypothesis that the money supply is truly exogenous, and not determined by feedback from any of the economic variables listed in table 1, would require that all of the coefficients on current and lagged values of those variables be insignificantly different from zero in an equation with money as the dependent variable. Because all variables of interest are included on the right-hand side of each equation, some are bound to be endogenous. Once it is determined that a variable, say money, is subject to feedback because some right-hand coefficients in its equation are nonzero, it is then possible that the coefficients on money in other equations are biased. This limitation must be recognized in interpretations of individual coefficients in the regression results presented below.

Several factors lead to the choice of the second method in this paper. First, the inclusion of lagged dependent variables allows serial correlation to be purged, in contrast to the disadvantages of the arbitrary 'prefiltering' performed by Sims in his frequently cited use of the first method. Second, the first method is extremely clumsy to use in multivariate applications, since both leading and lagging terms must be included for each independent variable; as a result, degrees of freedom are rapidly exhausted. Third, equations with leading variables cannot be subjected to postsample extrapolation experiments, which are often of interest to determine how well a given set of current and lagged right-hand variables account for movements of a dependent variable after the end of a given sample period [41].

To control its length, the paper contains equations for only three dependent variables for each country, the nominal money supply, wage rates, and the deflator for gross national product (or gross domestic product), all expressed as quarterly rates of change. Primary emphasis is placed on the money and wage equations. A price equation is estimated only to examine the extent to which domestic prices responded during alleged episodes of wage push[42].

DETAILED SPECIFICATIONS

The equation specifications have several important features[43].

1. In light of recent evidence that U.S. wage behaviour can be explained as well by the gap between actual (Q) and potential (Q^*) real GNP as by various unemployment concepts, I decided to use a single variable, the 'output ratio' (Q/Q^*), as a proxy for the effects of real output and labour-market conditions in the money, wage, and price equations[44]. Because the level of money should be related to the level of Q/Q^*, the equation for the rate of change of money uses as an independent variable the *rate of change* of Q/Q^*. On the other hand, the traditional Phillips-curve hypothesis postulates that the rate of change of wage rates depends on the level of excess labour demand, so the *level* of Q/Q^* was used in the equations for the wage rate and the price deflator.

2. There is no reason that an 'automatic stabilizer' increase in the fiscal deficit caused by a recession should put pressure on the monetary authority. Thus as a proxy for the full-employment deficit, the fiscal-deficit variable that is entered into the money equations is the *residual* from a separate equation (not exhibited below) that explains the actual fiscal deficit as a function of a constant, seasonal dummies, and current and lagged real GNP.

3. The 'basic equations' are uniformly estimated for the sample period 1958:3 to 1973:1. The first quarter is determined by the need to include lagged variables and by the 1957:1 starting date of the data file. The last quarter marks the initiation of the system of flexible exchange rates. Interesting features of the 1973–76 interval are identified both by examination of the residuals of a postsample extrapolation, and by re-estimation of an auxiliary equation for the full 1958:3–1976:4 period. Shifts in coefficients between the basic and auxiliary equations can be examined for evidence of changes in structure in the period of flexible rates.

4. The auxiliary equations for the rate of change of the money supply all include as an additional variable the rate of change of the exchange rate between each country and the U.S. dollar, entered in the form of a multiplicative dummy equal to zero up to 1973:1 and to itself thereafter.

5. Four lagged dependent and independent variables are included in the wage and price equations, and three lagged dependent and independent variables are included in the money equations.

6. For most countries the dependent variable in the money equation is M_1. Early investigations pointed to massive shifts between demand and time

deposits in Canada and France in 1967–68 as a result of banking reforms, and so M_2 was used for these two countries.

7. Preliminary results indicated that the coefficient on international reserves in the money equation should be allowed to shift at least once during the sample period. Thus separate coefficients on reserves are estimated in the money equations for 1958:3–1965:4 and 1966:1–1973:1, as well as for 1973:2–1976:4 in the auxiliary equations. The breaks for Canada are 1962:2 and 1970:2, corresponding to the end of the first experiment with flexible rates and the beginning of the second.

THE ROLE OF DUMMY VARIABLES

The use of dummy variables in the empirical results may require justification. The practice is generally accepted as legitimate when some *a priori* reason suggests treating a particular period as unique. But it can be questioned when the choice of time periods is arbitrary or based on a preliminary 'peek' at the data. By this criterion the use of seasonal dummy variables in all equations qualifies on the *a priori* criterion, but the wage-push dummies cannot enter any such plea of innocence. Even if particular events that might have caused a wage push can be identified—for example the Italian 'hot autumn' of 1969—there is no *a priori* criterion to determine how long the effect of wage rates might have lasted. With simultaneous, centralized, nationwide bargaining, the entire effect might occur in one quarter. With other bargaining mechanisms, it could be spread over several quarters.

Because the precise timing of the wage-push dummies in some cases was of necessity determined by 'peeking' at the data, separate versions of the wage equations with and without the wage-push dummies are exhibited. Although some readers might have preferred that the use of wage-push dummies be replaced by a detailed examination and discussion of individual residuals, this approach was rejected in order to avoid biasing other coefficients in an equation in which 'true' specification involves dummies. In fact, the inclusion of dummy variables does generally alter the coefficients on other variables in the wage equations presented below.

STRIKING FEATURES OF THE BASIC DATA

Figure 1 displays four-quarter overlapping rates of change of money, wage rates, and the price deflator for the United States, for a weighted average of the Other Seven, and for the World, consisting of the United States and the Other Seven[45]. The most striking aspect of the figure is the difference between the international-monetarist parable and the actual behaviour of the average for the World and for the Other Seven. There appears to be only a very loose relation between World wage and monetary changes between

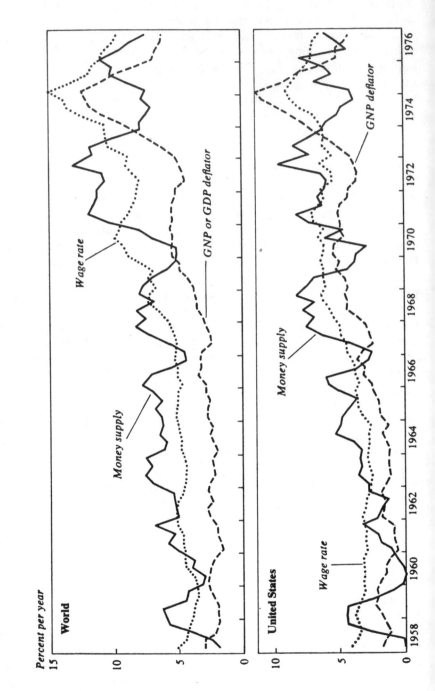

Figure 1. Four-quarter overlapping rates of change of money, wage rates and gross national product deflator, United States, Other Seven, and 'World', 1958–76[a].

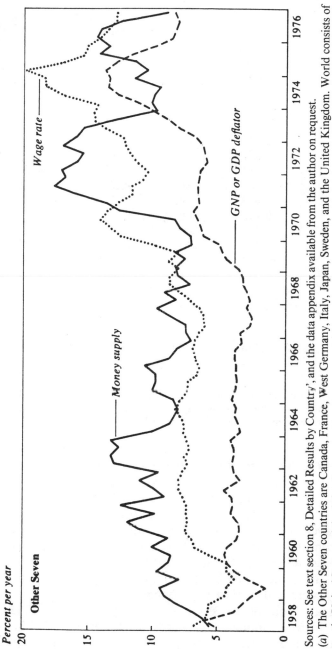

Percent per year

Other Seven

Sources: See text section 8, Detailed Results by Country', and the data appendix available from the author on request.
(a) The Other Seven countries are Canada, France, West Germany, Italy, Japan, Sweden, and the United Kingdom. World consists of the United States and the Other Seven.

Table 2. Coefficients and t statistics from two-way regressions on world money and wages, and on world money and prices[a].

Lag on independent variable and regression statistic	Independent variable			
	Money in wage equation (1)	Money in price equation (2)	Wage in money equation (3)	Price in money equation (4)
Lag				
Current period	−0.043	0.016	−0.371	0.197
	(−0.87)	(0.38)	(−0.87)	(0.38)
One period	−0.034	0.050	−0.331	−0.875
	(−0.68)	(1.36)	(−0.71)	(−1.60)
Two period	0.009	0.043	0.770	−0.647
	(0.16)	(1.06)	(1.58)	(−1.35)
Three period	0.001	0.006	1.683	0.588
	(0.01)	(0.15)	(3.52)	(1.12)
Four period	−0.036	0.055	−0.876	1.834
	(−0.85)	(1.48)	(−1.66)	(3.47)
Regression statistic				
Sum of coefficients	−0.103	0.170	0.873	1.097
	(−0.98)	(1.95)	(0.82)	(0.95)
Standard error (per cent)	0.266	0.229	0.777	0.808

Sources: See discussion in text.

(a). All variables are one-quarter percent changes. All equations include in addition a constant term, three seasonal dummy variables, and four lagged values of the dependent variable. The sample period for all regressions in this table is 1958:3–1973:1.

1958 and the end of 1972. The rate of wage change was essentially constant between 1960 and 1966, and showed no response to the temporary acceleration of money in 1963–66. Further, monetary behaviour appears able to explain little of the *doubling* of wage change between late 1967 and mid-1970, since the average rate of money growth during 1967–69 (7.1 per cent) differed little from that in 1963–66 (6.8 per cent). On the other hand, the lead of wage change relative to the monetary acceleration of 1970–71 suggests that at least part of the behaviour of money in this period might be explained by passive accommodation to wage change.

Although the primary focus of this study is on chains of causation and timing relationships between money and wages in the eight individual countries, table 2 displays the results of simple regressions relating wage, price, and monetary rates of change. As in all regressions estimated in this paper, four lagged values of the dependent variable are included, so the dependent variable is considered exogenous and influenced only by its own past values if the coefficients on all of the independent variables are zero.

Table 2 explores the international-monetarist contention that the world inflation rate depends on previous values of world monetary growth. In fact, only in the price equation (column 2) is the sum of money coefficients statistically significant, although the sum of coefficients is much too small to be consistent with the long-run neutrality of world monetary change. But the results in column 1 do not appear at all consistent with a monetary explanation of wage behaviour. Moreover, although the sum of coefficients on wages and prices in the two money equations is insignificant in columns 3 and 4, it is quite large, and one coefficient in each equation is very strongly positive. Thus the exogeneity of the world rate of monetary growth is not strongly supported, and the possibility is suggested that exogenous wage movements generated passive monetary accommodation.

Another interesting feature of figure 1 is the divergence of monetary-growth rates in the United States and the Other Seven. While the growth rate of money accelerated in the United States between 1962 and early 1969, that in the Other Seven decelerated between late 1963 and early 1970. And though the explosive period of monetary growth in the Other Seven between late 1970 and early 1973 does correspond to a period of relatively rapid U.S. monetary growth, the previous period of acceleration in the United States during 1967–69 was accompanied by relatively low monetary growth rates in the Other Seven. Again this pattern is consistent with the hypothesis that the United States was not the sole engine of world monetary growth, and that domestic wage behaviour within the Other Seven played some role in the 1970–71 monetary acceleration.

7. Summary of Basic Results

The signs and significance of several of the more interesting coefficients in wage and money equations for individual countries and the aggregate for the Other Seven are listed in table 3. The table starts with the United States and the weighted average of the Other Seven, and continues with the results for each of the Other Seven countries. The signs (+, 0, or –) refer to the sums of coefficients of the independent variables, and the superscripts a and b indicate statistical significance (using a one-tailed test) at the 10 per cent and 5 per cent level, respectively. A sign without a superscript stands at only the bare margin of significance, the 20 per cent confidence level.

WAGE PUSH, INTERNATIONAL RESERVES,
AND MONETARY ACCOMMODATION

The basic message of the results is that, while no simple subhypothesis accurately describes the behaviour of money and inflation in all of the eight

Table 3. Signs and significance of selected sums of coefficients, 1958:3–1973:1 sample period.

Equation and independent variable	United States	Other Seven							
		Total	Canada	France	West Germany	Italy	Japan	Sweden	United Kingdom
1. Money equation									
a. Wage rate	+	0	0	0	+	0	0	0	0
b. Output ratio	+	0	+[a]	−[a]	0[b]	+[a]	−[b]	−[a]	+[b]
c. Traded-goods prices	0	0	−[a]	0	−[a]	0	+[b]	0	0
d. Fiscal deficit	0	0	0	0	−[b]	0	+[b]	0	0[b]
e. Reserves, second half	0	0	0	0	+	0	+	0	+
2. Wage equation									
a. Money	+[b]	+[a]	0	+[b]	+[a]	0	+	−[b]	+[b]
b. Output ratio	0	+[a]	+	+	0	0	0	−[a]	0
c. Control and wage-push dummies[c,d]	−[b] −[a] …	+[b] +[b] +	… … …	+[b] … …	+[b] … …	+[b] +[b] …	+ + …	+[b] + …	−[b] +[b] −

3. *Price equation*

a. Wage dummy minus dummy contribution

contribution	1.022^b	0.859^b	...	0.488^a	0.055^e	-0.004^e	0.155^e	0.317	1.057^b
b. Dummy contrubution	0.810^e	0.135^e	...	0.764	0.649^e	0.056^e	-0.666^e	0.344^e	1.250^b

Sources: Tables 4 to 12.

(a) Significant at the 10 per cent level.

(b) Significant at the 5 per cent level.

(c) Dummy variables that appear in tables 4 to 12, but were not significant, are not reported in this summary table. See also discussion of dummies in text. The periods for which dummies are included are as follows:

United States—1963:1–1966:2; 1973:1–1974:1.   Italy—1962:1–1964:4;1970:1.

Total, Other Seven—1967:1–1969:3; 1968:2–1968:3; 1969:4–1970:2.   Japan—1967:4–1968:4; 1970:1–1970:4.

France—1968:2–1968:3.   Sweden—1969:4–1970:2; 1971:3–1972:2.

West Germany—1969:4–1970:2.   United Kingdom—1970:1–1971:1. Also see note 64.

(d) Insignificant dummy omitted

(e) Not significan:.

Note: Signs with no specific footnote are significant at the 20 per cent level. All significant levels are for one-tailed tests.

countries, nevertheless the international monetarists fare better than the wage-push group. The coefficient on international reserves in the second half of the sample period in the money equation (1966:1–1973:1) is strongly positive in three of the important countries, West Germany, Japan, and the United Kingdom, indicating that central banks in these countries were unable completely to sterilize shifts in money demand. Furthermore, in each of these three countries (as well as in the United States and France) money has a positive influence on the behaviour of the wage rate. The explosion of growth in world reserves during the 1970–72 interval thus appears to have contributed to an acceleration of growth in the money supply and indirectly to an acceleration of wage growth.

The wage-push hypothesis appears to be alive and well as an explanation of wage rates, but not as a theory of inflation or of monetary growth. Large positive coefficients on wage-push dummy variables emerge in the price equation for various periods in the Other Seven average, and in France, West Germany, Italy, Sweden, and the United Kingdom taken separately. The inflationary impact of the autonomous wage movements is measured in a price equation that contains two wage variables (each entered as a current value and four lags): first, the actual rate of change of wages minus the contribution of the dummy variables in the wage equation, and second, the contribution of the dummy variables themselves. For the Other Seven as a group, the coefficient on the dummy contribution is close to zero, as compared with a coefficient on 'normal' wage changes of close to unity. Only in the United Kingdom is the coefficient on the dummy contribution not only as large as the normal coefficient, but also statistically significant. In France, West Germany, Italy, and Sweden, the coefficient on the dummy contribution is larger than the normal one.

How can the generally small values of the sum of wage coefficients in the money equations be reconciled with the appearance of feedback from wages to money in the equation for the world as a whole (table 2, column 3)? The world response lies between the small response of the Other Seven and the large sum of coefficients for the United States. Thus passive monetary accommodation in the world appears to have been centred in the very country that exhibits no sign whatsoever of autonomous wage push. Only in the United Kingdom do the results display all of the ingredients required for wage push to be a valid theory not only of wages but also of continuing inflation; but, as discussed below, even this 'victory' for wage push is tempered by the finding that the 1970 wage push in the United Kingdom was not autonomous at all, but rather appears to have been a postcontrols rebound.

In general, the behaviour of monetary authorities in different countries has little in common, and no single subhypothesis receives strong confirmation. The Japanese appear to be inconsistent, pursuing a countercyclical policy relative to the output business cycle while simultaneously accommodating fiscal deficits. The Japanese money supply reacted positively to inflows of reserves, a result consistent with both the international-monetarist and countercyclical-activist approaches. Sweden exhibits countercyclical behaviour, while money in Italy and Britain appears to fluctuate procyclically. Both the Germans and the Canadians are inconsistent, resisting higher prices of traded goods but allowing the growth rate of the money supply to rise in response to higher wage rates. A positive co-efficient on a nominal variable does not indicate destabilizing behaviour in the money equation unless its value exceeds unity; by this criterion only the United States and Sweden (and the United Kingdom in the extended sample period) exhibit a destabilizing response of money to wage change.

In several countries the international-monetarist case is bolstered by the significantly positive coefficients on money in the wage equation. Yet the results summarized in table 3 understate the monetary effect, because some of the procyclical correlation of money and wages is soaked up by the out-put-ratio variable. When the output ratio is omitted from the basic wage equation, the money coefficients become larger in several countries[46]. This result denies the extreme wage-push view that wage claims are 'picked out of the air' and are totally independent of market forces, but is consistent with a more eclectic view that both market forces and autonomous 'push' episodes matter for wage behaviour.

8. Detailed Results by Country

Tables 4 to 12, grouped together at the end of the paper for easy reference, present the detailed empirical results. There is one table for each country, and one for the aggregate of the Other Seven. The first two columns of each table present equations in which the quarterly rate of change in the money supply is the dependent variable, with the shorter sample period up to 1973:1 in column 1 and the extended period through 1976:4 in column 2. The next three columns present wage-rate equations, with the short sample period in column 3, and with control and wage-push dummy variables added in column 4 for the short period, and in column 5 for the extended period. Finally, a single equation for price change is presented in column 6[47].
6[47].

THE UNITED STATES

A vast amount of empirical work on 'St. Louis equations' in the United States has treated the rate of growth of the money supply as exogenous in equations explaining the growth of nominal GNP. Sims' paper confirms the exogeneity of money in a simple bivariate test on the money supply and nominal income[48]. This result appears to be repeated in column 1 of table

4 for the United States, in the sense that no sum of coefficients on any independent variable is significant, even at the 10 per cent level. On the other hand, the sum of coefficients on the wage rate is very large, and one of the individual coefficients has a t ratio of 3.6. A Tinbergen analysis indicates that the wage variable does contribute almost all of the explanation of the acceleration of monetary growth in 1964–68[49]. It is the zigzag plus-minus pattern of the wage coefficients that reduces the significance of the sum of coefficients, suggesting that monetary growth responded in this period to the acceleration of wage growth, and less to the rate of growth of wages by itself[50].

The most interesting features of the U.S. wage equations are the strong role of money and of dummy variables for guidepost and restraint periods. The significant negative coefficients on the guidepost dummies confirm earlier results, of Perry and others, and so does the pattern of the other dummy variables in general. When the effects of all three dummies for the 1971–75 period in the extended wage equation in column 5 are cumulated, the sum of 0.18 per cent indicates that the rebound more than cancelled the mild restraining influence of the controls. The bottom line in the table lists the postsample cumulative extrapolation errors for three of the equations. These errors are remarkably small, both relative to my previous work on 'structural' wage and price equations, and compared to the results for some of the other countries.

THE OTHER SEVEN

The money supply in the Other Seven appears to have been exogenous, with no significant sum of coefficients on any independent variable. Despite the positive coefficients on international reserves in the money equations of several important countries, the money equation for the Other Seven bases its explanation of the 1970–73 money explosion (see figure 1) on a lagged response to changes in wage rates and tradable-goods prices. This in turn leads to horrendous postsample extrapolation errors, as the equation predicts huge rates of monetary growth, of 25 to 30 per cent in 1974–75, in response to the 1974 acceleration in wage rates and tradable-goods prices. The large positive coefficient on the fiscal deficit also leads to an expectation of rapid monetary growth, in contrast to the deceleration that actually occurred.

The wage and price equations in the Other Seven are more reasonable and interesting. As in the United States, money and dummy variables play a relatively strong role, although here most of the significant dummy variables have positive coefficients which support the wage-push sub-hypothesis, rather than the predominantly negative coefficients observed for the United States. It is important to note that the significance of money in the wage equation for both the United States and the Other Seven evaporates if the dummy variables are omitted (column 3). Thus one cannot claim *both* that dummy variables are unimportant or inappropriate *and* that money is an important determinant of wage change. The traditional Phillips-curve effect, in the form of a positive relation between the rate of change of wages and the *level* of the output ratio, shows up more strongly for the Other Seven than for the United States in column 4. Traded-goods prices also are more important, as would be expected.

The wage-push dummy variables are chosen for the same periods as in the major individual countries and are significant on lines 10c and 10d. But this lends little support to the wage-push hypothesis, because there appears to have been no significant positive impact of these autonomous episodes of wage change on the price deflator, or of wage rates in general on the money supply. The relatively strong positive impact of money-supply growth on wages supports the international monetarists. But the direct effect of money on prices is negative. Combining the estimated role of money in the wage and price equations for the Other Seven indicates that more than half of the impact of money on wage change does not feed through to price change.

CANADA

The Canadian money equations differ from the others by splitting the reserves variable according to the dates when Canada terminated and re-instated floating exchange rates, and also by including the exchange rate as a variable throughout the sample period. Further, in light of previous results and the overall domination of the Canadian economy by the United States, each Canadian equation includes as an independent variable the corresponding quantity in the United States[51]. The results yield few significant coefficients that would deny the exogeneity of the Canadian money supply. The influence of the U.S. money supply is surprisingly weak in light of the common periods of monetary restriction in the two countries in 1959–60, 1969–70, and 1974.

No dummy variables are included in the basic Canadian wage and price equations. U.S. wages and prices have relatively weak effects in the expected direction. In the extended wage equation through 1976 (column 4), a dummy variable is included for the Canadian policy of wage and price restraints announced in October 1975. The equation, which relies on the U.S. wage and traded-goods prices for almost all of its explanation of Canadian wage behaviour, attaches a strongly positive coefficient to this dummy variable. This perverse result apparently identifies the acceleration of wages in Canada relative to the United States that prompted the restraint programme, rather than the positive effects, if any, that the programme had.

FRANCE

France appears to have pursued a relatively countercyclical monetary policy. The negative sums of coefficients on the output ratio and traded-goods prices tend to confirm the OECD narrative of phases of French monetary policy which attributes restrictive measures introduced in 1963 and late 1968 to a reaction to the acceleration of inflation in those periods. Partially offsetting this verdict is a relatively large, albeit insignificant, sum of coefficients on wage rates. An inspection of the data indicates that the mid-1968 episode of autonomous wage increase was initially accommodated, but that within six months monetary policy had shifted to a stance of restriction.

Another interesting feature of the French money equation is the absence of any accommodation of reserve inflows. The expected positive correlation between money and international reserves in 1971–72 is offset by a dramatic negative correlation in 1968–70, when the initial monetary accommodation of the 1968 wage push caused massive reserve outflows, followed by a devaluation in August 1969, a period of tight money, and a reserve inflow. Another factor breaking the positive correlation between reserves and money was the mild restriction and a deceleration in monetary growth achieved by the French in late 1971, the period of maximum accumulation of reserves[52].

The wage equation of column 4 introduces two dummy variables, the second of which reduces the standard error of the equation. The restraint dummy refers to the eight quarters of 1964 and 1965, when a mild form of incomes policy was in effect[53]. The wage-push dummy is in effect in 1968:2 and 1968:3 and reflects the impact of June 1968 *Protocole de Grenelle* which resulted in a nominal wage increase of 11 to 13 per cent in manufacturing in the aftermath of the May general strike.

The price equation tends to support the wage-push approach, since the contribution of the dummy-variable coefficients to price change was even greater than that of 'normal' wage increases. But the wage-push episode did not lead to a continuing inflation because the final ingredient required for that development—a continuing accommodation by the central bank—was not present. By early 1969 the net influence of the countercyclical coefficients in the money equation—not just the negative coefficients on traded-goods prices and the output ratio, but also the positive coefficient on reserves—had swamped the influence of the positive coefficient on wages.

WEST GERMANY

The standard explanation of the explosion in German monetary growth between 1970:4 and 1973:1 is the flood of dollar reserves into the

Bundesbank beginning in early 1970; and the advent of the flexible-rate system is usually cited as the factor that allowed the Germans to 'regain control' of their money supply in early 1973. Indeed, the statistical significance of the second reserves variable is greater in the German money equation (table 8, column 1, line 8b) than it is for any other country. But an inspection of the other coefficients suggests that the story of German monetary movements is more complex than the simple international-monetarist story about a helplessly passive central banker drowning in dollars. Explaining the total acceleration in the four-quarter rate of change of money from 5.77 per cent in 1970:3 to 13.41 per cent in 1971:3, the equation assigns almost as much responsibility to the 1969–70 wage acceleration as to the 1970–71 inflow of reserves[54]. This single episode of monetary accommodation stands in sharp contrast to the evidence that during most of the rest of the sample period the central bank operated according to a simple countercyclical reaction function, inaugurating a restrictive policy when the inflation rate began to accelerate. The equation picks up this countercyclical behaviour by assigning a large negative coefficient to the change in traded-goods prices, which makes a substantial negative contribution in each of the phases labelled as 'restrictive' by the OECD (1959–60, 1965–66, and 1969–70)[55].

The large underprediction in the postsample extrapolation of the German money equation is a less extreme version of the Canadian problem; when a negative coefficient is assigned to the change in tradable-goods prices, a large negative growth rate of money is predicted in 1974. The extended money equation exhibits substantial shifts in coefficients as it struggles to explain the 1974 experience, providing evidence of a structural shift in German monetary policy when the era of flexible exchange rates began in early 1973.

Two dummy variables are included in the German wage and price equations. A restraint dummy is in effect in 1967–69, a period during which union leaders are claimed to have agreed to modest wage increases in the interests of economic stabilization[56]. Then a 're-entry', or wage-push, dummy covers the three quarters 1969:4–1970:2. The restraint dummy is insignificant, but the wage-push dummy is very large, contributing a cumulative wage increase of almost 6 per cent in column 4 and more than that in column 5.

Did the 1969–70 episode contribute to a continuing acceleration of inflation? The coefficient on the wage-dummy contribution in the price equation is relatively large, but at a very low level of significance. More important may have been the positive effect of the wage increases on monetary growth, and of money growth on price behaviour. Overall, the results seem to suggest that the inflow of dollar reserves was not the sole cause of the German monetary explosion of 1970–72, and that at least some of the responsibility rests with domestic wage developments.

ITALY

Although significance levels are low, most variables in the basic Italian money equation are positive, indicating, an accommodative rather than countercyclical monetary policy. An acceleration of the rise in wages, output, and traded-goods prices, and a larger fiscal deficit all appear to have stimulated monetary growth. In contrast to West Germany there is no accommodation of reserve inflows in 1971; quarterly rates of monetary growth in Italy were lower in every quarter of 1971 than in the corresponding quarter of the preceding 'wage-push' year, 1970. A structural change appears to have occurred in 1973, since the equation predicts more than *double* the monetary growth that actually took place after the end of the sample period.

The large and significant coefficients on the dummy variables in the Italian wage equations suggest that the Italian data are congenial to a wage-push interpretation. The first dummy variable applies to the period in the early 1960s often described by the term 'wage explosion'[57]. The second applies to the single quarter when the wage increases following the 'hot autumn' of 1969 took effect.

But, although wage push helps explain wages in Italy, the wage-push hypothesis suffers in the price equation, since wage increases had no influence at all on price increases. Nor did wage growth have a substantial impact on the monetary authorities. The Italian central bank appears to have behaved in a destabilizing procyclical manner, but more in response to domestic output than to wage rates. The absence of price response to the 1970 wage push is confirmed by an inspection of the data: the deflator for the Italian GNP exhibits a rate of increase in the first three quarters of 1970 that is almost identical to that of the same period in 1969. Perhaps the most surprising aspect of the Italian inflation performance was the absence of any acceleration during the entire 1969–72 period. Economic recovery between 1966 and 1969 had already caused a substantial acceleration in wage and price change before the 'hot autumn'.

Since 1973, Italian wage increases have been considerably more rapid than can be explained by the coefficients in the 1958–73 wage equation. A comparison of columns 4 and 5 of table 9 indicates that the coefficient on traded-goods prices has become larger and much more significant. More than those in most other countries, workers in Italy have fought to preserve their real wages in the face of a spiral in traded-goods prices caused by the food and oil supply shocks of 1973–74, and by the depreciation of the lira beginning in mid-1975. But the high positive coefficient on monetary growth in the wage equation when it is extended through 1976 suggests that the central bank may have considerable leverage over the behaviour of wage rates given changes in traded-goods prices.

JAPAN

Japan seems to be the model case in which monetary policy responded primarily to the growth rate of international reserves. Most analyses of Japanese postwar monetary policy cite deteriorations in the balance of payments as the single factor behind episodes of monetary restriction[58]. The basic money equation in table 10, column 1, is consistent with this overall interpretation, with the largest positive sum of coefficients on reserves of any country.

But there seems to be more to an explanation of monetary behaviour than a simple reserves effect. Beyond that, the money supply appears to have responded strongly in a countercyclical direction to output fluctuations. In fact, the accommodation of reserve inflows in 1971 might not have been so extreme had the economy not been experiencing a growth recession in that year, with the trough of the output ratio occurring in 1971:4.

Accounts of Japanese wage and price behaviour appear unanimous in denying any role for wage push[59]. Perry's test for autonomous wage change in 1968 yielded a positive coefficient on a dummy variable for that year but at a low level of significance[60]. Perry's conclusion is confirmed in table 10, where dummy variables for 1968 and for 1970 are positive but insignificant. Further, the absence of any positive impact of wage change on monetary growth argues against any lasting effect of autonomous wage movements on the inflation rate.

The pattern of postsample extrapolation errors is consistent with that in other countries and can be interpreted in the light of shifts in coefficients when the sample period is extended. The huge overprediction of monetary growth after 1973 is accounted for largely by the positive coefficient on traded-goods prices, which suggests erroneously that the oil shock would be accommodated rather than resisted. Further, the countercyclical behaviour during 1958–73 leads to the expectation that the central bank would do more than it actually did to counteract the unprecedented 1973–75 drop in the output ratio.

SWEDEN

The main feature of the Swedish monetary equation is a countercyclical output effect, similar to but larger in size than that in the corresponding Japanese equation. The recent problems of the Swedish economy, leading to the August 1977 devaluation, may date back to the unique Swedish response to the 1974 supply shocks and worldwide recession. In contrast to most countries, which failed to pursue vigorous monetary policies to counter the recession, the four-quarter rate of change of money in Sweden reached postwar peaks, around a 30 per cent annual rate of growth, throughout the 1974:3 to 1975:2 interval[61]. As in the case of Canada and Germany, a negative coefficient on traded-goods prices in the sample period 1958–73 causes a postsample prediction of a drop in the money supply, in contrast to the acceleration that actually occurred and that shifts the coefficient on traded-goods prices to a positive value in the extended money equation.

Appropriately enough, Swedish wage behaviour appears to adhere to the Scandinavian model of the international transmission of inflation[62]. The elasticity of wage change to changes in world prices is very large in all of the wage equations. A set of three dummy variables was introduced into the wage equations. First, following Perry's lead, a wage-push dummy was introduced for 1970. Second, a dummy was included for the subsequent year, to determine whether price restraint had any effect on wage behaviour[63]. Finally, a 're-entry' dummy was entered to test whether any restraining effect in 1971 was offset in 1972.

The signs are positive on all three dummy variables in the wage equations, and significant in the case of the first and third, indicating that wage change was faster than otherwise would have been expected during the entire 1970–72 period. The unsatisfactory forecasting performance of the 1958–73 wage equations is a consequence of the implausibly high co-efficient on traded-goods prices, which leads to the prediction of much faster wage increases in 1973–75 than actually occurred. The coefficient drops to a much more reasonable level in the extended equation in column 5. All wage equations exhibit the same negative coefficients on money and the output ratio, perhaps justifying the scepticism of Scandinavian economists about the monetarist approach, but suggesting a puzzle that requires further research.

UNITED KINGDOM

The results for the United Kingdom are perhaps the most interesting of all, and offer so many positive and significant coefficients that both inter-national monetarists and wage-push proponents will be pleased that their approach is vindicated, but dismayed that the opposite framework is validated as well! The basic money equation indicates significant accommodation of both output changes and inflows of reserves. The monetary authority appears to have behaved in a destabilizing manner, increasing the amplitude of the output business cycle until forced by a balance-of-payments constraint to shift to a restrictive policy.

The selection of dummy variables for the wage and price equations is designed to test whether alleged episodes of wage push actually represented a rebound in the aftermath of the various periods of wage freeze and restraint. Periods of applicability of the various dummy variables are those selected by the *Economist* as subject to a wage 'freeze', 'restraint', or 're-entry'[64]. In addition, a special dummy is included for the 1970 episode that has made wage push a byword among British economists. Indeed, autonomous movements during control and re-entry periods appear to be important in explaining British wage behaviour. Further, the behaviour of prices appears to have corresponded to that of wages, in contrast to the absence of price response to wage dummy variables in most other countries. And as final icing to the wage-push cake, the coefficient on wages in the money equation is positive and extremely large in the extended sample period.

But international monetarists might respond that though the icing may be impressive the cake within is cardboard. Somewhat remarkably in light of the antimonetarist orientation of many British economists, the influence of money on wage behaviour is stronger than it is in any other country. Moreover, the 1970 wage-push episode does not appear to represent any profound sociological phenomenon, but simply an attempt to catch up for losses in real income during the preceding period of restraint. Because the restraint dummy is in effect for so many quarters (line 10b), the cumulative effect of all the dummy variables taken together is strongly negative, implying that total wage change during 1958–73 was 26 per cent *less* than would have been expected on the basis of the contribution of the other coefficients[65].

As further support for the monetarist case, the equations for the United Kingdom clearly indict the Bank of England as the major culprit in the 1974–76 British wage explosion. Like workers in all other countries except the United States and West Germany, British workers tried to maintain their real wages in the face of the 1973–74 increases in traded-goods prices. The central bank then responded by accommodating these wage increases, and this monetary acceleration fueled a further increase in the rate of wage growth.

9. Conclusion

There is still considerable scope for research on the issues discussed here. The episodes of autonomous wage changes captured here by dummy variables may be attributable partially to factors unique to each country—tax changes, increases in the minimum wage, or changes in unemployment compensation systems. Moreover, the results may be sensitive to the particular wage series used in each country, and to errors in measuring wages. The attempt to fit a single money equation to the period 1958–73 overlooks the likelihood that monetary regimes may change. Further explorations into the behaviour of monetary authorities will require experiments to reveal such changes, and should be conducted on a variety of monetary aggregates and bases. Nevertheless, several interesting conclusions do emerge from the results presented here.

The paper began with three quotations setting out the conflict between the international-monetarist and wage-push explanations of the acceleration of world inflation during the latter part of the era of fixed exchange rates. Which of the quotations survives the confrontation with the data?

Harry Johnson attributed the acceleration of world inflation ultimately to U.S. monetary expansion. Table 2 confirms that world inflation is significantly influenced by the world rate of monetary growth, to which the United States contributes about half. U.S. monetary growth appears to have had a significant influence on the growth rate of U.S. wages, and U.S. prices then responded to wage changes with an elasticity of unity. The rate of wage growth in the Other Seven appears to have accelerated in 1969–70, well before the 1970–71 acceleration in monetary growth there, but this does not rule out a causal role for U.S. monetary behaviour. The statistical results attribute about two-thirds of this wage acceleration in the Other Seven to the influence of a high output level and an acceleration in the rise of world prices of tradable goods, both of which were caused partly by the prior U.S. monetary acceleration. As in the case of the United States, these wage increases in the Other Seven were then passed on as domestic price increases, and the domestic price level in the Other Seven was also pushed up directly by higher prices of tradable goods.

Nicholas Kaldor prefers to attribute the acceleration of world inflation to a wage push caused by trade-union militancy. The results here provide little support for this wage-push interpretation. About one-third of the 1967–70 acceleration in wage growth in the Other Seven is attributable to the contribution of dummy variables in the wage equation for the Other Seven. But, as the Harberger quotation points out, the other macroeconomic effects required for wage push to be a source of a continuing inflation were absent. The portion of the wage acceleration contributed by the wage-push dummy variables in the Other Seven did not feed through into price change[66]. Further, there is no sign of the passive accommodation of wage change by monetary authorities required if an inflation initiated by wage push is to continue. A positive effect of wages on monetary behaviour is close to statistical significance only in the United States, where there was no sign of any autonomous wage push. It is fitting that the wage-push hypothesis comes closest to fulfilling its macroeconomic requirements in the United Kingdom, where it has received such widespread attention; but even so the autonomous upsurge of wage change in 1969–70 appears to have represented a rebound in the aftermath of wage controls and restraint rather than a spontaneous event.

Is control of the money supply sufficient to control inflation? Money growth has a significantly positive impact on wage growth in four major countries making up 72 per cent of the 1976 GNP of the eight countries considered here[67]. Not only does this tend to deny the contention of some wage-push proponents that wage claims are numbers 'picked out of thin air', but it also supports the international-monetarist position that control of world monetary growth is a crucial requirement in the determination of the world inflation rate. A qualification is that in the remaining four countries the effect of money on wages is weak or nonexistent. A further qualification is that the estimated elasticity of wages with respect to money is small, and that of prices with respect to money is smaller still. Finally, this effect of money on prices apparently operates in conjunction with the effect of money on output.

The results indicate that the major competitor to the international-monetarist approach as an explanation of world monetary growth is not the wage-push hypothesis, but rather the countercyclical-reaction function. It does not appear to be true, as proponents of the international-monetarist view contend, that the money supply in these countries is automatically set equal to the demand for money by international movements of capital. Instead, in the money equations for most countries there are *negative* coefficients on either tradable-goods prices or the domestic output ratio, two important *positive* determinants of the demand for money. Further, the positive coefficients on international reserves in the money equations for several countries are consistent with the countercyclical-reaction approach as well as the international-monetarist view. Almost all countries experienced periods of monetary restriction as central banks responded to some combination of bouyant growth in output, imported inflation, and reserve outflows.

The study reveals differences among countries in the behaviour of money and wage rates that are as interesting as their similarities. Today's dichotomy between 'healthy' nations like West Germany and Japan, caught in a virtuous circle of appreciation and decelerating inflation, and 'sick' nations like Italy and the United Kingdom (pre-1977), caught in a vicious circle of depreciation and persistent inflation, shows up in differences in behaviour before the advent of flexible exchange rates in 1973. Growth cycles in the money supply in Germany and Japan appear to have followed a countercyclical-reaction pattern, whereas accommodation was the rule in Italy and the United Kingdom.

The results provide little support for the idea that central banks indirectly cause wage push through prior episodes of accommodation. In fact, the largest coefficient on wages in a money equation occurs in the case of the United States, which exhibits no evidence of wage push at all. On the other hand, one can apparently pick today's healthy and sick nations reasonably well by the response of wage rates to traded-goods prices[68]. This in turn may reflect in part a guess by trade unions in the sick nations that any attempt to maintain real wages in the face of the 1974 supply shocks would be accommodated by central banks.

The paper provides ample support for Lucas' criticism of econometric models as forecasting devices[69]. Policy regimes have changed in the face of novel events like the 1974 supply shock. In the case of almost every country, money equations estimated for the 1958–73 interval make huge forecasting

errors during 1973–76; it appears that the response of the monetary
authorities to changes in traded-goods prices shifted in the face of the
striking price increases of 1974. Further, the dramatic contrast between the
volatility of changes in the wage rate in some of the Other Seven countries
and the sluggish changes exhibited by the United States reminds us that we
all take for granted characteristics of the U.S. economy that depend ultimately on its labour-market institutions and that would change dramatically
if those institutions resembled the ones in Europe and Japan.

Notes to Tables 4 to 12

Unless otherwise indicated, all variables are one-quarter rates of change in percent. The numbers in parentheses are t ratios.

All coefficients and t ratios represent the sum of a series of freely estimated coefficients. The number of individual coefficients is as follows: All equations—lagged dependent variable, four coefficients. Money equation—wage variable, current and four lagged coefficients; other independent variables, current and three lagged coefficients. Wage and price equations—all independent variables, current and four lagged coefficients.

The money concept is M_1 for all countries except Canada and France, for which it is M_2.

In addition to the coefficients listed in the tables, each equation includes as additional independent variables a constant term and three seasonal dummy variables.

The money equations contain political dummy variables set equal to unity in the quarter of each national election and the three preceding quarters, with one political dummy coefficient per election.

In cases where the sum of coefficients is not statistically significant, one or more individual lagged coefficients nevertheless may be significant. The superscripts indicate significance at the 5 per cent level (one-tailed test) of one or more positive individual coefficients (*); one or more negative coefficients (**); and one or more coefficients of both signs (†).

Standard errors, cumulative extrapolation errors, and coefficients on dummy variables are listed as percentages.

Cumulative errors in line 12 do not include the effect of any dummies that are applicable only in the period after 1973:1—for example, the U.S. re-entry dummy in table 4, line 9d.

Table 4. Money, wage, and price equations, United States.

	Dependent variable and sample period					
	Money supply		Wage rate			Price index
				With dummies		
Independent variable and regression statistic	1958:3–1973:1 (1)	1958:3–1976:4 (2)	1958:3–1973:1 (3)	1958:3–1973:1 (4)	1958:3–1976:4 (5)	1958:3–1973:1 (6)
Independent variable						
1. Lagged dependent variable	−0.544** (−1.57)	−0.557** (−1.53)	0.816* (2.72)	0.400* (1.27)	0.650* (2.75)	−0.706 (−1.37)
2. Money supply	...	...	0.085* (1.07)	0.258* (3.04)	0.165* (2.39)	0.047 (0.73)
3. Wage rate	1.999† (1.19)	1.584 (1.00)	...	...	...	...
a. Wage rate minus dummy contribution	...	...	...	...	...	1.022* (1.88)
b. Dummy contribution	...	...	...	...	...	0.810 (0.35)
4. Output ratio (quarterly change)	0.371 (1.11)	0.430 (1.33)	...	...	...	...
5. Output ratio (level)	...	...	0.035* (0.36)	0.026* (0.28)	0.037† (0.48)	0.047 (0.72)
6. Traded-goods price index	−0.009 (−0.02)	−0.115 (−0.41)	0.020 (0.25)	0.144 (1.78)	0.029* (0.51)	0.009 (0.31)

	(1)	(2)	(3)	(4)	(5)	(6)
7. Fiscal-deficit residual (level)	−1.012** (−0.74)	−0.169** (−0.16)	...	...	...	...
8. International reserves	...	...	0.002† (0.08)	0.009* (0.40)	0.014† (0.84)	0.018 (0.69)
a. 1958:3–1965:4	−0.116 (−0.55)	0.089 (0.36)	...	...	...	...
b. 1966:1–1973:1	−0.092** (−0.72)	−0.037 (−0.34)	...	...	...	...
c. 1973:2–1976:4	...	0.023 (0.08)	...	...	...	...
9. Dummy						
a. Guideposts, 1963:1–1966:2	...	...	...	−0.237 (−2.45)	−0.173 (−1.93)	...
b. Controls, 1971:3–1972:4	...	...	...	−0.097 (−0.76)	−0.081 (−0.76)	...
c. Restraint, 1973:1–1974:1	...	...	...	−0.523 (−1.35)	−0.326 (−1.57)	...
d. Re-entry, 1974:2–1975:1	...	...	...	...	0.591 (1.81)	...
Regression statistic (per cent)						
10. Standard error	0.84	1.11	0.18	0.18	0.20	0.24
11. Cumulative error, 1973:2–1976:4	−3.01	...	0.95	−1.59	...	...

See notes to tables.

Table 5. *Money, wage, and price equations, Other Seven.*

	Dependent variable and sample period					
	Money supply		Wage rate			Price index
				With dummies		
Independent variable and regression statistic	1958:3–1973:1 (1)	1958:3–1976:4 (2)	1958:3–1973:1 (3)	1958:3–1973:1 (4)	1958:3–1976:4 (5)	1958:3–1973:1 (6)
Independent variable						
1. Lagged dependent variable	0.389* (1.04)	0.288* (0.83)	0.768* (2.21)	0.435* (1.47)	0.534* (2.32)	−1.022** (−3.34)
2. Money supply	⋯	⋯	−0.035** (−0.23)	0.200* (1.58)	0.374* (2.58)	−0.131** (−1.07)
3. Wage rate	0.474† (0.47)	0.440* (0.60)	⋯	⋯	⋯	⋯
a. Wage rate minus dummy contribution						0.859* (2.33)
b. Dummy contribution						0.135 (0.24)
4. Output ratio (quarterly change)	−0.235** (−0.60)	−0.100 (−0.30)	−0.058† (−0.35)			
5. Output ratio (level)	⋯	⋯	⋯	0.175* (1.31)	0.102* (0.71)	0.003** (0.02)
6. Traded-goods price index	0.398 (0.63)	−0.122 (−0.31)	0.403* (1.92)	0.362* (1.71)	0.149* (1.49)	0.348* (2.03)
7. Fiscal-deficit residual (level)	1.81*	−0.131**	⋯⋯	⋯	⋯	⋯

	(1)	(2)	(3)	(4)	(5)	(6)
8. International reserves	…	…	0.001 (0.02)	0.001 (0.03)	0.038 (−1.15)	… (1.82)
a. 1958:3–1965:4	0.09 (0.52)	0.094 (0.62)	…	…	…	…
b. 1966:1–1973:1	0.033 (0.24)	0.075 (0.78)	…	…	…	…
c. 1973:2–1976:4	…	0.281** (0.62)	…	…	…	…
9. Exchange rate, 1973:1–1976:4	…	0.849 (1.69)	…	…	…	…
10. Dummy						
a. First Italian explosion, 1962:1–1964:4	…	…	…	−0.037 (−0.27)	−0.20 (−1.15)	…
b. Restraint in West Germany and United Kingdom, 1967:1–1969:3	…	…	…	0.262 (1.58)	0.025 (0.13)	…
c. French general strike, 1968:2–1968:3	…	…	…	0.887 (2.54)	0.847 (2.34)	…
d. General wage explosion, 1969:4–1970:2	…	…	…	1.088 (2.99)	1.583 (4.86)	…
e. U.S. money supply	…	…	…	…	…	…
Regression statistic (per cent)						
11. Standard error	0.91	0.90	0.39	0.31	0.43	0.24
12. Cumulative error, 1973:2–1976:4	−46.4	…	−15.7	−3.3	…	…

See note to tables.

Table 6. Money, wage, and price equations, Canada.

Independent variable and regression statistic	Dependent variable and sample period			
	Money supply		Wage rate	
	1958.3–1973:1 (1)	1958.3–1976.4 (2)	1958.3–1973:1 (3)	1958.3–1976.4 (4)
Independent variable				
1. Lagged dependent variable	0.099 (0.25)	0.130 (0.39)	0.527* (1.54)	-0.116 (-0.40)
2. Money supply	⋯	⋯	-0.049 (-0.43)	0.028 (0.20)
3. Wage rate	0.869* (0.61)	0.387 (0.44)	⋯	⋯
4. Output ratio (quarterly change)	0.340 (0.89)	0.319 (0.97)	⋯	⋯
5. Output ratio (level)	⋯	⋯	0.094 (0.97)	0.109 (0.91)
6. Traded-goods price index	-0.906** (-1.31)	0.392* (1.00)	0.134* (0.62)	0.282 (1.40)
7. Fiscal-deficit residual (level)	-0.169 (-0.18)	-0.194 (-0.26)	⋯	⋯

8. International reserves	...	...	0.016 (0.60)	0.024 (0.72)
a. 1958:3–1962:2	0.058 (0.36)	0.172* (1.15)	...	...
b. 1962:3–1970:2	0.107 (1.38)	0.082 (1.12)	...	...
c. 1970:3–1976:4	−0.105 (−0.08)	0.007 (0.05)	...	...
9. Exchange rate, 1973:1–1976:4	0.464 (0.66)	−0.633 (−1.34)	...	...
10. Dummy				
a. U.S. money supply	0.269 (1.16)	0.202 (1.10)	...	...
b. U.S. wage rate	...	...	0.436 (1.09)	1.143 (2.79)
c. Restraint, 1975:4–1976:4	...	...	...	1.345 (2.50)
Regression statistic (per cent)				
11. Standard error	1.82	1.83	0.499	0.678
12. Cumulative error, 1973:2–1976:4	51.1	...	4.1	...

See notes to tables.

Table 7. Money, wage, and price equations, France.

Independent variable and regression statistic	Dependent variable and sample period					
	Money supply		Wage rate			Price index
				With dummies		
	1958:3–1973:1 (1)	1958:3–1976:4 (2)	1958:3–1973:1 (3)	1958:3–1973:1 (4)	1958:3–1976:4 (5)	1958:3–1973:1 (6)
Independent variable						
1. Lagged dependent variable	-0.011 (0.02)	0.149* (0.37)	-0.278* (-0.80)	-0.151 (-0.51)	0.364* (1.42)	0.222* (0.74)
2. Money supply	⋯	⋯	0.634* (2.37)	0.593* (2.61)	0.347* (1.68)	0.115* (0.58)
3. Wage rate	0.699 (0.89)	-0.004* (-0.01)	⋯	⋯	⋯	⋯
a. Wage rate minus dummy contribution						0.488* (1.39)
b. Dummy contribution						0.764 (1.27)
4. Output ratio (quarterly change)	-0.447 (-1.35)	-0.287 (-0.94)	⋯			⋯
5. Output ratio (level)			0.375 (1.61)	0.242 (1.24)	0.025 (0.12)	-0.027† (-0.18)

6. Traded-goods price index	-0.496 (-1.48)	-0.067 (-0.25)	0.036 (0.23)	0.196* (1.43)	0.323* (2.89)	0.032† (0.24)
7. Fiscal-deficit residual (level)	-1.085 (-0.56)	0.266* (0.19)	...	...	...	...
8. International reserves	...	...	0.002 (0.04)	0.006 (0.04)	-0.019** (-0.55)	-0.021** (-0.81)
a. 1958:3–1965:4	0.028 (0.22)	0.035 (0.30)	...	...	...	...
b. 1966:1–1973:1	0.069 (0.62)	0.097* (1.06)	...	...	...	...
c. 1973:2–1976:4	...	0.186 (1.22)	...	...	...	...
9. Exchange rate, 1973:1–1976:4	...	0.347 (1.03)	...	...	...	...
10. Dummy						
a. Restraint, 1964:1–1965:4	...	...	...	-0.257 (-0.88)	-0.341 (-0.99)	...
b. Wage push, 1968:2–1968:3	...	...	...	2.794 (3.73)	3.130 (3.92)	...
Regression statistic (per cent)						
11. Standard error	1.33	1.29	0.81	0.67	0.84	0.47
12. Cumulative error, 1973:2–1976:4	9.86	...	27.5	19.23	...	...

See notes to tables.

Table 8. Money, wage, and price equations, West Germany.

	Dependent variable and sample period					
	Money supply		Wage rate			Price index
				With dummies		
Independent variable and regression statistic	1958:3–1973:1 (1)	1958:3–1976:4 (2)	1958:3–1973:1 (3)	1958:3–1973:1 (4)	1958:3–1976:4 (5)	1958:3–1973:1 (6)
Independent variable						
1. Lagged dependent variable	0.301* (0.97)	0.251 (0.58)	−0.187 (−0.48)	−0.239 (−0.64)	−0.259 (−0.96)	−0.220 (−0.39)
2. Money supply	...	...	0.330 (1.00)	0.430 (1.36)	0.126* (0.65)	0.288 (0.70)
3. Wage rate	0.428* (1.08)	−0.123* (−0.24)	...	...	...	...
a. Wage rate minus dummy contribution	...	...	...	...	...	0.055* (0.09)
b. Dummy contribution	...	...	...	...	...	0.649 (0.19)
4. Ouput ratio (quarterly change)	−0.051** (−0.16)	−0.255** (−0.56)	...	...	...	...

5. Output ratio (level)	...	...	0.279 (0.60)	0.247 (0.56)	0.273* (0.76)	0.015 (0.02)
6. Traded-goods price index	−0.777** (−2.18)	0.155* (0.37)	0.410 (1.07)	0.296* (0.81)	0.025 (0.12)	0.734* (1.37)
7. Fiscal-deficit residual (level)	−2.330 (−1.51)	3.383* (1.60)	...	...	...	...
8. International reserves	...	...	−0.079** (−1.75)	−0.060† (−1.36)	−0.028† (−0.83)	0.027 (0.34)
a. 1958:3–1965:4	0.183 (1.34)	0.123 (0.69)	...	...	...	...
b. 1966:1–1973:1	0.137 (3.41)	0.056 (0.93)	...	...	...	...
c. 1973:2–1976:4	...	0.363 (0.93)	...	...	...	...
9. Exchange rate, 1973:1–1976:4	...	−0.494 (−1.47)	...	...	...	...
10. Dummy						
a. Restraint, 1967:1–1969:3	...	...	...	0.011 (0.02)	−0.240 (−0.51)	...
b. Wage push, 1969:4–1970:2	...	...	...	1.860 (2.43)	2.19 (3.30)	...
Regression statistic (per cent)						
11. Standard error	0.92	1.47	0.97	0.92	0.91	1.13
12. Cumulative error, 1973:2–1976:4	19.7	...	−12.1	−6.5	...	...

See notes to tables.

Table 9. Money, wage, and price equations, Italy.

Independent variable and regression statistic	Money supply		Wage rate				Price index
	1958:3–1973:1 (1)	1958:3–1976:4 (2)	1958:3–1973:1 (3)	With dummies			1958:3–1973:1 (6)
				1958:3–1973:1 (4)	1958:3–1976:4 (5)		
Independent variable							
1. Lagged dependent variable	0.012 (0.02)	0.638* (1.16)	0.081 (0.21)	0.009 (0.04)	−0.138** (−1.68)		1.037* (1.86)
2. Money supply	...	...	−0.016 (−0.04)	0.179* (0.77)	0.868* (2.50)		0.115 (0.64)
3. Wage rate	0.223† (0.34)	0.177* (0.32)	...	...	...		...
a. Wage rate minus dummy contribution	...	...	...	...	...		−0.004 (−0.01)
b. Dummy contribution	...	...	...	...	...		0.056 (0.19)
4. Output ratio (quarterly change)	0.714 (1.44)	0.302 (0.67)	...	...	...		...

	Col 1	Col 2	Col 3	Col 4	Col 5	Col 6
5. Output ratio (level)	...	...	0.270 (0.61)	0.107† (0.49)	−0.093† (−0.21)	0.004 (0.02)
6. Traded-goods price index	0.337 (0.56)	−0.046 (−0.11)	0.327† (0.73)	0.427† (1.51)	0.753* (2.86)	0.274* (1.12)
7. Fiscal-deficit residual (level)	0.659 (0.36)	−0.120 (−0.07)	...	...	...	...
8. International reserves	...	...	−0.068** (−0.54)	−0.057** (−0.74)	−0.092** (−1.18)	−0.012† (−0.18)
a. 1958:3–1965:4	0.178 (0.79)	0.039 (0.18)	...	...	...	...
b. 1966:1–1973:1	−0.181 (−0.61)	−0.347 (−1.17)	...	...	...	...
c. 1973:2–1976:4	...	−0.329 (−0.59)	...	...	...	...
9. Exchange rate, 1973:1–1976:4	...	−0.240 (−0.21)	...	...	...	...
10. Dummy						
a. Wage push, 1962:1–1964:4	...	...	...	1.318 (3.48)	1.823 (2.73)	...
b. Wage push, 1970:1	...	...	...	8.451 (6.69)	9.173 (4.06)	...
Regression statistic (per cent)						
11. Standard error	1.88	2.00	1.42	0.86	1.73	0.57
12. Cumulative error, 1973:2–1976:4	−61.4	...	14.4	13.6	...	...

See notes to tables.

Table 10. Money, wage, and price equations, Japan.

Independent variable and regression statistic	Dependent variable and sample period					
	Money supply		Wage rate			Price index
				With dummies		
	1958:3–1973:1 (1)	1958:3–1976:4 (2)	1958:3–1973:1 (3)	1958:3–1973:1 (4)	1958:3–1976:4 (5)	1958:3–1973:1 (6)
Independent variable						
1. Lagged dependent variable	−1.035** (−2.17)	−0.694** (−1.75)	0.866* (2.35)	0.714 (1.89)	0.581* (2.08)	−0.310** (−0.82)
2. Money supply	⋯	⋯	0.132* (0.71)	0.172* (1.12)	0.197* (1.15)	−0.019 (0.17)
3. Wage rate	−0.100 (−0.09)	−0.313** (−0.39)	⋯	⋯	⋯	⋯
a. Wage rate minus dummy contribution	⋯	⋯	⋯	⋯	⋯	0.155* (0.61)
b. Dummy contribution	⋯	⋯	⋯	⋯	⋯	−0.666† (−0.37)
4. Output ratio (quarterly change)	−1.020** (−2.74)	−0.751** (−2.27)	⋯	⋯	⋯	⋯

5. Output ratio (level)	...	...	0.001 (0.01)	0.010 (0.05)	0.006 (0.03)	0.074† (0.53)
6. Traded-goods price index	0.461 (0.88)	0.205 (0.51)	-0.032 (-0.03)	-0.029 (-0.11)	0.179* (1.28)	0.371† (2.22)
7. Fiscal-deficit residual (level)	5.211* (1.76)	5.655* (3.26)	...	...	...	...
8. International reserves	...	...	0.002 (0.06)	-0.001 (-0.02)	-0.001* (-0.02)	0.009 (0.40)
a. 1958:3–1965:4	0.434* (2.22)	0.391* (2.23)	...	...	...	...
b. 1966:1–1973:1	0.289* (2.51)	0.275* (2.87)	...	...	...	...
c. 1973:2–1976:4	...	0.458* (1.25)	...	...	...	...
9. Exchange rate, 1973:1–1976:4	...	3.698* (3.43)	...	...	...	...
10. Dummy						
a. Wage push, 1967:4–1968:4	...	...	...	0.677 (0.96)	1.064 (1.76)	...
b. Wage push, 1970:1–1970:4	...	...	...	0.720 (1.13)	0.502 (0.81)	...
Regression statistic (per cent)						
11. Standard error	2.04	1.97	0.99	0.98	1.15	0.64
12. Cumulative error, 1973:2–1976:4	-53.3	...	3.3	10.0	...	...

See notes to tables.

Table 11. Money, wage, and price equations, Sweden.

Independent variable and regression statistic	Dependent variable and sample period					
	Money supply		Wage rate			Price index
				With dummies		
	1958:3–1973:1 (1)	1958:3–1976:4 (2)	1958:3–1973:1 (3)	1958:3–1973:1 (4)	1958:3–1976:4 (5)	1958:3–1973:1 (6)
Independent variable						
1. Lagged dependent variable	0.333 (0.58)	0.670 (1.44)	−0.727** (−2.31)	−0.834** (−2.75)	−0.644** (−2.19)	−0.560** (−1.09)
2. Money supply	...	...	−0.280 (−2.14)	−0.260** (−1.99)	−0.255** (−1.57)	−0.021† (−0.17)
3. Wage rate	1.100 (0.76)	0.041 (0.04)	...	...	...	...
a. Wage rate minus dummy contribution	...	...	...	...	...	0.317* (0.92)
b. Dummy contribution	...	...	...	...	...	0.344 (0.35)
4. Output ratio (quarterly change)	−2.004 (−1.50)	−2.244 (−1.98)	...	...	...	...
5. Output ratio (level)	...	...	−0.580 (−1.10)	−0.816 (−1.60)	−1.307** (−1.76)	−0.042† (−0.10)

	(1)	(2)	(3)	(4)	(5)	(6)
6. Traded-goods price index	−0.841 (−0.46)	0.541* (0.44)	1.615* (2.69)	1.367* (2.37)	0.682* (1.62)	0.425* (0.87)
7. Fiscal-deficit residual (level)	−1.418 (−0.34)	−0.630 (−0.19)	...	...	...	...
8. International reserves	...	...	0.092* (1.48)	0.070* (1.14)	0.110 (1.53)	0.034 (0.69)
a. 1958:3–1965:4	−0.186 (−0.38)	−0.232 (−0.55)	...	...	...	...
b. 1966:1–1973:1	0.124 (0.49)	−0.080 (−0.39)	...	...	...	...
c. 1973:2–1976:4	...	−0.117 (−0.18)	...	...	...	...
9. Exchange rate, 1973:1–1976:4	...	−0.806 (−0.63)	...	...	...	...
10. Dummy						
a. Wage push, 1969:4–1970:2	...	...	...	2.662 (2.47)	2.788 (1.89)	...
b. Restraint, 1970:3–1971:2	...	...	...	0.663 (0.43)	2.709 (1.43)	...
c. Re-entry, 1971:3–1972:2	...	...	...	2.846 (1.94)	5.92 (3.16)	...
Regression statistic (per cent)						
11. Standard error	4.27	3.97	1.32	1.16	1.75	0.89
12. Cumulative error, 1973:2–1976:4	50.5	...	−46.0	−27.0	...	...

See notes to tables.

Table 12. *Money, wage, and price equations, United Kingdom.*

	Dependent variable and sample period					
Independent variable and regression statistic	Money supply		Wage rate			Price index
				With dummies		
	1958:3–1973:1 (1)	1958:3–1976:4 (2)	1959:3–1973:1 (3)	1958:3–1973:1 (4)	1958:3–1976:4 (5)	1958:3–1973:1 (6)
Independent variable						
1. Lagged dependent variable	−1.856** (−3.63)	−0.869** (−2.06)	−0.051 (−0.09)	−0.442 (−0.80)	−0.089 (−0.26)	−0.347** (−0.82)
2. Money supply	...	...	0.781* (3.77)	0.652* (2.89)	0.473* (2.17	0.011 (0.07)
3. Wage rate	0.413* (0.29)	1.741* (2.07)	...	...	...	...
a. Wage rate minus dummy contribution						1.057* (2.68)
b. Dummy contribution						1.250 (1.74)
4. Output ratio (quarterly change)	1.936* (2.56)	2.131* (3.37)	...	...	...	...
5. Output ratio (level)	...	...	−0.072 (−0.19)	−0.198 (−0.55)	−0.010† (−0.08)	−0.156 (−0.54)
6. Traded-goods price index	0.300 (0.28)	−0.373 (−0.44)	0.015 (0.03)	−0.137 (−0.29)	0.404† (1.08)	−0.478** (−1.48)

7. Fiscal-deficit residual (level)	−0.047 (−0.03)	0.954** (0.67)	...	...	...	−0.023 (−0.69)
8. International reserves	...	...	−0.045 (−0.91)	−0.058 (−1.25)	−0.040 (−0.81)	...
a. 1958:3–1965:4	−0.043 (−0.33)	0.056 (0.46)	...	...	...	...
b. 1966:1–1973:1	0.348* (2.59)	0.159 (1.36)	...	...	...	...
c 1973:2–1976:4	...	0.274 (0.63)	...	...	...	...
9. Exchange rate, 1973:1–1976:4	...	−0.019 (−0.02)	...	...	...	...
10. Dummy						
a. Freeze[a]	...	...	...	−0.525 (−0.69)	−0.388 (−0.53)	...
b. Restraint[a]	...	...	...	−1.493 (−1.82)	−0.600 (−0.73)	...
c. Re-entry[a]	...	...	...	−9.988 (−1.09)	−0.939 (−0.91)	...
d. Wage push, 1970:1–1971:1	...	...	...	2.197 (2.41)	0.854 (0.88)	...
Regression statistic (per cent)						
11. Standard error	2.28	2.42	1.20	1.11	1.43	0.67
12. Cumulative error, 1973:2–1976:4	18.9	...	25.2	56.9	...	...

See notes to tables.
(a) See note 64.

APPENDIX

Sources and Uses of Data

Unless otherwise noted, all variables were copied in level form from the data tape of *International Financial Statistics,* made available by the research department of the International Monetary Fund. Variables entered into the regressions were one-quarter rates of change calculated from these levels, with the exception of the fiscal deficit and output ratio in the wage and price equations (see below). All variables in level form are denominated in domestic currency.

Exchange rate. Quarterly average of market rate, or par or central rate, expressed as domestic currency per U.S. dollar.

Fiscal-deficit residual. The nominal deficit of the central government was divided by nominal gross national product to form the fiscal-deficit ratio. This ratio was then regressed on a constant, three seasonal dummies, and the real output ratio, current and lagged one period. The level of the residual from this regression was entered into the money equations as the variable labelled 'fiscal-deficit residual' in tables 4 through 12.

International reserves. Foreign assets of the central bank denominated in local currency. Because of implausible jumps in the data, this variable was defined for France and Italy as international reserves denominated in dollars multiplied by the exchange rate.

Money supply. M_1 was used for all countries except Canada and France. For those two countries, M_2 was used because of large shifts from demand to time deposits in 1967–68 as a result of changes in their banking regulations. The M_2 concept was defined as the M_1 series from the data tape plus the 'quasi-money' series. An implausible M_1 value for West Germany for 1968:1 was replaced by the average of 1967:4 and 1968:2, divided by an estimated seasonal-adjustment coefficient, 1.109.

Price deflator. Nominal GNP divided by real GNP (gross domestic product in some countries—see comments on actual output). Quarterly values for France and Italy for some years were interpolated by quarterly changes in the consumer price index, adjusted to maintain accurate official growth rates from year to year in the deflator.

Output ratio. The ratio of actual output *(Q)* to potential output *(Q*).* This ratio is entered in level form in the wage and price equations and as a one-quarter rate of change in the money equations.

Actual output (Q). Real GNP for Germany, Italy, Japan, and the United States. Real GDP for Canada, France, Sweden, and the United Kingdom. Where the data tape gave only annual data, quarterly data were constructed from annual series using as an interpolator the index of industrial production, adjusted by the relative annual growth rate of real output relative to industrial production. Interpolation was required for France

(1957:1–1969:4), Germany (1957:1–1961:4), Italy (1957:1–1974:1), and Sweden (1957:1–1973:4). Missing IMF data for 1975–76 for France and for 1976:4 for Italy were filled in from OECD, *Main Economic Indicators.* For Canada and Japan real output was derived by dividing nominal GNP by the GNP deflator from the data tape (GDP for Canada). Several quarters exhibiting sharp fluctuations in output were bridged to eliminate the effects of strikes and harsh weather. These included France (1959:1 and 1968:2), Germany (1963:1), Sweden (1963:1), and the United States (1959:3 and 1959:4, 1964:4, and 1970:4).

Potential output (Q*). The basic source was the biannual index of potential manufacturing output developed by Jacques R. Artus, 'Measures of potential output in manufacturing for eight industrial countries, 1955–78', International Monetary Fund, *Staff Papers,* **24** (March), 1977, pp. 1–35. Artus' indexes of potential output are derived from a production-function approach that allows the growth of potential output to vary annually in response to changes in the growth rate of capital and potential labour input, with the latter adjusted to take account of a gradually increasing full-employment unemployment rate. The resulting estimates are first interpolated here to a quarterly basis and then converted to a GNP (rather than just manufacturing) concept by multiplying the quarterly growth rates of potential output in manufacturing by the ratio of the growth of real GNP to the growth in manufacturing output between benchmark years. These years are those in which Artus' measure of the gap between actual and potential manufacturing output is approximately zero.

Traded-goods price index. An average of the rate of change of the import and export price indexes of each country.

Wage rate. The wage-rate series on the *IFS* tape is different for each country. For Canada it is average hourly earnings in manufacturing; France, index of labour costs, mechanical and electrical industries; Germany, index of wages, from the weekly statistical service of the Federal Statistical Office; Italy, index of minimum contractual wages for workers, excluding family allowance; Japan, index of contract cash earnings, all industries; Sweden, index of direct wages in all industrial groups; United Kingdom, index of average monthly earnings in all industries and services covered.

For the United States the wage index was taken from the data file of my paper, 'Can the inflation of the 1970s be explained?' *Brookings Papers on Economic Activity,* **8** (1), 1977, pp. 253–77. Since 1964 this index is the Bureau of Labor Statistics series on average hourly earnings of production or nonsupervisory workers on total private nonagricultural payrolls, adjusted for changes in overtime and the interindustry employment mix. Methods used to extend this index before 1964 are described in my 'Inflation in recession and recovery', *Brookings Papers on Economic Activity,* **2** (1), 1971 appendix C. The fringe-benefit adjustment used in the two cited papers was not applied to the wage index used in this paper.

NOTES

1. This research has been supported by the National Science Foundation. I am grateful to my colleague John Bilson for aiding me in the acquisition of data from the International Monetary Fund, and my research assistant James Glassman for an absolutely outstanding job. Also helpful were the suggestions of Victor Argy, Jacques Artus, Jacob Frenkel, Hans Genberg, Robert Hall, John Helliwell, Paul Krugman, David Laidler, Arthur Okun, Michael Parkin, George Perry, Richard Sweeney, and George Zis. Of special value were a number of discussions with Christopher Sims. An abbreviated version of this chapter appeared in the *Brookings Papers on Economic Activity,* **8** (2), 1977, pp. 409–68. I am grateful to the Brookings Institution for permission to reprint the portion of this paper which duplicates the Brookings version.
2. Harry G. Johnson, 'Inflation: a "monetarist" view', in Harry G. Johnson, *Further Essays in Monetary Economics* (London: Allen and Unwin, 1972), p. 335.
3. Nicholas Kaldor, 'Inflation and recession in the world economy', *Economic Journal,* **86** (December), 1976, p. 710.
4. Arnold C. Harberger, 'Inflation', in John Van Doren (ed.), *Symposium on the Emerging World Economy (Great Ideas Today* series) (Chicago: Encyclopaedia Britannica Educational Corporation, 1976), pp. 94–106.
5. Quotations from Harry G. Johnson, 'Panel discussion: world inflation', in Emil Claassen and Pascal Salin (ed.), *Stabilization Policies in Interdependent Economies* (Amsterdam: North-Holland, 1972), pp. 310–11.
6. Nicholas Kaldor, 'Inflation and recession in the world economy', *Economic Journal,* **86** (December), 1976, p. 710.
7. The 'Other Seven' countries are Canada, France, West Germany, Italy, Japan, Sweden, and the United Kingdom.
8. See, for instance, David I. Meiselman, 'Worldwide inflation: a monetarist view', in David I. Meiselman and Arthur B. Laffer (eds.), *The Phenomenon of Worldwide Inflation* (Washington DC: American Enterprise Institute, 1975), pp. 69–112. See also Hans Genberg and Alexander K. Swoboda, 'Causes and Origins of Current Worldwide Inflation', Discussion paper (Geneva: Graduate Institute of International Studies, November 1975; processed).
9. See M.R. Gray, R. Ward, and G. Zis, 'The world demand for money functions: some preliminary results', and Nigel Duck *et al.,* 'The determination of the rate of change of wages and prices in the fixed exchange rate world economy, 1956–71', both in Michael Parkin and George Zis (eds.), *Inflation in the World Economy* (Manchester: Manchester University Press and Toronto: Toronto University Press, 1976), pp. 151–78 and 113–43 respectively.
10. See Hans Genberg and Alexander K. Swoboda, 'Causes and Origins of Current Worldwide Inflation', Discussion paper (Geneva: Graduate Institute of International Studies, November 1975; processed).
11. See Robert A. Mundell, *International Economics* (London: Macmillan, 1968), chapter 18; also Harry G. Johnson, 'The monetary approach to balance of payments theory', in Harry G. Johnson, *Further Essays in Monetary Economics* (London: Allen and Unwin, 1972), pp. 229–49.
12. Rudiger Dornbusch, 'Devaluation, money, and nontraded goods', *American Economic Review,* **63** (December), 1973, pp. 871–80. The Dornbusch model is extended to the case of imperfectly flexible prices in Robert J. Gordon, 'Interrelations

between domestic and international theories of inflation', in Robert Z. Aliber (ed.), *The Political Economy of Monetary Reform* (London: Macmillan, 1977), pp. 126–54.

13.   An excellent general discussion of the channels through which inflation is transmitted can be found in Walter S. Salant, 'International transmission of inflation', in Lawrence B. Krause and Walter S. Salant (eds.), *Worldwide Inflation: Theory and Recent Experience* (Brookings Institution, 1977), pp. 167–227. See also Alexander K. Swoboda, 'Monetary approaches to worldwide inflation', in the same volume, especially pp. 33–44.

14.   This is the primary channel of international transmission in the 'Scandanavian' model of inflation. See Gösta Edgren, Karl-Olaf Faxén, and Clas-Erik Odhner, 'Wages, growth and the distribution of income', *Swedish Journal of Economics,* **71** (September), 1969, pp. 133–60. Also Odd Aukrust, 'Inflation in the open economy: a Norwegian model', in Lawrence B. Krause and Walter S. Salant (eds.), *Worldwide Inflation: Theory and Recent Experience* (Brookings Institution, 1977), pp. 107–53.

15.   See Irving B. Kravis and Robert E. Lipsey, 'Export prices and the transmission of inflation', *American Economic Review,* **67** (February), 1977, pp. 155–63. Also see Rudiger Dornbusch and Paul Krugman, 'Flexible exchange rates in the short run', *Brookings Papers in Economic Activity,* **7** (3), 1976, especially pp. 559–68.

16.   Peter Wiles, 'Cost inflation and the state of economic theory', *Economic Journal,* **83** (June), 1973, p. 378.

17.   A clear statement emphasizing the fairness issue is contained in John Hicks, *The Crisis in Keynesian Economics* (Oxford: Basil Blackwell, 1974), chapter 3.

18.   Richard N. Cooper, statement in 'Commentaries' on paper by Thomas D. Willet, 'The Eurocurrency market, exchange-rate systems, and national financial policies', in Carl H. Stem, John H. Makin, and Dennis E. Logue (eds.), *Eurocurrencies and the International Monetary System* (Washington DC: American Enterprise Institute, 1976), p. 252.

19.   Peter Wiles, 'Cost inflation and the state of economic theory', *Economic Journal,* **83** (June), 1973, p. 385; Stephen Marris, 'Panel discussion: world inflation', in Emil Claassen and Pascal Salin (eds.), *Stabilization Policies in Interdependent Economies* (Amsterdam: North–Holland, 1972), p. 303.

20.   Aubrey Jones, for instance, argues that 'a tightening of the supply of money is not, therefore, . . . a solution to the problem of rising prices', in *The New Inflation: The Politics of Prices and Incomes* (London: André Deutsch and Penguin, 1973), p. 39.

21.   See in particular George L. Perry, 'Determinants of wage inflation around the world', in Lawrence B. Krause and Walter S. Salant (eds.), *Worldwide Inflation: Theory and Recent Experience* (Brookings Institution, 1977), especially table 4, p. 424, in which significant coefficients are found for a dummy for 1968 in France and for 1970 in Italy, West Germany, Sweden, and the United Kingdom (a 1968 dummy for Japan is only marginally significant). A similar approach was followed by Erich Spitäller, who found significant dummy coefficients in various periods for France, West Germany, and the United Kingdom; see 'Semi-annual wage equations for the manufacturing sectors of six major industrial countries', *Review of World Economics,* No. 2, 1976, pp. 300–37.

22.   The most comprehensive tests of strike variables are presented in David Laidler, 'Inflation—alternative explanations and policies: tests on data drawn from

six countries', in Karl Brunner and Allan H. Meltzer (eds.), *Institutions, Policies and Economic Performance* (Amsterdam: North–Holland, 1976), pp. 251–306.

23.   A more formal and extended presentation of this framework is developed in Robert J. Gordon, 'The demand for and supply of inflation', *Journal of Law and Economics,* **18** (December), 1975, pp. 807–36. The paper provides additional citations and support for assertations made here. The presentation here reflects comments and discussion during the period since the drafting of the earlier paper.

24.   See Martin J. Bailey, 'The welfare cost of inflationary finance', *Journal of Political Economy,* **64** (April), 1956, pp. 93–110. Also Edward Tower, 'More on the welfare cost of inflationary finance', *Journal of Money, Credit, and Banking,* 3 (November), 1971, pp. 850–59.

25.   Arthur Okun points out that this two-way relation, if true, would provide the central bank an opportunity to conduct an 'incomes policy by terror'.

26.   This possibility is suggested in Mancur Olson's comment on my paper, 'The demand for and supply of inflation', *Journal of Law and Economics,* **18** (December), 1975, pp. 807–36. And it raises the standard question about cost push: why hadn't the senior workers already attained the optimum distribution relative to the junior workers?

27.   Mancur Olson puts forth this idea to explain the contrast between the rapid postwar real-output growth rates of Japan and Germany as contrasted to that of the United Kingdom in his 'The Political Economy of Comparative Growth Rates' (University of Maryland, October 1976).

28.   Albert O. Hirschman, *Journeys Towards Progress: Studies of Economic Policymaking in Latin America* (Cambridge, Mass.: Harvard University Press, 1963), pp. 208–9.

29.   A detailed analysis is contained in Robert J. Gordon, 'Alternative responses of policy to external supply shocks', *Brookings Papers on Economic Activity,* **6** (1), 1975, pp. 183–204.

30.   See Robert A. Mundell, *International Economics* (London: Macmillan, 1968), chapter 18.

31.   In the pure international monetary model with flexible prices, fixed output and perfect capital mobility, the Friedmanian central banker would have no control over the money supply, only over the division of the monetary base between international reserves and domestic credit. See several essays by Harry G. Johnson, in Jacob A. Frenkel and Harry G. Johnson (eds.), *The Monetary Approach to the Balance of Payments* (Toronto: University of Toronto Press, 1976), chapters 2,6, and 11.

32.   The seminal article was Grant L. Reuber, 'The objectives of Canadian monetary policy, 1949–61: empirical "trade-offs" and the reaction function of the authorities', *Journal of Political Economy,* **72** (April), 1964, pp. 109–32. A recent article containing a comprehensive set of references is Thomas M. Havrilesky, Robert Sapp, and Robert Schweitzer, 'Tests of the Federal Reserve's reaction to the state of the economy: 1964–74', *Social Science Quarterly,* **55** (March), 1975, pp. 835–52. Implications of endogenous stabilization reaction functions for reduced-form multiplier estimates are the subject of Stephen M. Goldfeld and Alan S. Blinder 'Some implications of endogenous stabilization policy', *Brookings Papers on Economic Activity,* 3 (3), 1972, pp. 585–640.

33.   Assar Lindbeck, 'Stabilization policy in open economies with endogenous politicians', *American Economic Review,* **66** (May), 1976, pp. 1–19.

34. William D. Nordhaus, 'The political business cycle', *Review of Economic Studies*, **42** (April), 1975, pp. 169–90.
35. Douglas A. Hibbs, Jr., 'Political parties and macroeconomic policy', *American Political Science Review*, **71** (December), 1977, pp. 1467–87.
36. Michael Parkin, 'The politics of inflation', *Government and Opposition*, **10** (Spring), 1975, pp. 189–202.
37. Robert J. Gordon, 'The demand for and supply of inflation', *Journal of Law and Economics*, **18** (December), 1975, p. 830.
38. Since consistency is not a necessary feature of the policies of columns 2 and 3, the entries on traded-goods prices in those columns are enclosed in parentheses.
39. Christopher A. Sims, 'Money, income, and causality', *American Economic Review*, **62** (September), 1972, pp. 540–52.
40. See C.W.J. Granger, 'Investigating causal relations by econometric models and cross-spectral methods', *Econometrica*, **37** (July), 1969, pp. 424–38. Christopher A. Sims, 'Macroeconomics and reality', *Econometrica*, (forthcoming), 1980.
41. I am grateful to Robert Hall for urging me to switch to the second method after a preliminary bout with the leading-variable technique.
42. The price equation includes two sets of current and lagged wage variables: (1) the contribution of the dummy variables in the wage equation, and (2) wage change minus the dummy contribution. If the two sets of coefficients are identical, then all wage changes alter prices in the same way, whereas a zero coefficient on the dummy contribution would indicate that the autonomous wage movements identified by the dummy variables did not influence price change at all.
43. Readers are referred to the data appendix, available from the author on request, for a detailed account of the construction of the data file developed for this project.
44. Robert J. Gordon, 'Can the inflation of the 1970s be explained?', *Brookings Papers on Economic Activity*, **8** (1), 1977, pp. 253–77.
45. The weights are current shares of real GNP, in U.S. dollars.
46. The money coefficients and t ratios (in parentheses), with and without the output-ratio variable, are as follows:

	With output	*Without output*
United States	0.258 (3.04)	0.327 (4.15)
Other Seven	0.209 (1.58)	0.156 (1.11)
Canada	–0.049 (–0.43)	0.019 (0.17)
France	0.593 (2.61)	0.526 (2.48)
West Germany	0.430 (1.36)	0.702 (2.52)
Italy	0.179 (0.77)	0.212 (0.94)
Japan	0.172 (1.12)	0.171 (1.00)
Sweden	–0.260 (–1.99)	–0.024 (–0.22)
United Kingdom	0.652 (2.89)	0.706 (3.55)

The decline in the coefficient for the Other Seven is puzzling, in the light of the increase in the average coefficient of the seven individual countries from 0.25 to 0.33.
47. The set-up of table 6, for Canada, is slightly different because no wage equations with dummy variables for the 1958–73 period were estimated for that country.
48. Christopher A. Sims, 'Money, income, and causality', *American Economic Review*, **62** (September), 1972, p. 547.

49.   The contribution of the wage terms rises from an average of 1.23 per cent per quarter in 1964 to 3.73 per cent in 1968.

50.   The coefficient on the fourth lag is strongly negative. The sum of coefficients on the current value and first three lags is 3.87 with a t ratio of 2.53. Figure 1 reveals the lead of wages relative to money in late 1965, and the contemporaneous movements in late 1968, mid-1970, and early 1971.

51.   See, for instance, Erich Spitäller, 'Semi-annual wage equations for the manufacturing sectors of six major industrial countries', Review of World Economies, No. 2, 1976, pp. 300–37.

52.   This restrictive reaction to the capital inflow is noted in Organisation for Economic Co-operation and Development, Monetary Policy in France (Monetary Studies Series) (Paris: OECD, 1974), p. 46.

53.   Lloyd Ulman and Robert J. Flanagan, Wage Restraint: A Study of Incomes Policies in Western Europe (Berkeley: University of California Press, 1971), pp. 161–63.

54.   Over the same period the contribution of the wage terms to the four-quarter rate of change of money rises by 5.23 per cent, and of the reserve terms by 6.72 per cent. Since this over-explains the actual acceleration, the contribution of the other terms decreases.

55.   OECD, Monetary Policy in Germany (Monetary Studies Series) (Paris: OECD, December 1973), pp. 43–50.

56.   Lloyd Ulman and Robert J. Flanagan, Wage Restraint: A Study of Incomes Policies in Western Europe (Berkeley: University of California Press, 1971), pp. 186–91. See also Gehard Fels, 'Inflation in Germany', in Lawrence B. Krause and Walter S. Salant (eds.), Worldwide Inflation: Theory and Recent Experience (Brookings Institution, 1977), pp. 619–20. Herbert Giersch dates the voluntary restraint back to a meeting between the German Council of Economic Advisers and representatives of the trade unions and the employers' associations on June 17, 1965, in A Discussion with Herbert Giersch: Current Problems of the West German Economy, 1976–1977 (Washington DC: American Enterprise Institute, 1977), p. 6.

57.   Lloyd Ulman and Robert J. Flanagan, Wage Restraint: A Study of Incomes Policies in Western Europe (Berkeley: University of California Press, 1971), pp. 202–3, include the interval 1961:3–1963:2 in their description of the 'wage explosion'.

58.   OECD, Monetary Policy in Japan (Monetary Studies Series) (Paris: OECD, December 1972), p. 58. See also Gardner Ackley with collaboration of Hiromitsu Ishi, 'Fiscal, monetary, and related policies', in Hugh Patrick and Henry Rosovsky (eds.), Asia's New Giant: How the Japanese Economy Works (Brookings Institution, 1976), pp. 169–171. Ackley and Ishi argue that it was the balance of payments alone, not domestic overheating of inflation, that guided the timing of the monetary authorities.

59.   See Gardner Ackley with collaboration of Hiromitsu Ishi, 'Fiscal, monetary, and related policies', in Hugh Patrick and Henry Rosovsky (eds.), Asia's New Giant: How the Japanese Economy Works (Brookings Institution, 1976), p. 176. See also Ryutaro Komiya and Yoshio Suzuki, 'Inflation in Japan', in Lawrence B. Krause and Walter S. Salant (eds.), Worldwide Inflation: Theory and Recent Experience (Brookings Institution, 1977), pp. 303–48.

60.   George L. Perry, 'Determinants of wage inflation around the world', in

Lawrence B. Krause and Walter S. Salant (eds.), *Worldwide Inflation: Theory and Recent Experience* (Brookings Institution, 1977), table 6, p. 427.

61.   This statement is equally valid for M_1 and M_2. The four-quarter rate of change of M_1 peaked at 27.2 per cent in 1974:3 and that for M_2 at 34.0 per cent in the same quarter.

62.   Gösta Edgren, Karl-Olof Faxén, and Clas-Erik Odhner, 'Wages, growth and the distribution of income', *Swedish Journal of Economics,* 7 (September), 1969, pp. 133–60; and Odd Aukrust, 'Inflation in the open economy: a Norwegian model', in Lawrence B. Krause and Walter S. Salant (eds.), *Worldwide Inflation: Theory and Recent Experience* (Brookings Institution, 1977), pp. 107–53.

63.   Lars Calmfors, 'Inflation in Sweden', in Lawrence B. Krause and Walter S. Salant (eds.), *Worldwide Inflation: Theory and Recent Experience* (Brookings Institution, 1977), p. 530.

64.   'Faith, five hopes, and Cassandra', *Economist,* 23 (July), 1977, p. 75. The freeze dummy is in effect in 1961:3–1961:4; 1966:3–1966:4; 1972:4–1973:1. The restraint dummy is in effect in 1962:1–1963:1; 1967:1–1969:4; 1973:2–1974:1; 1975:2–1976:4. The re-entry dummy is in effect in 1963:2–1964:1; 1970:1–1970:4; 1974:2–1975:1.

65.   Another serious defect in the wage-push argument is evident if account is taken of changes in the tax rate, a variable not included in this study. Large tax increases in 1967–69 would have justified a wage push by British workers even if wage restraint had not been in effect. See H.A. Turner and Frank Wilkinson, 'Real net incomes and the wage explosion', *New Society,* 17 (25 February), 1971, pp. 309–10.

66.   For the Other Seven the dummy contribution had essentially a zero sign in the price equation, and in all countries other than the United Kingdom its coefficient was insignificantly different from zero.

67.   The four countries are the United States, France, West Germany, and the United Kingdom. See note 46, which presents estimates of the money coefficients in the wage equation when the output-ratio variable is omitted.

68.   Compare the traded-goods coefficients in the extended wage equation in each of the tables. The size of the coefficients appears to be a rather accurate inverse indicator of the current economic health of the major economies:

Italy	0.753
Sweden	0.682
United Kingdom	0.404
France	0.323
Canada	0.282
Japan	0.179
United States	0.029
West Germany	0.025

69.   Robert E. Lucas, Jr.; 'Econometric policy evaluation: a critique', in Karl Brunner and Allan H. Meltzer (eds.), *The Phillips Curve and Labor Markets* (Amsterdam: North–Holland, 1976), pp. 19–46.

Is there a Wage Equation?[1]

Michael Artis

1. Introduction

Some observers would, I think, regard the title of this paper as embodying a
strictly rhetorical question and might argue that there is no such thing as *the*
wage equation (or set of wage equations) and that, as scientists of social
problems, economists are on the wrong track in trying to measure any such
equations. Indeed, it is worth emphasizing that, in contrast to the post-war
development of thought on the subject associated with the 'discovery' and
refinement of the Phillips curve and, to a lesser extent perhaps, of its main
rival the 'real wage' hypothesis[2], there exists a body of thought for which the
concept of a wage equation has no attraction because under conditions of
'full employment' the determination of wages becomes essentially a *political*
question. Such a view was made explicit in the Oxford Institute of Statistics
classic book *Studies in Full Employment,* published in 1944; the central
argument is that the post-war expectation of full employment, or more
generally, the (then, new) possibility of control of economic events by
rational economic policy removes the determination of money wages from
the influence of uncontrollable economic events and transforms it into an
essentially political question, for which the appropriate solution is also
political; i.e. incomes policy. Except in the guise of a normative rule for the
conduct of such a policy[3] the 'wage equation' as such is from this point of
view an illegitimate and misleading concept. It is interesting to reflect that
the main difficulty this viewpoint encounters in explaining the inflation of
the late 1960s and early 1970s is not why it occurred, but why it did not
occur much earlier. Moreover, it does not deny that unemployment *per se*
affects the rate of wage inflation but rather that it does so in a finely measur-
able manner when experience of its variation is confined to the relatively
narrow band known as 'full employment'. Neither should the logically inti-
mate connection of this viewpoint with the advocacy of incomes policy be
taken to imply that its advocates suppose that an incomes policy will always

be successful; rather the development of incomes policy is to be seen as a groping for a political solution, a process which inevitably takes time and proceeds by fits and starts. Incomes policy cannot, in this view, be very sensibly evaluated according to conventional econometric criteria[4].

The reason for drawing attention to this viewpoint at the outset is to make the point that economists may need to concede that 'economics', narrowly interpreted as positive economics with an econometric output, may have little to say, whereas 'political economy' has much to say on this question. The goals of inflation analysis are to understand the inflationary process and to contribute towards its control. There is nothing in this statement to persuade us that any bonus points are to be awarded to attempted *economic* explanations *per se,* if in fact these miss the essential point. Nevertheless, the economist should, by the rules of comparative advantage, at least start on his home ground even if he does so with a professional *memento mori* at the back of his mind. At any rate, this paper is constructed in that spirit.

2. The Phillips Curve: a Second Coming?

Seven years ago a conference was held at the London School of Economics to investigate the then current inflation. A centrepiece of that gathering was the clear confirmation of the empirical failure and theoretical inappropriateness of the Phillips curve as a means of predicting wage and price change in strongly inflationary conditions[5]. By that time the statements of Friedman and Phelps[6] were, of course, already available and some testing of the expectations-augmented Phillips curve hypothesis with U.K. data had already been undertaken[7]. Since then, further attempts have been made to implement this approach for the United Kingdom[8].

The exposition of the Friedman-style expectations-augmented Phillips curve, though based squarely on postulates of the 'new' microeconomics, is redolent of the 'classical economics' which bore the weight of Keynes' criticism and invective in *The General Theory.* As the analogue of the classical 'full employment' point, the argument provides for a natural rate of unemployment at which alone zero (or any steady) rate of inflation is feasible. A lower rate of unemployment involves accelerating inflation and a higher one decelerating inflation, given the existence of some learning process in the formation of inflation expectations. The gap between the actual unemployment rate and the 'natural rate' is endogenous to the gap between actual and expected inflation. Once the latter gap is closed, so will the former gap be. This implies that on the vertical axis of a Phillips curve diagram we should (or could) plot the difference between actual and expected inflation with the curve cutting the horizontal axis at the natural rate of unemployment (or, on the hypothesis that expected inflation is a positive function of past expected inflation and the previous error, the rate of change of inflation itself may be plotted on the vertical.)

Assuming that productivity growth is zero (for the sake of simplicity), the model described in the above remarks may be written down as follows. Denoting unemployment by U, the 'natural rate' of unemployment by U^N, and actual and expected price inflation by the symbols $\dot{p}$ and $\dot{p}^e$, we have:

$$(U - U^N) = -a(\dot{p} - \dot{p}^e). \tag{1}$$

Thus

$$U = -a(\dot{p} - \dot{p}^e) + U^N \tag{2}$$

and

$$(\dot{p} - \dot{p}^e) = k - U/a \tag{3}$$

or

$$\dot{p} = k - U/a + \dot{p}^e, \tag{4}$$

where $k = U^N/a$. The spirit of Friedman's exposition of the amended Phillips curve is conveyed by equations (1) and (2), although as a matter of observation (and typically of estimation), equations (3) and (4) are simultaneously true[9].

Variations in unemployment then, other than those caused by variations in U^N, are due to misunderstandings by workers (or employers) about the true value of the real wage to which their monetary contract commits them, which seems to exclude the possibility of involuntary unemployment as defined by Keynes, or, looked at the other way round, seems to run close to the classical view disputed by Keynes that the real wage is 'set' in the labour market. The 'amendment' of the Phillips curve implicit in the Friedman exposition thus involves much more than a slight change of dimensions as has been well explained by Tobin[10], who argues that 'Phillips curve doctrine is in an important sense the postwar analogue of Keynesian wage and employment theory, while natural rate doctrine is the contemporary version of the classical position Keynes was opposing'. This being so, it is hardly surprising that attempts to test the theory have provoked controversy. The prime issue involved in such tests concerns the search for a coefficient on $\dot{p}^e$ of +1 in equations like (4), for values of this coefficient of less than 1 are acceptable to 'Keynesian' re-interpretations of the Phillips schedule and to those who place a 'bargaining' interpretation upon the Phillips relationship. The premium placed on the evaluation of this coefficient points to an obvious practical difficulty, that of measuring 'inflation expectations'. No less a problem, however, is that of evaluating the value of U^N, the 'natural' rate of unemployment.

The theory does not require U^N to be a constant, though it is natural to suppose that it changes only slowly with respect to long-run factors rather than that it should exhibit substantial quarter-to-quarter variation. Nevertheless, the customary way of finding the natural rate of unemployment, which is to solve for it in an equation like (4) on the assumption of equilibrium equality between $\dot{p}$ and $\dot{p}^e$, gives scope to the procedure of subdividing the sample period according to tests of stability. This leads to the conclusion that the natural rate has (always for all countries?) increased during the late 1960s and 1970s, a result which engenders the suspicion that a moving intercept is being made to bear too much interpretative weight. The sceptic can hardly be expected to refuse the opportunity of claiming that, on this approach, changes in the natural rate of unemployment are to be identified with whatever change in the intercept of the equation will preserve the value of +1 on the $\dot{p}^e$ variable and a negative sign on unemployment, i.e. that the whole procedure slides into a tautological explanation of inflation in which the amended Phillips curves themselves are subject to upward shifting with respect to measured unemployment. Clearly the proponents of the augmented Phillips curve will carry more conviction if they are able to relate the alleged shifts in the natural rate of unemployment to changes in its economic determinants. The search theory of unemployment which underlies the basic model suggests that the level of unemployment will depend on the costs of being unemployed as opposed to working and therefore that the rate of dole as compared with employee compensation is an important variable. At the same time it is a well known and unsettled problem of British labour market behaviour that, towards the end of the 1960s, the status of unemployment as an indicator seems to have changed. This disturbance has been speculatively associated by a number of commentators with a change in the ratio of unemployment benefit to average earnings, mainly the result of the introduction of earnings-related unemployment benefits. Thus, in terms of the simplified linear model set out above, we might add

$$U^N = \gamma + \delta B/E,$$

$$(5)$$

where B/E is the ratio of the dole to average earnings and δ is expected to be positive. The estimating equation then becomes:

$$\dot{p} = \frac{\gamma}{a} + \frac{\delta}{a} B/E - \frac{U}{a} + \dot{p}^e. \qquad (6)$$

The linear specification provides for a parallel shifting of the augmented Phillips curves to the right, cutting the horizontal axis (for $\dot{p}^e = 0$) at a natural rate of unemployment dependent on $\delta B/E$.

This amendment to the simpler forms of the expectations-augmented Phillips curves commends itself for the reasons already implicit in the above. However, quite apart from whether it can be 'successfully' implemented (in the sense of providing a statistically respectable wage equation), the results of any such estimation need to be checked carefully for their microeconomic plausibility, especially in view of the rival hypotheses advanced in connection with the alleged disturbance of the figures of registered unemployed[11].

As regards inflation expectations, two difficulties in particular stand out:
(1) the relevant price indices for which expectations are taken;
(2) the source of, or mechanism assumed for, the generation of expectations.

The problems associated with (1) include the divergence between price indices relevant to employers and those relevant to employees. This includes, even at an aggregate level in an open economy, the divergence between import costs of final and of intermediate products, export and domestic prices, and between pre- and post-tax values of 'real wages'.

There appear to be two main ways in which a resolution to these problems has been sought. The first is to recognize the divergences implied by national boundaries and attempt to define the information sets characterizing the expectations of wage earners and employers[12]. The second is to abstract from the divergences implied by national boundaries and seek to define aggregates on a 'world' level[13]. While the former involves a degree of detail which may result in a lack of statistical significance associated with a majority of the estimated coefficients[14] as well as incompatibility with theoretically defined values, the latter also suffers from disadvantages[15] which considerably outweigh the gains that its simplicity promises. Among other things aggregation to a 'world' level is seriously incomplete and essentially still leaves commodity prices (and expectations about them) exogenous to the model, whilst the assumption of international labour markets and the concept of 'world' price expectations strains credibility.

As regards (2), the familiar problem is that of testing both for conformity with the theoretical prediction of the coefficient on $\dot{p}^e$ and for the validity of the source or generating mechanism imposed on the data. The substantial literature on the nature of the biases introduced through the assumption of autoregressive expectations-generating schemes, and the contribution of consistent and rational expectations schemes to a solution of the problem, will not be reviewed here[16]. However, it may be worth observing that the attractions of 'direct' observations are less obvious than they first appear. In particular, the so-called 'direct' observations actually available are qualitative and have themselves to be transformed[17] to yield data in an appropriate form. The joint hypothesis-testing problem is therefore technically not solved. Furthermore, the direct observations obtainable are not necessarily those actually entertained by the relevant economic agents (supposing these agents to be, for example, trade union negotiators rather than a Gallup sample of housewives).

A further problem arises in the treatment of expectations to the extent that both theory and applied work in this area focus on single-valued measures, presumably in concept a 'mean' of some kind. Yet in dealing with other aspects of inflation it has been thought important to incorporate variances in the analysis and indeed to refer to uncertainty regarding future prices as a major source of the costs of inflationary processes.

3. A Conspectus of Results

When the unaugmented Phillips curve is estimated over a period inclusive of the late 1960s and early 1970s, contrary to the results obtained for earlier periods, the unemployment variable turns out to have a positive association with the dependent variable. Simple emendation of the naive Phillips curve by adding an inflation expectations variable produces little improvement. Unemployment, typically, is either of the 'wrong' sign or insignificant, whilst inflation expectations variables, though usually carrying the correct sign, are not always significant or do not generally appear with the coefficient of +1 indicated by the underlying theory. (Figure 1 provides a summary of the behaviour of wages and unemployment over the period in a form which indicates the nature of the 'problem'.)

Table 1 represents a sample of estimates of augmented Phillips curves derived from three different studies[18]. In each case the independent variable is a version of the rate of change of wages and differences in definitions may help to account for part of the difference in results (the weekly wage rate of manual workers being used in both the Johnston and Timbrell, and Parkin, Sumner and Ward studies, and hourly earnings in the Nordhaus study). All three studies find 'wrong-signed' or insignificant coefficients on the unemployment variable. Neither Nordhaus nor Johnston and Timbrell obtain a significant coefficient on the inflation-expectations variable, which is represented in Nordhaus by an imposed distributed-lag scheme and in Johnston and Timbrell by a lagged average of the previous 12 months' change in the retail price index. The price-expectations variables in Parkin, Sumner and Ward are disaggregated into employers' estimates of export and home (output) prices and employees' estimates of domestic prices, of which only one (employers' estimates of home output prices) was significant. Additional variables listed in other studies, such as the proportion of workers receiving increases (n/N) in Johnston and Timbrell or the incomes policy dummies l_1 and l_2 (1961:3–1962:2, and 1966:3–1967:2, respectively) in Parkin, Sumner and Ward, are not significant and neither are the expected tax variables in the latter study, whose combined coefficient (the theoretical value of which is −1) is shown in the table.

Subject to a more complete evaluation of the work embodied in the last equation listed in the table, the augmented Phillips approach has not so far proven a particularly robust one.

Figure 1. Wages, prices, unemployment: (a) wages and unemployment; (b) inflation.

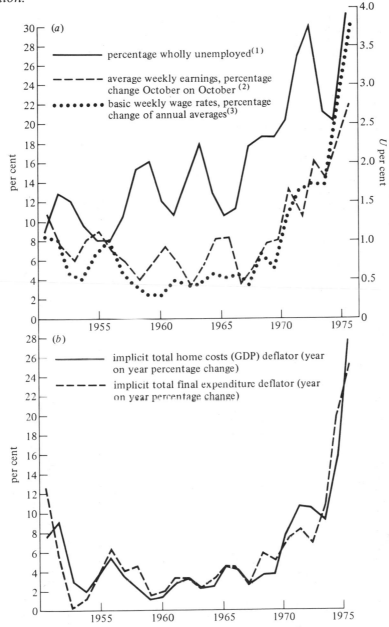

(1) Wholly unemployed (excluding school leavers) as percentage of labour force (annual average, seasonally adjusted).
(2) Male manual workers in manufacturing and certain other industries.
(3) All manual workers, all industries and services.

Table 1. Augmented Phillips equations: some sample results.

Equation key	Constant	Regression coefficients					$\bar{R}^2$	Estimation period and frequency of observations
		b_1 or b_2'	b_2	b_3	b_4	b_5		
Nordhaus	0.0543	$(1/U)$ -0.151 (0.389)	$(\dot{p}^e)$ 0.608 (0.890)				na	Annual: 1955–71
Johnston and Timbrell	-3.19	(U) 2.699 (1.96)	$(\dot{p}^e)$ 0.60 (1.39)	(n/N) 1.71 (0.41)			0.684	Annual: 1959–71
Parkin, Sumner and Ward	3.98	(U) -0.644 (0.70)	$(\dot{p}^e_F \dot{p}_E + \dot{p}_C)$ 0.854 (not sign?)	$(T_1 + (T_2 + T_3))$ -0.296 (not sign)	(l_1) 0.152 (0.10)	(l_2) -1.050 (0.70)	0.475	Quarterly: 1956:2–1971:4

Key: Regression coefficients b_1 or b_1' refer to U or $1/U$ respectively; b_2 to price expectations variables; b_3, b_4 and b_5 vary between studies (see text). Figures in brackets are t ratios, except in the case of Nordhaus, who gives standard errors. The dependent variable is a version of the rate of change of wages, on various definitions.

4. Real Wage Resistance?

At the London School of Economics conference referred to earlier, hopeful reference was made to a rival 'real wage frustration' hypothesis which, it was suggested, might provide a more fruitful source of explanation[19]. The principal idea was that the then current inflation (wage explosion) was essentially due to the appearance of a marked discrepancy between the real wage aspirations of labour and actual real wage achievement. Unwillingness to accept this discrepancy resulted in a money wage push. A discrepancy of this kind might, of course, arise from an upward revision of aspirations or from a downward revision (relative to an unchanged path of desired real wages) of real wages actually secured.

Sargan[20] reported some degree of success with a model of this kind, thus confirming his earlier work in 1964 and that of Gillion in 1968[21]. Since that time the real wage frustration hypothesis has been elaborated, but only incompletely tested, by other authors. Hicks set what he called 'real wage resistance' in a historic-doctrinal perspective[22], emphasizing its position as one of a trio of 'Keynesian' lineal descendents (the other two he distinguished being the Phillips tradition and the political-economy tradition) and argued its significance in converting the sharp increases in import prices in 1972–74 into an inflationary process. In 1972, Jackson, Turner and Wilkinson[23], and more recently (1976) Coutts, Tarling and Wilkinson[24], argued in favour of a net-of-tax version of real wages, thus pointing the way to a suggestion that increases in the effective tax rate in the late 1960s were responsible for widening the gap between aspiration and achievement, and thus for some (or all) of the increased inflation[25]. Johnston and Timbrell successfully incorporated a measure of this 'tax effect' into their model of wage determination[26], although their analysis does not involve a similar role for prices.

A basic model in this vein may be constructed as follows. Assuming invariance of settlement frequency to inflation or other economic variables[27], the objective of money wage rises secured at discrete intervals is to approximate a desired path for real after-tax wages. To secure such a path the size of the money wage increases on settlement day must take account both of the present discrepancy between desired and actual real disposable wages and, because of the discrete nature of the wage settlement process, the expected future rate of inflation over the settlement period and the expected change in direct taxation. Interpreted in a bargaining sense, the state of unemployment and of incomes policy is also relevant to the equation and might be thought to modify the speed of adjustment of nominal wages to changes in the gap between target and actual real wages. Thus, (in logarithms)

$$\Delta w = g\left[\left(\frac{w}{p}\lambda\right)^* - \left(\frac{w_{t-1}}{p}\lambda\right)\right], \tag{7}$$

$$(\tfrac{w}{p})^* = f(t, \dot{\lambda}^e, \dot{p}^e), \qquad (8)$$

$$g = h(U, F). \qquad (9)$$

Where, of the symbols which do not have an obvious meaning, λ = the ratio of the net-of-tax to the gross wage (the retention ratio), and F = incomes policy dummy. The relevant 'lagged real disposable wage' is expressed here as (w_{t-1}/p) rather than as $(w\lambda/p_{t-1})$ on the argument that the gap which workers seek to close by a new bargain over w is that between their currently aspired real disposable wage, and the current real disposable wage as determined by the interaction of the previously negotiated nominal wage and subsequent changes in λ and p[28]. However, this particular relationship has the disadvantage of defining the reactions to change in λ and p as identical both in value and in time, and further that the growth of the real after-tax wage, apart from the discrete jumps associated with fixed settlement intervals involving dependence on $\dot{\lambda}^e$ and $\dot{p}^e$, depends only on a time trend. Sargan, it may be noted, alternatively replaced t by $\dot{q}$ (the rate of productivity growth), producing an equation which could be rationalized along the lines suggested by Kuh[29].

Earlier results for equation forms approximating those suggested by a linearized reduced form of equations (7)–(9) were obtained by Sargan and Gillion, λ and F being suppressed, Table 2 shows the rather curious results obtained from estimating such equations from which the retention-ratio variable (λ) and the incomes-policy dummy variable (F) have been omitted. It is obvious that the equation is mis-specified and/or suffers from structural instability. Measured for the period as a whole (row I), the results suggest that neither the lagged real wage nor t and U are statistically significant determinants of wage rates. Indeed the inflation expectation proxies ($\Delta \dot{p}$, $\Delta \dot{p}_{t-}$) are the only statistically significant determinants.

When the period is broken into subperiods, however, as in the subsequent equations reported as rows II and III to rows X and XI, the lagged real wage variable is usually significant in both parts of the total period, though with a much higher coefficient in the second subperiod than in the first. Unemployment and inflation variables are never significant, but the time trend usually is; here again, however, there is a marked difference between the coefficient values obtained in the first and second subperiods, being much higher (to a multiple in excess of 10) in the latter. Subperiods VI and VIII are very similar in all major respects to the equation result reported by Sargan for the period 1949:4–1968:4[30]. It is therefore instructive to observe that whilst the corresponding equation form performs quite well for the remainder of the period (rows VII and IX)[31], the implied speed of adjustment trebles or quadruples whilst the implied desired trend path[32] of the real wage increases from something just over 1 per cent per annum to just over 5 per cent.

Table 2. 'Real wage' equations, 1953–74, quarterly: dependent variable $dlogw$ (hourly wage rates, male manual workers).

Equation Number	Constant	$\Delta\dot{p}$	$\Delta\dot{p}_{t-1}$	t	U	$w_{t-1}p$	$\bar{R}^2$	DW	Sample period
I	-0.008	0.40	0.49	-0.0002	0.008	0.06	0.49	1.67	1953–74
	(1.2)	(3.2)	(3.8)	(1.03)	(1.7)	(1.27)			
II	0.03	0.04	0.03	0.0003	-0.005	-0.15	0.08	1.75	1953–66
	(2.7)	(0.3)	(0.18)	(1.38)	(1.18)	(1.7)			
III	-0.06	0.016	0.30	0.002	0.003	-0.079	0.44	1.58	1967–74
	(2.1)	(0.06)	(1.03)	(1.4)	(0.21)	(0.64)			
IV	0.03	-0.16	0.001	0.0003	-0.005	-0.14	0.06	1.71	1953–67
	(3.25)	(0.11)	(0.009)	(2.03)	(1.17)	(2.22)			
V	-0.09	0.07	0.31	0.002	0.006	-0.16	0.43	1.63	1968–74
	(2.4)	(0.2)	(1.04)	(1.8)	(0.37)	(1.15)			
VI	0.04	0.010	0.02	0.0004	-0.003	-0.15	0.05	1.75	1953–68
	(3.26)	(0.07)	(0.15)	(2.21)	(0.08)	(2.34)			
VII	-0.22	-0.24	0.06	0.006	-0.0009	-0.46	0.47	1.54	1969–74
	(2.9)	(0.7)	(0.17)	(2.63)	(0.06)	(2.24)			
VIII	0.04	0.017	-0.02	0.0004	-0.004	-0.15	0.05	1.77	1953–69
	(3.4)	(0.13)	(0.12)	(2.4)	(0.86)	(2.52)			
IX	-0.30	-0.54	-0.11	0.008	-0.007	-0.63	0.35	1.37	1970–74
	(2.5)	(1.23)	(0.25)	(2.48)	(0.36)	(2.27)			
X	0.03	0.16	0.09	0.0005	0.0007	-0.15	0.12	1.53	1953–74
	(2.8)	(1.16)	(0.6)	(2.3)	(0.17)	(2.33)			
XI	-0.40	-0.27	0.18	0.007	0.04	-0.44	0.40	1.83	1971–74
	(2.6)	(0.53)	(0.38)	(2.12)	(1.03)	(1.4)			

Regression coefficients

This approach can therefore hardly be termed robust. We obtained results comparable with those reported by Sargan earlier, but note that for at least one subperiod in his sample (row II), the equation does not perform very well. Subsequently, we note that for later sample periods, whilst the same form of equation works more successfully, the crucial coefficient values undergo a marked change. This result may be interpreted as pointing to an upward revision of the 'aspiration' real wage in the mid-1960s as the proximate cause of (wage) inflation. It seems more likely, however, that the approximation of the real wage aspiration process by a time trend is unsatisfactory. The failure of the price expectations proxies to yield significant coefficients in any but the full sample period is not encouraging either. Whether the explicit incorporation of λ and F, omitted for consistency with Sargan, will improve the performance of this model remains to be seen.

5. Conclusions

Is there, then, no wage equation? In the narrow sense of this question, as to whether formal wage equations can be relied upon in, for example, macroeconomic forecasting simulation models, the answer seems to be no. It is not very satisfactory to answer the narrow question, however. Indeed, at a time when a number of macroeconomic-econometric relationships have been called to doubt[33], it would be surprising if one were able to say confidently that there is a reliable wage equation. The broader question is whether there are underlying economic forces determining the wage rate that are at least sufficiently important relative to social or political factors as to be capable, in principle, of being captured econometrically. This is not a possibility which we should reject yet, although it is evidently one which needs to be entertained with some humility. It would be appropriate to end by indicating the kinds of test which a successful wage equation might aspire to pass, and the kinds of problem to which attention might usefully be directed.

First, there are serious data problems. One of these is that wage rate changes, as measured by the official indices, comprise both changes in the rates at which individual settlements are made and changes in the numbers of those settling within a particular time period[34]. There is a clear disagreement about the determinants of settlement frequency. An index of settlement wages has been proposed, but to date no satisfactory measure has been constructed[35]. Similarly, if data were available, it would be interesting to examine whether public and private sector wages were determined according to different factors. Difficulties in measuring inflation expectations have already been referred to, but no reference has been made so far to the problems presented for successful analysis by the not infrequent application of varying shades of incomes policy and by pre-emptive anticipations of incomes policy. It is not at all obvious that dummy variables, whether confined to intercept shifts or extended to slope shifts as well (as in policy on/policy off analysis), are sufficiently subtle to capture these effects. Suffice it to say that simple diagnosis of the effects of incomes policy is severely handicapped by these problems as is the identification of any wage equation, except on the assumption that such policies are negligibly effective.

Secondly, it is important that wage equations be submitted to forecasting and stability tests[36]. The results in table 2 demonstrate the reason for doing this. Although refinements in our models and in the data employed to capture theoretical magnitudes[37] may entice greater support for our economic interpretations of wage determination, the confidence with which any hypothesis in this field can be entertained can hardly be but of a somewhat reserved nature in view of the bruising experience to which formerly well established relationships have been subject. But it may be that from time to time the importance of 'non-economic' factors may be recognized without such a concession being treated as professional suicide.

NOTES

1. I am greatly indebted to the research assistance and advice of Laurence Copeland. The usual disclaimer with respect to the opinions expressed in the paper is, however, applicable.

2. This term is used for want of a better one. What I have in mind is the genus of model first presented by Sargan in 1964, to which further reference is made below.

3. The analysis of the 'Nordic model' is in this vein (see Odd Aukrust, 'PRIM 1: a model of the price and income distribution of an open economy', *Review of Income and Wealth* **16** (1), 1970; Gösta Edgren, Karl-Olof Faxén, and Clas-Erik Odhner, 'Wages, growth and the distribution of income', *Swedish Journal of Economics,* **71** (September), 1969.

4. Thus the failure to detect incomes-policy impacts on wage inflation by these criteria does not invalidate the theory which leads to its advocacy, the more so in that the criteria by which incomes policy is usually judged econometrically are inappropriate to the theory leading to the policy. Specifically, the standard approach usually involves testing the 'Phillips curve' for shifts as a result of incomes-policy inputs, but the politico-economic approach implicitly rejects the Phillips curve.

5. The proceedings of this conference were subsequently published in Harry G. Johnson and A.R. Nobay (eds.), *The Current Inflation* (London: Macmillan, 1971).

6. M. Friedman, 'The role of monetary policy', *American Economic Review,* **58** (March), 1968; and E.S. Phelps, 'Phillips curves expectations of inflation and optimal unemployment over time', *Economica,* **34** (August), 1967.

7. R.H. Solow, *Price Expectations and the Behaviour of the Price Level* (Manchester: Manchester University Press, 1969).

8. Notably by W.D. Nordhaus, 'The worldwide wage explosion', *Brookings Papers on Economic Activity,* **3** (2), 1972; J.M. Parkin, M.T. Sumner, and R. Ward, 'The effects of excess demand, generalised expectations and wage-price controls on wage inflation in the U.K.', in Karl Brunner and Allan H. Meltzer (eds.), *Proceedings of the 1974 Carnegie-Melon Rochester Conference on Economic Policy.*

9.   It is interesting to note that Friedman (in his 'Unemployment versus Inflation', Institute of Economic Affairs, Occasional Paper No. 44, 1975) has entered a protest against estimating equations of the general form of (4), on the grounds that 'the estimation used, with $1/p\ dP/dt$ on the left-hand side, treats different observed rates of unemployment as if they were exogenous, as if they could persist indefinitely . . .' and '. . . The implicit assumption that unemployment can take different values begs the whole question raised by the accelerationist hypothesis' (*ibid*, p. 26). Perhaps those most prone to estimate just such equations should respond to this stricture, if stricture it is.

10.   J. Tobin, 'Inflation and unemployment', *American Economic Review,* **62** (March), 1972.

11.   Taylor, for example, has advanced the hypothesis that the distribution of unemployment between hoarded and registered unemployment categories has changed, but does not advance earnings-related benefit as the cause, hinting rather at a change in business expectations. (See J. Taylor, *Unemployment and Wage Inflations* (Harlow: Longman, 1974).) Other observers would deny that the unemployment/output relationship has changed significantly and attribute the observed change in the unemployment/vacancies relationship to vacancy recording improvements.

12.   See J.M. Parkin, M.T. Sumner, and R. Ward, 'The effects of excess demand, generalised expectations and wage-price controls on wage inflation in the U.K.', in Karl Brunner and Allan H. Meltzer (eds.), *Proceedings of the 1974 Carnegie-Melon Rochester Conference on Economic Policy.*

13.   See N. Duck, J.M. Parkin, D. Rose, and G. Zis, 'The determination of the rate of change in wages and prices in the fixed exchange rate world economy, 1956–1971', in Michael Parkin and George Zis (eds.), *Inflation in the World Economy,* Manchester: Manchester University Press, 1976).

14.   A. Deaton, 'Notes on the Parkin-Sumner-Ward Model of Wage Inflation', Department of Applied Economics, University of Cambridge, 1975, mimeo.

15.   See M.J. Artis, 'Comment on Duck, Parkin, Rose and Zis', in Michael Parkin and George Zis, *Inflation in the World Economy* (Manchester: Manchester University Press, 1976).

16.   A recent survey of some of the issues is available in D.W. Laidler, 'Expectations and the Phillips trade-off: a commentary', *Scottish Journal Of Political Economy,* **23** (February), 1976.

17.   See J.A. Carson and J.M. Parkin, 'Inflation expectations', *Economica,* **42** (May), 1975.

18.   W.D. Nordhaus, 'The worldwide wage explosion', *Brookings Papers on Economic Activity,* **3** (2), 1972; J. Johnston and M. Timbrell, 'Empirical tests of a bargaining theory of wage rate determination', *The Manchester School of Economic and Social Studies,* **41** (June), 1973; J.M. Parkin, M.T. Sumner, and R. Ward, 'The effects of excess demand, generalised expectations and wage-price controls on wage inflation in the U.K.', in Karl Brunner and Allan H. Meltzer (eds.), *Proceedings of the 1974 Carnegie-Melon Rochester Conference on Economic Policy.*

19.   See Harry G. Johnson, 'Introduction', in Harry G. Johnson and A.R. Nobay (eds.), *The Current Inflation* (London: Macmillan, 1971), p.x.

20.   J.D. Sargan, 'A study of wages and prices in the U.K., 1949–1968', in Harry G. Johnson and A.R. Nobay (eds.), *The Current Inflation* (London: Macmillan, 1971).

21. J.D. Sargan, 'A study of wages and prices in the U.K., 1949–1968', in Harry G. Johnson and A.R. Nobay (eds.), *The Current Inflation* (London: Macmillan, 1971); and C. Gillion, 'Wage rates, earning and wage-drift', *National Institute Economic Review,* No. 46, 1968.

22. John R. Hicks, *The Crisis in Keynesian Economics* (Oxford: Basil Blackwell, 1974), chapter 3; John R. Hicks, 'Whats wrong with monetarism', *Lloyds Bank Review,* No. 118, October, 1975.

23. D.A.S. Jackson, H.A. Turner, and S.F. Wilkinson, *Do Trade Unions Cause Inflation?* (Cambridge: Cambridge University Press, 1972).

24. J. Coutts, R. Tarling, and S.F. Wilkinson, 'Wage bargaining and the inflation process', *Economic Policy Review,* No. 2, March, 1976.

25. The suggestive evidence in the more recent presentation is, however, confined to a graph of real post-tax settlement wages and a commentary without accompanying statistical results.

26. J. Johnston and M. Timbrell, 'Empirical tests of a bargaining theory of wage rate determination', *The Manchester School of Economic and Social Studies,* **41** (June), 1973; and J. Johnston and M. Timbrell, Further Evidence on a Bargaining Theory of Wage Rate Determination, University of Manchester, 1976, mimeo.

27. This is contrary to the assumption made by Coutts, Tarling and Wilkinson (see note[24]) who argue firmly, but without demonstration, that settlement frequency reflects inflation, and seemingly feel able to assume, in consequence, that increased settlements frequency avoids the need for negotiations to take account of expected inflation. This seems to be an uncomfortably strong assumption, but one which is, in principle, testable. However, in the 1972 paper (see note[26]) Johnston and Timbrell have stated that they could find no economic determinants of settlement frequency.

28. Clearly then, the 'real wage resistance' model does allow real wages to decline to an extent and for a duration depending on the length of settlement interval and the value of g. On the less formal level, advocates of the real wage resistance hypothesis do not appear to maintain that real wages can *never* fall (and not only within the settlement interval) but only that there is a strong tendency for them not to do so. Real wage resistance, that is, *can* be broken. In this case Johnson's counter-arguments (see Harry G. Johnson 'What is right with monetarism?', *Lloyds Bank Review,* No. 120, April, 1976) seem over strong, though the political permissiveness to which he draws attention is no doubt a factor in fostering 'real-wage illusion' (the illusion of a 'right' to a real wage incompatible with productivity).

29. E. Kuh, 'A productivity theory of wage levels: an alternative to the Phillips curve', *Review of Economic Studies,* **34** (October), 1967; and J.D. Sargan, 'A study of wages and process in the U.K., 1949–1968', in Harry G. Johnson and A.R. Nobay (eds.), *The Current Inflation* (London: Macmillan, 1971).

30. Including the very low overall explanatory power of the equation; thus Sargan (see J.D. Sargan, 'A study of wages and prices in the U.K., 1949–1968', in Harry G. Johnson and A.R. Nobay (eds.), *The Current Inflation* (London: Macmillan, 1971), p.55) reports an uncorrected coefficient of multiple correlation of $R = 0.456$.

31. Indeed very much better to judge by the overall fit statistic!

32. Obtained by dividing the coefficient on the time trend by that on the lagged real wage and annualizing.

33. See, for example, G. Hacche, 'The demand for money in the United Kingdom: experience since 1971', *Bank of England Quarterly,* **14** (September), 1974; D.F.

Hendry and G.E. Mizon, 'Serial correlation as a convenient simplification, not a nuisance: a comment on a study of the demand for money by the Bank of England', *Economic Journal*, **88** (September), 1978; A.S. Courakis, 'Serial correlation and a Bank of England study of the demand for money: an exercise in measurement without theory', *Economic Journal*, **88** (September), 1978.

34.   Some time ago Gillion (see note 21) drew attention to this problem, which has received attention since from Johnston and Timbrell (see note 26), O. Ashenfelter and J.H. Pencavel, 'Wage changes and the frequency of wage settlement', *Economica*, **42** (May), 1975, and Coutts, Tarling and Wilkinson (see note 24).

35.   In particular the index measured by Coutts, Tarling and Wilkinson, but this appears to be defective in construction in that the series shown declines (on an annual basis) in two years in the 1960s, and it is consequently not attractive to attempt to explain it econometrically.

36.   The stability tests advocated here must be conducted with the caution that early sample-period data exhibit much less variance than later data. This readily leads to the appearance of structural instability which could, in fact, not be confirmed by appropriate statistical tests. There is a likelihood that early period results will tend to insignificance in the values of coefficients both from zero and from *those estimated for the later period.*

37.   A study by S.G.B. Henry, M.C. Sawyer and P. Smith ('Models of inflation in the United Kingdom', *National Institute Economic Review* No. 77, August, 1976) extended the testing of the 'real wage' hypothesis to incorporate the influence of tax deductions on the pressure for higher wage claims as compared with the results derived for this hypothesis in table 2. The authors found that the growth of the after-tax aspiration real wage seems to have been fairly steady over a similar sample period. It may thus be argued that it was the rise in tax deductions which largely provoked the wage inflation of the late 1960s and early 1970s. At the same time further work by M.T. Sumner ('Wage determination', in M. Parkin and M.T. Sumner (eds.), *Inflation in the United Kingdom* (Manchester: Manchester University Press and Toronto: Toronto University Press, 1976) building on the study of Parkin, Sumner and Ward (see note 12) reported a more robust Phillips curve, modified not only for the role of inflation expectations but also for the effect of changes in the benefit/earnings ratio on the measured figures of unemployment. Although these developments suggest that the search for a quantified explanation of wage determination has recovered some of its former confidence, it is as well to note that the hypotheses involved—the real wage hypothesis and the augmented Phillips curve—appear to be in some conflict both as to their findings with respect to crucial determining variables and as to their policy implications.

Measuring Economic Performance in an Inflationary Environment[1]

John A. Kay

It is desirable to eliminate inflation, but it also possible to learn to live with it. The early 1970s were a particularly painful period in Western economics because neither of these things had occurred. Inflation prevailed in most countries at unprecedented rates, but adjustments which might have made it relatively tolerable had not been made, and people were neither able to think consistently in real rather than money terms nor to make contracts on such a basis. As a result, both businesses and consumers suffered the uncertainty of a world in which the variance of the outcomes of plans was high and the new position of many previously accepted bearings was unknown. The most acute symptom in the United Kingdom was the liquidity crises which overtook the corporate sector in 1974.

Although the British inflation rate has been exceptionally high, many other countries have gone further in coming to terms with rapid inflation. The conservative behaviour of financial institutions may be a partial explanation, but the generalized opposition of the government has probably been the most important factor. This opposition is partly attributable to a belief that a form of wage indexation applied in 1974 had unfortunate consequences. But it is also likely that an important motive has been the feeling that if inflation is made more palatable the response to policies ostensibly designed to retard it will be less enthusiastic. Since exhortation to self-restraint is central to these policies, this factor is of special importance. The underlying view is that if you give protection to a man who is being assaulted, his opposition to his attackers will be less vigorous; a theory whose relevance is somewhat weakened by the fact that in this case it is the principal assailant who is denying the protection.

In the area which is the subject of this paper—company accounts—the need for adjustment to reflect inflation has, however, been accepted. This acceptance has been the consequence of the recommendations of the Sandilands Committee[2], but it has been gained only on the basis that it has no implications for anything else at all. Perhaps the most extraordinary chapter of that Report is the one entitled 'Implications for Indexation', whose purpose is to deny that the Report's proposals involve indexation of any kind. Indeed the vehemence of the denial leads to extravagant assertions that a general index of the purchasing power of money could not possibly be useful for any purpose whatever, and it is only grudgingly conceded that 'this period (since 1969) is conveniently and popularly described as a period of high inflation. There is no objection to the use of this term in the popular sense'. In fact, it is hard to imagine a question of less intrinsic interest or importance than whether a set of proposals which undeniably require the multiplication of historic cost figures by price indices can or cannot be defined as indexation, but the chapter is interesting for the insight it gives into what the Committee apparently thought necessary to win political acceptability for its recommendations.

The Report proposes a system called Current Cost Accounting (CCA). It rejects the Current Purchasing Power method (CPP) advocated by the Accounting Standards Steering Committee. The critique of this is powerful, and justified; the CPP system is extremely complex. Moreover what meaning (if any) the figures which emerge from it have, has never been satisfactorily explained. A number of other systems, combining some elements of both CPP and CCA, have also been proposed. The choice between them is of much more than academic significance. In 1976 Grand Metropolitan, among the top 20 U.K. companies in terms of assets, reported conventionally calculated profits of £33m. On a CPP basis, its profits would have been just over £100m. Under a CCA system, it is estimated that it earned around £6m. This is all rather disturbing. It ought not to be too difficult to decide whether a specific company is among the most or the least profitable in British industry. And did the £8m paid in dividends and the £15m of taxation represent a massive erosion of the group's capital or a derisory fraction of its available resources?

The Sandilands Report's definition of profit begins from the famous Hicksian dictum that 'income is the maximum value which (a man) can consume during a week, and still expect to be as well off at the end of the week as he was at the beginning'[3]; and by analogy the Committee suggested that profit should be defined as 'the value at the end of the year, less the value at the beginning of the year, plus the net cash flow arising within the year after making adjustments for the introduction of new capital'. It is worth noting how the forward-looking Hicksian concept of the first quotation is transformed into one which is backward looking in the second, but we defer comment on this for the time being. Profit defined thus the Committee calls the 'total gains' during the year.

In my view this is the right approach. But there are two difficulties which it raises. One is that profits so measured would be astonishingly volatile. We would discover, for example, that several property companies made profits in 1973 of some hundreds of millions of pounds, and losses of similar magnitude in 1974. The situation of manufacturing companies would be less extreme, but there would still be very large fluctuations in profit for reasons quite unconnected with the main operating activities of the company. The second difficulty is that such profits are typically higher, not lower, than profits as conventionally measured, mainly because increases in the value of fixed assets now enter the profit and loss account, and the Sandilands' Committee was set up to effect a reduction in the total of reported profit. This sounds a cynical comment, but it is not wholly intended as such. Interest in inflation accounting has arisen largely because business men felt, especially in 1974, that the overall state of health of many firms was worse than their profit figures indicated. It is unlikely that that feeling was altogether without foundation.

The Committee's solution was an ingenious one. It sought to distinguish two components of these 'total gains'. One it describes as 'holding gains'. These result from variations in the prices of inputs. They fluctuate substantially, and become relatively high in times of inflation. The other is 'operating gain'. This is the residual, the solid basic profit which provides the resources for distributions and is, by implication, the proper basis for taxation. When it is put in this rather vague way, it is easy to be sympathetic to the intention behind this distinction. For the majority of manufacturing businesses, price variations are at best a nuisance. They represent a distraction from the major objectives of the company, and their contribution to profit and loss is erratic and possibly unpredictable. 'We are fabricators of, not speculators in, the metal' is how the Chairman of British Insulated Calender's Cables, Britain's largest copper user, has described his company policy. As a statement of company policy it makes good sense. As a broad descriptive tool, the distinction between holding and operating gains is a useful one, but it is not a distinction which can be given precise and objective quantitative form. Therefore it is not one which can bear the weight which the Committee attempts to place on it. In fact several different definitions of the distinction are provided at different points in the Report, some of which we examine below.

The distinction is introduced by example.

A company manufactures gold watches and purchases a certain quantity of gold. At the time the watches are sold, the company measures the 'value to the business' as equal to its original purchase price. Any gain made from the sale of watches is an operating gain.

That seems reasonable. But immediately we are asked to imagine that

... the same company measure the 'value to the business' of the gold at the time the watches are sold at an amount higher by X than the original purchase price. In this case the gain from the sale of the watches is a combination of a holding gain of X and an operating gain, equal to the total gain less the holding gain.

This again seems quite reasonable, but which is the correct procedure? Quite correctly the Report points out that 'the extent of a holding gain thus mainly depends on the method adopted of measuring the value of assets', but does not tell us which method to adopt.

There are a number of possible ways in which we might divide the profit on the watch between holding gains and operating gains. We might decide that holding gains ceased when the gold began to be used in production, and the value added after that, during manufacture, was the operating gain. This interpretation, however, seems unlikely to be the one the Report intends. If the company is really eschewing speculation, it presumably does not hold gold which is not required for productive purposes, and therefore such holding gains would not arise. If it is not avoiding gold speculation, then the profits and losses from it ought, quite properly, to be included. Another possibile interpretation, which one might infer that the Report regards as the ideal, would be to measure the 'value to the business' of the gold in the watch at the moment the watch is sold. 'Value to the business' is presumably based on the principles previously enunciated and in order to prevent intolerable complexity, I shall assume it is equal to replacement cost. Of course, there is still a lot of ambiguity about deciding when exactly the sale takes place—when the watch is ordered, when the price is agreed, when it is handed over, when it is paid for—and the practical problems of applying this are obviously rather great. The difficulties of principle are, however, even more serious.

Let us suppose that the watch requires one ounce of gold, say costing about £70, and that it takes a year to make. The watchmaker is paid £10 for doing so, and there are no fixed assets. Watchmaking is a competitive business, so the return on capital employed in watchmaking is much the same as the return to be earned doing other things, let us say it is 10 per cent. In that case the manufacturer would hope to make a profit of £7, and so be aiming to sell the watch in a year's time for around £87. How would he expect this to be divided between operating and holding gains? Since there is a forward market in gold, we can see what the price of gold is expected to be in a year's time. It is easy to check that it typically exceeds the present price by much the same amount as the rate of return available in other things— again 10 per cent or so—so that the forward price is about £77. If this is the actual price next year, then the manufacturer will value the gold content of the watch at £77, add on his labour cost of £10, and so be left with total costs of £87 and an operating gain of zero. In other words, all his profit will be holding gain, and his expected operating gain, and consequently his expected tax payments and distributions, will be zero. Of course, things will probably not work out as he expects. Suppose the gold price rose sharply in the course of the year. Then the price he could obtain for the watch would probably rise, but not by as much as the price of gold, so he would make a larger holding gain, but an operating loss. The opposite would happen if the gold price fell. It is perfectly clear that all these measurements are preposterous. The 'operating profit', so calculated, is not a reliable or useful indicator of the outcome of the year's activities.

We should be grateful to Sandilands for providing an example which is simple enough to be analysed. More realistic cases are more complex, so that what is going on is much more obscure. But the same approach can be made, and the same result will be obtained. There is no distinction of principle to be made between gains which result from the holding of assets and gains which result from using them. The latter necessarily implies the former, and the reward for the combined operation must take the form of some sort of appreciation in the price of goods which the company holds. If this is the definition of operating gains which Sandilands intended, then on average, they are zero: and far from eliminating the effect of price fluctuation or profit it is only the existence of price fluctuation which brings them about.

Of course, when the Report comes to give practical examples, the operating gains which are found are positive. The reason is that it does not apply the definition above. Indeed it could not, since it would be much too difficult to use in practice. Instead another definition of the 'holding gain' and 'operating gain' distinction is employed. This is given by a formula, which determines an item called the 'cost of sales adjustment', to be added to the historic cost of stocks used in production for the purposes of measuring the value of inputs. It represents that part of the gain from stocks which is to be regarded as a holding gain; the remainder is operating gain. The formula which is given for computing it is actually quite complex, but to a close approximation it is equal to the average of the opening and closing values of stocks multiplied by the average increase in their price between the two dates[4]. Book value, it is suggested, will be an acceptable measure of value for this purpose, although current value might be preferable. The price change should ideally be determined by the firm's own experience, but index numbers may be used where this is difficult. Two features of this definition stand out immediately. The first, and the more extraordinary, is that if the firm is clever or fortunate in the timing of its purchases of stocks, the numbers in that formula will be affected little, if at all. The result of this is that speculative gains in stocks will be included under operating gains, not holding gains. Yet we are told that the function of the distinction was that it 'will enable management to assess the extent to which gains are due to luck or skill in the timing of purchases (holding gains) or to the productive efforts of the company (operating gains)'. The extent of the muddle between the numerous different explanations of the distinction contained in the Report is now almost complete. The 'cost of sales adjustment' is a rough indicator of the amount of money which the company must provide to maintain the value of its stocks at the new higher prices. As such, it is a figure of some importance for management purposes, but there is no necessary connection between the figure and any measure of holding gains. If the company has been averagely skilful in its purchases, it will probably have increased its profit by enough to enable it to make such provision. If it has been specially clever, it may have done better; if unlucky, worse.

The second, and more disturbing, feature of the formula is how easy it is to manipulate the elements of it. In a period of inflation, a company can increase its profits by the simple expedient of running down its stocks at the balance sheet date. This reduces the 'cost of sales adjustment' and hence boosts operating gains at the expense of holding gains. Under conventional accounting systems, manipulation of stocks has been a standard method of doctoring accounts but there it has usually meant shifting profits out of one year into another. Sooner or later, reality breaks through. Under the Sandilands system, there are no such difficulties. Reducing stock at the balance sheet date not only increases profits this year, it raises them next year as well. A lower *initial* stock valuation also has the effect of keeping the 'cost of sales adjustment' down and operating profit up. It is easy to show how the Sandilands model company could have earned a higher profit in every year by making sure the warehouse was empty when the auditors came round[5]. It is surely inconceivable that the tax system could be aimed at quite such a mobile target.

This discussion can be usefully summed up by citing yet another of the Report's definitions of the operating gain versus holding gain distinction. 'A useful guide to the investor', it suggests 'is the figure of the company's profit for the year drawn up on such a basis that if the company's revenues and costs remained unchanged, the same profit could be indefinitely repeated'. It would indeed be a useful guide, and it is probably to that objective that the attempt to isolate operating gains was directed. It is naive, however, to suppose that this figure can be extracted by some straightforward manipulations of the published accounts. If there had been price stability, the economic environment would have differed in many ways, and if the firm makes any response at all to its environment many of its actions would have differed also. The management of a firm might well be able to make some rough estimate of what profits might then have been, but we cannot for a moment expect that such estimates could command sufficient objectivity or precision to form the basis of a system of accounts.

The central source of the difficulty is that the Committee recognized but shied away from the fundamental problem with which it was faced. This problem is that there is a difference between profitability and liquidity, and that users of accounts are searching, in vain, for a single measure which will serve both functions. The distinction can easily be seen from everyday affairs. The man who takes out a large mortgage to buy a house has made a decision which, at current rates of interest and inflation, is almost certainly a wise one. It is a move which will prove rewarding in the long run, but may impose acute financial strains in the short term. He has improved his profitability, but reduced his liquidity. The difference between the two is the appreciation in the value of his non-monetary assets, the capital gain which he hopes to make on the house. The position of Grand Metropolitan is much the same. This is a company which has financed extensive purchases of fixed assets by heavy borrowings. In an age of inflation, this is a rational strategy, but it is one which leads to an adverse cash-flow situation at the present time. The widely disparate measures of its so-called profitability reflect the different emphasis which is given to its liquidity position, and the debate over the treatment of 'monetary gains' in reality reflects similar differences of emphasis.

Conventional profit and loss accounts have basically sought to measure profitability, but have substantially tempered their evaluation in the direction of liquidity. The most important contribution to this has been the refusual to bring unrealized gains into the profit and loss accounts. Although these two concepts have in this way been conflated in conventional accounting practice, until recently the results have not been too seriously misleading. The reason is that in the past assets typically depreciated in value. This meant that the cash-flow situation was at least as favourable as the profit and loss account suggested. Companies were therefore likely to have the cash resources to fulfil the demands for taxation and for distribution which their declared profitability brought about. The principal exception to this was property companies, but various accounting devices were constructed, primarily the capitalization of certain interest payments, to circumvent the difficulty. Two developments have changed all this. One is inflation, which means that assets frequently appreciate rather than depreciate in money terms. Thus a situation in which companies usually have more cash than they have profits has been transformed into one which they typically have less. Realizing this, they have sought to argue that their profits have been overstated. But the evidence that this is the case is not persuasive. What has occurred is essentially not a change in profitability but a change in the relationship between profitability and liquidity, and the crisis of 1974 was not primarily a profits crash but a cash shortage. The second recent development, which is of increasing importance, is the way in which the system of corporate taxation has developed. As a result of free depreciation and the 1974 stock-appreciation relief, the relationship between the tax liabilities which are charged in the profit and loss account and the amounts which are actually paid or are ever likely to be paid to the Inland Revenue has become extremely tenuous. These unreal tax charges pose a serious problem, since it is nearly impossible for any but the best informed of outsiders to unscramble what is actually happening on the basis of published information. It is a development which has further distorted the liquidity/profitability relationship, but generally in a direction favourable to the cash position of companies.

When the Committee obtained a measure of 'total gains', which we can regard as a pure indicator of profits, it concluded that it was not an indicator of company performance which would, in itself, be of interest to the users of accounts. Instead of accepting this, it sought to trim the definitions of profits to turn it into something closer to a measure of cash flow; so perpetuating the confusion between measures of profitability and measures of liquidity. If it had had the courage of its own radicalism, it would have concluded at this point that when you discover what profits really are you discover that they do not measure what you want to know. It defined them as the difference between two successive estimates of the present value of all future net cash flows of the business. The errors in such valuation estimates are potentially very great, and the difference between them is likely to be both erratic and subject to enormous error. Even if we had satisfactory information of this kind, it is not clear what we should wish to do with it. Here it is important to notice the difference between the forward-looking concept of income as defined by Hicks—the maximum which you can spend and still expect to be as well off at the end as at the beginning—and the backward-looking reporting concept which is contained in company accounts. It is useful to know how much you can spend next year without impoverishing yourself; it is much less useful to know how much you could have spent last year without impoverishing yourself. The latter is of interest only to the extent that it is a guide to the former, which in an unstable world it will rarely be.

The principal difficulties of profit measurement are all concerned with the measurement of changes in the value of assets held by the firm, with estimates of depreciation and stock valuation. In ordinary life, who bothers to make that kind of calculation? I have yet to meet anyone who makes annual estimates of the depreciation of his furniture, or puts a valuation on a one-year-old shirt, or makes regular checks on the prices of goods he has already bought and does not intend to buy again in the immediate future. The reason is not that the calculations are difficult—an accountant usually knows more about the state of his shirt than the state of the plant and machinery in the firm for which he works. It is rather that the answers would not be of any practical use. It is, of course, important to know when you will need new furniture, or a new shirt, or what are the prices of the goods which you shortly intend to buy. In other words, what individuals find it useful to know, and what they implicitly or explicitly attempt to estimate, is their cash position and their forecast cash flow. Their profit and loss account would not be worth the trouble it would take to compile.

Much the same is true of firms, and this is what the proponents of cash-flow accounting have realized. What is required—and all that is required—from companies is a statement of sources and uses of funds, a statement of assets, and a statement and forecast of the cash-flow implications which result from them. That means details of present and likely future capital commitments, the interest rates and maturity dates of borrowings, the size and timing of expected tax payments, and so on. Much, though by no means all, of this information is already contained in a scattered and unsystematic fashion in company accounts. If it were brought together, the financial position of secondary banks and property companies might have been rather more evident rather earlier than it appeared to be. But the overwhelming merit of such a scheme is its simplicity. Not only does it automatically 'account for inflation', but (unlike any other proposed scheme of inflation accounting) it is comprehensible. And it contains within it everything which is in present accounts which is of operational value.

We can illustrate this with reference to the two issues of distribution policy and taxation. There are two main questions relevant to distribution policy. Has the company generated enough cash to pay such a dividend, and can it expect to go on making payments at such a rate in future? The former question is answered by the sources and uses of funds statement. The second question depends in the short term on the cash requirements which the business will have in the next year or two, which will be given by the cash flow forecasts, and beyond that on the long-run earning capacity of the business, which is determined by the value of the assets shown in the balance sheet. On taxation policy, the rational basis for corporate taxation is surely net cash flow minus dividend payments plus net additions to monetary assets. This after all, is the potentially distributable surplus which the year's operations have generated. We have, in fact, virtually adopted this as the tax base already, since all expenditure on new plant and machinery and most expenditure on stocks is now deductible from taxable profit. This position has been reached almost accidently, as a result of measures to exempt businesses from profits taxation which they lack the cash resources to pay. There seems much to be said for explicit acknowledgement of this situation and its implications.

It is overwhelmingly likely that cash-flow accounting will win the day eventually, since it is the only way in which company accounts can ever be restored to a state in which ordinary people can understand them. But to the extent that the Sandilands Report has postponed this development, it has done a serious disservice to the cause of financial reporting. The outcome may be worse than that. Because the principles of profit measurement which it outlines are ambiguous and complicated, it is very difficult to see how little they mean. If 'operating profit' does become accepted as an indicator of business performance, the decisions of businessmen and investors are likely to be distorted in ways which can only prove economically damaging. If it is used as a basis for taxation, the detriment will be compounded further.

NOTES

1. I am grateful to Maurice Scott for his help in clarifying my thinking on this subject.

2.   See F.E.P. Sandilands (Chairman), Report of the inflation accounting committee (London: HMSO, 1976).

3.   J.R. Hicks, *Value and Capital* (Oxford: Oxford University Press, 1939), chapter 14.

4.   More precisely, it is the difference between the actual increase in the book value of stocks over the year and the increase in the book value of stock which is found when the opening and closing figures are restated at the average price of stock over the year.

5.   Except in the year when prices fell when it should have filled to overflowing.

The Failure of the Keynesian Conventional Wisdom[1]

Walter Eltis

It would be universally agreed today that Keynes' *General Theory of Employment, Interest and Money* is, together with Smith's *Wealth of Nations* and Marx's *Das Kapital,* one of the three truly great books that political economists have written. It would also be widely agreed that it made a significant contribution to human welfare in the quarter century after its publication. Those governments which, like Britain's, applied the tools that Keynes invented achieved full employment and, in addition, declining inflation rates for most of the 1950s.

But the 1960s and 1970s have been quite different. Inflation has accelerated throughout the world, and it must be particularly disturbing to Keynesian policymakers that the countries where their influence was greatest are those which have suffered most. These countries, and Britain and Italy can be singled out, have suffered from faster inflation, slower growth, larger budget deficits and severer international currency collapses than their principal competitors where pre-Keynesian methods of thought are still influential. So how is it, a sensible Keynesian might ask, that the countries where those in power and influence have the most correct understanding of how economics works manage to achieve the worst results and to be among the world's perpetual candidates for international financial support? Ironically, most of this has to come from countries which are managed in non-Keynesian ways.

One possibility is that Keynesian economists have been let down by the workers and managers of the countries they advise. This is a well known explanation of Britain's failures, much favoured by Keynesians in British universities and in Whitehall, but the reverse is also possible. The time has surely now come to consider the possibility that the Keynesian conventional wisdom, so uncritically used as a guide for policy in all situations, has flaws which have had a devastating adverse effect on those countries where Keynesian economists have been influential. A strong case can indeed be made out that, in the hands of lesser men and women, certain Keynesian propositions are a receipt for international poverty and economic breakdown, rather than for growing wealth and prosperity, for they depend on assumptions which made sense in the Britain of the 1930s, but make none today.

All economic theories necessarily rest on unreal assumptions, and it is therefore vital that the simplifications made are those which can most safely be made. Keynesian theory rests on unreal assumptions no more and no less than others. The particular Keynesian simplifications which will be critically examined below are the following. First, that where there are unemployed resources, extra public investment, i.e. public works, raises the national income and employment until planned saving has risen by a corresponding amount. Second, that the only price which an increase in the money supply influences is the price of bonds. Third, that the rate of interest is determined by the quantity of money and liquidity preference and, finally, that the major influence on the level of output and employment in an economy is effective demand, so that hard work and the efficiency of resource allocation in the public and private sectors has a less significant effect on the wealth of nations than correct demand-management policies. Sophisticated Keynesians are of course aware that these crucial propositions rest on particular assumptions which may or may not be the most appropriate ones. But most Keynesians, like indeed most neoclassicals and most monetarists, are less sophisticated than that. Many Keynesian economists, not to mention those of their former pupils who are now senior civil servants, trade union leaders, journalists, broadcasters, and politicians still accept these propositions as unquestioningly as the Tablets which Moses brought down from the mountain.

1. Public Expenditure and Employment

The proposition that extra government investment raises output and employment until planned saving has risen as much as planned investment is taught to British economics students at school or university as one of their first lessons in economics. More generally, it is explained at an equally early stage that extra government expenditure of any kind raises incomes and employment.

THE BASIC EQUATIONS

One of the basic diagrams which is used to explain this is shown in figure 1. The consumption + investment + government expenditure line shows the economy's aggregate expenditure, and the economy's equilibrium output must be where aggregate expenditure equals output, so it is at E where the

Figure 1

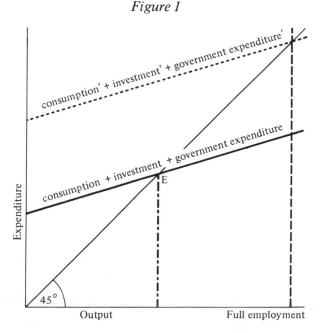

expenditure line cuts the 45° line (where expenditure and output are equal). It intersects this below full employment and, therefore, the higher dashed expenditure line, consumption' + investment' + government expenditure', is needed if full employment is to be achieved. Therefore, to achieve full employment, governments must raise private consumption and investment and their own expenditures. As policy tools to raise private investment are notoriously inadequate, governments in practice raise consumption + investment + government expenditure by raising government expenditure and by raising private consumption through tax cuts. These are the traditional Keynesian recipes for full employment.

But the weakness in the argument is that it ignores international trade. In other words, it is true for the world as a whole, for all countries acting together, or for a great power acting on its own, but it does not work for a small country in international trade as Britain now is, and this can easily be shown.

With international trade included, the complete version of one of the celebrated Keynesian national income identities is as follows:

$$\text{government expenditure} + \text{private investment} + \text{exports} \equiv \text{taxation} + \text{private saving} + \text{imports}$$

and this equation can be rearranged as:

$$\left(\begin{array}{l}\text{government}\\ \text{expenditure}\end{array}-\text{taxation}\right) \equiv \left(\begin{array}{l}\text{private}\\ \text{saving}\end{array}-\begin{array}{l}\text{private}\\ \text{investment}\end{array}\right)+(\text{imports}-\text{exports}).$$

In other words, the budget deficit equals the balance-of-payments deficit plus the excess of private saving over investment.

Keynesian governments, faced by the situation illustrated in the diagram, consider it orthodox to raise government expenditure and cut taxation for the reasons that have been mentioned. These policies can be described as follows:

$$\left(\begin{array}{l}\text{government}\\ \text{expenditure}\\ +3000\end{array}-\begin{array}{l}\text{taxation}\\ \\ -3000\end{array}\right) \equiv \left(\begin{array}{l}\text{private}\\ \text{saving}\end{array}-\begin{array}{l}\text{private}\\ \text{investment}\end{array}\right)+(\text{imports}-\text{exports}).$$

There is +3000 under government expenditure and –3000 under taxation to indicate that taxes have been cut by 3000 and public expenditure increased by 3000—policies like those which British and Italian governments have followed repeatedly in periods of unemployment. Now these policies which have added 6000 net to the left-hand side of the identity must also add to the right-hand side, and there is no doubt where the reader of an elementary Keynesian textbook would expect them to go. As in figure 1, a higher consumption + investment + government expenditure line will raise the national income and therefore private saving, and the national income will increase until private saving has risen sufficiently to finance the increase in the government's deficit. It does not need to rise by 6000 because, at a higher national income, tax revenue will also be higher, and it will be supposed in the examples here that private saving and aggregate tax revenues rise equally as the national income rises, so these will both rise by 3000. With 3000 added to private saving and to taxation (which makes good the previous tax cuts), the Keynesian identity becomes:

$$\left(\begin{array}{l}\text{government}\\ \text{expenditure}\\ +3000\end{array}-\text{taxation}\right) \equiv \left(\begin{array}{l}\text{private}\\ \text{saving}\\ +3000\end{array}-\begin{array}{l}\text{private}\\ \text{investment}\end{array}\right)+(\text{imports}-\text{exports}).$$

Here extra private saving finances the increase in government expenditure. But that is not the end of the story. Expansion in the national income raises private investment as well as saving, albeit one year to 18 months later, and in British booms since the Second World War it has raised it about as much[2]. Theoretical accounts which fail to take this into account omit the initial 'accelerator' or capital stock adjustment type effects of a change in the national income on investment.

The capital stock adjustment principle, which is perhaps the best econometric predicator of private sector investment[3], states in its simplest form that:

private investment = A previous national income level
$- B$ previous capital stock,

where A and B are constants. Now, in all booms, income rises faster than capital, and with this formula, it follows automatically that investment then rises faster than income. Hence there are good reasons to suppose that in expansion, *private investment* always rises faster than the national income. It is generally agreed that *private saving* also rises faster than the national income in periods of expansion for a variety of reasons. Hence both *private saving* and *private investment* can be expected to rise faster than income in any boom. Keynesian textbooks make the extraordinary error of admitting that *private saving* rises faster than income and then forgetting, because their policy analysis is static and not dynamic, that this is equally true of investment. If the British evidence allows it to be suggested that perhaps *private saving* and *private investment* rise about equally in periods of expansion, so that if 3000 is added to *private saving* it must be added equally to *private investment,* very striking results follow. This leaves 3000 too much on the left-hand side of the equation, unless we also add 3000 to (imports − exports), the balance-of-payments deficit, which is what we must do to balance the identity. Hence, what truly happens is this:

$$\left(\begin{array}{c} \text{government} \\ \text{expenditure} - \text{taxation} \\ +3000 \end{array} \right) \equiv \left(\begin{array}{c} \text{private} \qquad \text{private} \\ \text{saving} - \text{investment} \\ +3000 \qquad +3000 \end{array} \right) + (\text{imports} - \text{exports}) \\ +3500 \qquad +500$$

Private investment rises just as much as saving in the course of expansion, and imports rise far faster than exports. Expansion favours exports slightly, but to balance the equation imports must rise by 3000 more than exports. Hence, the ultimate effect of the Keynesian deficit-financed expansion is to destroy the balance of payments. This then brings these Keynesian booms to an end as soon as their balance-of-payments consequences become intolerable. This has happened many times in Britain. Moreover, after the collapse of the boom, British governments have had to maintain output at lower levels than it would otherwise have needed to be because of the balance of payments—so it is not clear that these Keynesian deficit-financed booms raise output and employment at all in the long term.

With further superficial thinking, orthodox Keynesian policies can be made to produce results which differ still more from what Keynesians expect to achieve. The problem with the expansion policies which have been outlined is that there is only one policy lever, demand expansion by unbalancing the budget, while there are two objectives, full employment and balance-of-payments equilibrium. So, given the rule that there must be at least one policy lever for each objective, an extra policy lever is needed. To meet this difficulty, it is widely supposed that, if the government increases its expenditure and devalues its currency at the same time, it will have the extra policy lever which will prevent the 3000 under government expenditure from going to (imports − exports) to destroy the balance of payments.

So we have the historical low point of British economic management, the Barber boom of 1971–73 with vast government expenditure increases and tax cuts and an 18 per cent devaluation in addition, the recipe for what may lay claims to be the most mismanaged boom since the publication of *The General Theory*. Of course private investment again rose about as much as private saving, so that the balance of payments again deteriorated as much as the budget, in spite of devaluation. And all that the extra ingredient of devaluation achieved was a 4 per cent addition to Britain's rate of inflation, with food and commodity prices rising faster in Britain than in any other major economy. The British Keynesians maintain that the rise in commodity prices in 1971-74 had nothing to do with their domestic policies, but it was these that contributed to the situation where commodity prices rose 40 per cent more in sterling than in Deutschmarks, which goes a long way to explain the greater inflationary strains that Britain experienced.

THREE WAYS TO INCREASE EMPLOYMENT

Some of Cambridge's most senior economists were among the first to see through the argument that budget deficits and devaluation should be combined to take the economy to full employment and balanced trade[4]. They saw that in expansion, if the balance of payments is not to be destroyed, government expenditure and taxation must rise together since private saving and private investment rise together. And there are just three ways in which Keynesians can seek to raise employment if they accept this.

First, employment can be raised through beggar-my-neighbour measures against foreigners. With the budget held stable, employment can be raised through a return to the competitive devaluations and tariff wars of the 1930s, which raise employment by raising exports or cutting imports. But in a world recession these policies will be as self-frustrating as in the 1930s if several countries attempt to follow them at the same time. The Cambridge economists who favour this approach must therefore be persuasive enough to convert the British government without being so persuasive that they also convert foreigners.

A second way in which employment can be raised is by raising government expenditure and taxation equally and at the same time, for effective demand and employment will be higher in an economy with more public expenditure and taxation than in one with a smaller balanced budget (as a result of the 'balanced-budget multiplier'). But this policy to achieve full employment through a large balanced budget entails more taxation at higher levels of public expenditure and employment. As taxes and public expenditure rise, a higher (and possibly growing) fraction of the labour force becomes dependent for its employment on the taxes paid by those workers who are not in tax-dependent public sector jobs. And if workers resist the payment of rising rates of taxation to keep others in employment, the result will be accelerating inflation and a profits squeeze, increasing still further the need for extra tax-dependent jobs. This can lead all too easily into a spiral where extra tax-dependent job creation results in the creation of fewer self-financing jobs in the private sector, with the result that still more tax-dependent jobs are needed, which raises required tax rates still further, and cuts job creation in industry and commerce where the self-financing jobs are yet again. This spiral in turn, can all too easily result in soaring rates of taxation, accelerating inflation as everyone tries to pass on extra taxes, and a growing fraction of the labour force which has to be found tax-dependent government jobs if full employment is to be maintained[5]. If governments are to avoid these dangers, then, as soon as they judge that taxation has reached acceptable limits, they must stop creating extra tax-dependent jobs in the public sector unless the private sector (and those nationalized industries which cover their costs) are still creating profitable jobs. With extra private sector jobs, more government jobs can of course be financed at constant rates of taxation. The British government judged that the limit to acceptable rates of taxation was reached by February 1976, and it has since been prepared to increase public sector employment only after employment in industry and commerce has risen[6]. So Keynesian job creation through a larger budget is ruled out, because taxes are too high to finance this without accelerating inflation leading to a possible hyperinflation.

There remains a third possible solution to the problem of unemployment which Keynesians could adopt, and this is precisely the one to which Keynes devoted the last years of his life. It is relevant to the problem of a world recession where unemployment is widespread. For the world as a whole there is no (imports – exports) term in the equations that were set out earlier, so if all countries together raise government expenditure and cut taxation, they will achieve expansion without collective balance-of-payments deterioration. World incomes will rise until, with more wages and profits everywhere, taxation rises as much as the initial rise in government expenditure. Hence, budgets will be restored at higher levels of world income, and private saving and private investment can rise equally in the course of expansion without destroying the balance of payments of the expanding countries, for the world as a whole cannot have a payments deficit[7].

Sadly, even all the OECD countries acting as a whole cannot take advantage of this proposition, for their joint expansion would greatly increase their total payments deficit with the OPEC economies, because of all the extra oil imports they would inevitably require. Hence even an agreement by every *developed* economy to pursue Keynesian expansionist policies in the world recession would not spare them large and growing payments deficits. The OPEC economies must be persuaded to expand at still faster rates than they are already expanding if international diplomacy is to allow Keynesian policies to work.

The argument suggests that the principal economic tools a small country, seeking to achieve full employment by Keynesian means in a world recession, has at its disposal are diplomatic ones if it is to avoid the beggar-my-neighbour policies which did so little good in the 1930s. It cannot fine-tune its way to full employment. Instead, it must persuade countries with economic power to act together if it is to achieve results. So it is the great and powerful that must follow Keynesian deficit-financing policies. It is they whom Keynes addressed in 1936 (when he addressed the powerful by addressing his own countrymen). So, while for the great powers acting together Keynesian policies are indeed a way of achieving full employment, and today the great powers must include OPEC, they can all too easily lead to the economic conditions of a banana republic if the economically insignificant use them on their own. Such countries may either destroy their currencies through repeated deficit-financed booms which destroy the exchange rate, or produce rubbish, which is unmarketable against the competitive products of others, behind the protection of tariff walls and import quotas. But the weaknesses in these policies were not much understood, so small countries like Britain in the 1960s and the 1970s, advised by Keynesian fine-tuners, accelerated domestic inflation and seriously damaged the international values of their currencies, either deliberately or accidentally, under the mistaken belief that they were pursuing full employment. And they may at any time move still nearer to true banana republic conditions by setting up the import-quota machinery which will destroy quality control in the manufacturing sector.

2. The Money Supply and Inflation

A second confusion of all but the more sophisticated Keynesians has stemmed from their failure to understand the role of the money supply in *The General Theory*. In that book, Keynes assumed, as a simplifying device, that portfolio holders—banks, insurance companies, pension funds, colleges and rich individuals—could hold their wealth in the form of only two kinds of asset, money and bonds. Extra money went in the first instance to portfolio holders (who held it in the form of what Keynes called larger 'speculative balances') and this meant that, with an increase in the money supply, portfolios became unbalanced. Portfolio holders, if they were formerly in balance, now had too much cash in relation to their bond holdings. They therefore attempted to switch from cash to bonds (which collectively they could not do), but in the process they bid up the prices of bonds until portfolio balance was achieved at new and higher bond prices, where interest rates were of course lower. The assumptions that all extra money went in the first instance to portfolio holders, and that these could react only by bidding up the prices of fixed-interest shares gave money a severely limited role, but the role is still considerable to anyone who understands that it is only an economist's simplifying assumption that bonds are the sole alternative to cash. Keynes's real assumption is that extra money goes in the first instance to portfolio holders, and bonds are merely a typical portfolio asset. With as many portfolio assets as in the real world, more money in the hands of portfolio holders must lead them to bid up the prices of assets in general, and not merely the bonds in their portfolios. So, when the money supply rises, bond prices will indeed be influenced, but so will the prices of equity shares, urban property, houses, farms, land, pictures, and even commodities. (And we all know that commodities often formed a considerable fraction of the portfolio of King's College Cambridge, while Keynes was Bursar)[8]. Therefore, in the true Keynes model that underlies *The General Theory*, an increase in the money supply will raise the prices of bonds, equity shares, houses, land, and commodities, as Leijonhofvud and others have suggested[9]. It will not raise their prices equally, and as we shall see some may even fall, but it will tend to raise their weighted average. As soon as it is recognized that all these prices will be influenced, analysis becomes far more complex than in *The General Theory* because a far more complicated theory of portfolio choice is needed if all these prices are to be included. But many Keynesians have failed to notice that bonds should be regarded merely as one portfolio asset out of many, wherever the theory is applied to the real world. They have therefore jumped far too quickly from the simplified presentation of the argument in *The General Theory* to the real world, and assumed that there, too, according to Keynes, money influences the price of bonds and nothing else. As evidence soon began to emerge that the price of bonds (or rather its inverse, the rate of interest) had a relatively insignificant effect on investment and consumption[10], it was assumed by these so-called Keynesians that the money supply had an equally insignificant effect on investment and consumption. Therefore, even though the great Keynesian book is called *The General Theory of Employment, Interest and Money* (which would suggest today to anyone unitiated that Keynes was a monetarist), the idea began to emerge that true Keynesians believed that the money supply influenced nothing of importance.

They should, of course, have traced the story back and appreciated that Keynes' insight was that extra money becomes a portfolio asset, and that an increase in the money supply therefore influences the prices of all other portfolio assets. Once this is understood, it immediately becomes clear that money is important, for no one can possibly imagine that government action which doubles the prices of housing and building land and puts pressure on commodity prices measured in domestic currency has negligible effects on the inflation rate. Apart from their immediate impact on the cost of housing which is up to one-third of the cost of living of owner occupiers (and 55 per cent of British families now live in houses they own) these will have effects on other prices and the wages of building workers which will affect other wages. Moreover, an increase in portfolio prices in general will have far greater effects on investment (equity finance cheaper, house-building more profitable, companies wealthier) than the mere increase in the bond price that follows from the superficial interpretation of Keynes with which so many have been content. And this wider interpretation allows basic Keynesian stories to be told which the no-money Keynesians cannot tell. Thus, it is part of Keynes' vision of the world that, even if there is no fall in the expected profitability of investment or in the propensity to consume, an increased psychological preference by the City of London for liquidity will produce falling share and property prices which can then move the economy towards a slump. This is straight Keynes: bankers can cause slumps[11]. But the no-money Keynesians could not possibly believe this. To them, bankers can influence only the bond price, and this has no influence on anything at all. These people therefore lost much of their Keynes and, in the process, those they advised including until recently the British Treasury believed that the money supply influenced nothing at all that was worth including in their equations. Hence, the British Treasury was until recently one of the most cavalier in the world about the influence of money on economies, and this damaged British economic management in all sorts of obvious ways.

In particular, the Treasury was persistently indifferent to the consequences for the money supply of its interest-rate policies, because money was assumed to influence neither investment nor consumption. Therefore, at times when it wished to keep interest rates down, for instance to economize in the cost of the national debt, or just to stabilize the rate of interest, it refrained from selling bonds in quantity. The national debt then had to be financed with excessive Treasury bill issues which made the banking system unduly liquid and allowed the money supply to grow. It will emerge that the long-term effect of these money supply increases was to put interest rates up, so the Treasury's increases in the money supply failed even to stabilize interest rates.

The money grew fastest in the dreadful Barber years when the Treasury allowed the budget deficit to soar and viewed the monetary consequences with indifference. Keynes would never have made this mistake. It cannot be emphasized too much that Keynes always considered money important.

3. Inflation and Rate of Interest

Keynes' simplification that money and bonds are the only portfolio assets has been even more damaging than has so far been suggested, because it has left Keynesians with an extremely unrealistic theory of the rate of interest. They insist and teach that an increase in the money supply will reduce the rate of interest. Now, from 1971 to 1974, when the money supply (M_3) about doubled in Britain, the prices of irredeemable government bonds fell by almost one-half, and the long-term rate of interest the government had to pay rose from 9 to 17 per cent. Therefore, orthodox Keynesian teachers were teaching the professors and economic advisers of the future the precise opposite of what was going on in the world around them. If they had explained that it was the prices of portfolio assets in general that would rise as a result of a doubling of the money supply, their students could have seen that any consequent increase in the expected rate of inflation would have adverse effects on the prices of bonds (which have mere money yields), in comparison with houses and land (which have yields that can keep pace with inflation). Because an increase in the expected rate of inflation will depress bond prices in relation to other asset prices, the money rate of interest will be higher, the higher the expected rate of inflation. This point is obvious as soon as it is appreciated that the money supply influences the prices of all portfolio assets, and by now many Keynesian economists have grasped this, but that was not the case even ten years ago.

Sir Roy Harrod has even attributed this lack of comprehension to Keynes himself. Writing in 1971[12]:

> I now come to my most important point. I am afraid that I shall be challenging a very widely held view, one held by many of you perhaps. It is painful to indulge in a head-on conflict, but it seems to be necessary in me to do so. I do not accept the Irving Fisher view that we should expect the money rate of interest to exceed what that rate would be if there were a prospect of stable prices by an amount equal to the expected rate of inflation. This view goes back beyond Irving Fisher to Alfred Marshall, who expressed it in his evidence before the Gold and Silver Commission in 1886. Keynes gave an outright denial of this doctrine and I am sure that Keynes was right[13].
>
> Bonds and cash are two forms of asset denominated in money. Neither has a hedge against inflation. Consequently, if after a period in which prices were expected to remain stable there arose a firm belief that prices will rise at a certain rate, the relative value of two kinds of asset neither of which contains a

hedge against inflation would not change. The rate of interest represents the rate at which bonds can be exchanged for cash. Since neither contains a hedge against inflation the new-found expectation that inflation will occur cannot change their relative values or therefore the rate of interest . . .

The idea that a new-found expectation can alter the relative value of two money-denominated assets, is logically impossible, and must not be accepted into the corpus of economic theory.

In fact, of course, an increase in the expected rate of inflation does not leave the cash and bonds margin unaltered. Cash gives a marginal convenience yield to those who hold it and, with faster expected inflation, holders will economize in cash so that the marginal convenience yield of money rises to match the higher money yield of bonds and the higher expected money returns from holding equities and physical assets. Hence money interest rates will very clearly rise with the expected rate of inflation.

A further and connected confusion in the Keynesian theory of the rate of interest is that, as in so much of Keynes, it relates to an economy that is cut off from the rest of the world. In an open economy the rate of interest will be influenced by the balance of payments and, in particular, countries with falling exchange rates will have to pay higher short-term interest rates on internationally mobile holdings than countries with exchange rates that are expected to rise. In so far as expected falls in the exchange rate are associated with expectations about rates of inflation, countries with rapid inflation will have high forward discounts on their currencies, and will therefore have to pay far higher short-term rates of interest than countries with slower inflation, so once again inflation influences interest rates. Joan Robinson, to her great credit, perceived as early as 1936 that the rate of interest of an individual country would be influenced by its balance of payments, and wrote something about this in her *Essays in the Theory of Employment* and sent the galley proofs to Keynes before publication. Keynes wrote to her, appalled, on 9 November 1936:

I beg you not to publish. For your argument as it stands is most certainly nonsense . . . You do not seem to realize that if you are right the whole theory of liquidity preference has to be thrown overboard. The rate of interest on English money no longer depends on the quantity of English money and the liquidity preference of the holders of it . . .

Four days later Joan Robinson wrote to Keynes, presumably to his great relief, 'I finally decided to cut all the controversial matter out of my exchange essay . . .'[14]. The leading Keynesians therefore preserved a united front to the world in defence of what was to become complete nonsense. But their great prestige kept it in British textbooks for a further 40 years.

Keynes' assumptions that the British interest rate is independent of foreign interest rates and that government bonds are a typical portfolio asset are comprehensible in the context of the Britain of the 1930s. London was then a great financial centre, so if he believed that world interest rates were determined in London, with sterling the *numéraire* against which other currencies were at a premium or discount, this would not have been absurd. And, with expectations of approximate price stability in London, bonds and equities and houses and land would not necessarily move in persistently divergent ways, so that in 1936 it might have been reasonable to regard bonds as a typical portfolio asset, for in 1936 commodity prices had risen relatively little in the previous century and a half. How much difference this makes is shown when Keynes' experience of centuries of relative price stability in his country is contrasted with that of Jean-Baptiste Say, the originator of Say's law. Say, writing in France after the Napoleonic wars, considered the possibility that a seller of commodities would hold on to the money he received and rejected it:

> When the producer has put the finishing hand to his product, he is most anxious to sell it immediately, lest its value should vanish in his hands. Nor is he less anxious to dispose of the money he may get for it; for the value of money is also perishable. But the only way of getting rid of money is in the purchase of some product or other. Thus, the mere circumstance of the creation of one product immediately opens a vent for other products[15].

So this Frenchman who lived through the currency collapse of the revolution, which had followed a series of currency devaluations under the Bourbons, believed that the value of money was perishable. Therefore, said Say, as soon as someone gets money from selling commodities, he buys other commodities. Money is therefore no more than a medium for transactions. Not so, said Maynard Keynes, an Englishman living in a country where for most of his life the gold value of sterling was exactly where Sir Isaac Newton had fixed it early in the 18th century. This Englishman saw money as the most secure store of value available to portfolio holders, and his prestige is such that many of his countrymen still believe and teach this, even while the commodity value of money halves every five to ten years.

Those who have been taught these theories of money and interest, which are contradicted by many of the observed facts of actual price and interest rate behaviour of the past 20 years, include those British civil servants who have learned some formal economics, many of the politicians in the Labour and Conservative parties who have held cabinet rank (in 1976 Britain had, for the first time since 1964, both a Prime Minister and a Chancellor without a British economics degree) and, in addition, senior trade union leaders, for two of the three most recent General Secretaries of the Trades Union Congress had Oxford Politics, Philosophy and Economics degrees. So it is no wonder that, with general assent, successive British governments fine-tuned their way to balance-of-payments crisis after crisis and increased the money supply under the mistaken impression that this would reduce the rate of interest at which British governments borrowed, which would ease the cost of Keynesian deficit financing. In practice, of course, the monetary expansion made inflation faster than it would otherwise have been, weakened sterling and therefore raised the rate of interest in London to the bewilderment of the British authorities, who were reduced to pleading with foreigners for lower world interest rates so that British interest rates could also be reduced. They would have been reduced, of course, if British inflation rates had been less, and most would now agree that a necessary (though not sufficient) condition for this would have been a slower rate of increase in Britain's money supply. But this would have contradicted everything our policymakers were taught while they were students.

4. Investment, Company Profitability and Growth

A final weakness in the Keynesian conventional wisdom which has dominated British economic management since the Second World War is a total lack of understanding of how growth and rising living standards are achieved. A vital point to note about *The General Theory* is that it was published three years before Sir Roy Harrod published his first essay on economic growth[16]. The model of production that underlies *The General Theory* is not far from a neoclassical stationary state. In this, full employment can be maintained continuously without perpetual investment in job creation, and the idea that economies must invest each year, possibly at a high rate, to provide enough new jobs to replace those which are destroyed by technical change seems never to have occurred to Keynes. He was always contemptuous of Marx. In *The General Theory,* largely following John Stuart Mill[17], he said that:

> . . . a properly run community equipped with modern technical resources, of which the population is not increasing rapidly, ought to be able to bring down the marginal efficiency of capital in equilibrium approximately to zero within a single generation; so that we should attain the conditions of a quasi-stationary community where change and progress would result only from changes in technique, taste, population and institutions . . .
>
> If I am right in supposing it to be comparatively easy to make capital-goods so abundant that the marginal efficiency of capital is zero, this may be the most sensible way of gradually getting rid of many of the objectionable features of capitalism. For a little reflection will show what enormous social changes would result from a gradual disappearance of a rate of return on accumulated wealth. (pp. 220–1)

To see an economy in long-term equilibrium as a quasi-stationary one requiring no profits to finance job creation was indubitably a serious error, and Marx's belief that a collapse of the rate of profit would destroy capitalism shows much more understanding of a market economy's long-term needs. In 1939 Sir Roy Harrod converted Keynes' model from a static to a dynamic one (though Keynes and his Cambridge colleagues found Harrod's work puzzling at first) but the damage was done.

The Keynesian conventional wisdom saw no need for continuing investment in job creation at a high level as a necessary condition for full employment. It was therefore not widely perceived in Britain that economies with a high potential for growth needed high investment, and therefore high profits to finance this. There was no technical need for profits because Keynes saw no objection to their being zero in the very long run, in spite of limited changes in population and technique. Also, as is evident from the quotation profits were seen not as a source of investment finance, but primarily as a source of social inequality. To Keynes, profits at any level at all were part of the unacceptable face of capitalism, for many of the objectionable features of capitalism would disappear if profits were zero. And the minimal investment necessary to maintain the economy in its long-term, General Theory, *quasi-stationary state* would presumably be induced by the mere expectation of profits. The 30 per cent investment share of Japan and the 25 per cent share of West Germany could not, of course, have been financed from expectations alone, while workers and the government took nearly 90 per cent of the national income as in Britain.

So the 'quasi-stationary state' economics of 1936 was unable to provide what was needed for Britain's growth opportunities of the 1950s, 1960s and 1970s. Here the Keynesian failure was not as great or total as it was in the field of monetary economics and fine-tuning, for several distinguished Keynesian economists did produce models where fast growing economies had higher shares of profits and investment than those with slow growth rates. However, the valuable models of Lord Kaldor, Joan Robinson and Luigi Passinetti[18] have been considered advanced and difficult by most students, the politicians and civil servants of the future, so they have not been widely absorbed into the ordinary thinking of men of affairs. But these did imbibe the quasi-stationary state world of *The General Theory,* so when they achieved power they destroyed the profitability of British industry (and this was true of both Labour and Conservative governments from 1964 to 1975) and then tried to boost investment by telling British industrialists that they could expect unprecedented growth.

This misconception of what is needed for growth should not have occurred for, with Roy Harrod's pioneering contribution, British economists should have become the first to understand the needs of a growing economy. But unfortunately Roy Harrod and many after him overlooked a vital point. He invented the 'natural' rate of growth, which was the growth rate that technical progress and population growth allowed, and the 'warranted' rate which was the rate the country's saving (less government investment) was able to finance. He concluded that if the 'warranted' rate was greater, countries would have excessive saving at full employment so that, '. . . we must expect the economy to be prevailingly depressed'. This is generally agreed. He described the situation where the 'natural' rate was higher, i.e. where saving was insufficient to finance the country's growth opportunities, as one with '. . . plenty of booms and a frequent tendency to approach full employment, the high employment will be of an inflationary and therefore unhealthy character'[19].

But that is not the end of the matter. If saving is insufficient, the investment the country needs for full employment may well be crowded out by other expenditures, so the country simply will not realize its growth opportunities. And this will not merely slow down growth. It will also mean that there is insufficient new investment to create enough new jobs for school-leavers and those made redundant by technical change, so inadequate saving (net of government investment) can lead to diminishing private sector employment opportunities as well as to inflation. Roy Harrod was therefore over-optimistic when he thought that there will be 'a frequent tendency to approach full employment'. He and most of the British growth theorists who followed him failed to include this line of argument in the conventional wisdom, so inadequate saving was seen merely as a cause of inflation, and not of structural unemployment in addition. A fall in private sector jobs can, of course, be made good if a growing number of public sector jobs is created, and this has happened to a great extent in Britain, but, as has already been pointed out, these extra public sector jobs are 'tax-dependent', so this process involves ever-rising taxation, or else budgets which become increasingly unbalanced. So Keynesians never had a theory of long-term job creation. They simply assumed that enough jobs would always be there if governments created sufficient demand.

Equally seriously, to most Keynesians the rewards from higher effective demand almost always exceeded those from greater efficiency and such old fashioned virtues as thrift with resources and hard work. Keynes ridiculed de Mandeville's thrifty bees and the Gladstonian virtues[20]. In the great slump of the 1930s output could indeed be raised massively by increasing effective demand (provided the balance-of-payments consequences could be managed or negotiated), but since the Second World War it is the economies with well organized beehives, thrifty bees, and a low ratio of drones in the hive that have prospered. Keynes' writings of the 1930s inadvertently set the economically literate in Britain on a course where hard work, efficient industrial organization, and the employment of a high fraction of the labour force on productive and profitable work were considered to be of only secondary importance in relation to correct demand management. And, because of their confused understanding of the functioning of economies at the macro-level, the British Keynesians were even unsuccessful managers of effective demand, so that average excess capacity rose as the rate of growth of output fell, thus doubly increasing the waste of resources that resulted from their demand-management policies.

5. The Misuse of Keynes in Britain

This has been an increasingly depressing account of the misinterpretation of the work of a very great economist, but it has an interesting historical parallel. In 1815 the Duke of Wellington was the world's most successful general. Because of his overwhelming prestige, those who were at Waterloo with him ran the British army for the next 40 years and insisted that everything must remain as it was under Wellington. The price for this conservatism was paid in the Crimean war. Since the Second World War British economic policy has been dominated by a desire to maintain the momentum of Keynes' very great successes, and the automatic transfer by Keynes' Colonels and Major Generals of his theories of the 1930s to a wholly different world in an attempt to do this was responsible for many of the disastrous policies of the 1960s and the 1970s.

To illustrate this, one need only quote from the memoranda that three of the greatest Keynesians who knew Keynes submitted to the Radcliffe Committee in 1958. This will allow us to see how Keynes' most distinguished successors were thinking at the start of the vital period in which the British economy was to decline so sharply in relation to its principal competitors.

First, Sir Roy Harrod, the author of some of the most notable and original contributions to economics after Keynes, wrote in a section of his memorandum entitled 'Normal Long Term Interest Rate in Britain should be 3%':

> The long term rate of interest is governed by the relation between the quantity of money and the money value of the national income. . . . If the quantity of money available were restored to a more normal relation to the money value of the national income, the long term rate of interest would come down to 3% quite naturally, without any fuss or bother[21].

Here, as in 1971, Roy Harrod's thinking was clearly locked into the simple two-asset Keynes model of 1936, where extra money cannot raise the rate of interest. In the real world, Lord Barber raised the money supply vastly faster than the national income, and the rate of interest did not fall to 3 per cent. It rose towards 17 per cent, and the increase in the money supply was partly responsible for this.

And Lord Kaldor, the great Keynesian who has had more influence over policy than any other since 1958, submitted a memorandum with a long section headed, 'The Dangers of a Regime of Stable Prices'. He was concerned that the British economy would stagnate if the inflation rate was too low[22]. This illustrates how the belief emerged that to Keynesians the objectives of full employment and growth must always have priority over the objective of price stability. But it did not then occur to Lord Kaldor that rapid inflation could have adverse effects on employment and growth.

And, finally, there is Lord Kahn, the Keynesian with the highest reputation for intellectual rigour. In 1958 he wrote in his memorandum that:

> Either interest rates are dangerously low, in which case they should be raised, or they are not dangerously low, in which case there is no harm in the increase in the quantity of money which is called for to keep them down[23].

We now know that raising the money supply may raise the rate of interest, so 'the increase in the quantity of money which is called for to keep [interest rates] down' is a meaningless concept—while raising the money supply in an attempt to achieve the unachievable has other adverse effects of which Lord Kahn is presumably now aware, but, like Roy Harrod, his thinking was clearly locked into the simplest version of Keynes' model of 1936 when he drafted this significant passage. Perhaps the statement in Lord Kahn's memorandum that most strongly foreshadowed what was to come is:

> To my mind the [government's] 'overall' deficit is of no significance[24].

Because Keynes was prepared to tolerate budget deficits in slumps, his great successors apparently felt it necessary to show how Keynesian they were by accepting budget deficits of any size. Presumably Lord Kahn would now consider Britain's deficit of 11 per cent of the national product in 1976 and Italy's of over 15 per cent significant.

The key point to note is that in 1958 three of the greatest Keynesians offered their countrymen monetary expansion, indifference to inflation, and the irrelevance of deficits. Their advice was accepted, but its disastrous effects have underlined an important lesson. In a changing world a particular economic model has only a limited life-span before its simplifications become dangerously wrong, and the evidence is overwhelming that the precise simplifications of Keynes' model of 1936 are now obsolete.

NOTES

1. I am grateful to Robert Bacon, Anthony Courakis, and Nicholas Dimsdale for helpful comments. An earlier version of this paper appeared in *Lloyds Bank Review,* October, 1976.
2. For instance, from 1962 to 1965, private saving rose by £1756m in Britain, while private investment (including investment in stocks) rose by £1452m. From 1971 to 1974, private saving rose by £8962m, while private investment (again including investment in stocks) rose by £9038m (National Income and Expenditure, 1973, table 70 and 1964–74, table 80).
3. See, for example, Dale W. Jorgenson, 'Econometric studies of investment behaviour: a survey', *Journal of Economic Literature,* **9** (December), 1971, for one recent survey of econometric work on the investment function.
4. See, for instance, Nicholas Kaldor, 'Conflicts in national economic objectives', *Economic Journal,* **81** (March), 1971; and R.R. Nield's articles in *The Times* on 19 and 20 July 1973.

5. This line of argument is set out in detail in Robert Bacon and Walter Eltis, *Britain's Economic Problem: Too Few Producers* (London: Macmillan, 1976).

6. This is made extremely clear in *Public Expenditure to 1979–80*, Cmnd 6393 (London: HMSO, 1976).

7. In terms of the Keynesian identity, a modest increase in government expenditure and reduction in taxation can be set out for the world as a whole as:

$$\left(\begin{array}{cc} \text{government} & \\ \text{expenditure} & -\text{taxation} \\ +1500 & -1500 \end{array}\right) \equiv \left(\begin{array}{cc} \text{private} & \text{private} \\ \text{saving} & -\text{investment} \end{array}\right)$$

and after world incomes have risen—with taxation and private saving rising equally—and private investment rising as much as private saving:

$$\left(\begin{array}{cc} \text{government} & \\ \text{expenditure} & -\text{taxation} \\ +1500 & +1500 \end{array}\right) \equiv \left(\begin{array}{cc} \text{private} & \text{private} \\ \text{saving} & -\text{investment} \\ +3000 & +3000 \end{array}\right)$$

so a country with a representative balance of payments would enjoy higher incomes without deterioration in either its balance of payments or its budget.

8. There is the famous story of Keynes walking past King's College Chapel, and saying, 'Too small, too small, far too small to hold all the wheat I have just bought for the college, if we have to take delivery'.

9. Axel Leijonhofvud, *On Keynesian Economics and the Economics of Keynes* (Oxford: Oxford University Press, 1968).

10. T. Wilson and P.W.S. Andrews (eds.), *Oxford Studies in the Price Mechanism* (Oxford: Oxford University Press, 1951) and *The Radcliffe Report*, Committee on the Working of the Monetary System, Cmnd 827 (London: HMSO, 1959) were influential in suggesting that interest rates were unimportant.

11. It is interesting in this context that, when Keynes became a member of the London Political Economy Club, the first question he put (in 1913) was, 'How far are bankers responsible for the alternations of boom and depression?' *(Political Economy Club Centenary Volume*, 1921).

12. See Sir Roy Harrod's comments on a paper by Milton Friedman in G. Clayton, J.C. Gilbert, and R. Sedgwick (eds.), *Monetary Theory and Monetary Policy in the 1970's* (Oxford: Oxford University Press, 1971), pp. 61–2.

13. Sir Roy Harrod may have had in mind here the passage on pp. 142–3 of *The General Theory* where Keynes criticizes Fisher's theory. See also, D.H. Robertson, 'Mr. Keynes and the rate of interest', in *Essays in Monetary Theory* (London: Staples, 1940), pp. 21–2.

14. *The Collected Writings of John Maynard Keynes*, Vol. 14, *The General Theory and After* (London: Macmillan, 1973), pp. 146–7.

15. Jean-Baptiste Say, *Traité d'Economie Politique,* Vol. 1, 4th edition, English translation by C.R. Prinsep (London, 1821), p. 167. The statement about the perishable value of money which prevents the circular flow of commodities from being blocked by 'hoarding' is not to be found in the early editions of Say's Treatise, so it has not been widely appreciated that a falling value of money is one of the presumptions on which Say's analysis is based.

16.   R.F. Harrod, 'An essay in dynamic theory', *Economic Journal,* **49** (March), 1939.

17.   John Stuart Mill, 'Of the tendency of profits to a minimum', in *Principles of Political Economy*, 1848, Book 4, chapter 4.

18.   Nicholas Kaldor, 'A model of economic growth', *Economic Journal,* **67** (December), 1957; Joan Robinson, *Essays in the Theory of Economic Growth* (London: Macmillan, 1962), chapter 2; and Luigi Pasinetti, 'Rate of profit and income distribution in relation to the rate of economic growth', *Review of Economic Studies,* **29** (October), 1962.

19.   R.F. Harrod, *Towards a Dynamic Economics* (London: Macmillan, 1948), p.88.

20.   *The General Theory of Employment, Interest and Money*, pp. 359–62.

21.   Committee on the Working of the Monetary System, Principal Memoranda of Evidence, Vol. 3 (London: HMSO, 1960), p. 114.

22.   *Ibid*, pp. 148–9.

23.   *Ibid*, p. 145.

24.   *Ibid*, p. 145.

Problems of Monetary Management: The U.K. Experience[1]

Charles Goodhart

1. Introduction

In 1971 the monetary authorities[2] in the United Kingdom adopted a new approach to monetary management, a change of policy announced and described in several papers on competition and credit control. The subsequent experience of trying to operate this revised system has, however, been troublesome and at times unhappy. The purpose of this paper is to examine certain aspects of recent monetary developments in order to illustrate a number of more general analytical themes, which may have relevance among several countries.

The outline of the paper is as follows. In the remainder of this section the previous, pre-1971, *modus operandi* of monetary management is sketched in, and reasons given why the authorities found it increasingly unsatisfactory. In the next section on the money supply and bank behaviour, the intended new method of credit control is described; the intention is then compared and contrasted with actual results. Part of the intellectual and theoretical basis for the change-over to a new *system* of monetary management[3] depended on the belief that it was possible to identify in the United Kingdom, as in other countries, a stable demand-for-money function. What became of that belief thereafter is recorded in the third section on the demand for money. The developments reported in the second and third sections posed some difficult problems for the conduct—even for the interpretation and assessment—of monetary policy. In order to deal with some of these problems a new instrument, the Supplementary Special Deposit, was introduced (in December 1973) in conjunction with guidelines for the growth of interest-bearing bank deposits, familiarly known as 'the corset'. Experience with this, in some ways novel, instrument is assessed in the final section on the operation of monetary policy.

Turning to the *modus operandi* of monetary policy prior to 1971, interest rate adjustments were mainly conditioned by the state of the balance of payments, with short rates being pushed up whenever sterling weakened, and allowed to fall—in order to encourage the housing market and company investment—when sterling strengthened. No attempt was made to peg long rates or to offset market trends in the gilt market entirely, but the Bank usually 'leant into the wind' to reduce the rate of change in market prices, in the interest of maintaining a broad, orderly market for government debt. The Bank was continually keen to sell marketable government (gilt-edged) debt, i.e. to fund the debt, in order to finance over time a 'reasonable proportion' of the government's current needs, and to refinance the steady stream of maturities. Such funding was done when market opportunities arose (i.e. when the market expected rates to fall); little or no attempt was ever made to press sales on an unreceptive market, even if the government's borrowing requirement was very large and/or if domestic credit and the money stock was growing unusually fast. This was partly because, until perhaps the last few years before 1971, the behaviour of the monetary aggregates played no part in deciding the authorities' actions, but even more because it was felt that there was no predictable relationship in the short term between gilt-edged sales and the level of interest rates.

With interest rates thus determined, the authorities turned increasingly in the years up till 1971 to direct control (by quantitative ceilings) of bank lending to the private sector. The purpose was to reduce private sector demand, mainly in the interests of the balance of payments. This was certainly the case in the series of requests (for the ceilings had no statutory backing) which began in December 1964 and continued in ever more precise form until 1971. These requests were occasionally supported by calls for special deposits which had to a large extent a symbolic character, and were intended to underline the Bank's intentions. In the final few years of this period, from 1969 onwards, such ceilings were also seen as playing a supporting role in restraining the broader monetary aggregates, i.e. the money stock as variously defined or domestic credit expansion (DCE), to which attention was increasingly turning[4].

Direct controls over bank lending had many disadvantages. Even leaving on one side the problems of administering them, their effect was naturally to reduce competition and efficiency within the banking system. These base-dated controls were in operation, fairly continuously from 1964 till 1971, so that for a prolonged period the main job of bank managers became to refuse new business (or to direct such business to subsidiaries with more leeway for lending), not to encourage it. In so far as such controls did not serve to freeze proportionate shares of banking business at its base-date position, it encouraged the growth of certain 'fringe' institutions outside the banking sector, and also the development of secondary money markets (e.g. an inter-company market was emerging at the end of the period) which allowed money and credit to flow around such quantitative credit barriers.

Not only was the amount of lending restrained by such direct controls, but also the rates charged on such loans were largely conditioned by the London clearing banks' cartel arrangements (effectively in force since 1917 with the support of the authorities), which tied the deposit and lending rates of these banks (eleven in number in 1964, reduced through mergers to six in 1971) to Bank rate. Other banks were free to set their rates at more competitive levels, and also did not have to observe the 8 per cent cash and 28 per cent liquid-asset ratios which the clearers maintained, which restricted the clearers from operating in the new parallel money markets, i.e. the eurodollar market and the sterling markets in inter-bank and local authority money, which operate on very small margins. In some part the clearers were able to respond to this situation by forming subsidiaries. Nevertheless, they would have been in an even more disadvantageous position after the abolition of ceilings controls—which in some ways had fallen less severely on them—unless such competitive disadvantages had been removed.

For such micro-level and structural reasons there would, in any case, have been an urge to seize the opportunity of a period of slack in the economy to get away, even if only temporarily, from the base-dated ceilings, and perhaps also to encourage the abandonment of the interest rate cartel. In the meantime, however, the rationale for this whole strategy was being queried at the macro-level. It was doubtful whether such direct controls on this one component of domestic credit creation were having a significant effect in restraining the money stock, or on real domestic expenditures. No evidence of any such effect could be observed from the studies made of the demand-for-money function. These studies showed that the demand for money, both narrowly and broadly defined, over the period 1963–70 (an observation period limited by the availability of data) could be well explained by current and previous movements in income and interest rates. In some part, potential borrowers refused loans from banks raised the

Figure 1. Bank lending (outstanding) to the personal sector.

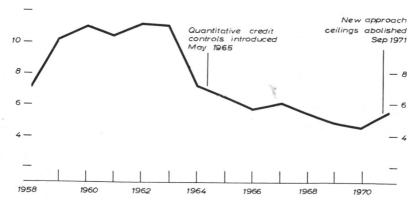

Percentage of annual Personal Disposable Income

Figure 2. Bank advances (outstanding) to industrial and commercial companies.

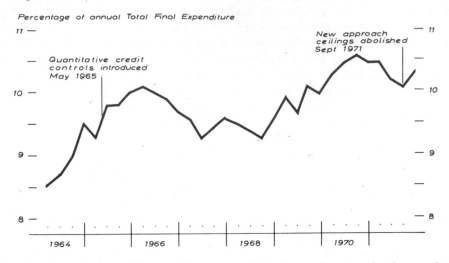

Percentage of annual Total Final Expenditure

money instead by selling public sector debt themselves, or by borrowing from other financial intermediaries who sold public sector debt in their turn, or by bringing in funds from abroad, a response which was at times most welcome. With interest rates determined along the lines already noted, this just led to a reshuffling of bank assets, with lending to the public sector replacing lending to the private sector with little effect on the money stock.

In any case, outside of the limitation of bank lending to persons which did appear to bite (see figure 1), the severity of the control was possibly exaggerated. At the time it was quite difficult to discern whether the ceilings were having any marked effect in restricting bank advances to companies (see figure 2). The Bank, in general, resisted the predictable pressures to exempt 'desirable' kinds of lending (e.g. exports, agriculture, house-building) from such ceilings. This was partly so that room should have to be made for expansion in these areas by restricting less desirable borrowers more severely, and partly because any such exemption is liable to provide a bigger loophole than intended. Definitional difficulties arise; moreover the exempted activities tend to be financed to the hilt by bank loans releasing funds for other uses, including on-lending. Even so, one important exemption was made in the interests of preserving the medium-term fixed-rate schemes for finance for exports and shipbuilding. In all the circumstances, measurement of the economic effect of such direct controls was hardly possible, and the selection of numbers for the ceilings was somewhat arbitrary.

In the meantime a number of academic econometric studies on the demand-for-money function in the United Kingdom had been completed both in the universities[5], and within the Bank itself[6], following mainly the example and methodologies of prior U.S. work. These all seemed to show that the development of the monetary aggregates during previous years could, after appropriate adjustment for the lagged relationships involved, be reasonably well explained by the movements in incomes and interest rates. As shown in figure 3, both M_1 and M_3 over the period 1964–71 varied fairly closely together and in line with money incomes, and after separation of incomes into real and price elements, the inclusion of an interest-rate variable and adjustment for lags, the fit could be much improved.

If these past relationships could be expected to hold in the future also, such findings seemed to carry a number of implications. First, velocity itself did not appear to be, as the Radcliffe Report had implied, unstable or unpredictable, so a change in the money stock would have a substantial effect either on money incomes or on interest rates; the question, however, of the transmission mechanism whereby either changes in interest rates or monetary aggregates then fed through onto income and expenditure decisions remained then, and since, wrapped in mystery in the United Kingdom. But at least monetary management would seem likely to have some effect. Moreover, if the level of interest rates was largely determined by external considerations, e.g. in a fixed exchange rate system, the equation(s) would seem to allow one to read off what rate of monetary growth would be consistent with (or more restrictive or expansionary than) the government's domestic income objectives. Alternatively, if exchange rates were floating or the external position did not represent a constraint (as in 1971/72), the equation could be used—though the relationships involved were more complex—to explore the effect of differing rates of domestic credit expansion on domestic incomes, interest rates, international capital flows

Figure 3. M_1, M_3 and GDP.

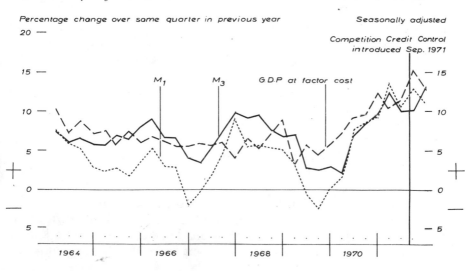

and exchange rates. Finally, the finding that interest rates appeared to have a significant and predictable effect on the demand for money tended to dissipate the previous pessimism that markets were too unpredictable to rely on variations in interest rates to control the monetary aggregates. The econometric evidence seemed to suggest that, one way or another, whether by restraining bank borrowing or by encouraging non-bank debt sales, higher interest rates did lead to lower monetary growth. In one fell swoop, therefore, these demand-for-money equations appeared to promise:

(1) that monetary policy would be effective;
(2) that an 'appropriate' policy could be chosen and monitored;
(3) that the 'appropriate' levels of the monetary aggregates could be achieved by market operations to vary the level of interest rates.

Ignoring Goodhart's law, that any observed statistical regularity will tend to collapse once pressure is placed upon it for control purposes, these findings, which accorded well with the temper of the times, helped to lead us beyond a mere temporary suspension of bank ceilings towards a more general reassessment of monetary policy. The main conclusions of this were that the chief intermediate objectives of monetary policy should be the rates of growth of the monetary aggregates, i.e. the money stock, in one or other of its various definitions, or DCE (and not particular components of these, such as bank lending to the private sector), and that the main control instrument for achieving these objectives should be the general price mechanism (i.e. movements in interest rates) within a freely competitive financial system.

2. Bank Behaviour and the Money Supply

Under this new approach the method of control was expected to be roughly as follows. When the authorities wished to act restrictively they would aim to push up interest rates either by raising the rate at which they relieved the normal cash shortages arising in the market (since the Treasury bill tender is usually set somewhat larger than necessary, in order to hold money markets under slight tension) or by a call for special deposits, etc. One of the previous limitations on the authorities' freedom of action was that Bank rate had been, and had been seen to be, an administered rate, subject to all the constraints that tend to restrain the flexibility of administered rates. In so far as Bank rate was sticky, this in turn had limited the flexibility of other money market rates, e.g. Treasury bill rate. It was the intention in 1971 to allow all rates, including Bank rate, to vary more flexibly. However several of the (political) constraints preventing administered rates from varying flexibly remained. In the hopes of enabling the market mechanism to work more nearly as planned, a subsequent change, made in 1972, was to link the (penal) rate for lending from the Bank, the minimum[7] lending rate (MLR), to Treasury bill rate, so that MLR would vary with changes in market rates[8]; the authorities, however, retained the option to make administered, fiat, changes in MLR at their own discretion.

The effect of operations which raise money market rates and place pressure on banks' reserve positions is to induce an upwards pressure on interest rates more generally. In practice banks do not respond to pressure on their cash positions by some large-scale, multiple cut-back in their asset portfolio, by calling in advances, etc. Instead their immediate response will be to bid for funds, by raising rates offered on deposits, or by selling liquid assets from their second line of reserves. With the cost of marginal funds rising, banks would, we believed, raise the rates charged on advances to maintain their profitability. Meanwhile with interest rates on public sector debt pushed higher, e.g. when banks had sold such assets to maintain their liquidity, persons might shift out of banks deposits into public sector debt[9].

The transmission mechanism whereby restrictive pressure on banks' liquidity positions became translated into a more general reduction in the rate of growth of their advances and deposits was seen to run via portfolio adjustments in response to changing relative prices (interest rates) by banks, persons, etc. Pressure on the banks' cash position was a means to this end. The adoption of a cash reserve (or high-powered money, or reserve base) target seemed to us to confuse ends and means. Apart from the fact that the provision of monetary data is too infrequent in the United Kingdom to make such a system possible (a feature which could, perhaps, have been changed at some considerable cost), such an approach would lead to much greater variance in short-term interest rates and subsequent structural changes. These would probably have had the effect of reducing the efficiency of the short-term money market since banks would tend to hold extra money balances rather than putting them into money market instruments. And if the authorities can control average short-term rate levels, there seems little to be gained by deliberately increasing the variance of such rates.

It was, indeed, partly for this reason that the new required reserve ratio, applied in common to all banks, covered a wider range of short-term assets, including Treasury bills, call money held with discount houses, gilts of under one year maturity. Given, however, the previous picture of the supposed control mechanism working through interest rates, the question arises, as to exactly what was the function or purpose of this ratio? Partly, I think, the desire to maintain some required ratio was due to uncertainty about bank behaviour in a more competitive, unconstrained system, a fear that perhaps bank behaviour would be unstable, or unpredictable. What if banks should come to feel able to work on much lower liquidity ratios for their own purposes? The existence of a required ratio held out a promise of a stable fulcrum against which the authorities might be able to press. Nevertheless the coherence of the inter-relationship between the cash-base/interest-rate mechanism spelt out earlier and the reserve–assets ratio has proved confusing to many. As Sir Leslie O'Brien stated, in his speech to the international bankers at Munich[10], the main method of control over the banking system was to be through the price mechanism, i.e. via interest rate adjustments. In this respect ratio control, through the required reserve–assets ratio, was to play only a supporting role.

When we embarked on this course in 1971/72, it was foreseen that the new control system would face certain initial, teething problems. In particular, there had been quantitative ceilings on bank lending since 1964, and within these ceilings there had been further qualitative guidance to banks to discriminate severely against certain types of borrower, e.g. persons. Once before when there had been 'a dash for freedom' in 1958–60, there had been a very sharp surge in lending to previously constrained groups. It was expected that this would occur again, but its magnitude was unpredictable. In the event it was very large, as shown in figure 4. With profitable lending business, which had been previously prevented, or diverted, by ceilings, returning to the banks, the banks would be in a position to raise the rates which they offered for funds to more attractive levels. Moreover the margin between the rates charged for advances and offered on deposits had been pegged for years by the clearing bank cartel. With the cartel abolished and competition encouraged, this margin could be expected to shrink, leading to re-intermediation by the banks, with a faster increase in both assets and deposits.

Moreover there was little or no previous experience to indicate how sensitively or rapidly the demand for bank borrowing might respond to

Figure 4. Bank lending (outstanding) to the personal sector.

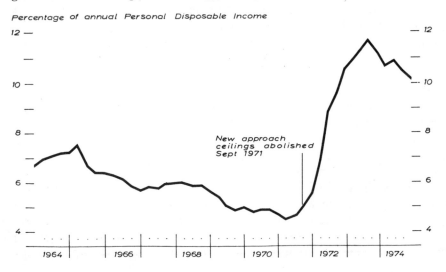

Figure 5. New house prices relative to average earnings.

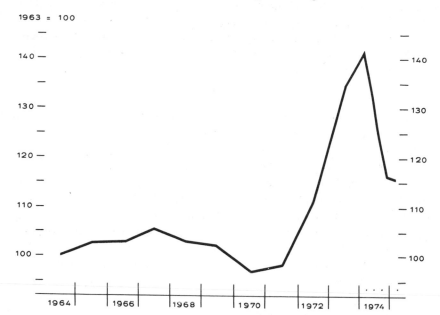

increases in interest rates, since such borrowing had been mainly affected by the alternate imposition and relaxation of ceilings in previous years. If the elasticity of demand for such loans was low, interest rates might have to be pushed to levels which would have serious adverse effects on the politically sensitive mortgage and housing markets. This was the more likely since the combination of tax arrangements[11] and accelerating inflation brought about an increasing divorce between 'real' and nominal bank borrowing costs. The authorities would have to pass presentational and psychological hurdles like going into double figures with nominal rates without bringing about any comparable rise in real rates. This problem was, of course, intensified, at least at the presentational level, by the adoption of prices and incomes policies from 1972 onwards.

Even so, it was, perhaps, the unforeseen problems that caused the greatest difficulties. At much the same time as the authorities were abolishing direct ceilings on bank lending, the government was also relaxing certain controls on commercial rents and property development. The combination of generally falling interest rates in 1971/72 with a suddenly unconstrained banking and property market led to a boom in housing and property prices (figure 5). By 1973, although interest rates began to rise, after June quite sharply, the rise in housing and property prices had become self-sustaining, in a quasi-speculative mania, which reached its bitter end at the turn of the year. The banking and financial community had not been immune from the lure of quick profits from participation in the property boom, although the involvement of the larger clearing banks was much less than that of several smaller 'fringe' financial institutions.

It was bad enough that the competitive process had been associated with instability in the housing and property markets. What was worse was that when the control mechanism was put to the test, especially in 1973, it appeared, at least in relation to the indicator by which its performance was commonly judged, which was M_3, the broad definition of the money stock, to have failed; indeed the results seemed actually perverse. In 1971 and 1972 the government was trying to bring about a faster rate of economic growth. An accompanying acceleration in monetary growth, especially when much of it could be ascribed to re-intermediation, seemed quite appropriate. But anxiety mounted as early as September 1972, and grew during the winter; by mid-1973 signs of overheating were apparent and the external position of sterling was becoming subject to stress. Accordingly interest rates were increased sharply, and the authorities wished to brake the rate of growth of the monetary aggregates. As interest rates rose in the latter half of 1973, the rate of growth of M_1, narrow money, slowed sharply, as was intended and expected. On the other hand, the rate of growth of M_3, the broad money aggregate[17], accelerated still further (see figure 6), and bank lending in sterling to the private sector surged ahead. Indeed in the period 1972–74 the relationship between the velocity of M_3 and the level of interest rates was perverse (figure 7), though the normal form of relationship continued to hold for M_1, (figure 8). Since 1972, therefore, the trends in the rates

Figure 6. M_3 and three-month inter-bank rate.

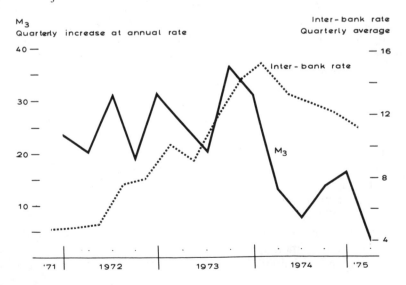

of growth of M_1 and M_3 have frequently been moving in markedly different directions.

It so happened, however, that M_3 was the monetary series to which most commentators in the United Kingdom paid closest attention. As an indicator it has several advantages over M_1. With M_3 comprising most

Figure 7. M_3 velocity.

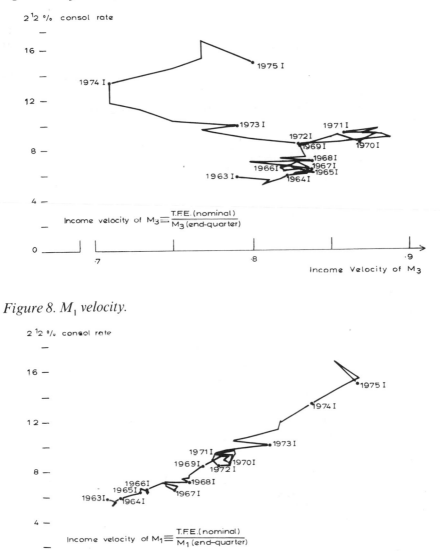

Figure 8. M_1 velocity.

domestic bank liabilities, it is possible to use bank balance-sheet and flow-of-funds data to relate M_3 to counterpart bank assets, domestic credit expansion and external balance-of-payments developments. Since policy measures tend to act more directly on the public sector borrowing requirement, on debt sales, and on bank lending to the private sector, than on the liabilities side of the balance sheet, it is easier to attach reasons for the change in the money stock, to ascribe praise or blame to this or that policy, if the indicator is M_3 rather than M_1.

Therefore, whether or not it was true in fact, a large number of commentators claimed that the rapid rise of M_3 in 1973 (while M_1 was falling away and interest rates were rising ferociously) was a sign of an irresponsibly expansionary, and inflationary, monetary policy. Even doubting the validity of such claims, the rapid monetary expansion—in bank lending and M_3—was having at the least an adverse presentational effect on expectations.

Figure 9. Base rate and three-month inter-bank rate.

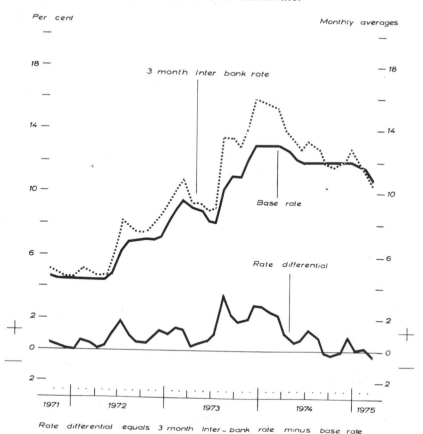

Rate differential equals 3 month Inter-bank rate minus base rate

Clearly the standard control mechanism had not worked; the first need was to discover why this was. An important factor, in my view, was that we had failed to foresee the likely course of bank behaviour in an unconstrained system (a failure which may be more easily understood since British banks had not had the chance of operating in such a *milieu* in living memory). In particular, in an oligopolistic banking system, with a large element of 'endowment' profits accruing on assets held against zero-yielding current accounts, the extent to which the banks might take the expansionary and competitive bit between their teeth and gallop off was unexpected. The practical point is that the cash-base/interest-rate mechanism only works as the textbooks claim if the margin between the rates which the banks offer for (additional) funds in wholesale money markets and charge on (additional) advances remains constant (or increases) as interest rates rise. If this holds, the interest *differential* between advances (and public sector debt) and deposit rates will at least remain constant, while the margin between rates on public sector debt (and advances) and on other assets should widen, thus causing the standard portfolio readjustment.

In the United Kingdom this did not happen. As shown in figure 9, over the period 1972–74, whenever rates were rising, money market rates, represented by inter-bank rate, rose relative to bank lending rates, (and to five-year bond yields). This, of course, made bank borrowing a relatively cheaper way of paying debts than running down liquid assets, as interest rates rose. Indeed, as Professor Sprenkle has noted[13], when the rates on overdrafts and deposits are equal, the precautionary demand for overdrafts will be infinite; for many months in 1972 and 1973 money market rates were in excess of bank lending rates to prime customers. During 1973 this pattern of rates encouraged a massive increase in bank lending, and a corresponding accumulation of time deposits, largely within the company sector (sometimes within a single company), where firms had command over large enough sums to take advantage of arbitrage opportunities.

Why did this happen? In the first place banks' base rates are administered rates, not market-determined and, for a number of well known reasons, administered rates tend to move more slowly than market rates, especially in an oligopolistic situation. In addition there was a technical problem. To prevent the discount houses creating reserve assets for the banking system on too large a scale, they were required to hold 50 per cent of their own assets in specified public sector reserve assets—quite largely Treasury bills—which would be especially attractive to the discount houses when longer-dated gilts were expected to fall in price. But this meant that in circumstances when bank liabilities and interest rates were rising, Treasury bill rates would be relatively held down by strong bidding from the discount houses; but MLR was tied to Treasury bill rates, and bank lending rates could not be raised far from MLR without incurring public odium.

This situation was put right in July 1973; in any case it probably only had minor influence. A much more important factor was that banks were not primarily concerned with short-term profit maximization. They had been encouraged to compete aggressively, and this was often taken to mean competition for business, market shares, etc. The extension of new lending facilities in 1972/73 was enormous, and undertaken with little or no concern for capital adequacy. Secondly, a rise in interest rates of itself tended to lead to an increase in bank profits because of the greater endowment effect on higher earning assets supported on an (albeit proportionately shrinking) base of zero-yielding current accounts. Thus as rates rose, banks could undertake additional business at a small loss and still turn in higher profits, as illustrated in figures 10 and 11. Certainly banking profits rose very sharply over the period 1970–73, despite the shrinking margins between deposit rates and advances rates[14]. Indeed this was so marked that it aroused at times some public hostility. So it was difficult for the banks to raise their base rates at a time when prices and incomes policies were in force and their profits had risen so fast. And once they had extended larger facilities, they could not, under the overdraft system, help lending more to customers taking advantage of relatively cheap borrowing rates. In any case, behaviour which increased banking growth even if profitless may then have seemed desirable.

Figure 10.   *Figure 11.*

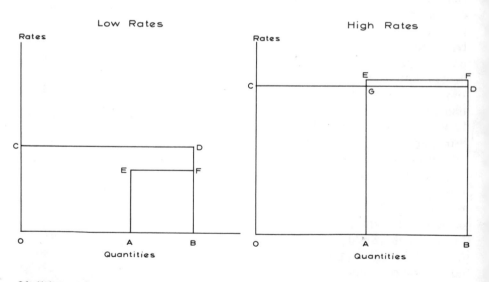

OA Volume of current accounts

AB Volume of time deposits

OC Rate on earning assets

AE Rate of interest on time deposits

OAEFDC net interest rate earnings

OA Volume of current accounts

OB Volume of time deposits

OC Rate on earning assets

AE Rate of interest on time deposits

OCGA-GEFD net interest rate earnings

Of course the details of this story are particular to the United Kingdom, but the economic moral is of wider application. This is that the determination of the money stock in any country depends crucially on banking behaviour and objectives. These can differ from country to country, and over time (as is discussed later, banking objectives in the United Kingdom in 1974 were very different from those in 1973). Professor Tobin in his famous paper[15] was among the first to remind us that banking behaviour and objectives matter. The U.K. experience is a lesson of the truth of this view. In particular a 'free market' system of control requires market-oriented and motivated participants—in their absence only a non-market control system can be effective. One can argue that the period, since 1971, marks a difficult stage of returning to a market system, or something approximating to it, and that this has required changes in institutional behaviour and structure that proved more difficult and prolonged than was initially expected.

3. The Demand for Money

The enormous increases both in bank lending and in interest-bearing time deposits in 1972/73 were largely due to the pattern of relative interest rates which the banks had allowed to develop. This was a new phenomenon. Prior to 1971 relative (bank) rates had been largely pegged by the cartel agreement: somewhat surprisingly it has not been possible to find in the econometric exercises any significant effect of such pegged own-rates in attracting deposits. After 1971, when, *inter alia*, the banks were able to compete for deposits more aggressively, the previous forecasting equations for M_3, and for the broad money holdings of persons *(MP)* and companies *(MC)* completely broke down, especially the latter (see figures 12, 13 and 14). In each case the extent of the monetary expansion was far in excess of that predicted by the equation in most of the quarters of 1972 and 1973. Everyone now agrees that the demand-for-money equations, using the broader definition of the money stock, have proved unstable.

The situation is not so clear cut in the case of the demand function for narrow money, M_1. The quarterly forecasts, using our 1971 equation, have *not* been notably accurate (see figure 15), but taking the period 1972–74 as a whole it is not clear that they have been biased. Moreover, re-running the equation as these new observations have arrived has not altered the form of the equation significantly. On these grounds we would argue that the relationship has remained fairly stable, but is subject to such considerable noise that it is only of limited help in monitoring quarterly, let alone, monthly developments. It is, however, only fair to add that this view that the demand for narrow money has remained a stable function (of current and past real incomes, prices and interest rates) has been disputed.

The interesting question then is not whether (most) demand-for-money functions in the United Kingdom ceased to be stable after 1971, but why this happened. The strict 'monetarist' analysis is, as I understand it, that the growth in the nominal money stock is exogenous to the private sector. The public has a demand for 'real' money balances, and as the nominal stock of

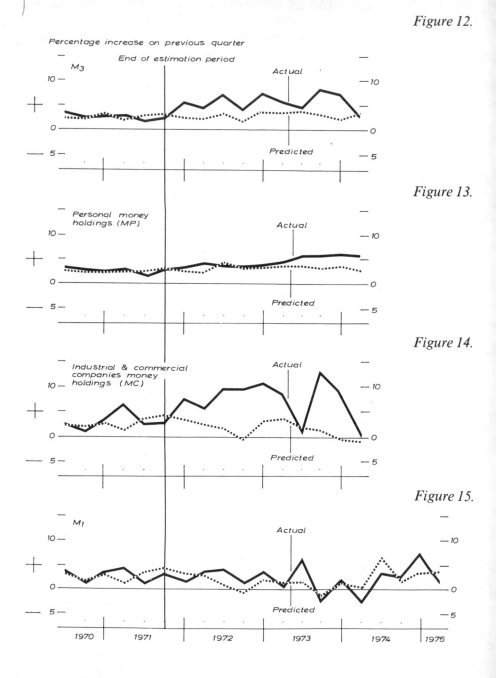

Figure 12.

Figure 13.

Figure 14.

Figure 15.

money increases the public will then adjust its spending on real goods (thereby affecting both prices and real incomes) and financial assets (thereby affecting interest rates) until incomes, prices, and interest rates have adjusted to a level consistent both with exogenous nominal balances and the demand function for real money balances.

Somewhat in this vein it has been argued, for example by Artis and Lewis[16], that the extension of advances by the banking system in 1972/73 was so large that the above adjustment mechanism just could not work (see figure 16). The system moved into disequilibrium. The underlying demand function may not have changed, but the public could not reach their desired position.

One can make a number of remarks about such a line of approach. First, if movements in the nominal money stock are indeed the exogenous, causal force, the appropriate relationship to fit is a money multiplier, not a demand-for-money function. Second, if an exogenous monetary shock causes people to adjust until *real* balances are some function of current *and past* real incomes and interest rates, one should observe considerable over-shooting and instability in the economy in response to variations in monetary growth rates. Finally, if the lags between injections of nominal money balances and their effect on real incomes and prices are long and

Figure 16. Bank lending in sterling to the private sector and total final expenditure.

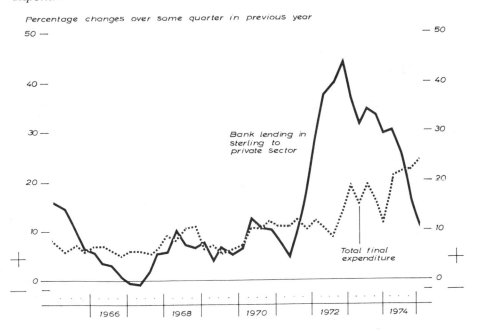

variable, it is difficult to see how people can ever normally be close to their underlying demand function for real money balances.

For practical purposes, however, these can be treated largely as debating points. The question essentially at issue in assessing monetary developments at this time was whether the volume of interest-bearing time deposits that had been accumulated so hugely in 1973 by the private sector, especially by companies, was voluntarily held at existing levels of incomes and interest rates, or whether at those existing levels money holders were preparing to move into other assets. Whether, or not, such deposits were willingly held is perhaps to some extent a semantic issue. What is held at any point of time must in a sense have been chosen, otherwise something else would have happened. Moreover even those of us who believed that this unprecedented build-up of time deposits was an explicable function of relative interest rate movements recognized that under changed circumstances this did represent a disturbing overhang of purchasing power.

Nevertheless I did not, and do not, accept the Artis–Lewis explanation that the huge rise in interest-bearing deposits in 1973 was largely a dis-equilibrium phenomenon. Instead I would explain it largely in terms of a rational response to movements in interest rate differentials. In particular, I would refer again to the theoretical case that when the return on bank deposits rises to equal the cost of bank borrowing, the demand for both bank loans *and bank interest-bearing deposits* will be infinite, since one can obtain additional precautionary balances at zero cost. They become a free good. It was, moreover, noteworthy that throughout 1973 the increase in company sector bank deposits kept quite largely in step with the increase in company sector borrowing (while there was little growth in company sector real expenditures) (see figure 17).

One conclusion which we have reached is that our equations purporting to explain the movements in the holding of broad money balances (M_3) prior to 1971 were badly mis-specified. They were mis-specified because they did not contain an own-rate, and also left out some of the more important interest differentials, especially the margin between bank lending rates and deposit rates[17]. We have run a number of revised equations in this vein, and indeed get quite good fits over the period 1971–73 (see Appendix). However as Artis and Lewis[18] very rightly point out, it has not generally been possible to find the same kind of result within the earlier period 1963–71[19]. With only a few observations in the later period it is perfectly possible that the interest differential variables introduced then, and only then, were in fact acting as proxies for other factors. So for the time being I remain agnostic whether the experiences of 1971–74 reveal that the demand for money suffered a major structural change (after the introduction of the new system in 1971), or was not in equilibrium in these years, or was simply unstable. Either way reliance on the stability of the demand for money has been severely shaken. For our own internal forecasting purposes we have, at

Figure 17. Industrial and commercial companies—money holdings and bank lending.

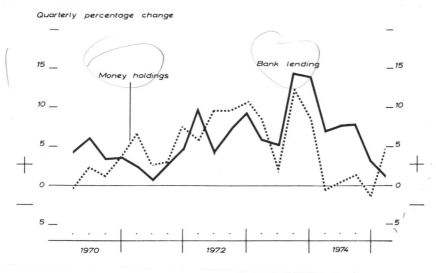

least for the time being, ceased to place *any* reliance on these equations except in the case of M_1, and to a lesser extent as a check on the judgmental forecast of persons' money holdings.

In the monetarist prescriptions for the appropriate conduct of monetary policy, a great weight depends on the stability of the demand-for-money function(s). Except, perhaps, in the case of M_1 we have not found these to be stable in use. It is not true that it does not matter which aggregate one looks at. The trend rates of growth of M_1 and M_3 have been moving in markedly differing directions for quite a lot of the period since 1972 (see figure 18). Moreover, in trying to understand and to interpret the movements in interest-bearing bank deposits we have come to the conclusion that holdings of these respond sensitively to interest rate differentials. In so far as this is so, the grounds for drawing a sharp distinction between such 'monetary' liabilities and all other substitute sources of liquidity, including overdraft and trade credit facilities, as well as alternative liquid assets, seems weaker. This naturally raises the question of the appropriate monetary indicators. It may well be that a broad monetary indicator, M_3, is by its nature particularly unreliable. In the EEC committees concerned with monetary developments, for example, attention is concentrated on a primary liquidity total, nearly the same as M_1, and a much broader secondary liquidity total, which includes deposits with building societies, savings deposits, etc. It may not be sensible to pay much attention to anything between the narrow concept of money and a broad, Radcliffe-type, liquidity measure. If so, the concentration on M_3 figures in the United Kingdom has been a bad mistake. In any

Figure 18. M₁ and M₃ trend rates of growth*.

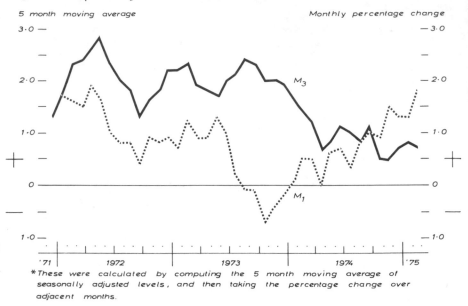

*These were calculated by computing the 5 month moving average of seasonally adjusted levels, and then taking the percentage change over adjacent months.

case the unreliability of most of the demand-for-money functions and the disparate readings provided by the movements of the monetary aggregates have forced us, in some cases none too unwillingly, back to a more pragmatic approach to monetary analysis and policy.

Only with respect to M_1 can it still be argued that a fairly stable demand for money may exist. As already noted, with M_1 being only a component of total bank liabilities, its movements cannot be related to the various elements of domestic credit expansion. And in view of the ease of shifting between time and current accounts, the ability of the authorities to control M_1 at all tightly under any regime would seem limited. But the main disadvantage of the M_1 series in the United Kingdom is its extremely erratic nature. We only obtain once monthly (and end-quarter) data, so we have 16 observations a year. The monthly changes of the seasonally adjusted data from July 1971 till March 1975 are shown in table 1 together with the

Table 1. M₁ monthly changes.

	Change over previous month	Five-month moving average	Seasonally adjusted deviation Deviation
1971 July	+ 42	–	–
August	+176	–	–
September	+119	+106.2	+ 12.8

October	+ 38	+144.2	−106.2
November	+156	+107.4	+ 48.6
December	+232	+ 89.0	+143.0
1972 January	− 8	+136.2	+144.2
February	+ 27	+151.0	−124.0
March	+274	+131.4	+142.6
April	+230	+175.2	+ 54.8
May	+134	+162.4	− 28.4
June	+211	+118.4	+ 92.6
July	− 37	+ 89.8	−126.8
August	+ 54	+ 98.8	− 44.8
September	+ 87	+ 52.4	+ 34.6
October	+179	+105.8	+ 73.2
November	− 21	+ 91.0	−112.0
December	+230	+ 86.0	+144.0
1973 January	− 20	+ 68.4	− 88.4
February	+ 62	+145.0	− 83.0
March	+ 91	+101.8	− 10.8
April	+362	+120.4	+241.6
May	+ 14	+158.6	+144.6
June	+ 73	+142.8	+ 69.8
July	+253	+ 21.6	+231.4
August	+ 12	− 24.4	+ 36.4
September	−244	− 15.8	+228.2
October	−216	− 61.8	+154.2
November	+116	− 47.4	+163.4
December	+ 23	− 17.0	+ 40.0
1974 January	+ 84	+ 14.6	+ 69.4
February	− 92	+ 53.4	−145.4
March	− 58	+ 31.4	− 89.4
April	+310	− 5.8	+315.8
May	− 87	+ 46.2	−133.2
June	−102	+ 86.8	+188.8
July	−168	+ 29.2	+138.8
August	+145	+ 82.6	+ 62.4
September	+ 22	+123.8	−101.8
October	+180	+133.4	+ 46.6
November	+104	+206.2	−102.2
December	+216	+172.0	+ 44.0
1975 January	+509	+190.2	+318.8
February	−149	−	−
March	+271	−	−

The standard deviation: 135.775.

residuals from a five-monthly moving average. The standard deviation from the moving average is large in relation to the calculated values of that moving average. We receive the data several weeks after the monthly make-up date. The noise in the series is so loud that it takes us several months to discern a systematic trend with any confidence. In any case the demand for M_1 is a function of current *and past* incomes and interest rates. So the movements in the series, when the systematic trends can be interpreted, tell you where you have been, not necessarily where you are going. That at least is something. For example it would suggest that monetary policy was becoming excessively tight at end-1973, easing thereafter in the latter half of 1974; and most British commentators believe the reverse.

The monetarist edifice rests largely on the stability, and predictability, of the demand-for-money function. Econometric study of the data in the 1960s had suggested that in the United Kingdom we too could build parts of our monetary policy on this basis. Subsequent experience has revealed weaknesses in this foundation.

4. Policy Response

We had intended, in the new approach to competition and credit control, to control the monetary aggregates through the price mechanism by lowering or raising interest rates. This worked reasonably well in the case of M_1, since, with rates on most current accounts held at zero, an increase in rates engineered by the authorities represented, *ipso facto,* an increase in the interest differential between current accounts and other assets. This was not the case with M_3. Patently, the control mechanism in 1973 was failing. This occurred, we believed, because a rise in market rates does not, under certain circumstances, lead to a revision of interest *differentials* in a manner which would cause a fall in advances and deposits. Indeed differentials were moving perversely as rates were being pushed up.

Since the problem was caused in large part by banks' aggressive bidding for interest-sensitive funds, the appropriate solution seemed to be to make such behaviour increasingly costly. That was the purpose of the Supplementary Special Deposit scheme. Under this scheme a limit to the rate of growth of interest-bearing liabilities was fixed, admittedly rather arbitrarily. If banks bid so strongly for funds that they grew faster than this allowable rate (on a three-monthly average calculation to smooth out unpredictable variations), they paid an increasing penalty, in the form of having to place zero-yielding deposits with the Bank of England, the further over the limit they went—a progressive penalty.

There are a number of good features about this scheme. A major problem of running a more competitive banking system had been that the banks had been so keen on expansion, extending facilities on a large scale, bidding aggressively for funds to support expansion, that credit control had been gravely weakened. The existence of this new instrument, even when it is not actually in use, should serve to restrain bank behaviour, in a manner that market disciplines failed to achieve. This instrument should prevent any future recurrence of the arbitrage 'bubble' that blew up in the autumn of 1973.

There are a number of features about the scheme that may be considered good or bad. The imposition of a tight 'corset' can go beyond forcing interest rate differentials back to normal relativities. It could be used to make deposit interest rates unusually low in relation to rates on lending and on other assets, thereby bringing about artificial dis-intermediation. According to the monetarists, the resulting fall in bank lending and in time deposits, and the faster growth in personal sector holdings of short-term public sector debt, has little or no economic effect, only a presentational one. Similarly the use of the corset could be so severe, especially if the banking system has only small reserves of public sector debt to run off, that it could force banks to ration advances themselves in order to avoid penalties.

Then there are some clear disadvantages in this mechanism. It has the inherent defects of a base-dated mechanism, tending during its periods of imposition to fix the banking system into a rigid mould. It shares with other ceiling controls the problems of choosing arbitrary ceiling, guideline, limit numbers, and the many problems of administration.

Figure 19 shows (for the clearing banks and other banks separately) the path of interest-bearing eligible liabilities (IBELs) relative to the free limit.

Figure 19. Interest-bearing eligible liabilities by groups of banks*.

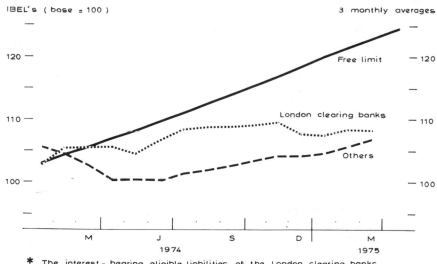

* The interest - bearing eligible liabilities of the London clearing banks are adjusted for interest throughout.

The scheme did have an effect, more or less as intended, during the early months of 1974. Banks became considerably more conservative in extending facilities, and the competition for funds among themselves abated. Interest differentials reverted to a more normal level, and the arbitrage bubble was largely run off.

By the autumn of 1974, however, the effect of the 'corset' had been overtaken by other independent forces within the system. One of the factors bringing an end to the speculative boom in property development and housing towards the end of 1973 was the sharp rise in interest rates (changes in tax regulations were another). Some of the newer 'fringe' financial institutions had over-extended themselves, especially in their involvement in the property business. An inter-related property development/secondary banking crisis developed at the turn of the year; a number of property companies and some financial institutions became insolvent, and the loss of confidence in a larger group of smaller banks (with or without justification) caused widespread withdrawals of funds and liquidity problems, which the Bank in concert with the clearing banks took steps to counteract.

This crisis led banks throughout the system to reassess their objectives, and to attach much greater weight to prudential considerations and safety, and less to growth for its own sake. This tendency was reinforced by further developments throughout 1975, e.g. bank failures in other countries, losses in international exchange markets, etc. Moreover the growth of both sterling and foreign currency deposits was making banks' equity–deposit ratios (in several countries) look exposed. A general concern about banks' capital adequacy developed, for the first time for many years. In 1974, however, equity markets were so depressed that new issues were effectively ruled out. Anyhow a good profit record would be a desirable basis for a new issue. With interest rates falling during 1974/75, and with running costs, especially the wages and salary bill, rising at an inflated rate, profits were becoming harder to earn. So, during 1974/75, banks' objectives shifted markedly from growth to profit maximization and retrenchment.

Meanwhile, during 1973/74, companies' cash flow positions had been severely weakened by a combination of rampant inflation, price controls, additional taxation, the three-day week in early 1974 and, for many industries, stagnant output. Owing to the usual long lags before investment expenditures react to economic developments, companies moved into increasing and enormous deficit. With capital markets severely depressed, there was virtually no alternative source of external finance during 1973/74 except recourse to the banks. Figure 20 shows the growing indebtedness of the company sector to the banks. By the middle of 1974, however, the gearing of company sector balance sheets was becoming adverse; indeed interest payments were taking a much larger share of company profits (see figure 21). By then companies were becoming increasingly hesitant about borrowing more from the banks, and began to trim back their stockbuilding

Figure 20. Industrial and commercial companies outstanding advances, liquid assets and net liquidity relative to total final expenditure.

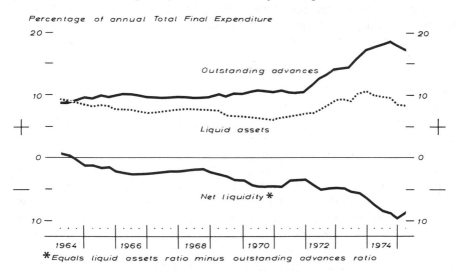

Percentage of annual Total Final Expenditure

Outstanding advances

Liquid assets

Net liquidity *

*Equals liquid assets ratio minus outstanding advances ratio

Figure 21. Interest charges and gross trading profits.

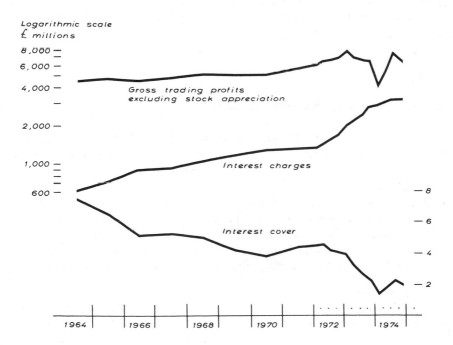

Logarithmic scale
£ millions

Gross trading profits
excluding stock appreciation

Interest charges

Interest cover

(and fixed investment plans) quite severely. Towards the end of 1974 the price controls were relaxed and tax relief—on stock appreciation—was given, so their cash flow began to recover. In any case from mid-1974 the pressure of demand by companies for advances slackened off.

In this context with the banks more concerned with profit maximization, slack demand for advances and a plentiful supply of reserve assets from the ever-growing budget deficit, banks sharply reduced the rates bid for deposits. The margin between bank deposit rates and lending rates widened. Under such conditions it was much cheaper to pay bills by running down deposits than by increasing overdrafts, and more profitable to hold public sector debt, or building society deposits, than bank deposits.

To some extent owing to these factors the 'corset' ceased to become binding for most banks after the autumn, and by the winter appeared otiose. Accordingly in February 1975 the opportunity was taken to suspend it.

This again illustrates the main theme of this paper, which is the sensitivity of the financial system to interest differentials. In seeking to manage this system it is not sufficient to have a regard to *the* interest rate. One has to go further and keep an eye on the pattern of relative rates. The Supplementary Special Deposit scheme was in a sense an instrument aimed at influencing this pattern. It is too soon, however, to attempt a balanced judgment of the likely usefulness of this novel instrument.

For the rest, the experience of the last few years has gone a long way, at least in the United Kingdom, to undermine confidence in the stability of the demand for money and the applicability at least of the stricter monetarist prescriptions. In these conditions of uncertainty, there has been some return to a more eclectic, agnostic approach.

APPENDIX

Demand for Money Equations since 1971

The failure of the demand-for-money equations (with the possible exception of the M_1 equation) estimated up to 1971:3* to predict money stock growth subsequently, stimulated, within the Bank, further research into the nature of the relationships.

Attempts to re-instate the equations have essentially taken the form of introducing new variables into existing equations† with a view to modelling more satisfactorily the structural changes in the demand for money which followed the introduction of competition and credit control in September 1971. (See the descriptive account of post-1971 developments in the text.)

---

*Estimation period 1963:1–1971:3.

†A stock adjustment model is used throughout estimated in first differences with a Cochrane–Orcutt transformation.

Research has been directed towards both the broad (M_3) and narrow (M_1) definitions of money and towards its sectoral allocation between the personal sector (MP) and the industrial and commercial company sector (MC). Equations have been re-estimated over the period 1963:1–1973:4.

Two developments following the structural change in 1971 may have affected the growth of M_3 and MC in 1972 and 1973. These were:

(1)   the growth in the banks' issues of negotiable Certificates of Deposit (CDs) and the subsequent expansion in the market for these instruments.

(2)   the distortions created by the inflexibility of banks' base rates (which determine lending rates) relative to borrowing rates (which are market determined). At times during 1972 and 1973 volatile market rates rose to levels above lending rates and made profitable arbitraging possible. As a result, both M_3 and MC aggregates were sometimes severely distorted by the response to the pattern of rates.

Equations were estimated (1963:1–1973:4) for both M_3 and MC which included a CD rate as an own-rate alongside the competing rates which featured alone in the earlier equations—this was an attempt to capture the increasing attractiveness of such interest-bearing deposits in M_3 and MC. Indeed there is strong theoretical support for including an own rate in a demand-for-money specification. Further, attempts were made to incorporate a variable representing the return to interest arbitrage*. Table 2 compares the results of estimations over the period 1963–73 with those of the earlier period 1963–71. The CD and arbitrage variables, it should be noted, were included in the estimations for the final observations only. Both variables proved statistically significant and improved the fit of the equations over the longer observation periods for both equations. However, experience in the use of these equations for forecasting purposes up to 1975:1 suggests that they may still be mis-specified. Both equations have consistently failed to predict accurately the subsequent growth of MC and M_3. Attempts to introduce further explanatory variables—such as the net acquisition of financial assets in the MC equation—have been fruitless.

Further research on the MP equations has been undertaken. The inclusion of the four quarters of 1973 in the estimation period yields real income elasticities well outside the plausible range†, although a better fit overall is produced (see table 3). It is clear that the exceptional growth of MP in 1973 has not, and perhaps cannot, be explained properly—at least with reference to past experience. Attempts to improve the MP equation by the

---

*An adjusted differential between the three-month CD rate and banks' 'prime' lending rate.

†Similar equations estimated over the period up to the end-1972, however, had real income elasticities of unity.

Table 2. M_3 and MC equations.

Dependent variable	Estimation period	Coefficients						$\bar{R}^2$	SE (%)	DW	Long-run elasticities			
		TFE	P_t	$1+LA_t$	$1+CD_t$	D_t	M_{t-1}				p^b	Real income	LA^c rate	CD^d rate
M_3	1963:4–1971:3	0.175 (1.46)	0.391	−0.491 (2.47)			0.609 (4.50)	0.51	0.911	2.20	−0.5	0.449	−0.08	
M_3	1963:4–1973:4	0.149 (1.42)	0.225	−0.665 (3.59)	1.139 (4.44)		0.775 (8.53)	0.88	1.032	2.36	−0.6	0.661	−0.19	0.47
M_3	1963:4–1973:3	0.197 (1.98)	0.272	−0.661 (3.70)	1.287 (4.59)	1.196 (2.97)	0.728 (8.51)	0.89	0.945	2.37	−0.5	0.724	−0.16	0.38
MC	1963:4–1971:3	0.199 (0.81)	0.841	−1.306 (2.50)			0.159 (1.09)	0.16	1.873	2.13	0	0.236	−0.10	
MC	1963:4–1973:4	0.296 (1.31)	0.595	−1.122 (2.74)	3.465 (5.30)		0.405 (3.71)	0.72	2.112	2.09	−0.3	0.497	−0.14	0.47
MC	1963:4–1973:4	0.325 (1.52)	0.574	−1.244 (2.79)	3.145 (4.90)	2.215 (2.34)	0.426 (4.05)	0.72	2.005	2.05	−0.2	0.567	−0.14	0.44

All variables are in natural logarithms.

SE: Standard error.

TFE: Total Final Expenditure at 1970 prices, £m, s.a.

PDI: Personal Disposable Income at 1970 prices, £m, s.a.

P_t: The TFE deflator or PDI deflator where appropriate.

LA_t: The interest rate on three-month deposits with local authorities (quarterly averages of working days).

CD_t: The interest rate on three-month sterling certificates of deposit (quarterly averages of working days).

CON_t: The yield on $2\frac{1}{2}$ per cent consolidated stock (quarterly averages of working days).

D_t: A variable representing the return to interest arbitrage—an adjusted differential between the three-month CD rate and bankers' 'prime' lending rate.

M_{t-2}: The appropriate money stock series lagged one quarter.
(a) t values are shown in brackets beneath the coefficients.
(b) For an explanation of p transformation see appendix to G. Hacche, 'The demand for money in the United Kingdom: experience since 1971', *Bank of England Quarterly Bulletin*, **14**, (September), 1974.
(c) Calculated at the mean values of the estimation period
(d) Calculated at the rate for 1972:4.

Table 3. MP equations.

Dependent variable	Estimation period	Coefficients						$\bar{R}^2$	SE (%)	DW	Long-run elasticities		
		Constant	PDI	P_t	$1+CON_{t-1}$	M_{t-1}	$NAFA^a$				p	Real income	Consol rate
MP	1963:4–1971:3		0.344 (4.13)	0.343	−0.433 (1.15)	0.657 (5.62)		0.75	0.754	2.47	−0.6	1.002	−0.08
MP	1963:4–1973:4		0.269 (3.26)	0.093	−0.223 (0.63)	0.907 (9.81)		0.85	0.854	2.23	−0.6	2.900	−0.17
MP^b	1963:4–1973:4	0.00225	0.250 (2.67)	0.104	−0.303 (0.76)	0.896 (9.27)		0.76	0.864	2.17	−0.6	2.411	−0.02
MP^b	1963:4–1973:4	0.00325	0.236 (2.54)	0.171	−0.442 (1.08)	0.829 (7.70)	0.00001 (1.35)	0.77	0.854	2.18	−0.6	1.385	−0.03
MP^b	1963:4–1973:4	0.00217		0.147	−0.92 (2.12)	0.853 (7.25)	0.00002 (1.64)	0.68	0.899	2.07	−0.4		−0.06

(a) Net acquisition of financial assets by the personal sector.
(b) The three equations cannot be compared directly with previous ones as they are estimated with a constant term.

See also footnotes to table 2.

Table 4. M_1 equations.

Dependent variable	Estimation period	Coefficients					R^2	SE (%)	DW	p	Long-run elasticities		
		TFE	P_t	$1 + LA_t$	$1 + CON_{t-1}$	M_{t-1}					Real income	LA Rate	Consol Rate
M_1	1963:4–1971:3	0.205 (1.16)	0.749	−0.868 (2.35)	−1.227 (1.34)	0.252 (1.67)	0.37	1.385	2.09	−0.4	0.274	−0.07	−0.11
M_1	1963:4–1973:4	0.237 (1.64)	0.562	−0.709 (2.48)	−0.986 (1.12)	0.438 (3.05)	0.50	1.635	2.09	−0.7	0.422	−0.08	−0.12

See also footnotes to table 2.

addition of a net acquisition of financial assets variable has also been investigated—its inclusion has been found to add to the explanatory power of the equation. However, like the M_3 and MC equations, the MP equation (all specifications) has been markedly unsuccessful in explaining post-1973 developments.

Little further research has been done on the M_1 equations which have remained fairly stable over differing estimation periods (see table 4). Although the M_1 quarterly series moved erratically during 1974, the M_1 equation performed tolerably well—at least to the extent of not exhibiting any noticeable predictive bias.

The reasons for the poor performance of the re-estimated equations since the end of 1973 are difficult to pin-point. It might be thought, however, that the introduction of the Supplementary Deposit Scheme (and distortions thereby created) coupled with the rapidly accelerating rate of inflation (which could have significantly altered the behaviour of money holders) may have contributed to the equation failures.

If any conclusions can be drawn at this stage on the Bank's continuing research in this area, it is the rather negative one that with all but the M_1 equations exhibiting considerable instability and little predictive ability, the equations cannot be used with any confidence in an operational forecasting context.

NOTES

1.   This paper represents the personal viewpoint of the author, and should *not* be regarded as representing an official position.
2.   A term encompassing the Bank and the Treasury, the responsible Minister being the Chancellor of the Exchequer.
3.   It is probable that the opportunity—provided by a period of recession during 1970/71 and the accession to office of a new government dedicated to competition— to remove bank lending ceilings, at least temporarily, would have been taken in any case. It was not this step, but rather the attempt to construct a completely alternative *system* of monetary management—alternative to a continuation of long periods of ceilings interspersed with (shorter) periods of relaxation—in which the work on the demand-for-money function played a role.
4.   This is set out in more detail in 'The operation of monetary policy since the Radcliffe report', *Bank of England Quarterly Bulletin,* 9 (December), 1969.
5.   See for example D. Fisher, 'The demand for money in Britain: quarterly results 1951 to 1967', *The Manchester School of Economic and Social Studies,* 36 (December), 1968; and D. Laider and J.M. Parkin, 'The demand for money in the United Kingdom, 1955–1967: preliminary estimates', *The Manchester School of Economic and Social Studies,* 38 (September), 1970.
6.   C. Goodhart and A.D. Crockett, 'The importance of money', *Bank of England Quarterly Bulletin,* 10 (June), 1970; and L.D. Price, 'The demand for money in the United Kingdom: a further investigation', *Bank of England Quarterly Bulletin,* 12 (March), 1972.

7. 'Minimum' in the sense that this was the lowest rate at which the Bank would provide support to the market in this way. The Bank reserved, and has at times made use of, the right to exact a greater penalty for last resort lending.

8. MLR is set $\frac{1}{2}$ per cent higher than the average rate of discount for Treasury bills established at the weekly tender, rounded to the nearest $\frac{1}{4}$ per cent above.

9. In so far as people have extrapolative expectations, at least in the short run (a condition which many of those close to the market believe to be the case), then a period of *rising* interest rates, while the banks sell gilts, would discourage, and *not* encourage, larger debt sales to the non-bank public. If at some, unforeseeable, point, however, the market subsequently reaches a plateau, where prices are no longer expected to slide down, *then* the higher yield level may encourage an increased demand.

10. Sir Leslie O'Brien, 'Key issues in monetary and credit policy', *Bank of England Quarterly Bulletin,* **11** (June), 1971.

11. Interest payments have always been tax-deductible for companies. Shortly after their return to office in 1970, the new Conservative government also made interest payments tax-deductible for persons. Moreover, there was for a time a tax loop-hole that could be exploited by borrowing to re-invest in CDs.

12. There had been a further definition, M_2, but this had depended on an assumed broad difference in character between the smaller, retail-type, time deposits in clearing banks, which were in practice transferable to current accounts on demand, and larger, money-market, wholesale time deposits in other banks. After 1971 when the clearing banks entered the market for CDs and wholesale time deposits under their own names, the grounds for making such a distinction disappeared, and the M_2 series was dropped.

13. C. Sprenkle, 'Effects of large firms and bank behavior on the demand for money of large firms', American Bankers Association, 1971, mimeo, especially Appendix C; also he has a research paper in process on this subject with M.H. Miller, initial versions of which were prepared at the London School of Economics, 1974, mimeo.

14. *Clearing bank pre-tax profits**

	1970	1971	1972	1973	1974
£m	255.1	299.3	413.0	618.7	471.3

*Figures taken from clearing banks' annual published statements.

15. J. Tobin, 'Commercial banks as creators of "money"', in D. Carson (ed.), *Banking and Monetary Studies* (Homewood, Ill.: Irwin, 1963).

16. M.J. Artis and M. Lewis, 'The demand for money: stable or unstable?', *The Banker,* **124** (March), 1974; and 'The demand for money in the United Kingdom: 1963–1973', *The Manchester School of Economic and Social Studies,* **44** (June), 1976.

17. In most demand-for-money functions only own-rates and yields on other alternative *assets* are included. Our experience suggests that yields on alternative liabilities, advances or trade credit, should enter as well; indeed portfolio theory suggests that this should be so.

18. M.J. Artis and M. Lewis, see note 16.

19. When own-rates and yields on other relevant assets and liabilities are included in such an equation over the period 1963–71, they do not appear very significant.

Floating Exchange Rates:
A Study of Sterling 1972–76

Peter Sinclair

1. Introduction

In August 1971, the United States suspended the convertibility into gold of the U.S. dollar. This link broken, the dollar began to float in relation to gold (which was *de jure,* if not *de facto,* the *numéraire* of the Bretton Woods system) and to the world's other major currencies. An era had ended. When a new vector of currency par values was established (in December 1971, at the Smithsonian in Washington), the spread between the upper and lower intervention points for each currency against the dollar was doubled. This increased the maximum area of permitted fluctuation between two currencies (other than the U.S. dollar) to nearly 10 per cent, the 'tunnel'. It represented, therefore, a partial victory for the advocates of floating. Most Western European countries decided, however, to cut the margin of permitted fluctuations between their own currencies, thus creating the 'snake'. But neither the tunnel nor the snake were to survive unmodified for long. The United Kingdom and Eire were forced to leave the snake in June 1972 and sterling has been floating since then. Italy left the snake in February 1973, and France in January 1974, and again in March 1976. The snake itself has become increasingly a Deutsche mark bloc; and it has been contorted by numerous changes in par values between its surviving members. The tunnel was strained beyond break-point on several occasions (the U.S. dollar devalued in February 1973), and, in 1974, it finally disappeared.

This paper addresses itself to the fortunes of sterling in the period of floating. The period has witnessed the largest balance of payments deficits (on most definitions) since the Second World War; it has seen sterling lose half its internal purchasing power, and nearly half its external value; it has recorded the sharpest increase in unemployment since 1938, and a deterioration in the public finances unparalleled in peacetime since the commencement of reliable statistics in the 17th century. The adverse movements in each of these economic variables are bewildering in their speed and magnitude, and in their conjunction. A number of important questions suggest themselves and this paper is an attempt to answer them.

(1) Why have the balance-of-payments deficits persisted (at least until the time of writing), *despite* the falls in sterling
(2) Is the inflation better treated as a cause or a consequence of the falls in sterling?
(3) What significance attaches to the large and growing budget deficits of the public authorities?
(4) Are there serious grounds for thinking that floating exchange rates (for Britain, at least) are unstable?

But before these questions are answered, a brief survey of the changes in sterling's external value over the period is required.

Britain's experience of the floating pound in the first four and a half years after June 1972 can be divided into seven slides and seven pauses. Table 1, which shows monthly averages of daily values of an effective exchange rate for sterling, based on a geometrically weighted average of 21 countries' exchange rates (1972 trade flows providing the various weights[1]), reveals the picture clearly.

Table 1. *Effective exchange rate index (December 1971 = 100; value of sterling against a geometrically weighted average of 21 other countries).*

	1972	1973	1974	1975	1976
January	99.2	80.9	82.4	81.5	72.8
February	99.7	88.9	82.9	81.6	72.7
March	99.8	87.7	83.9	81.9	70.5
April	99.7	88.8	84.6	81.0	67.2
May	99.7	89.8	84.7	78.8	65.8
June	97.7	89.2	84.8	77.4	64.3
July	92.9	85.3	84.8	76.0	65.1
August	93.3	84.6	84.2	74.9	64.8
September	93.0	82.6	83.6	74.6	62.5
October	91.4	82.6	83.7	73.4	59.2
November	89.7	83.7	82.6	73.0	59.1
December	89.5	82.6	81.6	72.6	60.5

The dates of the slides and the pauses that can be discerned are as follows:

Slides		Pauses	
(1) Beginning of float–July 1972	– 6.8	July–September 1972	+0.1
(2) September–November 1972	– 3.6	November 1972–June 1973	–0.3
(3) June–September 1973	– 7.2	September 1973–October 1974	+1.3
(4) October–December 1974	2.5	December 1974–April 1975	–0.8
(5) April–October 1975	– 9.3	October 1975–February 1976	–1.0
(6) February–June 1976	–11.5	June–August 1976	+0.7
(7) August–October 1976	– 8.6	October 1976–	minimal change

The slides identified lasted, on average, a little under three months, while the first six pauses were on average twice as long. The statistics point to substantial variance in periodicity; the pauses seem to have been getting briefer, and the slides more prolonged. But closer inspection shows that most of the falls in the slide periods (particularly the last three slides) were accomplished quickly, in only a few weeks. Over half of sterling's decline in slide 6, for instance, occurred in March, and almost all of slide 7 can be attributed to the month of September. All the slides identified contain many briefer periods, sometimes lasting only a day or so, which witnessed sharp drops, recoveries, or little change. The pauses exhibit some pronounced daily changes, as well. But the overall difference between slide and pause periods is conspicuous enough: sterling fell by a monthly average of $2\frac{1}{2}$ per cent in the former, while the average monthly change in the later period was imperceptible.

2. Why have the Balance-of-Payments Deficits persisted, *despite* the Falls in Sterling?

There are two extreme interpretations of sterling's experience. They can be treated as polar opposites. One is to continue regarding the exchange rate as a policy parameter controlled, and changed from time to time, by the authorities, in which case the float is 'dirty'. The other is the 'clean float'.

In the dirty float, deficits are met by official purchasers of spot sterling; by foreign currency borrowing by central government (or the nationalized industries and local authorities, acting as its agents); by loans from the International Monetary Fund; by private short-term capital movements deliberately engineered by the authorities' intervention in domestic interest rates and forward foreign exchange markets. Surpluses would be absorbed by the same mechanisms, operating in reverse.

If this were an accurate account of the history of the exchange rate and the balance of payments after June 1972, several questions would emerge. The foremost, and most paradoxical, would be why the balance-of-payments deficit on current account grew remorselessly for the first two years of the 'float', despite substantial depreciation, and remained heavily in deficit for three years thereafter. Three possible answers suggest themselves. One is that the exchange rate has a perverse effect on the current account, at least initially. The second is that other factors were responsible for the increasing deficits, swamping any favourable effects from the depreciation; and the third that the exchange rate changes were inadequate to combat Britain's relatively high inflation, so that sterling was effectively appreciating over the period, when converted into real terms.

Of these, the third answer is clearly at variance with the facts. From June 1972 until December 1973, the depreciation markedly exceeded Britain's relative rate of inflation. During 1974, sterling moved little, while inflation accelerated; prices rose rather faster, but not much faster, in Britain than in most other countries. In 1975, depreciation neatly matched relative inflation, while in 1976 it exceeded it. The second answer has much to commend it, as will be seen below, but it is equally consistent with the 'clean float' interpretation, to which we shall turn shortly. It is the first answer that would be most alarming. It would suggest that a clearly floating exchange rate would be subject to instability, at least in the short run. As far as the current account is concerned, an initially perverse response to depreciation is certainly a possibility: the alleged phenomenon (known as the J curve) can be produced by sufficiently unfavourable price-elasticities of demand and supply for exports and imports, in the short run. The J curve is investigated in section 5. The point is that if Britain can now be treated as a sufficiently small participant in world markets for traded goods, she will be effectively a price-taker. In these circumstances, the long-run effect of depreciation on the current account can never be perverse; while in the short run, a perverse effect can only arise if delivery lags, and imbalance in the currency price-quotations for exports and imports, are sufficiently large, and depreciation itself sufficiently unexpected. Recent changes in currency-quotation make the J curve increasingly improbable.

The second, opposite approach to the float is to treat the exchange rate as an endogenous variable, purely determined by market forces. This is 'clean floating'. The combination of deficits and depreciation would now cause no difficulty. Causality would run from the former to the latter. This would accord with the general hypothesis for the adjustment of prices in disequilibrium: the hypothesis, attributed to Walras, that price moves in the direction of excess demand. A British balance-of-payments deficit implies an excess supply of sterling, which should therefore entail a drop in its value. This interpretation makes the deficits logically primary; consequently we would still need to explain why the 'initial' deficits arose, and also try to distinguish them from any secondary effects upon them produced by the depreciations. These problems and others related to them, are discussed in section 3.

The history of sterling after June 1972 cannot be understood properly without relying on *both* interpretations. For a year after November 1973, for instance, there was substantial intervention by the authorities to hold the exchange rate when it might otherwise have fallen heavily. Furthermore, both before and after this, there were many briefer intervals when the exchange rate was broadly static, and effectively pegged. In addition, some of the declines of sterling, most of which occurred sharply and quickly, taking only a few weeks at most, seem to have been initiated by the authorities—in March 1976, for instance, the slide began when the Bank of England sold sterling. Lastly, the heavy and clearly non-zero 'balance for official financing' (usually but not always negative) is simple testament enough to the fact that the exchange rate was not floating freely.

Despite all this, the second interpretation (depreciations follow deficits) is essential too. When the Bank of England decides to allow market forces to depress sterling, and even when it gives it a downward nudge, it should be thought of as responding to market pressures. A sequence of large monthly deficits on current account convinces the authorities of the costs (in reserve losses, unemployment, or future imports sacrificed to mounting foreign debt charges) of holding the exchange rate somewhere above what is apparently its equilibrium level. At times the sheer magnitude of outward capital flows may force a depreciation the authorities are powerless to prevent; such outflows can normally be attributed to accumulating evidence of a weak, and/or deteriorating current account, and to a growing conviction on the part of market participants that the exchange rate will have to slide to counteract this.

The pattern of events discernible from the evidence—the 'stylized fact'—is a series of staggered depreciations, separated by periods of tranquillity during which the exchange rate alters little. The depreciations, when they occur, often amount to 5 per cent or more, and the periods between them last about six months. It is, therefore, unreasonable to treat the exchange rate as being wholly exogenous or wholly endogenous. The longer the time period under consideration, probably the greater the justification for stressing its endogenity. Although it is, in principle, possible to see the market as determining rates in the short run within a trend-corridor chosen by the authorities, the history of Britain's managed float since June 1972 suggests the reverse: dirtier in the short run, cleaner in the long run.

In the analysis that follows, we shall suppose that the 'clean float' interpretation is a helpful model with which to consider sterling's experience, but the reader is invited to recall its disadvantages, which will be investigated closely. The 'clean float' hypothesis predicts that sterling depreciates if it is in excess supply, and appreciates if in excess demand. An approximate measure of the market excess supply of sterling in an interval of time is the balance-of-payments deficit. One might expect a relationship of the sort shown in figure 1, but before the evidence is inspected, a number of difficulties must be noted.

Figure 1. Balance of payments surplus or deficit (B) versus change in external currency value of domestic currency ($\hat{R}$).

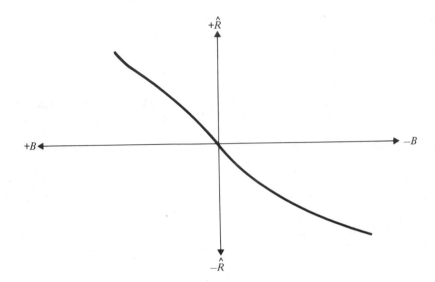

First, the ϕ curve in figure 1 is a black box, it is a hypothesis, and no more than that. If the provision of foreign currency exchange services were given to a private international monopoly, the ϕ curve (or something like it) might easily be derived from conventional wealth-maximizing considerations. The monopolist's price-setting behaviour would depend on deviations in his inventories of currencies from some optimal mix. Such deviations would result from excess demands and supplies of currencies on the part of all other market participants. In practice, however, foreign exchange services are supplied by a large number of agents who act independently. All of them can be treated as price-takers; their customers would conduct substantial arbitrage flows between currencies if the prices they posted diverged from prices known to rule elsewhere in the market.

Second, a rigorous treatment of ϕ would involve an elaborate specification of the stock and flow equilibrium conditions governing the behaviour of the holders of currencies. Under fixed exchange rates, central banks intervene to satisfy excess demand and supply: the price of a currency is allowed to fluctuate, at most, between narrow limits either side of the par rate. Floating rates transfer this function (in whole or part) to private holders of currencies. These private holders may be thought of as having demand functions for stocks of escudos, lire, sterling, and so on. Demand for a particular currency would be expected to vary positively with wealth, interest rates available on deposits denominated in that currency, the expected appreciation of the currency, and net disbursements in that currency expected in the near future; it would vary negatively with anticipated returns on other currencies, and probably, too, with the transactions costs in spot and forward currency markets, and the variance of expected changes in the currency's value. Yet, in addition to the stock demands, flow demands for currencies on the part of private holders would be indispensable elements underlying ϕ. We would need to know how *quickly* they would be prepared to run down or accumulate holdings. Here the speed of actual exchange rate changes would be a major influence. One should note the marked difference in behaviour between holders with regressive expectations for the relevant exchange rates, and those with extrapolative expectations.

A third problem surrounds the choice of deficit on the balance of payments as proxy for the excess supply of sterling. Three candidates present themselves (the current account; the current account plus long-term capital account; the account left for official financing) and each has disadvantages. The third has the grave demerit of being definitionally zero under 'clean' floating exchange rates, since the authorities will then abstain completely from intervention in the foreign exchange market. Official financing will, furthermore, tend to boost the exchange rate when all else is equal. The second comes closest to the Meadean concept of 'autonomous'[2] balance, but suffers from the difficulty, in practice, of distinguishing long-term or autonomous capital movements, and those which are short-term or accommodating. The statistics are shaky, and even the distinction, itself, is rather artificial since it requires an arbitrary incision into what may logically be a continuum. The first measure—the current account itself—is an imperfect proxy for other reasons. It excludes capital account transactions which may be far larger, particularly over a short interval, and far more instrumental in inducing exchange rate changes[3]. One recalls the £3000m outflow which occurred in one week in late June 1972, which forced the British authorities to abandon the Smithsonian parity and the 'snake in the tunnel' arrangement with the EEC currencies. Furthermore, the current account conventionally includes one elusive but important item that ought to be in the capital account: the component in nominal interest payments made across frontiers which reflects expected inflation. This component is a concealed capital repayment and should not count as true, recurrent income ('what you can keep spending without getting poorer'). There is obviously no reason for including some elements of the capital account and not others of similar 'autonomy'. Lastly, the flow of goods and services across national boundaries is not synchronized with the flow of the receipts and disbursements to which they relate; much trade is financed by credit, never of uniform length. It is the currency payments on which ϕ is based, not the transfer of goods and services themselves.

A fourth difficulty posed by any attempt to apply ϕ concerns the $\hat{R}$ term (the rate of change of the currency's external value). A *numéraire* is called for. The complex gyrations to which all major currencies have been subject since August 1971 obviously preclude a single currency (even the dollar) from being taken as an adequate *numéraire*. Accordingly, a wider backcloth is sought. We employ the effective exchange rate index, which was applied in section 1 (see table 1). Strictly, this is not a true measure of the change in sterling's value between two dates, but an answer to the question: 'Given plausible estimates of the direct- and cross-elasticities of demand and supply for exports and imports, what unilateral change in the value of sterling against 21 major currencies would have the same effect on the United Kingdom's current account on the balance of payments, as the actual vector of exchange rate changes that have occurred?'.

Another difficulty with ϕ is that it is, in theory, a correspondence between the *ex-ante* excess supply of sterling and the actual decline in sterling's external value. In practice, all we have is *ex-post* measures of the excess supply—and imperfect ones at that—in the balance-of-payments statistics. There are two-way causal links here: price changes may be a function of excess demand, but excess demand is also a function of price. Since the current account is likely to display considerable viscosity in the short run (one quarter, for example), while even some portfolio movements normally treated as long-run may exhibit the effects of very recent exchange rate changes, the *ex-ante/ex-post* problem may lend some justification for concentrating exclusively on the current account.

Yet another objection which is prompted by ϕ relates to expectations. Suppose the exchange rate for some currency is expected to fall by 2 per cent in the coming quarter. It would be odd to insist upon a zero intercept in figure 1. If B were zero, it would be more reasonable to expect a 2 per cent fall in R, if three months was the relevant time-interval. An analogy for this can be seen in the expectation-augmented Phillips curves advanced to explain how the inflation–unemployment trade-offs change over time. There would be a unique ϕ for each 'market' expectation of $\hat{R}$ over a given interval of time (see figure 2). Exchange rate changes could then be decomposed into 'equilibrium' (or predicted) and disequilibrium components. Functionally, one might hypothesize an equation of the form:

$$\hat{R} = a + \beta \hat{R}^e + f'(B),$$

where $\hat{R}^e$ = expected change in the exchange rate, $\beta > 0$ and $f' < 0$.

If a were set to zero and β to unity, and $\hat{R}^e$ were regressive in $\hat{R}(t)$, we should derive a long-run a curve coincident with the $\hat{R}$ axis. This would

Figure 2. Expectations-augmented φ curves.

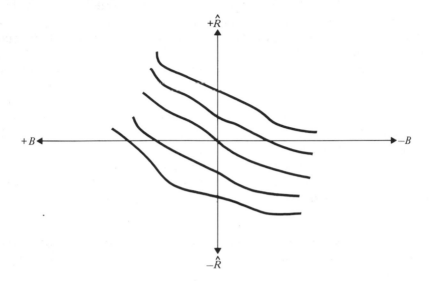

signify that the equilibrium long-run surplus (deficit) on the balance of payments would be zero, but the change in the exchange rate could have any value. It would correspond with Friedman's vertical long-run Phillips curve for the labour market. If all exchange rate changes were perfectly anticipated, tax complications ignored, and real interest rates equalized between countries, one would expect to see actual exchange rate changes mirrored exactly in previous premiums or discounts on forward exchange, interest rate differentials, inflation differentials and, under even stricter conditions, the differential growth rates of domestic money supplies. In these circumstances, currency depreciations could be regarded as neutral (or nearly so) in their effects on all real variables. The only qualification would relate to the optimum quantity of money argument, that the welfare-maximizing exchange rate path would have to be consistent with equality between the nominal interest rate and the social marginal cost (zero?) of creating real balances.

There are two final difficulties with our φ relationships: the question of official intervention, and the choice of time interval. The period of floating has seen official intervention on a large scale and the British authorities have intervened frequently (although not continuously). Intervention has taken a wide variety of forms. These include sales of foreign currency spot and forward, manipulation of domestic interest rates to stimulate short-term capital inflows or curb outflows, loans from the International Monetary Fund and other central banks, an extension of sterling balance guarantees (from 1973 to 1974), and substantial foreign exchange borrowing by nationalized industries under the so-called 'Treasury scheme'. The twelve months from November 1973 to October 1974 saw particularly heavy official inter-vention to protect sterling from dropping. At other times, depreciations have been engineered, or at least initiated, by conscious policy actions. We should therefore be very wary of treating the exchange rate as a fully endo-genous variable since June 1972.

The choice of time-interval is also problematic if the ϕ function is either non-linear or volatile. The shorter the interval, the greater the importance of the lumpy, non-recurrent movements on which statistical records are necessarily imperfect. Daily exchange rate changes of up to 3 per cent were witnessed in 1976 at periods of exceptional strain, but there is no way of determining the gross or net flows of sterling over such a short period, let alone of singling out the autonomous elements from the accommodating. A long time interval suffers from other drawbacks; above all, the ϕ curve is increasingly likely to be smudged by feedback from the exchange rate on B.

Table 2. *Current account balance-of-payments surplus as proportion of total imports (B), and change since previous quarter in the effective exchange rate for sterling ($\hat{R}$).*

Quarter		1972	1973	1974	1975	1976
1	B	+ .033	− .030	− .126	− .069	− .009
	$\hat{R}$	−	−1.5	+0.1	−1.1	−1.4
2	B	+ .032	− .006	− .118	− .039	− .044
	$\hat{R}$	−0.06	+0.6	+1.9	−3.2	−8.6
3	B	− .028	− .043	− .101	− .069	− .051
	$\hat{R}$	−6.0	−5.7	−0.6	−4.9	−2.6
4	B	− .001	− .057	− .107	− .027	− .033
	$\hat{R}$	−3.1	−1.4	−1.9	−2.9	−7.0

The evidence is presented in table 2 and figure 3. Nearly all observations from the first quarter of 1972 to the fourth of 1976 lie drearily in the deficit–depreciation quadrant. The first three quarters of 1974 are highly deviant, displaying very large deficits and only small changes in the exchange rate; this can be attributed, in part, to heavy intervention by the Bank of England in this period[4], which was designed to sustain sterling and prevent a trig-gering of the cost-of-living thresholds for wages in force for the majority of employees at that time. (Earnings could rise by 40 pence for every 1 per cent increase in the retail price index above 7 per cent from November 1973 to

Figure 3. B versus $\hat{R}$ showing most observations in the deficit–depreciation quadrant.

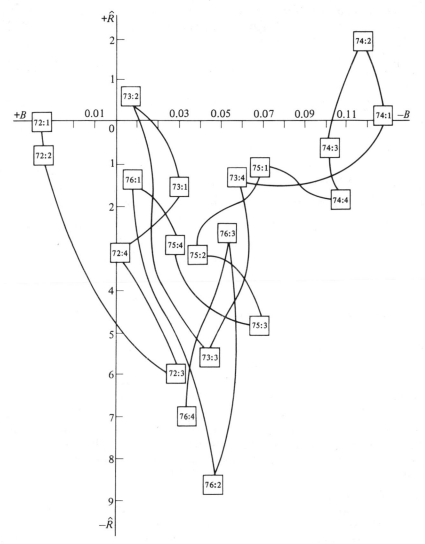

October 1974.) It is also relevant that sterling had depreciated substantially in the previous 18 months, and that foreign exchange markets may have been expecting a sharp, but delayed, current account improvement similar to that in the 30 months following Britain's 14.3 per cent devaluation in November 1967. Finally, 1974 was the first year of dearer oil. Over half Britain's current account deficit that year could be put down to the oil price increase of winter 1973–74, which was seen to be a burden faced (in varying degrees) by all advanced countries and hence not an argument for switching out of sterling as such. Indeed, the oil producing countries appeared happy to receive about one-quarter of their revenues in sterling, so that the immediate effect upon sterling was probably favourable.

Most of the other observations (1972:4 to 1973:4 and 1974:4 to 1976:1) provide mild support for the ϕ hypothesis. The association is far from perfect, but nonetheless discernible.

However, if the ϕ hypothesis is correct (i.e. the depreciation of sterling is the consequence of deficits, rather than the latter a perverse consequence of the former) we still need to establish why the deficits occurred. Perhaps the greatest insight into the possible causes of imbalance in external payments can be obtained from a consideration of another economic principle attributed to Walras (Walras' law). This hypothesis is generally taken to state that for all possible price vectors—in and out of equilibrium— the market value of the sum of all excess demands (for commodities, factors of production, and assets including money) is zero:

$$\sum_{j}^{n} p_j \sum z_{ij} = 0,$$

where i indexes $1, \ldots, m$ agents and j indexes $1, \ldots, n$ goods including factors of production, assets, and money. It is sufficient for Walras' law that each agent respects his budget restraint, and faces an identical set of prices over which he can exercise no control. Let us suppose that Walras' law holds for each country.

A balance-of-payments deficit on current account represents an excess demand for one sub-set of goods—current tradable commodities (including services). The value of excess demand for importables exceeds the value of excess supply of exportables. By Walras' law, at least one other sub-set of goods (at least one other market) must be in excess supply. Four candidates suggest themselves: nontraded goods; money; labour; and claims on future goods.

An excess supply of nontradables cannot, by definition, be sold to nonresidents. It may co-exist with an excess demand for tradables which will, on the other hand, manifest itself in a trade deficit[5]. The reason must be a disequilibrium relative price of tradables in terms of nontradables. If the system is stable, it is the nontradables which are (relatively) too dear, the tradables (relatively) too cheap. A decline in the relative price of nontradables would stimulate opposite effects in the tradables sector (assuming sufficient substitution). This explanation of Britain's weak current account has often proved appealing. One way it might work is this: suppose that Britain experiences (for whatever reason) faster inflation than other countries, while the exchange rates are fixed. Commodity arbitrage among *tradable* goods will tend to preserve the equilibrium condition:

$$P_t = \frac{P_t^*}{R},$$

where P_t is price of tradable goods, * denotes abroad, and R is exchange rate (price of home currency in foreign exchange). The domestic price of tradables will be held down, but the domestic price of nontradables does not suffer from this constraint, and will drift upwards. The consequences may include a reduced profit margin in tradables, a blunted incentive to produce, a drop in Britain's share in world exports, and a large and growing deficit on current account. This (or similar) reasoning underlay Kaldor's espousal of a selective employment tax (SET). SET had other aims as well (notably, to raise the growth rate by switching labour from services into manufacturing)[6], but because the export–output ratio for manufacturing greatly exceeded that of the services sector it could act as an instrument of external balance, similar to currency depreciation. (SET was in operation between 1966 and 1973, and taxed labour in services sector only.) Bacon and Eltis attribute Britain's economic ills to a high and growing output of unmarketed goods provided by the public sector, and a low and falling share of resources devoted to producing marketable goods for export, investment, and private consumption[7]. Their explanation for the current account deficits is, again, a variant of the nontradables hypothesis.

Some evidence can be adduced in favour of this. Export prices have generally dropped relative to the GDP deflator, until arrested by currency depreciation. The share of services in output and employment rose while that of the more tradables-dominated manufacturing sector fell. Government current expenditure had been rising as a share of GDP. All these three movements were visible over at least some of the period 1970–75, but international comparisons reveal that Britain is by no means unique in these respects (see table 3).

However, we saw that excess demand for tradables—and the current account balance-of-payments deficit that must accompany it—may be associated with excess supply in markets other than that for nontradables. Money, labour, and claims on future goods were instantiated.

An excess supply of *money* must imply portfolio disequilibrium[8]. This will presumably coincide with excess demand for other financial assets, real assets, commodities, or factor services—perhaps all four. The first two should affect the capital account of the balance of payments, as agents attempt to restore equilibrium by acquiring foreign financial or real assets if domestic supply is insufficient. The third represents the real balance effect, which, in an open economy, should lead to a deterioration in the balance of payments on current account. The fourth may produce effects similar to the third by raising factor prices and excess demand for traded goods.

Turning to the evidence, it is hard to identify an excess supply of money as such. All that can be seen directly is the level (and rate of change) of

Table 3. International comparison of export prices relative to GNP or GDP deflator, current account surplus as percentage of total imports, and share of public consumption in GNP at market prices.

	United Kingdom			France			West Germany			Italy			Japan			United States		
	A	B	C	A	B	C	A	B	C	A	B	C	A	B	C	A'	B	C
1969	100.7	4.6	17.2	95.7	(8.6)	12.4	104.1	5.9	15.7	102.8	16.4	13.3	102.5	12.7	8.3	79.7	0.3	22.2
1970	100.0	6.7	17.7	100.0	1.3	12.4	100.0	1.8	15.9	100.0	5.1	12.8	100.0	7.4	8.2	100.0	4.0	22.3
1971	97.0	8.9	18.1	100.1	2.0	12.5	155.0	0.7	17.1	98.3	10.6	14.2	96.3	26.0	8.7	98.3	(2.2)	22.0
1972	94.5	1.0	18.6	95.4	0.9	12.3	91.4	1.9	17.6	95.5	10.2	14.6	89.7	24.8	9.0	97.0	(7.6)	21.6
1973	99.1	(4.5)	18.3	97.8	(1.5)	12.2	90.7	5.7	18.2	101.3	(8.1)	14.3	87.4	(0.3)	9.1	107.2	8.0	20.0
1974	112.2	(13.5)	20.3	110.5	(9.0)	12.4	98.4	9.8	19.9	123.3	(17.5)	14.0	98.4	(6.6)	10.0	123.7	1.9	21.5
1975	103.3	(6.1)	22.2	101.5	0.4	13.3	95.9	3.5	21.3	120.4	(1.0)	14.1	91.4	(1.0)	11.2	127.3	14.5	22.4

Key Export price index relative to GNP or GDP deflator (both in local currency; 1970 = 100). Current account surplus as percentage of total imports (bracketed numbers indicate deficits). Share of public consumption in GNP at market prices.

Sources: United Nations, *Yearbook of National Income Accounts*; International Monetary Fund, *International Financial Statistics*. The author will supply an explanation on how the data are derived, on request.

159

Table 4. Growth rates of broadly and narrowly defined money stock in local currency, percentage per annum.

	United Kingdom	France	West Germany	Italy	Japan	United States
1971	13.1, 12.8	17.4, 13.8	10.8, 12.3	16.4, 22.8	24.2, 25.3	12.1, 7.9
1972	28.0, 16.8	19.5, 13.0	15.3, 13.6	22.9, 18.6	24.8, 22.2	11.4, 5.7
1973	27.5, 10.1	14.9, 10.0	12.0, 5.6	22.4, 20.4	16.8, 26.4	12.2, 7.3
1974	12.8, 3.5	18.1, 11.8	7.5, 5.9	16.3, 16.0	11.5, 13.3	9.4, 4.0
1975	7.4, 15.5	14.4, 10.8	7.3, 14.1	23.0, 9.2	5.3, 10.3	6.6, 4.5

Note: Definitions of broad and narrow money differ. Left-hand of each column is broadly defined money, right-hand, narrowly defined.
Source: International Monetary Fund, *International Financial Statistics.*

various definitions of the money stock. We should be wary of interpreting even rapid growth of the money supply as evidence for the emergence, or existence, of an excess supply of money. The increase in supply might be a passive response to rising demand (due perhaps to inflation or a rise in real income), and even if it were not, the money stock might effectively be in continuous equilibrium if there were a sufficiently rapid adjustment in the price and volume of other variables affected. The evidence shows that 1971–73 was a period of rapid monetary expansion in Britain, followed by a year of very slow growth. Other countries' experience was not wholly dissimilar, although there are substantial divergencies (see table 4).

We are certainly in no position to reject the hypothesis that the fast rise in the money supply in the United Kingdom between 1971 and 1973 was, in part, responsible for the severe deterioration in the balance of payments between 1972 and 1974. Much of the steep climb in the volume of imports from 1971 to 1973 can be attributed to the trade cycle upswing in these years. Few economic relationships in post-war Britain have been better attested than the strong dependence of imported manufactures, semi-manufactures, and materials on national income in the middle to late phases of a boom. The extent to which the boom itself can be explained by the growth of the money supply from the second quarter of 1971 is less easy to assess; not least, there remains the question (still quite open) of which caused which. More detailed research is needed before any definitive answer can be given.

Excess supply of *labour* can be measured, with varying degrees of accuracy, in unemployment and unfilled vacancies statistics. If real wages are above their equilibrium levels, there is likely to be non-Keynesian unemployment and an excess demand for commodities. An increase in real wages from equilibrium will tend to depress production and labour hiring and, given a sufficiently low elasticity of demand for labour or a sufficiently high rate of unemployment benefit, expand consumers' expenditure. Unemployment fell in Britain from the winter of 1971/72 until mid-1974, only to rise sharply thereafter. Real wages grew modestly in the 1971–73 boom, and have behaved erratically since then, with the uneven incidence of rises in, and controls upon, nominal wage rates and prices. The period from 1974:1 to 1975:2 witnessed pronounced increases in real wages. Labour had been insulated from much of the terms of trade between 1972 and 1974 (the ratio of export to import price deflators for goods and services fell 19.8 per cent between these years); the operation of the prices and incomes policies then in force was largely responsible for this, and the wage explosion that followed the removal of the wage controls in spring 1974 took two to three quarters to be reflected in price rises. These developments probably aggravated the balance-of-payments deficits in 1974 and 1975, while also serving to add to other pressures raising unemployment from mid-1974. But against this, real consumers' expenditure appears to have registered absolute declines of nearly 1 per cent in both 1974 and 1975—which undoubtedly moderated the growth in imports—and the depreciation in sterling raised profit rates, production, and quite possibly labour hiring in the export industries.

Errors and omissions aside, the overall balance of payments must balance. In an accounting sense, therefore, a current account deficit will be accompanied by an excess supply of *claims on future goods* (or future money), which will appear as net capital imports. Such a phenomenon, clearly, could not persist indefinitely, but it is quite consistent with short-run flow-equilibrium conditions on asset and commodity markets. No implications for policy need follow, unless the authorities consider the excess supply of claims to be sub-optimal because of externalities, deficiencies in information, or some other source of imperfection in capital markets. The excess supply of claims may or may not be accompanied by a loss in reserves of foreign exchange. Since the relationship between the current and capital accounts of the balance of payments is an accounting identity, no direct inference may be made about the direction of causation. Spontaneous inward investment (direct or portfolio) by foreign residents may raise imports through its effects on wealth, expenditure, and income at home. Alternatively, domestic residents may wish to trade away some future consumption for present consumption at prevailing international interest rates; or capital imports may best be taken to represent the passive, financing counterpart to a heavy current demand for goods and services at home, the intertemporal significance of which is imperfectly perceived by domestic agents. The evidence available does not permit us to adjudicate between these competing interpretations; matters are made very difficult by the fact that A may borrow from B by exchanging claims on C. Despite this, a sectoral distinction between private and public overseas borrowing is interesting (see table 5).

These figures suggest that 1974 and the first months of 1975 were a period of sizable public sector borrowing from overseas, motivated (in part) by the authorities' wish to prevent sterling from falling substantially in the foreign exchange markets. It was seen earlier that sterling's depreciation in 1974 was lower than might have been predicted, given the large current account deficit. In fact, £1067m was borrowed directly by the government in foreign exchange in the fourth quarter of 1974 and the first quarter of 1975, and the nationalized industries were also borrowing heavily in Deutsche mark, Swiss francs and U.S. dollars from 1973 onwards (although this began to fall off in 1975). From mid-1972 to end-1973 and from mid-1975, however, official overseas borrowing was less pronounced. Private sector overseas borrowing also peaked in 1974—as one would expect, given that 1974 recorded the largest current account deficit—but seems to have exceeded public sector overseas borrowing substantially in each of the three years 1973, 1974 and 1975. This evidence is consistent with the hypothesis that the current account deficits were (at least in part) occasioned by an excess supply of 'claims on future goods' by the U.K. private sector, but it does not prove it. It may be more plausible to treat the overseas sector's transactions in assets with both the public and private sectors as an accommodating item which, together with the exchange rate itself, absorbed the strain of current account deficits that arose for other reasons.

In sum, the fall in the external value of sterling since June 1972 is better regarded as the consequence of Britain's balance-of-payments deficits, than their cause. The deficits arose from a number of factors. First, Britain's

Table 5. Overseas sector's transactions, with U.K. public and private sectors.

	A	B
1972:2	+855	– 978
3	+171	– 62
4	+188	– 171
1973:1	–152	+ 374
2	–379	+ 607
3	+ 47	+ 175
4	–	+ 396
1974:1	+107	+ 715
2	+ 68	+ 817
3	+171	+ 632
4	+593	+ 317
1975:1	+110	+ 342
2	+421	– 55
3	–522	+1083
4	+122	+ 172
1976:1	+502	– 463

A: Overseas sector's transactions with (increase in claims on) the U.K. public sector.
B: Overseas sector's transactions with (increase in claims on) the U.K. private sector.
Units: £m.
Source: *Bank of England Quarterly Bulletin.*

terms of trade deteriorated sharply from mid-1972 to 1974, with the increase in the prices of primary commodities (of which Britain was a large net importer), culminating in the four-fold rise in oil prices between 1973 and 1974. Second, the period 1971–73 witnessed a cyclical upturn in the British economy, associated with unparalleled growth in the domestic money supply (June 1971 to mid-1973), and major fiscal reflation (particularly in 1972); Britain has always exhibited a high marginal import propensity in the middle and late stages of a boom, and the rise in the volume of imports of manufactures and semi-manufactures from 1972 to the end of 1973 was quite consistent with previous experience. Third, there is also some evidence to suggest that nontradables had been rising in price relative to tradables at the beginning of the decade, and that this could have contributed to the current account deterioration in 1972, 1973, and 1974. Lastly, the rapid rise in real wages in 1974 may have had a similar effect later.

3. Is Inflation the Cause or the Effect of Sterling's Depreciation?

In principle, the answer to this question is that it could be either. If a *small* country experiences more rapid inflation than the rest of the world at a constant exchange rate, the prices of tradables will sink in relation to nontradables. Given sufficient substitution in consumption and production, the current account of the balance of payments will deteriorate. All else equal, this will increase the probability of an excess supply of its currency. In this event, pressure will develop for a formal devaluation by the authorities to restore the balance, or for a currency depreciation if the exchange rate is floating. For a *large* country, on the other hand, tradables' prices may not be parametric in foreign currency. Some of its relative inflation may be transmitted into the prices of its exports, or imports, or both, in foreign markets. But its balance of payments is likely to worsen on current account, again given sufficient substitution, as foreign and domestic agents switch expenditures towards foreign-produced tradables. Repercussions on the exchange rate will then be the same, at least qualitatively.

In the cases of both small and large counties, if the relative inflation is initiated by different rates of monetary expansion, these effects on the exchange rate may well be compounded by a mechanism operating on the capital account of the balance of payments. An excess supply of money in one country will induce portfolio disequilibrium, and an excess demand for non-monetary assets. If the supply of domestic assets is not raised, this can easily lead directly to the acquisition of foreign assets by domestic residents; and any increase in the price of domestic assets (real and nominal) may also induce substitution—by both domestic and foreign agents—towards foreign assets. Furthermore, even wage-led inflation may generate similar results if domestic profit rates are seen to drop in consequence, and direct and port-folio capital exports are likely to emerge or increase.

But depreciation may also stimulate domestic inflation. A small country will experience an immediate rise in the domestic prices of exportables and importables. If all else is equal, they should rise by $x/(1 - x)$ per cent for each x per cent drop in the exchange rate. The prices of nontradables will also drift upwards, to the extent that they employ (or continue to employ) tradables as inputs. Traded-goods industries will increase their bids for factor services, the prices of which should start to rise unless there is sub-stantial excess supply, or the nontradables sectors release them rapidly. Increases in money wage rates will be strengthened if labour consumes tradables since constant nominal wages must imply lower real wages. Furthermore, the drop in the exchange rate is highly likely to increase every-one's expectation of the overall domestic price level in future, which will once again tend to encourage upward adjustments of nominal factor prices in anticipation. If the domestic money supply is kept constant, the inflation-ary impetus of exchange depreciation may be blunted: real balances at home will be cut; asset prices will be checked, or even cut; unemployment will tend to rise at least relative to the levels it would otherwise have reached; the rate of rise of money usage rates should be moderated; and there may even be a favourable direct effect on expectations of inflation. But it is worth noticing how likely it is that the domestic money supply will rise in response to exchange depreciation. An increase in domestic interest rates will encour-age switches from currency to bank deposits; tempt banks to move out of more liquid into less liquid assets; and perhaps, also, entice the central bank into open market purchases of bonds to moderate its national debt servicing charges, bankruptcies, and disruptions in credit flows and balance sheets.

It can be seen that the depreciation–inflation mechanisms are too numerous and too intertwined to permit any easy answer to the question of which caused which. Spectral analysis may turn out, in future, to provide a clear answer. This technique involves comparing the waves of inflation over time against the waves of exchange rate changes, to establish whether the former are a better predictor of lagged than of previous values of the latter. If they are, there is *prima facie* evidence that inflation causes exchange rate changes; if inflation is a better predictor of previous than of later deprecia-tions, there is *prima facie* evidence that the depreciations cause inflation. The exchange rate and inflation statistics reveal that British inflation 'peaked' in 1971 and 1974–75, both relative to other countries, and absolutely, while depreciations 'peaked' in 1972–73 and 1975–76. It would be very naive, however, to infer that this constitutes decisive proof that in-flation is the cause rather than the consequence of exchange rate changes. A larger interval of time is needed before spectral analysis could be expected to produce any reliable results. Even then, theoretical considerations make one pessimistic about the chance of deriving unambiguous answers: reaction speeds may change over time; the way expectations are found may change over time; the extent to which the money supply responds to interest rate pressures may change over time; and even if fluctuations in the variable y do always precede fluctuations in the variable x, it may often be possible to construct a theoretical model which predicts this but has fluctuations in x the cause of fluctuations in y[9].

4. The Balance of Payments and the Budget

The third question prompted by our analysis of the floating pound relates to the connection between the current account of the balance of payments and the government's budget position. One hypothesis—known as the New Cambridge—that has received considerable attention recently[10] is that these two variables should normally be closely correlated. It is supposed that the combined net acquisition of financial assets of the household and corporate sectors is small in relation to the public authorities' financial surplus or deficit and the balance of payments on current account, and that it varies little with national income. The major implication for policy is that the exchange rate should probably be regarded as an instrument for attaining internal, not external, balance. Devaluation, it is suggested, will not, by itself, induce an appreciable long-term improvement in the current account of the balance of payments since the multiplier effects of an initial improvement will be to raise income, and consequently imports, substantially. On the other hand, on the assumption that the sectoral balances of the public authorities and the rest of the world are closely associated, the financial policy parameters that help to shape the government's overall budget surplus or deficit are thought to have a comparative advantage as an external balance instrument. The conditions under which the New Cambridge instrument assignment is stable and the corresponding 'Old Cambridge' assignment (of exchange rate to external balance and financial policy to internal balance) is unstable turn out to be rather restrictive[11]. One major difficulty is the fact that the public authorities' net acquisition of financial assets should be regarded as a *state* variable, not a *control* variable; it is government spending, transfer payments, public sector prices, and tax rates that constitute the set of budgetary policy instruments. Another problem is that, under floating, the exchange rate ceases (in whole or part) to be an exogenous policy parameter. Nonetheless, it is worth investigating the evidence for the claim that the current account of the balance of payments and the public authorities' surplus or deficit have been closely related in practice.

Figure 4 shows that there is certainly some apparent association from 1972 to 1974. The sign is as predicted, and a deterioration in the current account of £100m is associated with an increase in the public sector borrow-

*Figure 4. Current account surplus or deficit versus public sector borrowing,
1972:1 to 1976:1.*

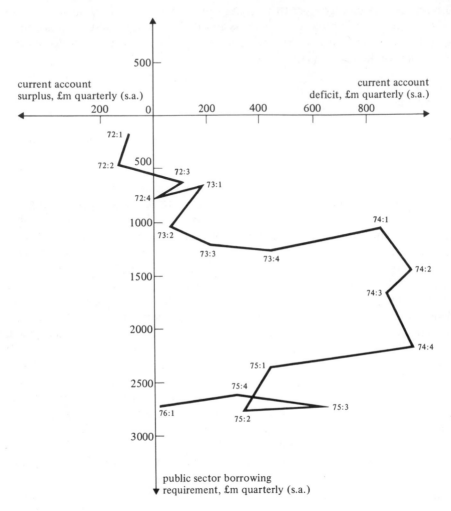

ing requirement of rather under £200m, rather than £100m as the strictest
version of the New Cambridge hypothesis requires. Similar results follow
from a comparison of the current account with the public sector's net
acquisition of financial assets.

1975 and 1976, however, do not provide support for the hypothesis. The
current account deficit was halved, in 1975, and registered further slight improvement in 1976. The public sector borrowing requirement continued to
rise steeply until mid-1975. In 1976 it was more than five times as big as the
current account deficit. The counterpart to these movements in the flow of
funds has been the very large rise in the private household sector's saving,

and the restoration of the corporate sector's cash flow from its very depressed levels in 1974. The period 1973–76 witnessed a fall in the real value of consumers' expenditure on durable goods of a severity unparalleled in post-war Britain, influenced no doubt by the sharp check to household real disposable income, the fall in real wealth, and tightening credit conditions. Corporate sector cash flow fell in 1974 as price controls delayed, and less than fully compensated for, substantial increases in the costs of labour and material inputs, and committed fixed investments and stock appreciation rose strongly to approach and even overtake retained after-tax earnings. The improvement in 1975–76 is explained by falls in the rate of rise of labour and materials costs, relaxation in price controls, falls in fixed and inventory investment, and above all the deferral of corporation tax due on profits attributable to stock appreciation. These are the principal reasons for the recent breakdown of the New Cambridge relationship.

For completeness, mention should be made of the special factors which have swollen the public sector borrowing requirement since 1972, and more particularly over the period 1974–75. First, the 1973–76 recession raised transfer payments and cut tax and nationalized industry receipts by perhaps as much as £2000m in 1975 prices, compared with the figure they would have reached at 'full employment'. Second, various limits on earnings rises for high-income recipients who face high marginal tax rates were in force from November 1972 to Spring 1974, and from July 1975 and this, coupled with the flat-rate limit on wage rises, may have lowered income tax receipts by about £600m. Third, the rises in public sector subsidies for food and agriculture, and housing in 1975, were some £881m and £381m higher, respectively, than they would have been had they mentioned a constant ratio to GDP at factor cost since 1970. Lastly, the rise of £1931m in nominal debt servicing charges paid by central and local authorities between 1970 and 1975 is of particular importance in this context. A large proportion of this—perhaps one half—should be attributed to the increase in the expected inflation component in the nominal interest coupons offered on new and reissued debt. This element in the increase of the public sector borrowing requirement is rather spurious. In steady-state growth, the real value of public sector debt will represent constant fractions of real wealth and income, and if taxes are levied to meet the full nominal interest charges when positive inflation is expected, the community will presumably find that these fractions fall over time. There is no compelling case for penalizing *current* tax-payers in this manner. When full account is taken of the effects of inflation on the accounts of public authorities, whose debts are typically nominal and whose assets are typically real, the public sector borrowing requirement looks very different. There are notorious difficulties with gauging real interest rates, *ex-post* or *ex-ante* and, of course, the fact that nominal interest payments are fully liable to tax complicates matters still further. However, it might be safe to assume that as much as 60 per cent of

Table 6. Annual estimates of the current accounts and government budget deficits of the six largest Western countries from 1975.

	United Kingdom		France		West Germany		Italy		Japan		United States	
	B	F	B	F	B	F	B	F	B	F	B	F
1968	− 1.822	−1.283	− 1.92	−1.059	− 0.977	+2.964	− 3.225	+2.688	− 1.953	+1.048	−25.16	+ 0.374
1969	+ 2.144	+1.078	− 0.688	−1.798	+ 0.428	+1.931	− 2.697	+2.406	− 1.692	+2.119	+ 3.23	+ 0.155
1970	+ 1.605	+1.759	+ 0.666	+0.297	− 0.154	+0.729	− 5.144	+0.902	− 0.886	+1.97	− 2.85	+ 2.156
1971	− 1.55	+2.577	− 0.626	+0.53	− 0.301	+0.323	− 7.695	+2.041	− 0.516	+5.797	−23.04	− 1.323
1972	− 4.033	+0.35	+ 1.253	+0.297	− 1.141	+1.041	− 9.866	+2.266	− 4.731	+6.624	−23.23	− 5.55
1973	− 5.741	−2.04	+ 1.646	−0.691	− 1.066	+4.341	−13.674	−2.51	− 6.705	−0.136	−24.41	+ 7.156
1974	− 8.271	−8.441	+ 0.896	−5.943	− 3.897	+9.759	−13.78	−7.817	− 6.168	−4.693	− 3.49	+ 2.33
1975	−18.634	−3.86	−10.034	+0.33	−13.843	+3.881	−25.373	−0.528	−23.76	−0.682	−44.22	+17.361

All data in U.S. $ billion. B = government budget balance; F = current account balance.
Source: International Monetary Fund, *International Financial Statistics*.

the public authorities' interest payments in 1975 (£3957m) is effectively a concealed repayment of capital. This adjustment would reduce the true public sector borrowing requirement for 1975 by about one-quarter. Similar adjustment to the current account of the balance of payments, the deficit in which was augmented by the effects of heavy borrowing in nominal terms, might improve the balance by some £500m in 1975 prices. All these considerations explain or mitigate the bad performance of the New Cambridge hypothesis, but they do not seriously affect the grave doubts one must entertain about it.

Table 6 gives the annual estimates for the current accounts and government budget deficits of the six largest Western countries from 1968 to 1975. A linear regression of F on B, with no lags, produced the following result:

$$F = 0.4836 - 0.0562\,B \qquad\qquad R^2 = 0.01642$$
$$(0.604)\ (0.0633) \qquad\qquad \bar{R}^2 = -0.00496$$

while a linear regression of the ratio of F to national income on the ratio of B to national income, again with no lags, fared little better:

$$F/Y = 0.0057 + 0.12449\ B/Y \qquad\qquad R^2 = 0.61857$$
$$(0.00324)\ (0.0998) \qquad\qquad \bar{R}^2 = 0.041462$$

Standard errors are given in brackets. The null hypothesis is not rejected at the 75 per cent probability level. The second equation is probably a fairer test than the first, since the former suffers from heteroscedasticity. These statistical tests justify extreme scepticism about any reliable direct link between F and B. It is the experience of 1974 and 1975 in particular which serves to throw doubt on the validity of the New Cambridge hypothesis.

5. Stability?

The fourth question posed by the analysis of sterling's float since 1972 focuses on stability: Is there evidence that the floating pound has been unstable? If we are to assume that Walras' adjustment hypothesis is correct, the answer must be that everything depends on whether the excess demand for sterling is a decreasing function of its value in foreign currency. If yes, sterling will be stable, in that a chance departure from equilibrium will set in motion forces whose net effect will be to push the exchange rate back towards equilibrium. If no, sterling will exhibit instability, at least over certain intervals of time or exchange rates.

We shall confine our attention to two aspects of the stability problem: the so-called J curve, and the movement of forward exchange rates as proxies for the market's expectation of the future spot rates.

The J curve sets out to describe the time-path of the balance of payments (on current account) after a devaluation or exchange depreciation. The change in the current account is measured vertically, and time horizontally. It is widely suggested (partly on the basis of the experience of the sterling devaluation in November 1967) that the current account first deteriorates, next recovers, and then finally begins to register a net improvement over its initial level, which grows as time goes on. The initial deterioration is supposed to last perhaps six months; a year or so must elapse, it is thought, before any net gain is recorded. If the downward tail of the J does exist, sterling will display temporary instability when other factors combine to swamp the initially perverse effect of exchange rate changes—unless, in fact, autonomous elements in the capital account of the balance of payments swing in the opposite direction by more than the deterioration on current account.

The essential point behind the J curve is the fact that the current account registers the delivery of goods and services for the period in question, and not the orders placed for them[12]. Deliveries follow orders, often by many months; the lag may be up to three years for some heavy capital goods (aircraft, ships, power stations). The full trade volume responses to exchange rate changes cannot, therefore, show at once. A substantial slice of deliveries in the two or three months after a devaluation, for example, will represent orders agreed before devaluation in the light of the then prevailing set of prices. But it must be emphasized that the lag in volume responses (in all probability, a distributed lag) does not imply that the current account must *deteriorate* immediately after a devaluation; the point is that the volume changes will take time to build up. Initial deterioration is a possibility, but no more than that. It is necessary for an initial deterioration that the devaluing country experience a deterioration in its terms of trade.

Devaluation cannot permanently affect the terms of trade of a small country for which tradables prices are parametric in foreign currency. Nor is it likely to have any enduring effect on them if it takes place when all world markets are in full equilibrium, or the devaluation is fully expected. In disequilibrium, however, unexpected devaluation by a large country may improve or worsen its terms of trade. One simple condition for improvement in a two-country world is that the product of the two countries' import-demand elasticities exceed the product of export-supply elasticities; if it falls short, the devaluer's terms of trade will suffer. In the British case from 1972 to 1976, much of the depreciation of sterling that occurred was widely expected. In most of the relevant tradables markets, Britain must be treated as a price-taker in foreign exchange and to the extent that she is not a price-taker, there cannot be any prior expectation either way about the sign of the difference between the two elasticity products. There is no reason, therefore, for expecting that sterling's depreciation led to any sizeable, long-lasting effect on Britain's terms of trade. (It is quite probable, however, that the substantial terms of trade deterioration which Britain experienced in 1973–74—attributable chiefly to the sharp jump in the prices of primary commodities, especially oil—led to a greater depreciation in sterling than would have come about otherwise.)

But the depreciations, if unexpected, can still have had an appreciable *temporary* effect on the terms of trade. If the prices of exports and imports are quoted in the destination country's currency, unexpected devaluation will produce a temporary boost to the terms of trade. It will induce a temporary deterioration if export and import prices are quoted in the supplying country's currency. A simple, formal model can illustrate this.

Suppose that, at date 0, a small country devalues once-and-for-all and, in so doing, multiplies the domestic price of foreign exchange by δ. The exchange rate had previously been constant. The foreign exchange prices of its exports and its imports are constant throughout. Deliveries are exponentially lagged behind contracts agreed; λ and μ are the inertia coefficients for exports and imports, so that

$$\text{exports in period } 0 = (1-\lambda) \sum_{i=0}^{\infty} \lambda^{-i} z_{xi},$$

$$\text{imports in period } 0 = (1-\mu) \sum_{i=0}^{\infty} \mu^{-i} z_{mi},$$

where z_{xi} and z_{mi} are export and import contracts agreed in period i, θ is the proportion of exports invoiced in foreign currency, and π is the same proportion for imports. The home country's functions for z_{xi} and z_{mi} for date i are loglinear in own-price expressed in home currency (elasticities are η and $-\epsilon$ respectively), but cross-price-elasticities are zero, and neither function is affected by changes in the money stock, real or nominal income, or factor prices.

At period n, the relative rise in the home-currency value of exports since period -1 is

$$(1-\lambda^{n+1}) \delta^{1+\eta} + \lambda^{n+1} (1 + \theta (\delta - 1)) - 1,$$

and for imports

$$(1-\mu^{n+1}) \delta^{1-\epsilon} + \mu^{n+1} (1 + \pi (\delta - 1)) - 1.$$

If trade was balanced at period -1, and $\lambda = \mu$, the length of the J curve (the number of periods that must elapse after devaluation at period before the current account returns to balance) is

$$\frac{\ln A}{\ln \lambda} - 1 \text{ where } A = \left[1 - \frac{(\theta - \pi)(\delta - 1)}{\delta(\delta^u - \delta^{-\epsilon})} \right]^{-1}.$$

It is necessary that $\pi > \theta$ for the J curve to exist at all, assuming that ϵ and η are positive.

For the sake of illustration, the length of the J curve has been computed for various values of δ, $-\epsilon, \eta, \theta, \pi,$ and λ (table 7). If the length of period is taken as one quarter (three months), and $\lambda = 0.8$, the median delivery is some 13 months after the contract is agreed. This does not seem an inappropriate figure, although it may somewhat overstate the average lag. The table shows that even with modest values for the elasticities, and this long delivery lag, initial deterioration in the current account will not exist at all unless there is a pronounced excess of π over θ. Even when this gap is at its highest possible value, the length of the J is less than six months. The length of the J (and probability of any initial deterioration) is slightly sensitive to the size of δ but the sign is indeterminate. If there are reasons for expecting λ to exceed μ (and there may well be in Britain's case) the length of the J and the probability of any initial deterioration may be somewhat larger. Allowing the current account to be in deficit when devaluation occurs makes a very minor difference in the same direction.

Table 7. Length of the J curves for various values of δ, $-\epsilon, \eta, \theta, \pi,$ and λ.

	δ	$-\epsilon$	η	θ	π	$\lambda (=\mu)$	Length of J curve
Case A	1.1	1	1	0.4	0.5	0.5	zero
Case B	1.2	1	1	0.3	0.5	0.8	zero
Case C	1.2	1	1	0	1	0.8	0.679
Case D	1.2	0	1	0	1	0.8	1.718
Case E	1.1	0	1	0	1	0.8	1.899
Case F	1.2	0	1	0.3	0.5	0.8	zero
Case G	1.2	0	1	0.3	0.8	0.8	0.5614

We must conclude that the mere existence of the J curve for Britain[13] is open to doubt. Devaluation or depreciation may not induce any temporary deterioration in the trade balance at all. Even if it does exist, it will not be long before the balance returns to its initial value; two quarters might be an upper estimate. It should also be noted that θ (the proportion of British exports quoted in foreign currency) has been rising, and could well have reached 0.5 in 1976: Britain's largest private company, I.C.I., moved to a policy of invoicing all its exports in foreign currencies. On the other hand, θ was presumably much lower in 1972 or 1973, and lower still at the time of the 1967 devaluation. British companies have been learning to avoid foreign exchange losses. It is interesting to note, however, that the rest of the world's demand for sterling as a transactions medium is negatively related to θ. The trend to foreign currency pricing of exports may have exacerbated the weakness of the capital account of the balance of payments in late 1975 and 1976, but no statistical measures of the size of this effect are available.

Further factors working against the significance of the J curve as a potential threat to the stability of the floating pound include the fact that some of the fall in sterling will have been anticipated by traders. Sterling-denominated export prices will no doubt have begun to include some allowance for expected depreciation. Furthermore, the fact that the J curve has been widely believed to exist has made international companies more sanguine about holding sterling (and perhaps even increasing their holding of sterling) at a time when the depreciations seemed to be having little effect on the current account.

We now turn to the forward exchange market.

If we are prepared to make some rather inhibiting assumptions, forward exchange rates can be treated as perfect proxies for the market's current expectation of future spot rates, for the dates at which the forward contracts mature. These assumptions are that all agents concerned have uniform expectations; that they are prepared to be in (collectively) limitless amounts whenever the relevant predicted spot and forward rates diverge; and that commissions and other transactions costs, and contract default risk, are all negligible. The analysis that follows assumes that these conditons hold.

A floating exchange rate may exhibit instability in expectations if its values in future periods are *extrapolative.* An unexpected depreciation will then generate expectations of a faster rate of depreciation than had previously been anticipated. Unless the relevant short-term interest rates in the devaluing country are raised smartly, or happen to fall heavily elsewhere, an adverse covered-interest-arbitrage margin is likely to grow or open up. This may well stimulate outward flow of short-term capital, in response to which the spot rate will probably decline further. *Regressive* expectation of the exchange rate will have opposite effects. Depreciation will cut the spot price of the currency in relation to its forward price. The forward discount on the currency will drop (or the premium will rise). Unless interest rate movements at home or abroad wipe out this effect, there must be an increased probability of favourable short-term capital movements. This will tend to boost the spot value of the currency. If the lags on past values happen to be geometrically distributed, the difference between regressive and extrapolative expectations can be demonstrated very simply in a discrete-time model[14]: we find that

$$\frac{\triangle^n \log R^e \text{ (at 0)}}{\triangle t^n} = (1-\lambda) \sum_{i=0}^{\infty} \lambda^i \frac{\triangle^n \log R_{-i}}{\triangle t^n}$$

where R is the exchange rate, e is the expectations superscript, λ is the inertia coefficient, i is the date index, and t is time. If $n = 0$, expectations for R are regressive; if $n = 1$, expectations for R are extrapolative, and expectations of the trend in R are regressive. If $n = 2$, expectations of the trend in R are extrapolative.

There is one reason for expecting that n may equal one. The condition for arbitrage in international commodity markets[15] not subject to trading impediments is

$$p_j = p_k R_{jk},$$

where p_j is the local currency price of any tradable commodity in country j; p_k is the local currency price of the same commodity in country k, and R_{jk} is the price of country k's currency in terms of country j's. In rate of change terms,

$$\hat{p}_j^e = \hat{p}_k^e + \hat{R}_{jk}^e,$$

where the e superscript denotes expected value. If we allow ourselves to ignore trade taxes and costs, non-traded goods, and relative price changes, $\hat{p}_j^e$ and $\hat{p}_k^e$ will represent the expected speeds of domestic inflation in countries j and k. There is now widespread evidence testifying to the existence of extrapolative price expectations within particular economies. The assumptions of consistent expectations and perfect international commodity arbitrage now point inescapably to the result that expectations of R must be extrapolative, too.

Various exploratory tests have been conducted on forward exchange rates and sterling and the results obtained were:

$$\triangle f_1 = -0.0000164 + 1.035 \triangle s, \qquad \bar{R}^2 = 0.9849$$
$$(0.11516)$$

$$\triangle f_3 = -0.0000677 + 1.03366 \triangle s, \qquad \bar{R}^2 = 0.9463$$
$$(0.11729)$$

$$\triangle f_{12} = -0.000277 + 1.0297 \triangle s, \qquad \bar{R}^2 = 0.9461$$
$$(0.11659)$$

$\triangle f_1$, $\triangle f_3$ and $\triangle f_{12}$ are the daily change in the central closing dollar price in New York of sterling for delivery respectively one, three and twelve months later. $\triangle s$ is the daily change in the central closing price in New York for spot sterling. The period covered is March 2 to June 24, 1976, which provides 82 observations. The data source is the *Financial Times*. The standard errors are given in brackets. It will be seen that the regression coefficients are highly significant, and slightly exceed unity. The difference from unity is not, however, significant at any acceptable probability level. The conclusion to be drawn from this is that sterling appears to be on a random walk in this period; the forward markets are 'efficient' at least in the sense that whatever factors depress or raise the spot rate in a day appear to be fully and immediately reflected in broadly parallel movements in the forward rates. There is no evidence in favour of regressive expectations, unless the inertia coefficient is taken to be vanishingly small. If anything, there is some slender support for the view that expectations are not merely close to the borderline between regressive and extrapolative expectations, but have—at least during this period—been mildly extrapolative. 1975 and 1976 witnessed a steady rise in the forward discount on sterling against the dollar as its depreciation gathered pace. Alternative explanations for these findings might be that the relevant short-term interest rates in London rose instantaneously as spot sterling fell and went down when spot sterling rose, or that New York interest rates moved in the opposite directions at these times. If one could then assume that arbitrage kept the covered-interest margin negligible at all times and effectively determined the forward exchange rates (and this would in its turn require arbitragers' elasticity of demand for forward exchange to exceed very substantially the elasticity of traders' and speculators' demand), it would follow that changes in the price of spot sterling would be accompanied by changes in the forward exchange rates in the same direction. But such alternative explanations are highly unsatisfactory. A rise in London short-term interest rates on, for example, three-month Treasury bills might well induce some fall in the forward currency—as arbitragers switched covered funds to London—but it would tend to hoist the spot rate, not weaken it. Furthermore, interest rate changes of the required magnitude, on a daily basis, simply did not occur.

Some slight support for the presence of extrapolative exchange rate expectations comes from other tests. It might be anticipated that changes in forward exchange rates are related to the difference between the forward exchange rate for a particular date and the actual spot rate that turned out to rule on that date. If the strict expectations hypothesis—the view that speculators 'rule the roost' in the forward exchange markets, and that forward exchange rates for date T at date t are unbiased estimates of the market's expectation at t of the future spot rate at T—is correct, it would not be implausible to suggest that expectations of future spot rates are revised in the light of errors. Accordingly, the following equation was tested.

$$\triangle f_3 = a + \beta\, e,$$

where $\triangle f_3$ is (as before) the change in the three-month forward exchange rate (but measured this time over a three-month, not a daily, interval), and e is the difference between the spot rate and the three-month forward exchange rate three months earlier. The results for sterling in terms of the U.S. dollar, over the period April 1972 to February 1976, were:

$$\triangle f_3 = -0.0228 + 1.01737e, \qquad \bar{R}^2 = 0.9797.$$
$$(0.1448)$$

(All exchange rates are central closing rates in London, for 41 end-of-the-month observations. Source of data: *Bank of England Quarterly Bulletin*.)

The same equation was also tested for the U.S. dollar–Deutsche mark rate, using monthly averages of New York central closing rates:

$$\triangle f_3 = -0.0103 + 1.0389e, \qquad \bar{R}^2 = 0.9814.$$
$$(0.16375)$$

(Source of data: International Monetary Fund, *International Financial Statistics*. Period: June 1972 to October 1975).

In both these equations, the regression coefficients are highly significant, exceed unity, but do not differ significantly from unity. The inference to be drawn is that forward exchange rates do respond closely to what might be taken to represent errors in predicting spot rates, and, once again, that the balance of probability slightly favours extrapolative over regressive expectations. In these circumstances, the authorities cannot look to depreciation as a stimulus to stabilizing inward short-term capital movements. On the contrary, if they are anxious to minimize the chance of further depreciations in the near future, depreciation should be followed by increases in domestic interest rates, or other devices designed to create a temporary inflow on the capital account.

The analysis of stability of the exchange rates has not produced grounds for anxiety about the response of the current account. The current account should respond favourably to depreciation and there is no inherent reason why even the immediate effect should be adverse. The effect on the current account may, of course, be minimal if the depreciation has been anticipated or if the money supply and money wage rates are adjusted upwards at the same time; but an unexpectedly rapid depreciation, accompanied by offsetting movements in the money supply and money wage rates should still work in the correct direction.

The capital account, however, may exhibit some instability. A fall in the spot value of sterling is accompanied, so it appears, by parallel falls in its forward value; in fact, the falls in the forward exchange rate seem to be, if anything, absolutely larger than the spot falls that occasion them. This is potentially worrying: it implies that, over the short run, the authorities may need to react to an unexpected depreciation by immediately raising interest rates to prevent the falls gathering pace.

6. Conclusion

This study of Britain's experience of floating exchange rates began by posing a number of questions. Have the persistent deficits on the balance of payments led to sterling's depreciation, or have they been an unexpected result of it? What is the causal connection between inflation and depreciation? What is the external significance of the government's budget deficits? Has the exchange rate exhibited signs of instability? Answers have been proferred to these questions, some tentative, some firm. There are grounds for treating depreciation as the outcome of deficits on external payments, which were themselves attributable to a number of factors: rapid growth in domestic aggregate demand, unmatched by productive potential, in the period 1971–73; rapid rises in wage rates in 1974 and 1975; and above all the 25 per cent deterioration in Britain's terms of trade from 1971 to 1974, over which she had minimal control and which was without parallel since the Korean War. But the causal dependence of the exchange rate upon the balance of payments has been suspended or modified at times by official intervention, which was designed to hold the exchange rate in 1974 (to restrain internal inflation). In 1975 and 1976, however, the exchange rate was allowed to sink—perhaps even encouraged to do so—in order to check rises in unemployment and improve the balance of payments.

It was seen that the causal connections between inflation and depreciation were complex and bi-directional, and that it is premature to offer any simple answer in the absence of detailed econometric analysis and more evidence. No support at all was found for the New Cambridge hypothesis that the current account surplus (deficit) is determined by—or even closely related to—the budgetary position of the public authorities. As regards stability, reasons were found for doubting the significance of the J curve, but there were clear signs that exchange rate expectations were highly and immediately sensitive to current spot movements. It was more likely than not that they had become slightly extrapolative, so that an unexpected spot movement was associated with a slightly larger movement in forward rates. This pointed to the need for the Bank of England to be prepared to raise short-term interest rates quickly in the face of a foreign exchange crisis.

The floating of sterling has not proved to be the panacea its keenest proponents had hoped. External payments have remained weak and worrying. Internal balance targets (both unemployment and inflation) have proved increasingly difficult to attain. But it would be wrong to attribute these failures to the exchange rate regime itself. The huge absolute and relative price rises in Britain's key importables (food, metals and oil) and the major international recession which followed in its wake from 1974 to 1976 are the major explanations for sterling's decline and the other macroeconomic problems with which Britain has been faced. A rigid exchange rate would have proved totally indefensible.

NOTES

1. Details are given in H.M. Treasury, *Economic Progress Report,* 9 March 1977, and the International Monetary Fund's multilateral exchange rate model is discussed in R.R. Rhomberg, 'Indices of effective exchange rates', International Monetary Fund, *Staff Papers,* March, 1976.
2. See J.E. Meade, *The Theory of International Economic Policy,* Vol. 1, *The Balance of Payments* (Oxford: Oxford University Press, 1951), pp. 11–2.
3. See P. Kouri, 'Capital flows and the dynamics of the exchange rate', Seminar paper 67 (Stockholm: Institute of International Economic Studies, December, 1976).
4. One measure of the extent of this intervention is the foreign currency borrowing by public authorities, which was as follows:

1971:1, 51; 2, 31; 3, 0; 4, 0
1972:1, 0; 2, 0; 3, 0; 4, 0
1973:1, 45; 2, 281; 3, 364; 4, 309
1974:1, 306; 2, 435; 3, 189; 4, 821 (including direct borrowing by central government, 644)
1975:1, 468 (including direct borrowing by central government, 423); 2, 162; 3, 43; 4, 137
1976:1, 276; 2; 582, 3, 492; 4, 441

5. W.E.G. Salter, 'Internal and external balance: the role of price and expenditure effects', *Economic Record,* **35** (August), 1959, is the classic seminal article on the significance of nontradables for the balance of payments.
6. See N. Kaldor, *Causes of the Slow Rate of Economic Growth in the United Kingdom,* Inaugural lecture (Cambridge: Cambridge University Press, 1966), for an analytical account of Kaldor's thinking on this issue.
7. R.W. Bacon and W.A. Eltis (ed.), *Britain's Economic Problems: Too Few Producers* (London: Macmillan, 1976). See also E. den Dunnen, 'Dutch economic and monetary problems in the 1970s', the next paper in this volume.
8. See S.P. Magee, 'The empirical evidence on the monetary approach to the balance of payments and exchange rates', *American Economic Review,* **66** (Papers and Proceedings), 1976.
9. J. Tobin, 'Post hoc: ergo propter hoc?', *Quarterly Journal of Economics,* **84** (May), 1970, provides two models, in the first of which monetary cycles are 'caused' by endogenous income cycles, but precede them, and in the second model monetary cycles 'cause' income cycles, but lag behind them.
10. The reader is referred to two papers by W. Godley and F. Cripps, 'Demand management and the balance of payments', *London and Cambridge Economic Bulletin,* January, 1973; and 'Demand inflation and economic policy', *London and Cambridge Economic Bulletin,* January, 1974; and a paper by R. Neild, 'The case for a change in financial policy: mid-1977', *London and Cambridge Economic Bulletin,* July, 1974; and S. Bispham, 'New Cambridge and monetarist criticism', *National Institute Economic Review,* No. 67, 1975.
11. See P.J.N. Sinclair and R.G. Smethurst, 'Demand management', in D.J. Morris (ed.), *The Economic System in the United Kingdom* (Oxford: Oxford University Press, 1977).
12. See S.P. Magee, 'U.S. import prices in the currency contract period',

Brookings Papers on Economic Activity, **5** (1) 1974, is a pioneering study of this issue.

13.   The model is constructed specifically for a small country unable to influence the level of foreign currency prices for the goods in which it trades. This assumption may be a little restrictive for Britain, but repealing it does not create a presumption that the J curve is likelier to exist. Depreciation of the currency, in a simple elasticity model, leads to an improvement in the terms of trade if the product of the supply elasticities is larger, and to a worsening if it is smaller. The small country assumption ensures that devaluation has no permanent effect on the terms of trade, which alter in the short run only when devaluation is unexpected, deliveries lagged, and θ and π are unequal. It is the possibility of a temporary adverse effect on terms of trade which can give rise to the downward-sloping tail of the J. If the small country assumption is relaxed, however, the possibility of a long-run perverse response of the trade balance to devaluation does arise, although econometric evidence casts doubt on this as a serious possibility.

14.   See J.S. Fleming, *Inflation* (Oxford: Oxford University Press, 1976), who introduces the important concept of expectation gears.

15.   This is the central concept in purchasing power parity theories of exchange rates. See L.H. Officer, 'The purchasing power parity theory of exchange rates: a review article', International Monetary Fund, *Staff Papers,* **23** (March) 1976.

Dutch Economic and Monetary Problems in the 1970s

Emile den Dunnen

1. Introduction

In the early 1970s, after a protracted period of excess demand, the Dutch economy moved fairly abruptly towards a level of demand which was insufficient to meet employment objectives. This was partly due to a shift in the state of public finance. The main cause, however, was a gradual process of profit erosion, due to increases in unit labour costs, encouraging at first a shift towards capital intensity and hence a high rate of investment, but ultimately resulting in stagnation of investment.

In spite of the deficiency of (investment) demand and the reduction in employment, aggravated by the 1974–75 depression, inflation accelerated. In the first half of the 1970s, wages gross of tax rose under the stimulus of increases in the 'collective burden' (i.e. taxation and social insurance contributions) by about 14 per cent compared to about 9 per cent for prices. Profits dropped to such a low level as to impair fundamentally the propensity to invest. Coupled with this was a critical deterioration in international competitiveness, which would have manifested itself in a worsening of the balance of payments but for the considerable increases in income accruing from sales of natural gas that sustained the already large current account surplus.

These tendencies resulted in a growing consensus on the need for recovery of industrial profits in order to provide for a growth rate sufficient to ensure full employment as well as a simultaneous increase in income from employment and higher social security benefits. To secure such objectives it is necessary to accept a rate of growth in wages which in contrast to earlier experience, does not exceed increases in productivity. In addition, the rate of inflation must be reduced in order to protect, and possibly improve, the competitive position of the country. Both ends would be furthered by a reduction in the collective burden, directly to help industry and more generally to curb the rise in costs and prices. Raising consumer and public expenditure—the usual remedy for a cyclical drop in investment—should be adminstered with caution. Because of the decline in profits and investment, there is not much excess capacity which means that excess demand and faster inflation may be expected to ensue.

Yet the political climate in the Netherlands is not conducive to a reduction in the collective burden. Indeed, if spending is not cut back sharply, public outlays—and hence the collective burden—will increase even faster than before. Increasing the government's borrowing requirement, as a substitute for increases in the collective burden, is not possible either as there is little room for doing so. Granted these constraints, no rapid recovery can be expected.

Monetary policy, which in the 1960s was heavily relied upon to combat excess demand, in the present circumstances can play only a modest role. This role consists of preventing any inflationary impetus from emanating autonomously from the monetary sphere, as this would impede the anti-inflationary incomes policy. Such a task is not easy. Monetary control is hampered by large surpluses on current account, the continuation of which is—temporarily—accepted because they are largely due to the natural gas proceeds, which in a few years are bound to decline. Furthermore, the sluggish economy makes it difficult to use the instrument of credit control. Both factors contributed towards a sharp growth in the money supply in 1973–75.

In what follows a description of some of the characteristics of the Dutch economy and policy will be presented together with an outline of the origins of the current economic situation, so as to obtain greater insight into the economic and monetary problems envisaged for the next few years.

2. Characteristics of Dutch Economy and Policy

An important feature of the Dutch economy is its great openness. Imports and exports of goods and services each amount to around 55 per cent of GNP. This implies great sensitivity to economic developments abroad and heavy dependence on international competitiveness. Of primary importance are developments in Germany since the latter accounts for one-third of Dutch foreign trade.

This openness is reflected in a strong preference for fixed exchange rates, and the consequent need for discipline in domestic economic policy. To support a policy, quantitative targets have been devised. Externally, the Netherlands seeks to achieve an underlying annual current surplus of about 1 per cent of net national income (NNI), corresponding to the amount of development aid on capital account, while balance is sought in other capital flows.

In order to achieve the external objective under conditions of balanced economic growth, the 'collective sector' (i.e. the public sector plus social insurance) should gear its basic borrowing requirement[1] to the private sector's savings surplus. In calculating the basic borrowing requirement, the impact of fiscal measures taken to offset temporary, cyclical, disturbances to the private sector is not taken into account. From the early 1960s to the mid-1970s, because of structural changes in the private sector, the basic borrowing requirement varied between 3 and 4 per cent of NNI; more recently it has been 4 per cent.

Public finance also plays a part in keeping capital movements in balance. Net inflows or outflows, in principle, lead to offsetting reductions or increases in long-term borrowing by the central government. The extent to which this happens depends partly on monetary considerations; the public sector's financing behaviour (i.e. the extent to which its borrowing requirement is financed long or short) is used as a monetary instrument.

The success of monetary policy, which is aimed at keeping the value of the guilder as stable as possible, greatly depends on the outcome of net current external transactions and on the sensitivity of international financial flows to the relative movements in domestic and foreign rates of interest. Deviations from external equilibrium in a small, open economy like the Netherlands, soon have a relatively large impact. Therefore, with fixed exchange rates, it is almost impossible to conduct a monetary policy that is at variance with monetary policies pursued in other countries. This dependence has hardly diminished by participation in the European exchange rate arrangement—the so called 'snake'—which for the small countries means a situation of fixed exchange rates. The extent to which their currencies float against those of non-snake countries is, in practice, determined by the movement of the Deutsche mark, a feature which increases the dependence of the Dutch economy on Germany.

Another characteristic of the Dutch economy is the fast rate at which the collective sector expanded: from 35 per cent of NNI in the early 1960s to 55 per cent in 1975. This growth is nearly exclusively in transfers and social insurance benefits; economic activity continues to take place predominantly in the private sector, by private enterprises. Meanwhile, because of the passing-on mechanism, the fast rate of growth of the collective burden means a significant increase in industrial costs, as the rapidly increasing tendency towards income equilization has resulted in additional increases in statutory minimum incomes, and hence in extra burdens particularly for industries employing a large proportion of unskilled labour.

In the early 1960s, fairly substantial natural gas reserves were discovered in the north of the country. Exploited and subsequently sold at home and abroad, the contribution of natural gas to the domestic energy balance amounted in 1973—before the oil price explosion—to about F1.4 billion (or $2\frac{1}{2}$ per cent of NNI). In 1975, with the rise in prices, in terms of oil equivalent not yet fully passed on, this had gone up to F1.11 billion (or 6 per cent of NNI). However, if the current rate of extraction continues, the natural gas

Table 1(a). Industrial production and real income (averages of annual percentage rates of increase).

	1955–60	1961–63	1964–70	1971–73	1974–75	
1. Industrial production	4¾	4	6½	4½	¾	
2. Employment in industry[a]	1	1½	¾	−¼	−1	
						(−)
3. Productivity	3¾	2½	5¾	4¾	1¾	
4. Improvement in terms of trade[b]	¼	¼	–	–	−1¾	
						(+)
5. Real income* (3+4)	4	2¾	5¾	4¾	–	
6. Inroads on profits*[c]	–	2¾	¾	¾	3¼	
						(+)
7. Real wages and salaries* (5+6)	4	5½	6½	5½	3¼	
8. Increase in collective burden[d]	1¼	1	2	3	3	
						(−)
9. Real disposable wages and salaries (7+8)	2¾	4½	4½	2½	¼	
(of the typical employee)*[e]	(3)	(4¼)	(5)	(2¼)	(1¾)	
Industrial fixed investment (net)	8	4	9	1½	−4	

*Per worker, i.e. employees plus self-employed.
(*a*) Including self-employed.
(*b*) As percentage of industrial production.
(*c*) The extent to which increases in labour costs cause profits to grow slower than real income (line 5).
(*d*) Taxes and social insurance contributions; including the central government's share in natural gas proceeds. As percentage of the private sector's share in NNI. The decline of this share is reflected in the rise of the collective burden after 1963; as percentage of NNI the collective burden rose at a fairly constant rate of 1½ points per annum.
(*e*) That is a married man with two children and an income just below the lowest of the earnings ceilings in force for the various types of social insurance (in 1975: Fl.23,400). The fairly large difference between the two incomes mentioned under item 9 shown for 1974–75 is due partly to the equalization of incomes policy conducted in these years.

reserves are estimated to become exhausted in 15 to 20 years, and a decline in their economic significance is expected after 1978.

3. Economic Developments before 1976

BACKGROUND TO THE DEFICIENCY OF DEMAND

The deficiency of demand since 1972 can be partly related to saturation in demand for house-building for the first time since the Second World War. In addition, the basic borrowing requirement of the public sector temporarily dropped below its target as a result of attempts to reduce the excessive borrowing requirements of the 1960s. At the same time, industrial fixed investment slowed down in response to the gradual process of declining profits. This slowdown highlighted the strong causal link between (cost) inflation, erosion of profits, erosion of investment activity, and increase in unemployment: a sequence that had remained concealed for a long time.

Profit erosion began in the period 1961–63 when the guilder was revalued by 5 per cent, the five-day week was introduced with no loss of pay, and a wage explosion (at the end of 1963) had to be absorbed. Thanks to a very strong profit position at the outset, such tendencies could be met without great deterioration of the already strong external position. But, together with an increasing level of demand and an overstrained labour market, they gave rise to a steadily increasing cost inflation in that real wages rose faster than productivity (table 1(a)). Price increases were, however, thought desirable in moderating excess demand[2].

However, since 1964 the steady decline in profits caused employment in the private sector to increase less rapidly in relation to growth in input and investment than previously, and after 1971 an absolute decline set in[3]. The rate of replacement of existing capital increased in an attempt to take advantage of labour saving. This led initially to an accelerated rise in productivity, but gradually, as the economic life of existing machinery and equipment had to be shortened further, the gains to be had from such substitution diminished. This meant that in a growing number of cases it became more advantageous to cease production, and thus employment became more seriously affected.

The growing inability to protect profitability, resulting in a decline in profit expectations, inevitably reduced the propensity to invest, as did increasing inflation with its adverse effects on corporate finance.

The results of the process outlined above did not become apparent until later. A large shortage of labour at the beginning of the 1960s caused the unemployment figures to remain low, as did the policy, started in the late 1960s, of gradually raising the school-leaving age, and a rapid rise in the number of persons entitled to benefits under the Incapacity to Work

Insurance Act (WAO) introduced in 1967. Both factors held the increase in labour supply down. Only when the Dutch economy appeared hardly to participate in the international boom of 1973 and unemployment did not fall from the cyclically high level of 3 per cent reached in 1972, did concern arise. By then economic growth had already slowed down. In 1974 and 1975 there were further adverse effects on profitability from the depression and the post-oil crisis policy of maintaining domestic demand, resulting as it did in profits bearing the deterioration in terms of trade. A critically low level of profitability was reached. The Central Planning Bureau estimated that if the existing trends and policies were to continue, the structural element in unemployment, which amounted to $1-1\frac{1}{2}$ per cent of the working population in 1975, would rise to 4 per cent by 1980. Even in the absence of cyclical unemployment, the overal figure is, of course, higher since frictional and other unemployment of some 2 per cent must also be taken into account. Apart from some cyclical recovery, the growth rate of GNP would drop to a bare 3 per cent per annum, and that of investment to 1 per cent.

INFLATION

The faster growth in productivity, caused by the accelerated replacement of machinery and equipment in the second half of the 1960s, led to a considerable increase in prosperity. Attention became increasingly focused on improving the economic position of the non-working section of the population, and this was reflected in a rapidly increasing collective burden (table 1(b)). This trend continued until, at the beginning of the 1970s, economic growth declined. The consequent reduction in room for improvement of real disposable wages led to (successful) attempts to pass the collective burden on to profits. The rate of inflation, which had already risen, was thus given further impetus.

The inflationary process in the Netherlands has gradually taken a strongly autonomous character. This began in 1969 with the introduction of a retroactive wage adjustment on the basis of price trends. Ironically, this adjustment was intended as a non-recurrent measure to break the inflationary spiral in that year. Indexation, which now takes place twice a year, focused more attention on the development of real wages and, in its wake, on real disposable wages. The latter also became important politically. Greater concern for the lowest income groups led to statutory minimum wages for adults, those for young persons under the age of 23 being increased over and above average wages. As these extra increases were not taken into account in wage negotiations, they pushed up costs and inflation further. The effect of statutory minimum pay increases on social security benefits, which are largely linked to minimum wages, reinforced the inflationary process via a rise in the collective burden.

Table 1(b). Supplementary economic indicators (averages of annual figures).

	1955–60	1961–63	1964–70	1971–73	1974–75
Percentage rate of increase					
1. Wage and salary bill per industrial employee	$7\frac{1}{4}$	$7\frac{1}{2}$	$11\frac{1}{2}$	$13\frac{3}{4}$	$14\frac{1}{4}$
2. Consumer prices	$2\frac{1}{2}$	3	$4\frac{1}{2}$	$8\frac{1}{2}$	10
3. National income implicit price deflator	$3\frac{1}{2}$	$3\frac{1}{2}$	$5\frac{3}{4}$	$8\frac{1}{2}$	$11\frac{1}{4}$
Ratios					
4. Unemployment (as percentage of total labour force)	2	1	$1\frac{1}{2}$	$2\frac{1}{2}$	$4\frac{1}{4}$
5. Collective burden (as percentage of NNI)	$32\frac{1}{2}$	$35\frac{1}{2}$	41	$47\frac{1}{2}$	$51\frac{1}{2}$

Source: Central Planning Bureau, Central Economic Plan 1975 and 1976.

Figure 1. Corporate financing as a percentage of NNI.

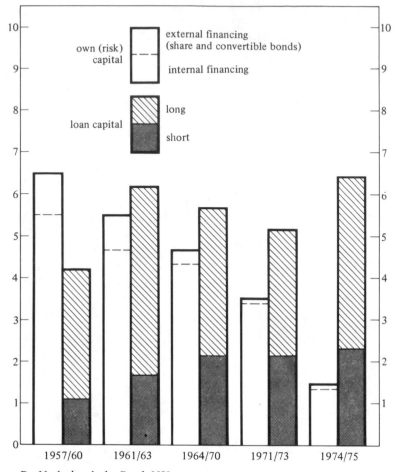

Source: *De Nederlandsche Bank NV.*

As inflation accelerated, in addition to the burden of increasing wage costs, industry was faced with the need to make ever greater upvaluations of invested capital and back-up services, and also to maintain the real value of pensions and other retirement benefits. This increased the inflationary pressure and, because of the limited scope for raising prices, led above all to additional pressure on profitability. As a result, the possibilities for internal financing dwindled further and with them the ability to attract equity capital. The loan capital component in the structure of financing became increasing large and this, in turn, reduced creditworthiness. In 1974–75, this trend accelerated so strongly (figure 1) that in September 1975 the government launched a scheme under which industry could acquire subordinated loans with a state guarantee for the repayment of the principal.

INTERNATIONAL COMPETITIVENESS

Price policies, which traditionally have been directed at reducing inflation, make it difficult to pass costs on fully in prices. International competition is another, and perhaps more significant, reason for being unable to do so. According to the Central Planning Bureau, prices of foreign competitors have in the past risen far less rapidly than the costs of Dutch exports. In 1970–75 the appreciation of the guilder (about 3½ per cent per year on average) was a further contributive factor.

In the past it was often possible to continue trading and to maintain or even enlarge the share of foreign markets by narrowing profit margins. Given the present level of profitability, the Central Planning Bureau now feels there is very little room left for doing so any longer. Thus, if Dutch production costs continue to rise more rapidly than those of competitors, the external position of the country will soon be adversely affected[4].

The unabatingly high inflationary trend in 1974 and 1975 may well have affected the external position. If so, this has been concealed by the rapidly increasing contribution of natural gas to the current account of the balance of payments. Proceeds from gas exports alone went up from F1.1½ billion (1 per cent of NNI) in 1973 to F1.4 billion (over 2 per cent of NNI) in 1975. Thus the surplus on current account, albeit probably adversely affected by the depression, continued to be greater than 2 per cent of NNI.

THE MID-1970s

As early as 1973, the decline in profitability already had far greater repercussions on employment than in other countries (table 2). As the gravity of

Table 2. Percentage unemployment in a number of countries[a].

| | Average | | | Increase on 1962–72 | |
	1962–72	1973	1975	1973	1975
Germany	1.0	1.3	4.2	30	320
France	1.7	2.1	3.8	24	124
United Kingdom	2.3	2.6	4.0	13	74
United States	4.7	4.9	8.6	4	83
Netherlands	1.1	2.4	4.7	118	327
WAO benefit recipients[b]	(4.6)[c]	(6.2)	(7.4)		

(a) Various sources. Because of differences in concept the ratios for the various countries are difficult to compare.
(b) Number of recipients under the Incapacity for Work Insurance Act (WAO), as a percentage of the working population.
(c) Average for 1967–72.

this trend was realized, attention focused more sharply on the need to restrict the rise in costs. However, efforts in this direction in recent years have been unsuccessful. Despite temporary reduction, the collective burden continued to grow. In addition to social security benefits, real disposable wages went up, especially in the lower, specially favoured categories. Under these conditions, the worsening in terms of trade due to oil price rises, and the decline in production associated with the depression, had to be entirely absorbed by profits. Consequently, profitability dropped to a level which made it highly unlikely that the Netherlands would be able to participate in the international economic recovery[5]. Hence in the first half of 1976, the government determined that in principle no wage increases should be allowed other than the indexations already agreed. The burden of taxes and social insurance contributions was stabilized, but further fiscal reliefs for industry were not introduced.

It has now become apparent that, in addition to restraints on cost increases to stem the accelerating replacement of existing machinery and equipment, there is also a need, at least at present, for additional incentives to encourage the revival of industrial investment. It is essential that such measures form part of a comprehensive, medium-term strategy, about which there is social agreement. Only then will entrepreneurs be confident that, unlike previously, resolutions to improve profitability will be realized. In outlining such a strategy, problems of distribution, inflation and exchange play a vital role.

4. Economic Problems

DISTRIBUTION OF REAL INCOME

In the 1960s excessive competing claims on real national income were perceived as a cause of excess demand and inflation. The 1970s have made it clear that, if in their urge to eat out of the national pots, wages and social security benefits leave insufficient food for profits, these will in due course become undernourished and cause a deficiency of demand and an even higher rate of inflation. Thus it has become imperative that social agreement be reached on how economic growth should be distributed. At the same time this has become more difficult to secure for three reasons. First, there is less to share now that the annual growth in output will be $3\frac{1}{2}$–4 per cent instead of 6 per cent. Secondly, room must be left for a recovery in profitability, i.e. for a more than proportionate share of profits in the growth of output. Thirdly, as people have become more and more accustomed to getting fairly substantial real improvements in disposable wages and social security benefits, it will be more difficult to make them accept lower, or no real improvements at all. The last point is illustrated by the so-called multiannual expenditure programme up to 1980, which had been agreed upon within the government. This programme provided for an average increase in collective outlays of 7 per cent in volume terms. On current estimated growth in income, the collective sector's share in net national income would consequently rise by 1¾ points per annum. Given a share of 55 per cent in 1975, this would mean that the collective sector would take in the full annual *increase* in NNI. In these circumstances any hope for a recovery in profits and investment would become illusory. The government has, therefore, decided to adjust its expenditure policy in such a way as to hold the annual increase in the collective burden down to 1 percentage point of NNI per annum. This still means that no more than 1½ per cent growth of income per annum remains to be divided between wages and profits in the private sector; the collective sector, on the other hand, will grow by 5½ per cent per annum (table 3). Central Planning Bureau estimates show that under these conditions, even when the annual growth of average real disposable wages is kept between 1 and 1½ per cent, only a slight recovery in profitability may be expected, and this will mean no reduction in unemployment.

Table 3. Growth in the collective and private sectors.

	As percentage of NNI			As percentage of sector
	proportionately	additional	total	
Collective sector	0.55 × 3.75 = 2.06	1.00	3.06	1/0.55 × 3.06 = 5.57
Private sector	0.45 × 3.75 = 1.69	−1.00	0.69	1/0.45 × 0.69 = 1.53
Total economy	3.75		3.75	

Additional measures are therefore needed, and the question is to what extent they could be taken at the expense of the current account surplus, which is estimated to be somewhere in the order of 3–4 per cent in the next few years. As stated earlier, the objective of Dutch policy is to obtain an average annual balance-of-payments surplus of about 1 per cent of NNI. Consequently there would seem to be room for increasing the collective sector's basic borrowing requirement by 2–3 points above the presently acceptable level of 4 per cent of NNI. Such an increase would mean that a corresponding increase in the level of expenditure or decrease in the collective burden could be met by extra borrowing.

However, such an adjustment cannot be made as the freedom of manoeuvre conveyed by the external position is largely fictitious. This is because the contribution of natural gas to the national energy account is estimated to fall by 2 per cent of NNI between 1980 and 1985. As economic prospects for this period are even worse than those for the years up to 1980, it is imperative that an external surplus be maintained to meet this reduction. Thus, the borrowing requirement of the collective sector may be increased by only 1 point at most, to 5 per cent of NNI. As the margin of 1 point-at-most has arisen from the shortfall in investment activity, which will have to be restored so as to raise employment (through recovery of profits), the measures to be taken will have to improve profits directly. Once a recovery of investment is well under way these extra stimuli may—and must—be terminated.

If the additional measures to be taken at the expense of the current account surplus do not ensure a sufficient recovery of profitability and investment, the most obvious further action, in view of the strong resistance to encroachments upon real disposable wages, would be a further restraint on the collective sector's growth rate. However, political resistance to this has been strong, despite the fact that such restraint—for the sake of the recovery of profitability—would make a higher rate of economic growth possible, and hence eventually the same level of social security benefits could be more easily attained.

INFLATION AND EXCHANGE RATE PROBLEMS

Even if agreement is reached in talks between the government and both sides of industry on how the expected growth in real income should be distributed so as to enable a sufficient recovery of profits *ex ante,* the rate of inflation (currently varying between 9 and 10 per cent on an annual basis) will have to be drastically reduced if improvement in profitability is to be realised *ex post.* This is because of trends in other countries, like in Germany, where the rate of price rises is being successfully slowed down. With wage indexation based on price increases recorded in the past, Dutch costs may easily rise faster than those of foreign competitors. And because there is at present insufficient room for raising prices, profits will be eroded.

The rate of inflation in Germany, the main trading partner, is not the only factor to be considered. The possibility that the 'snake' will appreciate against other currencies is also of importance. Such an appreciation will be to the detriment of profits, even though the dampening effect on prices will eventually lead to a slower rise in costs.

Against this background the government prohibited the 5 per cent price adjustment of wages as from July 1 1976. Instead, it authorized a Dfl.30 increase per worker, combined with some compensational reduction in the burden of social-security contributions. Together these measures provide an average increase in disposable wages of about 2½ per cent, bringing the wage and salary bill per industrial worker to about 9½ per cent above the 1975 level.

The exchange rate instrument cannot be used to tackle present inflationary problems. Revaluation in respect of snake partners would confront industry immediately with lower prices in terms of domestic currency, and hence have an impact on profits which would only be partly compensated for by smaller rises in costs. In the present precarious profit situation this means a risk the country cannot afford to take. Moreover, the strength of the external position is only temporary. For this reason also, the Netherlands has decided that, for the time being, it must go on living with a large surplus on current account.

More generally, the Netherlands is willing to accept the national policy discipline which a system of fixed exchange rates demands, and advocates the same for other countries. It feels that such a discipline is indispensable to the free international movement of trade. This is not to deny that the system of floating exchange rates of the last few years has facilitated the necessary radical adjustment of parities, which had moved out of line during the 1960s. Experience has shown, however, that even larger countries must have a national policy discipline when exchange rates are floating, since a depreciation in the rate of exchange can all too easily trigger cumulative inflationary responses. Sooner or later matters will have to be put right. The longer this is postponed, the more painful and the more drastic the operation will have to be. The Netherlands may well keep this in mind in conducting its present incomes policy.

POLICY PROPOSALS

In a number of White Papers submitted to the Dutch Parliament in June 1976, the government revealed its plans on what policy it intends to conduct in the coming years in respect of the present economic problems. These plans indicate that, in addition to the previously announced restraints on the growth rate in the collective burden (the implementation of which is elaborated in the White Papers), direct incentives will be provided for industry, amounting to 2 per cent of NNI per annum. The expected ensuing accelerated growth in NNI—up to 4 per cent per annum—would ultimately increase the flow of funds to the government by 1 per cent of NNI per annum, so that in 1980 the public authorities' basic borrowing requirement will on balance be 1 per cent larger than it would otherwise be, and amount to 5 per cent of NNI. This will bring the economy into a danger zone with respect to the maintenance of economic equilibrium. Yet the government feels the risk ought to be taken, an opinion which could be shared if there were reasonable certainty that the percentages mentioned would not be exceeded and thus bring the borrowing requirement to a level that would lead to overheating and faster inflation. On this point a few reservations seem justified.

According to calculations made by the Central Planning Bureau, the proposed financial injections into industry would be large enough to bring about a recovery in profits and investments sufficient to keep structural unemployment in 1980 at about the same level as in 1975, i.e. 1½ per cent of the working population. The calculations are, however, largely based on past experience with comparable incentives. But the character of the stimuli was different then, not linked to social *desiderata*. This time the government wants to try to localize the subsidies and burden-reducing measures in such a way as to achieve a maximum effect on employment. To reach this goal, special steering powers with regard to investment are being legislated. In addition, the government seeks to increase the influence of employees on company management by widening the powers of the existing works councils (joint consultative committees of managers and workers), and to increase labour's commitment in company performance by introducing VAD, (a retained capital gains tax to cream off 'super profits') and placing the proceeds in a fund under union management for worker benefit. Yet these factors will not encourage the propensity to invest, and thus could limit the intended stimulus to growth, while the increase in the flow of funds to the government could be less than expected.

The above mentioned 'social' policy proposals are an important condition for acceptance by the trade unions of the pressure the policy programme is to bear on wages. Average real disposable wages would increase by 1–1½ per cent per year. Allowing for the effects of promotions, etc., the possibility of increasing contractual wages would on average be virtually zero. Given the government's policy of equalization of incomes, there would be a real improvement for workers in the lowest income groups, but this would be at the cost of a drop in real income for the other groups for some years to come. This would seem to be asking a very large contribution of wages indeed, and failure to secure it will be at the expense of profitability and growth.

5. Monetary Problems

POLICY CONSTRAINTS

Traditionally monetary policy in the Netherlands has been sensitive to developments abroad. Since the 1960s it has been recognized that a restrictive policy 'becomes ineffective when, as a result of increasing financial pressures, capital starts flowing in from abroad, or when, as a result of a reduction in domestic expenditure, a surplus arises on the balance of payments current account'[6]. Now that a large surplus on current account has been accepted as being for a number of years inevitable, and no implications are desired for the exchange rate of the guilder, there is a need for capital outflow, the more so as the position of the guilder in the snake is stronger. Direct restrictions on external capital transactions, however, can be imposed only to a limited extent because of the advanced liberalization of capital movements which the Netherlands is reluctant to relinquish. At present the

Netherlands employs chiefly two instruments in this field: (1) there is limited approval of loans taken up abroad for domestic purposes and (2) non-residents have been permitted access to the Dutch capital market. The impact of the latter instrument, as well as the net outcome of non-restricted capital flows, depends greatly on relative movements in interest rates at home and abroad and on national and international expectations of the prospective movement in the guilder rate. As long as exchange rate expectations do not result in an outflow of capital, the Netherlands will have to take particular care—in the 1970s even more so than before—not to cause interest rates at home to move up faster than those abroad. At times when monetary policies elsewhere, notably in Germany, move in an opposite direction, a restrictive policy in the Netherlands is bound to be unsuccessful.

The domestic situation also imposes constraints on monetary policy. It will be hard to introduce severe measures of credit control without causing heavier pressure on investment and greater unemployment. Also, because of its uneven impact on industry (apt to produce inequities to the detriment of the small and weak enterprises), credit control should preferably not be imposed unless as a last resort and hence only when the other important policy medium—i.e. the public sector's financing behaviour—proves to be unsuccessful.

THE PUBLIC SECTOR'S FINANCING BEHAVIOUR

The financing behaviour of the public sector comes under the responsibility of the Minister of Finance, whereas credit policy chiefly falls under the responsibility of the Bank of Netherlands. The two authorities keep close contact on the policy to be conducted, not only as regards the coordination of implementation, but also as regards the basic principles. The common objective is to control the national liquidity ratio, that is the ratio between the money supply[7] and national income. This objective is pursued by influencing domestic money creation by both public authorities and banks.

As for the financing behaviour of the public sector, policy is based on two principles; one relating to the criteria for the management of the public sector's own income and expenditure, the other to the central government's borrowing on the capital market. With regard to the former, there is agreement by the authorities that the public sector should manage its income and expenditure in such a way that, averaged over a longer period, it will not be necessary to resort to financing by money creation, except for a small amount to meet local authority needs. This principle accords with the more general principle of policy, mentioned earlier, that the public sector's basic borrowing requirement should match the private sector's savings surplus. If so, the borrowing requirement could always be fully met in the capital market, and thus there would be no risk of public finance exerting inflationary pressures through money creation.

However, for reasons of monetary policy this rule may be departed from, notably in the event of cyclical or secular disturbances of economic equilibrium, or in the case of disequilibrating capital flows. For example, in an overheated economy it will normally be desirable to engage in long-term borrowing in excess of central government's basic borrowing requirement in order to strengthen monetary policy. On the other hand, a borrowing requirement that has been enlarged by cyclical or secular recovery measures should preferably be financed entirely in the capital market if it is accompanied by a surplus on the balance of payments current account (i.e. a surplus of national savings). Financing by money creation would then lead only to unnecessary and undesirable monetary expansion, the more so if no credit control is possible. Disequilibrating capital flows, whether autonomous or induced (such as the desired outflow of capital in the 1970s) may inhibit the government from making the best possible use of capital available in the home market.

MONETARY EXPERIENCE 1972–75

The period 1972–75 illustrates the difficulties to be encountered in conducting monetary policy when a deficiency of demand is combined with a surplus on current account, while the national currency is highly valued internationally. This has almost continually been the case with the guilder (except for (chiefly) some speculative activity around the turn of 1973 caused by the oil crisis). In addition, experience in this period, particularly in the summer of 1974, shows that a high rate of inflation and strong inflationary expectations give rise to a desire for shorter maturities and indexation. Should such loans become a permanent feature of the financial system, this would greatly blur the distinction between short-term financial assets that are relevant for purposes of the Dutch monetary analysis and those that are not, and thus would deprive monetary policy of its analytical base.

At the beginning of the period in question, money was not very easy in the Netherlands. The restrictions imposed during 1969–71—years of excess demand—had caused the liquidity ratio to drop from $36\frac{1}{4}$ to $33\frac{1}{2}$ per cent. However, in view of the high rate of inflation already prevailing, prevention of monetary expansion was considered desirable. In 1972 and 1973, the first two years of the period, the restrictions applied to stem the inflow of capital dated partly from 1971 when uncertainties about the value of currencies often were extremely great owing to the drastic currency realignments at the time. In addition to the regulation prohibiting any net acquisition of guilder-denominated bonds by non-residents, a whole range of measures was adopted, for varying lengths of time, to ward off speculative inflows of foreign money generated by anticipations of appreciation of the guilder. On balance, some outflow of capital could be maintained, which quickly strengthened when the international boom and the resulting upward movement in interest rates began to lead to substantial purchases by residents of foreign bonds and shares. However, because the Dutch economy did not share in the international boom, the surplus on current account widened at the same time, and the influx of liquidity from abroad (the overall surplus on the balance of payments derived from the monetary statistics) remained substantial (table 4).

Table 4. Balance of payments and monetary data (amounts in millions of guilders).

	1972	1973	1974	1975
(1) Balance on current account (transactions basis)	4.150	6.400	5.500	4.150
(2) Capital market transactions	−1.350	−3.100	−1.350	−1.300
(3) Other capital transactions and miscellaneous	400	−950	−850	1.050
(4) Balance of payments surplus[a] (1 to 3)	3.200	2.350	3.300	3.900
(5) Money creation on behalf of public sector	−3.400	−1.400	−1.050	2.150
(6) Money created by banks[b]	5.150	9.350	9.200	−2.150
(7) Changes in the money supply (4 to 6)	4.950	10.300	11.450	3.900
(8) National liquidity ratio[c] at end of period	$32\frac{3}{4}$	$35\frac{1}{2}$	$38\frac{1}{2}$	$37\frac{1}{4}$

(a) As recorded in the monetary statistics. These figures sometimes differ substantially from those recorded in the balance of payments statistics.
(b) Short-term lending to the private sector, net long-term operations of the money-creating institutions, and miscellaneous.
(c) The ratio of M_2 (Dutch concept) to NNI.

Source: De Nederlandsche Bank NV.

In these years, the public authorities themselves contributed to the deficiency of demand (witness the small borrowing requirement of less than half the size that would have been consistent with the underlying trend of the economy). In contrast, their borrowing on the insulated bond market was heavy, particularly in 1972. Thus liquidity was absorbed to such an extent as to largely offset the inflow of liquidity from abroad. Bank lending, which in the light of slackening investment activity had been freed from the restrictions imposed in 1969–71, did not expand very much in 1972, causing the liquidity ratio to drop a littler further, to 32¾ per cent. Thereafter, however, credit expansion began to increase quickly. This was partly due to special factors caused by sharply increasing money market rates—in line with the movement in international rates—with bank rates initially lagging behind. This led to the re-intermediation of short-term lending by non-banks and to a 'merry-go-round', i.e. overdrafts being used for investment in time deposits which carried higher rates of interest. In addition, demand for credit was stimulated by very sharp, but presumably partly temporary, volume and price increases in stocks. Against this background, and also with a view to the weak economic situation, the Bank of Netherlands did not restrain bank lending. In consultation with the banks it did introduce, in the summer of 1973, a liquidity requirement, but this was applied in such a way as not to restrict lending.

The uncertain prospects, temporarily caused by the oil crisis of late 1973 and early 1974, were a reason for continuing to be cautious. However, when the rate of credit expansion continued to increase, the Bank of Netherlands, in the summer of 1974, took a first step towards using the liquidity requirement as a restriction on lending. Only because of the unexpectedly fast emerging depression was this initial step not followed by a real restriction in the autumn.

Meanwhile, partly because of renewed sales of guilder bonds to non-residents after some restrictions on capital inflow had been removed at the end of 1973 and in early 1974, the net outflow of capital abated. Initially these sales were primarily due to an international overvaluation of the guilder when, after the oil crisis, the Netherlands appeared to have large gas reserves and therefore could count on a corresponding surplus on current account. Later the sharp decline in international interest rates generated by the depression, followed, but only after some lag by Dutch interest rates, provided an additional incentive. The balance-of-payments surpluses widened and the guilder moved almost continually at the top of the snake. In this situation the central government's capital market policy had to be directed first of all to maintaining interest rates at such a level that capital outflows would not be hampered and inflows not encouraged. Money market policy aimed to keep short-term rates at home to a level conducive to absorption of the balance-of-payments surplus by increases in banks' net foreign assets. This reduced the risk of speculative inflows of capital being generated by a strong growth in official reserves.

Because demand management policies had been directed initially at preserving domestic demand, and later at countering the depression, public finance showed a rapidly growing borrowing requirement which, because of the necessary constraints on capital market borrowing, ultimately had to be financed by substantial money creation. One cause for resorting to such means of financing was the rather long time it took for central government to widen the scope of its borrowing by entering the private placings market, which makes up about three-quarters of the capital market. It finally did so early in 1976.

Also during this period judgement of monetary trends had been greatly obscured by sizable shifts of savings between savings deposits, which are not counted among the money supply, and time deposits, which are. These shifts were prompted by the abnormal interest rate differentials, mentioned earlier. Another distorting element was that the full effect of the sharp import price increases in 1973 and 1974 was recorded only with a lag in the national liquidity ratio's denominator, i.e. the net national income. When, by the end of 1975, these factors had been more or less reversed or had ceased to operate, the liquidity ratio appeared to have gone up by $4\frac{1}{2}$ points compared with end 1972, to $37\frac{1}{4}$ per cent. A cyclical increase in the liquidity preference might have contributed to this rise, but this did not mean that, with economic recovery gradually gathering pace, the liquidity ratio would go down spontaneously. Considering the gravity of the persisting inflation, however, such a drop was certainly desirable.

AT THE 'BIT OF AN UPTURN'

Developments in the last few years have shown that 'block' floating, like the 'snake' since March 1973, renders the monetary policy of a non-dominating partner, such as the Netherlands, generally less vulnerable to speculative inflows of capital, but not to flows directed specifically at such country's own currency. Moreover, dependence on economic developments and the monetary policy of a major partner, like Germany, has become greater. Both factors contributed to the monetary ease in 1974 and 1975. More recently external conditions would seem to have become more favourable to the conduct of a restrictive monetary policy.

In the spring of 1976 the international valuation of the guilder seems to have been reversed. This may have been occasioned by the consultations held between the 'snake' partners, early in March, on a reform of their cross parities; talks which ultimately resulted in the French franc abandoning the snake. During these consultations it became clear that if the Deutsche mark were to be revalued, the guilder would not follow suit. Next, the rate of inflation in the Netherlands proved to be faster than in Germany, and a reversal of this trend appeared doubtful. These factors may have contributed towards the guilder moving at the bottom of the snake in the second half of March 1976 and staying there notwithstanding the relatively sharp rise in domestic interest rates in May–June. If this situation were to continue, an important constraint on capital market borrowing by central government would have to come to an end.

How much need there is for increasing long-term government borrowing may be evident from the behaviour of the public sector's borrowing requirement in 1976 when compared to that of 1975. A continued, strongly expansionary economic policy, and the impact of the 1975 depression on 1976 tax receipts are the two major causes of this growth. In the first half of 1976 long-term borrowing did not increase nearly as fast as the growth in borrowing requirement, as it was still dominated by caution in view of the guilder's position in the snake. For 1976 as a whole avoidance of financing by money creation by the public sector has thus become an illusion; it is to be hoped that this kind of financing will not become too large. Thus, in contrast to experience after previous recessions, public finance will in this upturn not lead to any tightening of the currently very great monetary ease.

Bank lending to the private sector, which in 1975 had expanded by only 6 per cent due to the depression and to funding of short-term debt, increased in the first few months of 1976 at an annual rate of over 20 per cent. This contributed to a further increase in the liquidity held by the non-bank public. In view of these developments, the Bank of Netherlands took a first step towards what might, if necessary, become a restrictive credit policy, by reducing the banks' margin of free liquid reserves. This action would seem to indicate that the Bank of Netherlands—despite a low level of investment—will impose credit restrictions if the liquidity ratio remains high even in a period of strengthening economic activity.

How concerned the Bank of Netherlands is about the present and future monetary situation is evidenced by the following quotation from its 1975 annual report[8]:

> [The Bank] will have to keep a close watch on the national liquidity ratio and if necessary influence it in such a way as to avoid any autonomous inflationary impetus from the monetary sphere. The available range of policy instruments will be applied if need arises. In this context a question which merits special attention is whether the borrowing requirement of the public sector will in time return to its normal basic level, thus eliminating the need for financing by money creation, which is not entirely avoidable in the present circumstances.

The Bank's implicit concern about the trend in public finance also, and especially, after 1976 is not without cause, as was indicated in the previous section. There is a serious danger that this sector's borrowing requirement will remain larger than is compatible with the maintenance of economic equilibrium and with the avoidance of financing by money creation.

NOTES

1. The difference between the underlying trend in expenditure and current receipts.
2. A government proposal to curtail severely increases in real wages in 1973 was considered unwarranted by the Social and Economic Council's Commission of Economic Experts because it was feared that this would result in too favourable a competitive position, thereby leading to a renewed overheating.
3. Cf. H. den Hartog and H.S. Tjan, 'Investments, wages, prices and demand for

Labour', *De Economist,* (1/2) 1976. The conclusions reached by these authors from a clay–clay vintage model describing the production of the Dutch private sector lend support to what follows.

4.   Central Economic Plan 1976, pp. 98–9.

5.   The Central Planning Board calculated roughly that for the Dutch industry as a whole net return on own capital has become rather negative.

6.   Bank of Netherlands, *Annual Report,* 1965, p. 17.

7.   The Netherlands' concept of money supply (or stock) is an M_2 concept. The main difference from most other M_2 concepts lies in the fact that short-term claims on the central government and the local authorities are included, whereas only a small proportion—a calculated 'liquid' part—of savings deposits at credit institutions and savings banks is taken into account. The national liquidity ratio as an object of monetary policy is more extensively dealt with in my article 'Monetary policy in the Netherlands', in Karel Holbik (ed.), *Monetary Policy in Twelve Industrial Countries* (Boston: Federal Reserve Bank of Boston, 1973). Also available as No. 5 of the Reprint Series of the Bank of Netherlands.

8.   Bank of Netherlands, *Annual Report,* 1975, 'General survey', penultimate paragraph.

Monetary Policy and Economic Activity in France[1]

Jean-Claude Chouraqui

1. Introduction

The aim of this paper is to examine the role of monetary policy in short-term demand management in France during the first half of the 1970s. To this end I begin by providing an account of the economic context within which monetary policy has been deployed and of the way in which such policy has been combined with other tools of short-term management. The use of instruments of policy for the attainment of specific objectives is then considered and the conclusions drawn contrasted with earlier findings.

2. A Broad Description of Experience

THE ECONOMIC CONTEXT

In line with experience during the 1960s the French economy continued to enjoy a high and steady rate of growth until 1974. As figure 1 reveals, the average annual rate of increase in GDP in the early 1970s was in the region of 5.8 per cent per annum and, as such, in accord with the growth in productive potential. Furthermore, owing to sustained investment expenditure and the competitive advantage provided by the August 1969 devaluation of the French franc (which made it possible to avoid the slowdown in world economic activity in 1971–72) cyclical deviations from this trend were small. A continuance of earlier trends was, however, observed in the case of labour markets where structural imbalances sustained the slow rise in unemployment begun in the mid-1960s, while prices continued to rise at a relatively high rate compared to that recorded in other European countries.

After 1973 a sharp break from trend occurred. The rate of growth of GDP slowed down considerably to 3.9 per cent in 1974 and became negative in 1975. This sharp fall in economic expansion was accompanied by a serious

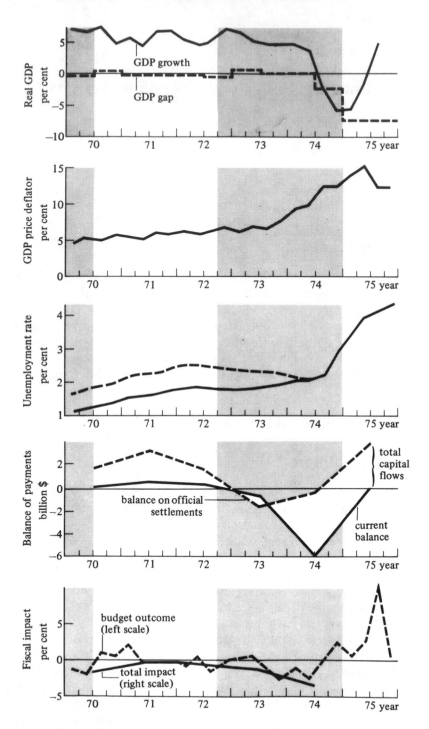

worsening of the labour market. The rapid rise in unemployment induced an increase in precautionary savings, thus depressing consumption by households, while the deterioration in the financial position of firms led them to revise their investment plans downwards. Such tendencies did, of course, contribute to a more moderate rate of inflation than may have been experienced otherwise, and also helped to improve the current account of the balance of payments after the large 1974 deficit that followed the increase in oil prices[2].

SHORT-TERM DEMAND MANAGEMENT

Three distinct phases of monetary policy can be distinguished for the years 1970–75. On the basis of measures announced by the monetary authorities and intentions expressed by them with regard to conduct of policy, the 1970s began with a relatively easy monetary environment, followed by a restrictive phase and then monetary expansion. In particular

(1) from mid-1970 until nearly the end of 1972 monetary policy responded to the expansion in economic activity in an accommodating fashion;

(2) from late 1972 to end 1974 a restrictive stance was adopted in an attempt to curb inflationary pressures and, since late 1973, the deterioration in the current account of the balance of payments;

(3) an expansionary policy has been applied since early 1975 with the aim of stimulating economic activity.

Figure 1. Indicators of economic trends and economic policy.
Key Source: INSEE and OECD.
- *(a) GDP growth (seasonally adjusted) is expressed as percentage change over previous quarter at annual rate.*
- *(b) GDP gap is the difference between actual and potential GDP. Potential output data have been derived from production functions estimated by the OECD Secretariat.*
- *(c) Movements in GDP price deflator are shown as change over the corresponding quarter of the previous year.*
- *(d) The dotted line in the third panel represents the unemployment rate adjusted for the progressive implementation of the Agence Nationale de l'Emploi created in 1968.*
- *(e) Indicators of fiscal impact are expressed in terms of ratios to GDP. Budget outcome refers to seasonally adjusted figures of the government budget actual surplus or deficit (three quarter moving average). Budget deficit is + in the figure. Total fiscal impact has been estimated by the OECD Secretariat by using the Bent-Hansen method.*
- *(f) Shaded areas indicate phases of restrictive monetary policy as described in the text.*

Over the same interval fiscal policy operated in a similar direction. In the first subperiod an expansionary balanced-budget policy was implemented. The fiscal impact became neutral in 1973 while the effects of a distinctly deflationary budget in 1974 were partly delayed until 1975. Finally the monetary ease of 1975 was paralleled by a large deficit in the central government budget.

Yet, as in some other countries, monetary and fiscal policies were not thought sufficient to deal with certain aspects of the overall economic situation. Thus monetary and fiscal actions were supplemented by a system of *price programming* impinging on various sectors of the economy.

3. The Conduct of Monetary Policy

Monetary policy was *formulated* (as is to be expected) in the light of general economic and social objectives and *expressed* in terms of specific monetary targets.

GOALS

In 1970–72 the government's main concern was to maintain a high level of employment. Hence, despite anxiety caused by the persistence of inflationary pressures, monetary policy remained easy. The fight against inflation and the restoration of current account balance were, however, the primary objectives in the next two years. With regard to inflation, the specific aim was to reduce the rate of increase in prices to a level comparable to that of France's main trading partners. For external balance a reduction in imports and a stimulus to exports was sought by moderating domestic demand. The emphasis on combating inflation and correcting the current account position was reinforced by the oil crisis. But from 1975 onwards the rise in unemployment, caused by the deepening of recession, led to a gradual change in priorities leading first to ease and subsequently to more actively expansionary policies. In so doing, however, due regard was paid to the need to restructure the productive sector in the light of the change in relative prices resulting from oil price increases.

TARGETS

In pursuing these objectives, attention focused primarily on bank credit and on behaviour of short-term rates. The fact that bank credit rather than the money supply appeared as the intermediate target variable relates to specific characteristics of the French financial system. In particular, French banks do not hold excess reserves and are permanently indebted to the central bank. On the other hand, they have at their disposal a large volume of potential liquidity in the form of assets discountable at the central bank or eligible in the money market. In such a context, banks respond to market incentives by extending credit without paying particular attention to their liquidity position, and meet any need for reserve money by borrowing from the central bank or by selling short-term securities in the money market[3]. Thus, unless prepared to withdraw from the market and cause a serious shortage in bank liquidity, the central bank is unable to ration the supply of reserve money to the banking system, and therefore is unable to control the money supply in the short run. Accordingly, its actions are directed towards controlling bank credit which emerges as the main target for policy, while the money supply can only be considered as a broad indicator of the thrust of that policy.

INSTRUMENTS

Three main instruments are employed to influence credit: money market intervention, compulsory reserves, and quantitative controls[4].

The banks' dependence on the central bank for provision of reserve money enables the authorities to influence bank lending rates by varying the cost of refinancing. Since 1971 open-market operations have displaced rediscounting at the central bank as the principal channel of central bank accommodation[5]. By raising or lowering its intervention rates on the money market, the Bank of France is able to move lending rates in the direction required to influence demand for credit. To contain bank credit the Bank of France has, since mid-1973, intervened less frequently in the money market. Less frequent intervention, it was reasoned, would encourage banks to pay more attention to their liquidity position before extending credit and less prone to take central bank support for granted[6].

In practice, however, the Bank's freedom of action has been somewhat limited by considerations relating to government objectives in the sphere of investment and employment, stability of financial markets, and external considerations which compel that money market rates be kept in line with those of other countries. The free handling of exchange rates since 1973 has not fundamentally changed this behaviour as the monetary authorities have tried to prevent any excessive appreciation or depreciation of the franc. Thus experience has shown that, in order to avoid sudden pressure on money market rates, the Bank of France chooses to provide the banks with the means of restoring their liquidity positions even when these have been disturbed by excessive credit extension.

As in the case of money market intervention, compulsory reserve ratios have been applied and varied primarily with the aim of influencing bank lending rates and bank lending. Changes in compulsory reserve ratios have caused variations in banks' indebtedness to the central bank, resulting in increases in bank's operating costs that are reflected on lending rates.

Initially compulsory reserves were related to bank liabilities only, but in February 1971 credit ratios were introduced. These took the form of requirements for:

(1) ordinary reserves at a uniform rate, which apply to the change in credit outstanding relative to the position at a given reference date; this type of reserve requirement was temporarily suspended in June 1974;

(2) supplementary reserves, at a progressive rate, which apply to total credit outstanding; this form of reserves affects institutions whose credit growth rate over a certain period exceeds the norm set by the authorities.

These new arrangements were designed to 'play an educative role in establishing a direct link between the credit operations of financial institutions and their obligation to place reserves at the central bank'/. It was thus envisaged that this instrument would act as a direct disincentive to bank lending without generating the distortions implicit in the rigid system of credit ceilings (*encadrement*) used in the past. Banks may choose to exceed the recommended norms provided that they pay the penalty in the form of supplementary reserves. Higher costs are then reflected in higher rates charged to borrowers and/or lower bank profits.

In practice the high progressivity of the supplementary reserves against credit, intensified in June 1974, and the continuance of official directives to banks (especially to the three larger, nationalized banks) have brought the new system very close to a scheme of credit ceiling. Furthermore, such constraints have been accompanied by selective action on the distribution of credit. Special norms have, with some exceptions, been set for the expansion of short-term export credits. More direct selective controls have been used for medium-term loans, the rediscounting or money market eligibility of which require prior agreement by the Bank of France. There have also been special regulations for consumer credit applying, in particular, to the duration of the loan and the proportion of the value of the goods which can be financed by credit. The increase in personal loans by banks came under close scrutiny since there had been a tendency to use these instead of the usual forms of financing purchases and sales of durable goods.

In addition to credit controls, direct controls on interest rates were pursued. These impinged on both domestic and international placements of funds. In the latter sphere, namely international capital movements, attention focused primarily on exchange controls. Most long- and short-term capital operations were controlled in varying degrees, both for the bank and non-bank sectors. One of the main techniques used was regulation of banks' net foreign positions, sometimes combined with a prohibition of franc loans to non-residents, and limitation on the timing of commercial payments. Exchange controls were used in order to curb capital inflows in the period 1970–72 while in 1974–75 they were used to encourage such movements. However, the monetary authorities also took action to increase financial disincentives against short-term capital foreign transactions. Thus at the beginning of the 1970s, in order to discourage capital inflows, higher reserves were required against non-resident deposits while banks were prohibited from paying interest on such deposits.

Finally from August 1971 to March 1974 a two-tier foreign exchange market was operated to prevent both inflows and outflows of capital. Under that system intervention by the central bank was, in principle, confined to the official franc market through which most current transactions in goods and services passed, while the rate of the financial franc which applied to capital transactions varied with supply and demand. When, in 1974, the French authorities chose to leave the European 'snake', the floating of the franc was extended to the official market and, since it no longer served any useful purpose, the two-tier exchange market was abolished.

4. The Impact of Monetary Policy

SOME EVIDENCE FROM THE 1960s

Empirical studies on the 1960s and the turn of the 1970s provide a good guide to how effective French monetary policy has been in the past in short-term demand management. Both in periods of ease and monetary restraint, the behaviour of monetary aggregates and interest rates has closely reflected changes in the direction of policy. Furthermore, although the magnitude of effects has been smaller in periods of ease than of restraint, a significant direct impact of monetary policy on private domestic demand and output can be identified with a relatively short (six to nine months) lag. Among the components of demand, private fixed investment, residential construction, and consumption of durables by households have been the most responsive to changes in policy, while (surprisingly) stockbuilding does not appear to have been directly influenced by monetary conditions.

As regards the transmission mechanism, econometric studies suggest that policy effects relate primarily to changes in the availability of bank credit. This reflects the low degree of substitution between alternative forms of finance resulting from strict controls by the authorities on domestic non-bank sources of funds (i.e. specialized institutions and the bond market) and on borrowing abroad. The relatively small role played by cost (interest rate) effects, compared to credit availability, is essentially due to the nature of policy in the 1960s since, until 1968, the authorities had tended to keep interest rates more or less constant.

EXPERIENCES OF THE 1970s

Monetary experience since 1971 was rather different to that of the 1960s. In the easy-money phase of 1971–72, the monetary aggregates grew strongly

Figure 2. Indicators of the thrust of monetary policy (percentage change over previous quarter at annual rate, seasonally adjusted data, three quarter moving average).

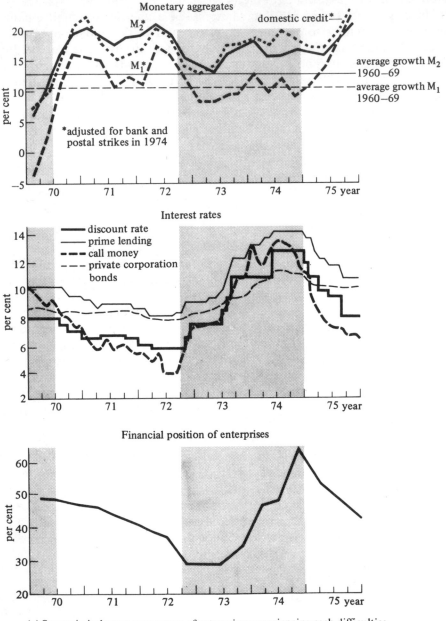

(*a*) Survey in industry: percentage of enterprises experiencing cash difficulties.

Source: Conseil National du Credit, INSEE and Morgan Guarantee Trust.

compared with past trends (see figure 2), so that the accommodating policy pursued by the authorities turned out to be expansionary. The main cause of this development was a rapid growth in bank credit, which was reflected in increased indebtedness of enterprises and households. The appreciable rise in the demand for credit was to some extent due to the concern of the private sector to hedge against the possibility that credit ceilings might be reintroduced. Although intervention by the monetary authorities to neutralize this behaviour seems in retrospect to have been only moderate, it must be remembered that the government was at that time giving priority to the maintenance of a high level of employment rather than countering inflation. Moreover, the action of the monetary authorities was undermined by large

Figure 3. (a) Short-term interest rates. (b) Short-term capital flows (including errors and omissions) (inflow, positive; outflow, negative).

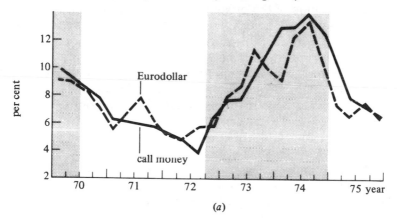

(a)

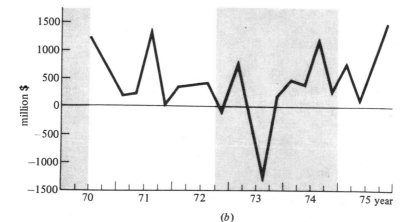

(b)

Source: OECD.

short-term capital inflows, the effect of which was to limit their room for manoeuvre in the field of interest rates (see figure 3). In this connection, it must be pointed out that the two-tier foreign exchange market did not succeed in making internal monetary policy entirely independent of external influences. In fact, to avoid excessive appreciation of the financial franc compared with the official franc—which might have provided an incentive to shift transactions from one market to the other—the Bank of France tended to keep money market rates slightly below Eurodollar rates.

In the period of monetary restriction of 1973–74, the expected tightening of bank credit did indeed take place, although the banks sometimes had difficulty.in complying with the official credit expansion norms. On the other hand, the lags in the effect of monetary policy proved to be longer than in similar circumstances in the past. This can be explained by the fact that, when the monetary restrictions were introduced towards the end of 1972, the financial position of the private sector was particularly easy and, more generally, the degree of liquidity of the economy was very high. It was, therefore, only at the end of 1973—a year after the adoption of the restrictive policy—that a tightening of enterprises' cash positions was observed (see figure 2). The impact on demand and prices being also delayed in consequence, the restrictive measures were reinforced in mid-1974.

At a time when the international situation was becoming unfavourable, the *cumulative* effects of monetary policy on the economy began to be felt, leading to the serious fall in production and employment recorded in the second half of 1974 and the greater part of 1975. More accurate anticipation of the delayed action of monetary policy measures might have prevented the authorities from strengthening the monetary restrictions in 1974, though it must be remembered that they were then faced with increasing inflationary expectations, the rise in prices taking on disquieting proportions.

What also distinguishes the last phase of monetary tightening from the earlier restrictive periods is official action with regard to business investment (see figure 4). Whereas in the past the monetary authorities had been very selective in limiting credit, even productive investment was not spared by the credit restrictions of 1973–74 (and in particular those included in the mid-1974 stabilization plan). However, the authorities' interest rate policy did take account of the high level of indebtedness of firms. The net result of all this was that productive investment did not, on this occasion, constitute a positive element in demand, its decline having helped to accentuate the overall fall in production. Similarly, in contrast to what had generally occurred in the 1960s, stockbuilding appeared to have been affected to some extent by the monetary restrictions. The very considerable financial difficulties experienced by enterprises in 1974 led them to manage their stocks more cautiously; this attitude was reflected *inter alia* in the heavy destocking movement which took place in 1975.

Contrary again to what had happened in the past, the relaxation of

Figure 4. Investment by enterprises (change over previous quarter at annual rate, seasonally adjusted data at constant prices, three quarter moving average.

  (a) Percentage of enterprises replying 'well filled' minus percentage replying 'insufficient'.

  (b) Percentage of enterprises replying 'higher than usual' minus percentage replying 'lower than usual'.

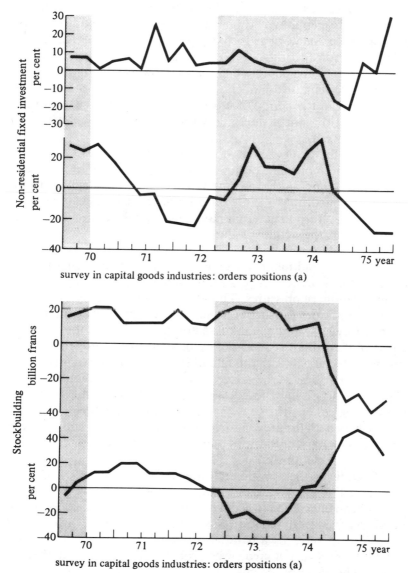

survey in capital goods industries: orders positions (a)

survey in capital goods industries: orders positions (a)

Source: INSEE, Quarterly National Accounts, and 'Tendances de la Conjoncture'.

monetary policy in 1975 was not followed by a faster rise in bank credit to the private sector. Having learned the lesson from the experience of the early 1970s, the monetary authorities continued to limit the expansion of bank credit to norms calculated to prevent too big a rise in the demand for credit. In fact, this demand remained low because of the slowdown in economic activity, so that the growth in bank credit stayed within the recommended limits. Nevertheless, the money supply broadly defined (M_2) again expanded rapidly as a result of the increase in claims on the Treasury created by the exceptionally large central government budget deficit. This deficit was in fact financed by increased borrowing by the Treasury from the banking system in the form of direct advances by the Bank of France and bond purchases by the commercial banks. However, government indebtedness as a whole remained moderate in relation to GNP as the government took advantage of the period of more or less balanced budgets in the years 1971–74 to get its indebtedness down to a level lower than that of most industrial countries.

As regards the achievement of internal and external equilibrium, the effectiveness of monetary policy was limited by the repercussions on domestic prices, and on the current balance, of the upsurge of raw material prices and the quadrupling of the oil price in particular. On the whole, however, while the return to external payments equilibrium in 1975 can partly be attributed to the action of the monetary authorities, the results they obtained in the struggle against inflation tended to be disappointing. The combination of rapid monetary expansion and rapidly rising prices in the first half of the 1970s even suggests that monetary policy may have helped to feed the inflationary pressures. This thesis is supported by the fact that the monetary authorities pursued a policy of accommodating the rises in production costs which were the main factor in accelerating the inflation. This was part of their more general policy of aligning the growth in the money supply broadly defined with the rate of increase in nominal GDP. Thus, the monetary authorities, in fact, accepted the rate of inflation resulting from market forces, while these forces were also affected by official price control of varying degrees of stringency. Thus, by allowing monetary expansion to keep pace with both the growth in volume of transactions and the increase in prices, the monetary authorities were unable to curb the development of inflationary expectations.

Finally as far as the transmission mechanism of monetary policy is concerned, past findings about the relative importance of credit availability effects and cost effects do not seem to require much modification in the light of recent experience. In the restrictive period of 1973–74, the rise in interest rates was largely offset by a parallel rise in prices so that, on the whole, the impact of the real cost of credit was probably less strong than that of credit rationing. The effect of the cost of credit on housing investment, however, seems to have been appreciable; similarly rates of interest on savings and time deposits probably had a considerable influence on short-term saving behaviour by individuals, and hence on private consumption of manufactures.

5. Concluding Remarks

Monetary policy in France during the first half of the 1970s covered a wide variety of official actions through interest rates and credit rationing. Given the range of instruments available, the main problem for the monetary authorities was how to select and combine them. To judge from the disturbed course of economic and monetary developments, it has to be admitted that the policy pursued did not have all the desired effects over the whole of the period under review. In terms of short-term demand management, however, significant results were achieved, as is shown by the clear impact recorded in the restrictive period 1973–74.

The main reason for the inadequacy of monetary policy was the banks' attitude towards their liquidity positions. Despite the efforts of the authorities to induce banks to gear their supply of credit more closely to their liquidity positions, they continued to behave as if they had unlimited refinancing possibilities with the central bank. Faced with a *fait accompli*, and anxious to prevent heavy pressures on the money market, the Bank of France was unable to regulate the volume of its credit to the banking system. On the other hand, it was able to influence the rates of interest at which it provided that credit. The central bank made more use of this ability to control interest rates than in the past, but its room for manoeuvre in this sphere was circumscribed by external considerations. Thus, although the task of the authorities was facilitated by the at first partial and later full floating of the franc, and in spite of the more widespread use of exchange control, international capital flows played an increasing role in determining interest rates. Moreover, in a wider medium-term context, policy considerations (the need to encourage investment) and short-term developments (accelerating inflation) tended to limit the effectiveness of interest rate policy.

In order to keep monetary expansion under control, the authorities set up a mechanism very similar in effect to ceilings on bank lending, a technique which they had already adopted frequently in the past. In this way they were able to influence money creation at the source, while exercising independent control over interest rates. As a general rule, the authorities consider that credit ceilings enable them to contain bank credit within desired limits, and with greater precision and rapidity than if they were to act solely through the traditional monetary instruments of refinancing policy and compulsory reserves. However, the use of this system of direct rationing of bank credit over a long period of time reveals disadvantages in the form of distortions of the credit market mechanism.

NOTES

1.   This paper reflects the opinions of the author and does not purport to represent the views of the organisation to which he belongs.

2.   A detailed description of short-term economic developments can be found in the OECD annual reports on France, and in *Profil Economique de la France*, Documentation française, 1976

3.   See P. Berger, 'Emission monétaire et multiplicateur de crédit', *Revue Banque*, July-August, 1974; and A. Coutière, 'Un modèle du système monètaire français', in *Statistiques et Etudes Financières*, No. 17 (Paris: Ministère de l'Economie et des Finances, 1975).

4.   See OECD, *Monetary Policy in France* (Paris: OECD, 1974), and Banque de France, *Les Instruments de la Politique Monétaire en France*, 1971.

5.   The change in emphasis was primarily due to criticism directed towards the previous arrangements in that a system of monetary control based on discount rates was not sufficiently flexible while the multiplicity of rates at which 'last resort' assistance was provided resulted in distortion and inefficiency. See Banque de France, *Compte Rendu des Operations*, 1972.

6.   To this end the Bank of France has modified its intervention techniques and procedures on the money market; it now makes outright purchases of money market paper at intervals rather than daily advances against paper on a sale and repurchase basis.

7.   More explicitly, the authorities considered that 'the traditional system [of reserve requirements on bank liabilities] establishes a link between reserves and domestic liquidity that is not geared to specific cause of the change in money supply . . . Consequently banks are not induced to relate their credit expansion to the additional reserves which they must hold when their deposits increase . . . A system based on credits, permits a more direct constraint on credit expansion particularly if a high *marginal* requirement is imposed . . . '. See Banque de France, *Compte Rendu des Operations*, 1971, p. 43. Similar arrangements, we may note, were considered by the Bundesbank but not adopted. See A.S. Courakis, 'Monetary thought and stabilization policy in the Federal Republic of Germany, 1960–1976', in S.F. Frowen, A.S. Courakis and M. Miller (eds.), *Monetary Policy and Economic Activity in West Germany* (London: Surrey University Press, 1977), chapter 2.

8.   See in particular, OECD, *Monetary Policy in France* (Paris: OECD, 1974) parts III and IV, and J.H. David, 'Un modèle de l'economie française inspiré des thèses monétaristes', *Bank of France, Quarterly Bulletin*, No. 5, 1972.

Structural Changes and Cyclical Behaviour of the Italian Banking System

Mario Monti and Tommaso Padoa-Schioppa

1. Introduction

The way specific targets such as price stability and employment have been combined in defining the course of monetary policy has varied greatly at different times and in different countries. But from a more general point of view one can say that in the last 15 years monetary policy in most countries has focused on the objective of stabilizing economic fluctuations.

The way policymakers and economists have explained the working mechanism of monetary policy has also varied greatly in time and space; some have even suggested that no explanation is necessary. But here again, at a general level, widespread agreement exists on the view that two essential elements of the mechanism are the monopoly of the central bank over the production of legal tender and the role played by financial institutions in linking ultimate borrowers to ultimate lenders. Conceptually, each of these two elements could exist without the other, as they do in models with money and no financial intermediaries, and in models where money is entirely endogenous.

This reveals both the distinctions and the relationships between different functions performed by the financial system: an allocative function that represents the very reason of its existence, the function of managing the mechanism of payments, and, finally, the function of transmitting to the economy the impulses of monetary policy. The last function may be performed in so far as the banking system stands at a crossroads between savers, investors, and the central bank, i.e. in so far as it performs the first two functions. On the other hand, and looking at this same reality from the point of view of a central bank, not only the need for stabilization policy, but the technique of monetary action itself, strongly depend on the structure of the economy and the financial system. It is so, firstly because cyclical instability stems from that structure, secondly because, to be effective, policy has to be tailored on the existing 'transmission box', and finally because economic stabilization cannot be achieved while disregarding other objectives for which the monetary authority is responsible, such as the stability of financial institutions.

The purpose of this paper is to analyse, through Italian post-war monetary experience, some aspects of the relationship between the structural and the cyclical aspects of the financial sector, and to attempt to show how *financial intermediation* and *credit policy* relate to them.

In the next section we briefly summarize some of the institutional aspects of the Italian financial system that are both peculiar to Italy and relevant to the subsequent discussion. We shall then (in section 3) show how the conditions surrounding financial intermediation and monetary policy have evolved in the post-war period, and how such evolution has accelerated in the most recent years. The effects of such an evolution on banking will be then analysed both from the point of view of the balance sheet structure and of bank behaviour over the cycle (section 4). The three episodes of monetary restraint which we have experienced in the last 15 years are then reviewed to show how they differ as a result of the underlying evolution of the financial structure (section 5). Finally some conclusions are drawn in the last section.

2. Some Relevant Features of Italy's Financial System

No attempt can be made here to illustrate the Italian financial system. Instead we shall review some of the main features that have been relevant in its recent development.

The services of financial intermediation in Italy are mainly produced by two types of institutions: banks and so-called special credit institutions (we do not consider insurance companies here). According to the principle of specialization, which is one of the cornerstones of the Bank Law of 1936 that still regulates our financial system, each type of institution is required to hold assets and liabilities of equivalent maturity. Banks (i.e. commercial and savings banks) raise deposits and hold loans and securities. Loans are mostly short term, up to 18 months, as are deposits. Securities have different maturities, most of them having been issued for four years or more. Special credit institutions raise their funds by issuing securities and invest them in long-term loans, with maturities of five years or more.

Because of the progressive decline in self-financing by non-financial enterprises and the high liquidity preference of the public, a large share of household financial assets is held in the form of bank deposits, while a large proportion of the stock of capital is financed with long-term loans extended by special credit institutions. The missing link in the chain of transmission of funds from ultimate lenders to ultimate borrowers is provided by banks that, against the deposits of the public, hold securities of special credit institutions.

This distinctive feature of the Italian financial system takes the name of 'double intermediation'. Three of its determinants, which we have just mentioned, are the principle of specialization, the lack of self-financing, and the liquidity preference of the public. In addition two other important factors have to be taken into account: the payment of interests on bank deposits, and the various obstacles to direct transmission of funds from savers to investors.

Although interest rates both on loans and deposits are regulated by an interbank agreement, there are no effective ceilings to prevent deposit rates from adjusting to market conditions. This is true not only for savings deposits, but also for demand deposits, whose maximum rates, to give an example, rose by more than 6 percentage points between January and June 1976, when they reached the level of 16.5 per cent. The high level of interest paid on money balances reinforces the tendency of the public to hold a high proportion of its financial wealth in liquid assets. It also discourages the development of short-term assets, such as commercial paper and certificates of deposits, that could establish a direct link between lenders and borrowers. Such links are also less developed than in other countries in the long end of the market. A primary reason for this position is the preferential tax treatment of securities issued by financial institutions compared to those issued directly by enterprises. A second reason relates to imperfections in the securities market and, in particular, the stock exchange. Insufficient information on firms' accounts and the small amounts traded help to discourage the less sophisticated investor from buying company securities.

Thus, in the process of resource allocation, financial intermediation plays a role that in relative terms is far greater than in other countries. A way of looking at this feature is to consider the net financial position of different sectors of the economy, comparing it to GNP. As in most industrialized countries, in Italy net savings are concentrated in the household sector. But, taking the 1971–73 data for the seven larger industrial countries, the ratio of household net savings to GNP in Italy was just three times the average for the other six (15.9 per cent against 5.3 per cent). In contrast, the comparison for the two major deficit sectors, i.e. central government and the business sector, shows an identical but inverted situation: –16.0 per cent in Italy against an average of –5.5 per cent in the other six countries[1].

As regards policy, it has to be pointed out that Italian legislation offers a variety of instruments for monetary and credit control that go beyond the scope of using monetary policy for short-term stabilization purposes. Thus, in addition to such traditional instruments as compulsory reserves and the discount window, there are others that may be used to influence investments and resource allocation in the longer term. Two of the most important are the authorization of issues of securities, and the system of subsidized long-term credit.

Table 1. Conditions surrounding monetary policy.

Year	X + M	Treasury deficit	Bank deposits	Bank deposits	Debts of the private sector		Short-term
				Total assets	Total		Total
		(ratios to GNP)			Total liabilities		
1952	24.4	5.0	28.9	33.3	54.3		64.8
1953	24.7	3.8	30.6	34.8	57.9		64.3
1954	23.9	4.1	32.9	33.4	54.0		62.9
1955	24.2	3.7	34.5	32.6	52.0		62.1
1956	26.2	2.0	35.7	33.7	54.9		60.8
1957	29.2	1.5	37.0	33.4	53.1		59.2
1958	26.5	2.6	40.0	34.1	52.8		55.0
1959	26.8	2.6	43.9	29.4	42.4		54.5
1960	31.7	1.8	46.7	28.1	40.9		54.8

1961	32.3	1.5	49.1	29.8	43.9	55.0
1962	32.9	2.1	51.9	33.5	51.3	55.1
1963	33.7	2.5	51.3	36.1	57.9	55.1
1964	32.4	2.4	51.1	40.5	67.1	51.2
1965	33.7	1.5	55.8	40.4	63.6	49.3
1966	35.4	4.6	59.4	40.5	63.7	49.4
1967	35.6	2.8	61.9	43.3	69.0	49.6
1968	36.7	4.3	65.1	44.6	71.2	48.3
1969	39.3	3.2	66.2	44.1	70.0	48.5
1970	41.1	5.5	68.7	47.7	74.6	48.8
1971	42.5	7.5	74.8	50.6	79.0	46.2
1972	44.7	8.2	81.0	51.1	78.6	46.0
1973	49.2	10.0	86.0	51.7	79.5	45.1
1974	61.4	9.2	83.0	56.8	81.8	46.6
1952–60	26.4	3.0	36.6	32.5	51.3	59.8
1961–70	35.3	3.0	58.1	40.1	63.2	51.0
1971–74	49.5	8.7	81.2	52.6	79.7	46.0

3. A Changing Financial Environment

In the post-war period, financial conditions progressively departed from those consistent with orderly functioning of markets. Initially there was considerable compatibility between saver and investor preferences regarding duration of financial and real capital, and hence the process of capital accumulation. Granted the then size and distribution of financial wealth, the stock market was efficient enough to secure the raising of the necessary amounts of equity finance, while company savings comprised a large part of the total capital requirements. Consequently 'transformation' by financial intermediaries was necessary to a limited extent only, a fact conducive to intermediary specialization. *Credit allocation,* it may be said, dominated over *credit transformation.* Furthermore, since government and the foreign sector were small in size and generally in balance, compatibility of financial preferences had only to be preserved in the relatively narrow and, as already suggested, homogeneous domain of interaction between households and businesses.

In this environment, policy of an orthodox character was within the authorities reach. Operating as 'the banks' bank', the Bank of Italy, itself, specialized in short-term credit, and supplied base money by lending to banks to the extent required by the needs of production and trade. The system of compulsory reserve ratios strengthened the relationship between the monetary base and credit expansion, while funds raised by long-term credit institutions were controlled through the authorization to issue securities. The instruments available to the monetary authority were thus sufficient to secure the objective of stabilizing the internal and external value of money, the only objective deemed relevant in the circumstances that prevailed.

countries have so many of the conditions for bliss changed so rapidly and as much as they did in Italy. The increasing openness to international trade, the growing intervention of government in the economy, income redistribution, and stronger claims for security of employment, and real value of incomes, altered the conditions surrounding financial activity. Table 1 summarizes some of those changes. The value of foreign trade, $X + M,$ compared to that of GNP, has risen from an average of 26.4 per cent in the 1950s to 35.3 in the 1960s, to 49.5 in 1971–74. The current deficit of the Treasury was decreasing until the mid-1960s, and then started an accelerated growth up to 10 per cent of GNP in 1973 and 1974. In the meantime, an increasing divergence emerged in the maturity structure of assets and liabilities of the various sectors. The share of bank deposits in total financial assets rose from an average of 32.5 per cent in the 1950s, to 40.1 in the 1960s to 52.6 in the early 1970s; in the same periods the share of short-term liabilities in total liabilities of the private sector fell from 59.8 to 51.0 to 46.0 per cent.

Such structural changes may be attributed to the same causes that have permitted Italy to reach, over the last quarter of a century, a higher level and a more even distribution of income. At the same time, however, they have fundamentally altered the original picture, and have produced conditions in which financial disequilibria are both more frequent and more serious, while available instruments to cure them are less effective.

4. Effects on Banking

Looking at the balance sheet of the banking system we find the mirror-image of the disequilibria of non-financial operators. Given the institutional principle by which banks are not allowed to make long-term loans, and given the limited amount of securities issued by non-financial firms, such an image has acquired the following contours in Italy (table 2):

(1) the ratio of securities held by banks to bank deposits has risen sharply from an average of 13.1 per cent in the 1950s, to 20.5 per cent in the 1960s, to 29.0 per cent in the 1970s;

(2) of the total funds provided by the credit system as a whole, the share directly or indirectly financed with bank deposits increased from 71.1 per cent in 1971 to 76.2 per cent in 1974;

(3) banks have reduced their share in total financing by credit institutions to ultimate lenders from 72.5 per cent in the 1950s, to 65.3 per cent in the 1960s to 59.3 per cent in the 1970s.

Banks thus became increasingly specialized in creating money, while progressively leaving contacts with firms to the long-term credit institutions. A decreasing share of the liabilities they created was absorbed by extending short-term loans to their private customers. On the other hand, the very nature of the relationship between credit institutions and their borrowers was altered by two phenomena: the increasing share of borrowers belonging to the public sector, and the increasing share of 'subsidized' credit. The former depends on the expansion of the deficits of central and local governments, on the deficits of public and semi-public bodies such as hospitals or social security agencies, and, finally, on government intervention in private firms to prevent defaults and to protect employment. The latter is one of the chief instruments by which, in the post-war period, policies were pursued to encourage investments in particular areas or industries of the Italian economy. Both these phenomena have the effect of stimulating credit expansion outside and independently of the price (rates) mechanism, and hence in conditions in which the assessment of allocative efficiency is particularly difficult.

The structural change in the composition of banks' balance sheets has reconciled the diverging financial structures of surplus and deficit sectors. It has also made it possible to finance private and public demand to an other-

Table 2. Asset composition of banks and banks' share in total credits.

Year	Asset composition of banks (ratios to deposits)				Banking system and credit system (ratios to total credits by credit institutions)	
	Total securities	Treasury bonds	Short-term loans	Foreign assets	Total bank credit	Bank credit to final lenders
1951	10.1	5.4	61.3	..	....	....
1952	11.6	6.1	63.4	..	....	....
1953	13.7	7.0	65.1	..	....	....
1954	13.2	7.1	65.2	..	....	....
1955	14.0	9.0	65.1	..	....	....
1956	14.2	9.3	66.2	..	....	....
1957	13.3	8.6	64.0	0.4	....	....
1958	13.0	7.6	56.3	0.7	....	....
1959	13.9	7.7	54.0	1.1	....	....
1960	14.0	6.5	57.4	2.5	....	....

1961	13.9	6.1	58.6	3.0	75.3	70.1
1962	15.3	5.3	59.7	4.0	75.0	68.9
1963	15.6	4.5	64.4	2.6	75.2	68.6
1964	17.0	4.1	60.4	3.0	72.9	66.1
1965	19.9	5.5	53.5	5.9	73.1	65.0
1966	22.8	7.8	53.2	6.7	73.2	63.9
1967	23.6	7.9	53.8	6.3	72.9	63.1
1968	25.8	9.7	53.7	8.8	72.4	61.9
1969	26.4	9.2	55.5	11.5	71.6	60.9
1970	24.7	8.1	54.2	14.3	71.3	60.3
1971	25.9	9.8	51.0	15.1	71.1	59.2
1972	26.2	10.3	51.6	18.7	71.9	59.3
1973	30.7	9.6	50.0	20.6	73.3	57.7
1974	33.3	7.8		9.5	76.2	59.2
1951–60	13.1	7.4	61.8	1.2	74.9	72.5
1961–70	20.5	6.8	56.7	6.6	73.8	65.3
1971–74	29.0	9.4	50.9	16.0	73.7	59.3

wise impossible extent. The cost of this service that the banking system has offered to the economy has been a reduction in the system's operational flexibility, the consequences of which are felt particularly when stabilization policies are required.

When stability of interest rates is maintained for sufficiently long periods, it does not make much difference whether the share of deposits invested in long-term securities is high. Difficulties arise, however, when interest rates rise. While rates on deposits and short-term loans adjust fairly rapidly to the changing conditions of liquidity under the pressure of bank competition, the time required for the adjustment of the average yield of the securities portfolio depends on the rate of increase of the portion of securities whose yield corresponds to the new market conditions. The larger the portfolio of securities in the initial stage of interest rates upswing, the slower the adjustment in the average yield and the stronger the threat to bank stability. If a bank refrains from offering higher rates on deposits, it is the liquidity position which is threatened; if it offers much higher rates, the burden of the adjustment falls on the profit and loss account.

The widening of the spread between loan and deposit rates is also the result of such tensions and, *ceteris paribus,* it is greater the greater the share of deposits that is invested in securities. If, in addition, the rates on newly issued bonds are less flexible than the rates on loans when the general level of rates is rising, banks try to invest a larger share of their new assets in loans, thus reducing the access of long-term credit institutions to the capital market.

While this loss of operational flexibility was making equilibrium in banking activity more vulnerable to policy actions, in the financial sector monetary policy was charged with increasing responsibilities. The spectrum of targets was broadened so as to include full employment, growth of output, and selective investment policies. And this was happening while the public sector was becoming less efficient and policy instruments, other than the monetary ones, were becoming increasingly ineffective. It, therefore, became more necessary to tackle financial instabilities with emergency provisions in the field of credit, as well as in that of foreign exchange. Financial institutions, and banks in particular, carried the main burden of such provisions. At each cycle, interest rate movements and changes in the assets composition became larger.

5. Interest Rates in Three Restrictive Phases

Recent Italian monetary history presents three episodes of credit restrictions. A fourth one started at the beginning of 1976 and is yet too recent to be described.

The first two episodes occurred in 1963–64 and 1969–70 respectively. On both occasions it was observed that, at the end of the restriction, the positive margin of the rate of loans over the bond yield reached a minimum, while the spread between the latter yield and the rate on bank deposits reached a maximum (figure 1 and table 3). The loan–bond rate differential shrank by 0.75 percentage points in both episodes. The bond–deposits rate differential widened by 1.4 in the first and by 1.8 points in the second. These movements reflected the greater mobility of the bond rate compared to the other rates, and this depended also on the fact that the bond market was relatively freer than the loan and deposits markets. The rate on loans, on the other hand, was more flexible than that on deposits. The spread between the two increased by about 0.6 points in 1963–64 and, given greater rigidity of bank balance sheets, by more than 1.1 points in 1969–70.

Parallel to the movements in interest rate differentials, there was a shift towards loans in the assets composition of banks, mainly due to their tendency, in times of stringency, to support their customers rather than to invest in bonds. For the non-bank public, on the other hand, investments in

Figure 1. Interest rates and credit policy.

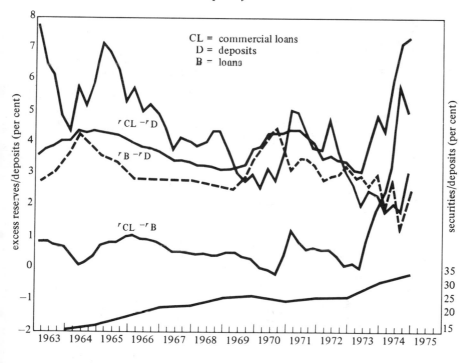

Table 3. *Three credit restrictions: interest rates and bank balance sheet structure.*

| Periods | Interest rates | | | | | | Balance sheet ratios | |
| | Levels | | | Spreads | | | Bonds | Loans |
	r_{CL}	r_B	r_D	$r_{CL}-r_B$	r_B-r_D	$r_{CL}-r_D$	Deposits	Bonds+Loans
1963–64								
1963:2	7.01	6.11	3.21	0.90	2.90	3.80	15.69	83.09
1964:3	7.67	7.54	3.25	0.13	4.29	4.42	16.04	82.95
Δ	0.66	1.43	0.04	-0.77	1.39	0.62	0.35	-0.14
1969–70								
1969:2	7.33	6.77	4.15	0.56	2.62	3.18	26.55	71.93
1970:3	9.58	9.72	5.28	-0.14	4.44	4.30	26.04	72.21
Δ	2.25	2.95	1.13	-0.70	1.82	1.12	-0.51	0.28
1973–74								
1973:2	7.56	7.46	4.49	0.10	2.97	3.07	25.81	71.59
1974:3	16.38	10.58	9.25	5.80	1.33	7.13	32.80	65.38
Δ	8.82	3.12	4.76	5.70	-1.64	4.06	6.99	-6.21

CL = commercial loans; B = bonds; D = deposits.

securities were becoming relatively more profitable than holding bank deposits. Loans were 71.9 per cent of bank credit (loans + securities) at the end of 1962, while their share of the 1963 increase in credits was 89.6 per cent.

In the cyclical experience of 1973–74, both the size and the direction of these movements was different from the previous two episodes. Monetary policy in 1973–74 was directed not only to a target in terms of the total volume of bank credit to be attained through the indirect instrument of creating base money, but also to one in terms of credit distribution by means of direct credit controls. The latter target was pursued in the framework of a permissive policy of monetary base creation in 1973 and in a severely restrictive context in 1974. In particular, in order to remove bottlenecks in the financing of the investment boom of 1973 and to protect the securities market in 1974, measures were taken to sustain the demand for securities and to prevent banks from liquidating their portfolios. Such measures consisted of what was later to be labelled as 'portfolio constraint'. Banks were required each statutory period to invest part of their deposits in long-term securities; the amount of the compulsory investment was proportional to the stock of deposits at a previous date. Introduced as an emergency device, portfolio constraint was to become, with some modification, a permanent component of the set of instruments of credit policy. At the beginning of 1975 the compulsory investment was made proportional to the flow of deposits, while other investments in securities, that were due as part of the system to reserve requirements, were suppressed.

The effects of this policy on the spreads between interest rates and the assets composition have been opposite to those observed in previous periods of credit restrictions. The positive differential between the rate on loans and the rate on bonds, instead of shrinking, widened by more than 5.5 points. The bond–deposit rate differential, by contrast, instead of widening shrank by more than 1.5 points. As to the composition of credit, the share of loans fell from 65.3 per cent at the end-1972 stock, to 55.7 per cent in the 1973–74 flow, in the same circumstances in which banks previously tended to enlarge it.

As in the two past episodes, the loan–deposit rate differential increased, but the size of the increase, of about 4.0 percentage points, was almost four times that of 1969–70 and more than six times that of 1963–64. This difference shows one of the important links between the cyclical behaviour of interest rates and the structure of banks' balance sheets. In 1973–74, the ratio of securities to deposits was twice that of ten years before, and a correspondingly smaller share of deposits was invested in commercial loans. While all the rates on the liability side are flexible, only a decreasing share of assets is available to generate the flexibility necessary to restore profits. Financial disequilibrium of private and public borrowers, in the meantime, increases the risk of banking activity.

6. Concluding Remarks

The purpose of this paper was to discuss some of the interrelations between the structural and cyclical aspects of financial intermediation, as they emerge from Italian experience. Although it is not in the nature of this exercise to draw any far-reaching conclusions, we believe that a few patterns have been highlighted that may lend themselves to discussion with reference to other countries also. Indeed it will appear that Italian experience provides a fruitful case study since this country has been experiencing, with particular intensity, structural changes which have been observed in most other industrial economies and their financial systems.

Our own reading of the material presented here may perhaps be summarized as follows. The increasing budget deficit, the greater role of foreign trade and capital flows, and the widening gap of portfolio preferences as between domestic surplus and deficit sectors, are among the factors which simultaneously make monetary policy ever more necessary as a stabilization tool, more heavily dependent upon financial intermediaries for its implementation, and less viable and/or effective if it has to rely on its traditional operating instruments. The joint effect of these trends, and of the more and more exacting attitude of public opinion *vis-à-vis* the monetary authorities, is that of forcing the latter to devise new forms of intervention. These are increasingly characterized by direct and administrative elements of control over the activity of financial intermediaries in general, and banks in particular.

While new controls are usually applied during restrictive phases and subsequently relaxed, their effects on bank balance sheets and profit and loss accounts tend to persist; the 'liberalization' which often occurs during expansionary phases usually does not fully offset the effects generated while the controls were in existence. There are thus carry-over effects from one cycle to the next and they make for permanent changes in the structure.

Two consequences of this pattern of events have to do with the price (interest rate) mechanism and its role in the allocation of financial resources. They both emerge neatly from the Italian experience, as shown above, but are probably shared by several other countries. One is the shrinking area of the total credit market, which still warrants the word 'market' in the sense of relying upon the interest rates for the purpose of allocating credit. The other consequence is that, in this very residual section in which rates perform an allocative function, their contribution to an efficient allocation becomes increasingly questionable. The former phenomenon is the result of the growing absorption of credit by the state deficit, of the increasing—though hard to measure—financial intermediation discharged by the state itself in favour of other public entities, and of the expanding role of subsidized credit. Acquisitions of assets, bonds in particular, by the banks under the portfolio constraint is another example of non-market behaviour in the credit market.

As to the efficient functioning of interest rates in guiding allocation when allocation can be freely selected, doubts are cast both by the coexistence of demands for credit characterized by very different interest elasticities (which are probably the result of the fact that not all of them are derived from reasonable economic calculations and perhaps that these are impossible for some borrowers, like certain public bodies), and by the movements in the level and structure of interest rates, generated not by aggregative or allocative considerations but by administrative controls on banking assets.

It may not be inappropriate to conclude, at least on the basis of Italian experience, that the original function of financial intermediaries—to provide an efficient allocation of funds—has been 'crowded-out' by the other functions which public opinion and the authorities have been assigning to these intermediaries over time. If the case of Italy has some general validity, it may be expected that in several countries a basic issue of financial reforms in the years to come will be that of either reinstating an acceptable degree of market allocation through interest rates, or moving much closer to central planning of financial flows. A 'mixed finance' is a more delicate creature than a 'mixed economy'.

NOTES

1.   The other six countries are Canada, France, Japan, the United Kingdom, the United States and West Germany.

The Interaction between Money, the Exchange Rate and Prices: the Italian Experience in the 1970s

Rainer Masera

1. Introduction

The principal aim of this paper is to review critically the economic experience of Italy during the 1970s. Monetary and financial factors are singled out as crucially relevant to an understanding of the serious economic imbalances that developed during the period under consideration. To this end, an exploratory version of a short-run econometric model of the interaction between equilibrium in the money market and the determination of the effective exchange rate for the lira and of domestic prices has been developed.

The main contention of the present study can be summarized as follows. The rising deficit of the public sector coupled with the economic authorities' almost absolute aversion to a rise in long-term interest rates led, on the one hand, to far-reaching distortions in the long-term end of financial markets—which seriously hampered the saving/investment process—and, on the other, to binding constraints on the conduct of monetary policy. The excessive monetary creation stemming from the financing needs of the Treasury, however, was not associated with the expansionary results commonly related to the existence of wealth and substitution effects. Thus, even in the short run, the results of a reputedly 'expansionary' monetary policy amounted only to rapid falls in the external and internal value of the lira.

The transmission mechanism of a monetary base expansion rests on the fact that, from the point of view of the representative economic agent finding himself with new excess monetary balances, wealth has increased (at least temporarily). The adjustments in spending, which therefore result, play a vital role in the dynamic adjustment process leading to a new equilibrium position. According to the transmission process which is regarded in this study as applicable to the Italian situation (i.e. to the workings of a relatively small and inherently open economy), the stress is laid on the direct increase in demand for foreign financial assets stimulated by domestic monetary expansion. This will result either in offsetting monetary contraction via the intervention policy of the monetary authorities, or in a fall of the exchange rate of the domestic currency, until an equilibrium position is re-established.

What must be emphasized is that the transmission process set out in the present study is significantly different, at least in the short run, from both the Keynesian and the monetarist theories; the adjustment role played by direct and indirect spending on domestic goods and services in order to remove the discrepancy created by a monetary expansion is drastically reduced. Indeed, if allowance is made for inflationary expectations[1], and assuming a relatively greater speed of adjustment of domestic costs and prices with respect to import and export volumes to the new exchange rate configuration, a monetary expansion is also unlikely to have any significant short-run impact on real magnitudes in a highly open and relatively small economy.

2. The Econometric Model

MAIN FEATURES

The analytical framework of this study is essentially short run in character which makes it possible to consider real income as exogenously determined. The model presented here is specified on a monthly basis and covers the experience of the 1970s. One of the aims is to provide a tentative assessment of the interaction between money supply and demand processes and the determination of the exchange rate. It might therefore appear preferable to restrict the empirical analysis to the period from January 1973 to March 1976; however, the shift to the floating exchange rate system has been more formal than substantial, in the sense that the extent of the Bank of Italy's intervention on the foreign exchange market has increased on average in the period 1973–76 compared to 1970–73. On the other hand, the effective exchange rate for the lira began to show a certain variability from 1970. Indeed, the 1970s as a whole may be said to have been characterized by an *a priori* freedom of the Bank in selecting monetary targets not necessarily dependent upon the constraint of maintaining a given exchange rate.

The model, which is presented in table 1 and figure 1, is composed of three parts describing, respectively, (1) the monetary base, (2) the balance of payments, and (3) the process of price determination.

(1) The monetary base
Under a system of truly fixed exchange rates, prices and interest rates have to be accepted, for a small open economy, as largely determined in world markets. Hence changes in the demand for monetary balances will dominate variations in the stock of money[2]. Under these conditions the true degree of

Figure 1. Simplified flow chart of the model.

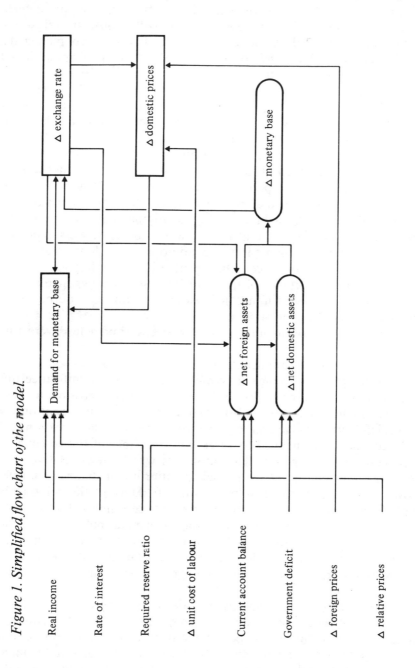

freedom of the central bank is represented by the ratio of net foreign assets to total reserve money, in the sense that attempts to force supply-determined changes in net domestic high-powered credit will be offset by adjustments of market operators via the balance of payments. In a system of managed floating the central bank has the option, in the short run, of shaping the adjustment process by allowing it to take place to the desired degree as a combination of movements in the exchange rate and in net foreign assets. Under these conditions, it becomes important to assess the dynamics of the process of market adjustment to monetary disequilibria in order to obtain indications of the direct effect of monetary policy[3].

The transmission mechanism of monetary policy differs significantly as between the monetarist and Keynesian approaches. The former would indicate, for instance, that a policy-engineered increase in nominal monetary balances will stimulate total nominal expenditure until the stock of real money balances is brought back to its original equilibrium level. The separation, in the short run, of price and real output effects depends on a number of factors, including initial conditions; in the longer run, however, the impact is mainly on prices. On the other hand, the Keynesian approach singles out the importance of nominal interest rate adjustments and their interaction—via the accumulation process—with real output changes, which affect the structure of prices.

In their original formulations, these two basic approaches[4] were aimed at describing the workings of an essentially closed economic system and were, therefore, not directly applicable to the analysis of open economies under fixed exchange rates, though they may again acquire significance under a system of clean floating. It does not, however, appear possible to use them directly in the context of substantial central bank intervention, which immediately impinges upon the process of nominal money creation.

In general I am inclined to agree with the lines of the so-called 'asset approach' to exchange rate determination, which views relative currency rates as prices consistent with stock equilibrium in financial portfolios[5]. However, the exploratory and highly simplified formulation adopted in this study focuses directly on the interaction between the stock of base money created by the monetary authorities and the general public's willingness to hold it. This is essentially due to the difficulties inherent in setting the analysis in terms of overall portfolio balance[6] and detailed specification of equilibrium conditions in the private sector's desire to accumulate net financial wealth.

The monetary sector is directly specified in this study in terms of demand and supply of central bank reserve money. According to the reduced-form short-run adjustment process postulated here, an excess supply of nominal base money balances elicits offsetting shifts toward foreign financial assets, by disturbing portfolio equilibrium. To the extent that policies adopted by the central bank do not result in a sufficient contraction of nominal base money, the adjustment will take place directly in terms of an exchange rate fall. The specific hypothesis made in this study is that the short-run demand for 'real' monetary balances is not formulated exclusively in terms of domestic goods but, more immediately, with respect to command over foreign-currency-denominated balances. Taking for instance the extreme case of clean floating, the injection of excess reserve money into the system will be met by an attempt to move out of domestic currency. The process will last until the resultant exchange rate fall has made the public content with the new nominal amount of high-powered money. It should be noted that the adjustment mechanism postulated here need not be inconsistent with the monetarist process outlined above. If purchasing power parity (PPP) relationships[7] hold in the long run, the difference in the two approaches might essentially lie in the duration of the period over which equilibrium conditions are explicitly considered, although the short-term causal links are reversed here with respect to the standard monetarist interpretation of the PPP.

The demand for base money, RM^d, is thus assumed to be a function of nominal income, Y, a short-term rate of interest, i, the required reserve ratio to be satisfied by the banking system, RR, and the exchange rate, e, expressed as the 'effective price of domestic money', of the form[8]

$$RM^d = a_0 + a_1 Y + a_2 i + a_3 RR + a_4 e. \tag{1}$$

It is further assumed that the economy adjusts its actual holdings of reserve money, RM, to its desired level according to a partial adjustment mechanism:

$$\triangle RM = \lambda(RM^d - RM_{t-1}). \tag{2}$$

By substituting (1) into (2) we get, for purposes of econometric estimation,

$$RM = \lambda a_0 + \lambda a_1 Y + \lambda a_2 i + \lambda a_3 RR + \lambda a_4 e + (1-\lambda)RM_{t-1}. \tag{2a}$$

The adjustment factor $\lambda (0 < \lambda \leqslant 1)$ measures the fraction of the difference between the desired demand and the actual stock in the previous period, which the public succeeds in adding to the previous period's stock over the time considered. The coefficients a_1 and a_3 are expected to be positive, whereas a_2 and a_4 should be negative reflecting, respectively, the opportunity cost of holding reserve money relative to short-term interest-bearing assets and the 'real' demand approach postulated in this study.

The nominal supply of monetary base balances, RM^s, can be changed through variations in net domestic, NDA, and net foreign, NFA, assets of the central bank,

$$\triangle RM^s = \triangle NDA + \triangle NFA. \tag{3}$$

It is assumed here that there are no adjustment lags on the supply side so that changes in the supply of money coincide with variations in the actual stock,

$$\triangle RM^s = \triangle RM. \tag{4}$$

Changes in the two monetary base components are explained by two policy reaction functions. In the supply function of net domestic assets I have attempted to allow for the government budget constraint: the extremely crude assumption made here is that a constant fraction of the government deficit, GD, is financed via net reserve money creation. The monetary authorities will also engage in offsetting operations with respect to intervention in the foreign exchange market. Finally, *ceteris paribus*, an increase in the required reserve ratio will allow a larger creation of net domestic assets[9].

$$\triangle NDA = b_0 + b_1 GD + b_2 NFA + b_3 \triangle RR. \tag{5}$$

In equation (5) we thus expect $-1 < b_1 < 0$, since the variable GD enters with a positive sign in the case of a surplus and with a negative sign in the case of a deficit. One may regard b_2 as the neutralization coefficient of intervention policies and it should therefore be negative, while b_3 is expected to be positive.

Domestic short-term rates of interest are considered here to be exogenously determined. The rationale for this might be found by assuming that the level of domestic rates is determined by interest rates in foreign financial centres, expected nominal discounts (premiums) on foreign currencies and a vector of scale, growth and integration variables. Endogenization of the links between foreign and domestic rates through these variables was not thought possible in this exploratory study, although efforts along these lines should obviously be made.

(2) The balance of payments
We start with the payments (transaction basis) identity:

$$CA + KF = \triangle NFA, \tag{6}$$

where CA and KF denote respectively the current account and the *autonomous* capital account balance.

Over the period considered in this study, substantial amounts of 'compensatory financing' were undertaken by public entities at the instigation of the monetary authorities with the proceeds sterilized in special accounts with the Bank of Italy. For present analytical purposes, account is taken of such compensatory borrowing in the definition of net foreign assets by regarding it as 'below the line' and thus imputing it to the monetary authorities.

The current account balance is regarded here as exogenously determined, on the grounds that it depends essentially on *lagged* (predetermined) values of such variables as domestic and foreign income levels and their relationships to potential values, monetary demand–supply imbalance, and relative cost, price, and effective exchange rate developments. Taking into account the balance-of-payments identity, this simplifying assumption makes it possible to consider the autonomous capital balance as determined by the intervention policy adopted by the monetary authorities. In the extreme case of no change in net official foreign assets, the exchange rate will adjust in such a way as to induce balancing autonomous capital flows, so as to ensure the attainment of short-run equilibrium in the money market and in the balance of payments.

The policy-reaction function describing intervention policy treats the monetary authorities as attempting, on the one hand, to finance a fraction of the current account outcome and, on the other, to lean against the wind in respect of short-run changes in the effective rate. Over the longer period, however, the fall in the exchange rate is allowed to take place when past movements in domestic prices relative to those in the main industrial countries, $\triangle CP$, have led to a deterioration of the competitive position. We thus have the following equation:

$$\triangle NFA = c_0 + c_1 CA + c_2 \triangle e + c_3 L\,(\triangle CP), \tag{7}$$

where we expect $0 < c_1 < 1$, indicating a partial financing of the current account; $c_2 > 0$ expressing the attempt to moderate short-run variations in the effective price of the domestic currency relative to foreign monies; and $c_3 > 0$, because if domestic prices have grown more rapidly than those abroad the intervention policy, *ceteris paribus*, will allow the downward adjustment of the exchange rate to take place.

(3) The process of price determination

The analysis of prices in an open economy should in principle include four different indexes relating to output, absorption, imports, and exports[10].

Changes in export and domestic output prices should reflect the difference in inflation rates between tradables and nontradables, whose relationship may make movements in relative competitive positions based on overall inflation indexes inaccurate. The absorption deflator can be thought of as a weighted average of import prices (in domestic currency) and market prices of domestically produced goods.

The rate of inflation on domestic output can be viewed as determined by: (a) direct demand pressure in domestic and foreign markets; (b) internal factor costs; (c) foreign input prices, which derive from movements in the effective exchange rates of the domestic currency and the average foreign currency price of imported goods and services; and (d) expectations of future price developments, which should also play a relevant role in shaping the inflationary process in the short run.

The obvious measure of the overall inflation is represented by the GNP deflator. An attempt was therefore made to obtain this measure on a monthly basis by interpolating the quarterly GNP deflator. However, the resultant index turned out to be practically coincident with the consumer price index; hence the simplified equation actually tested takes the form:

$$P = f[L(\Delta ULC), L(\Delta PM), L(\Delta e)]. \tag{8}$$

The actual monthly change in domestic (consumer) prices is explained in terms of distributed lags of previous changes in unit labour costs (ULC), foreign import prices (measured in foreign currency) and the effective exchange rate for the lira[11].

EMPIRICAL RESULTS

The model is composed of eight independent equations: the two identities (3) and (6), the partial adjustment function (2), the equilibrium condition (4), the two behavioural equations (1) and (8), and the two monetary policy functions (5) and (7) (see table 1). All testable equations were estimated on seasonally-adjusted variables by employing two-stage least-squares regression methods. The econometric results are given in table 2 where the ratios of coefficients to standard errors are given in parentheses; R^2, $\bar{R}^2$ and DW are the coefficients of determination, the coefficient of determination adjusted for degrees of freedom, and the Durbin-Watson statistic respectively. Lagged structures were estimated by means of the Almon technique; in the regression results the constant term was constrained to zero.

All structural parameters a_i in equation (1), as derived from the estimated coefficients in equation (i) of table 2, have the expected sign and plausible values. The long-run (partial) elasticity of the demand for high-powered money with respect to nominal income—calculated at the point of means—is 1.29. Those with respect to the interest rate and the effective exchange rate

Table 1. The model.

---

1. The market for monetary base
(1) RM^d $= f_1(Y, e, i, RR)$
(2) ΔRM $= \lambda[RM^d - RM_{t-1}] \; 0 < \lambda < 1$
(3) ΔRM^s $= \Delta NDA + \Delta NFA$
(4) ΔRM^s $= \Delta RM$
(5) ΔNDA $= \Delta NDA + \Delta NFA$

2. The balance of payments
(6) $CA + KF = \Delta NFA$
(7) ΔNFA $= f_3[CA, \Delta e, L(\Delta CP)]$

3. The price equation
(8) ΔP $= f_4[L(\Delta ULC), L(\Delta PM), L(\Delta e)]$

List of variables
Endogenous variables:
P = domestic price level
RM^d = demand for monetary base
RM^s = supply of monetary base
RM = monetary base stock
e = effective exchange rate (price of domestic currency)
NDA = net domestic assets held by the central bank
NFA = net foreign assets held by the central bank
KF = total net autonomous capital flows

Exogenous variables.
i = domestic short-term rate of interest
CA = balance of payments on current account
y = real GNP ($y = Y/P$)
RR = required reserve ratio
GD = government deficit (−) or surplus
CP = level of domestic (consumer) prices relative to a weighted average
                        of those in main competitor countries
ULC = unit cost of labour in industry
PM = foreign price level
All lagged variables

Other symbols
$L(\quad)$ = lag operator
Δ = first-difference operator

---

are –0.26 and –0.51 respectively. Nearly one-fifth of the total adjustment occurs in the first month.

The two policy-reaction functions explain a relatively high proportion of the variance despite their obvious weakness (mainly related to the fixed-parameter assumption). The very simple formulation describes a rather mechanical behaviour of monetary policy[12], which is dominated on the external side by the short-run desire to finance the current account to a large extent (over one-half), while attempting to moderate short-run exchange rate fluctuations (a one-point fall in the effective exchange rate would, ceteris paribus, entail sales of net foreign assets amounting to some 90 billion lira).

The policy function describing creation of net domestic assets indicates that, on average, four-fifths of the outcome of intervention policies are neutralized. Consequently, the financing of the Treasury deficit accounted for around 90 per cent of the creation of total base money during the period under consideration.

Finally, the inflation equation stresses the rapid impact of changes in the exchange rate and in foreign prices on the domestic price formation process, compared with variations in unit labour costs. The model should, however, be extended to capture the indirect effects of exchange rate and foreign input cost movements on labour costs. It may be mentioned that import prices, measured in foreign currency, and the exchange rate were introduced as separate variables to allow for possible differential impacts on the domestic price behaviour stemming from both expectational and pricing-policy factors. In the price equation a dummy was included to deal with the price control measures introduced in mid-1973 and subsequently relaxed[13]. The regression results indicate that such measures altered the time profile of inflation but did not have any lasting effect on the trend.

3. Some General Considerations on Recent Economic Developments in Italy

It is only possible here to make a cursory examination of the lessons to be drawn from Italian experience in the light of the analytical framework presented in the previous section. A general point to be made is that the acquired 'freedom' in the conduct of exchange rate and domestic economic policy proved to be only freedom to inflate at a higher rate than competitors. Indeed, as a result of the constraints imposed upon the financial structure there was a progressive increase in the malfunctioning (and inefficiency) of the economic system. Whereas between 1955 and 1969 both the effective exchange rate and the relative price performance had shown a remarkable stability, from 1970 to the end of March 1976 the effective exchange rate of the lira fell by some 40 per cent, while consumer prices, wholesale prices

Table 2. The estimated behavioural equations and policy functions (1970: January–1976: March).

	R^2	$\bar{R}^2$	DW
(i) Demand-for monetary-base equation	0.999	0.999	1.88
(2.a)' $RM = 26.33\, Y - 87.20\, i + 176.10\, RR - 16.34\, e + 0.813\, RM_{t-1}$			
$\quad\quad (3.24)\quad (-3.64)\quad (3.53)\quad\quad (-4.79)\ (12.77)$			
(ii) Net-domestic-asset-creation policy function			
(5)' $\Delta NDA = -0.346\, GD - 0.814\, \Delta NFA + 751.8 \Delta RR$	0.707	0.594	1.96
$\quad\quad\quad\quad (-5.43)\quad\quad (-5.25)\quad\quad (3.40)$			
(iii) Intervention policy function			
(7)' $\Delta NFA = 0.551\, CA + 86.6\, \Delta e + \sum_{i}^{6} a_i (\Delta CP)_{t-i}$	0.617	0.599	1.84
$\quad\quad\quad\quad (4.84)\quad\quad (6.0)\quad\quad \sum_i i\alpha_i = 43.8$			
(iv) Inflation equation			
(8) $\Delta P = \sum_{0}^{17} a_i (\Delta ULC)_{t-1} + \sum_{0}^{3} \beta_i (\Delta PM)_{t-i} + \sum_{0}^{8} \gamma_i\, (\Delta e)_{t-i} + 0.795\, DCP^*$	0.945	0.940	1.27
$\quad\quad\quad\quad\quad\quad\quad\quad\quad\quad\quad\quad\quad\quad\quad\quad\quad\quad\quad (6.117)$			
$\quad \sum_i a_i = 0.551 \quad\quad \sum_i \beta_i = 0.110 \quad\quad \sum_i \gamma_i = -0.492$			

* DCP is a dummy variable introduced to allow for the adoption of temporary price control measures in 1973. The variable takes the values of –1, –1, –2, –1, –1, in the months August–December 1973 and +1 in January, February, March, August, September, October 1974. For details and explanations see text.

and unit labour costs in industry went up by 15, 35 and 45 per cent, respectively, relative to developments in main competitor countries[14]. However, with a view (based on (pseudo)-Keynesian considerations) to fostering investment and growth, the surge in prices was not allowed[15] to be reflected in an adjustment of long-term domestic interest rates. As a result, real interest rates became strongly negative. For instance, holders of long-term Treasury securities, who had obtained an average real (ex-post) yield of 2.8 per cent between 1955 and 1969, were confronted with an average loss of 10 per cent per annum in the six years 1970–75[16]. In the 1970s holders of fixed-interest securities saw the real value of their assets more than halved, and those who held equities fared even worse.

In this process the role of financial markets in allocating resources was destroyed and no replacement created. The sharp rise in wage costs led to a progressive, rapid increase in the financial surplus of the household sector, which had as counterpart the deterioration in the financial position of both the enterprise and the public sector. However, nominal surpluses were not even capable of maintaining the real value of the household sector's assets, and the economy entered a vicious circle of rapid, but variable and unpredictable inflation combined with a sharp decline in net saving and investment and a progressive deterioration in the growth record, leading to the present phase of near stagnation.

The sharp acceleration of monetary aggregates[17] and the rhythem of inflation in the 1970s is largely attributable to the growing constraint imposed upon monetary policy by swelling public sector deficits, given the interest rate objectives pursued by the Treasury. According to the regression results presented here (equation (ii), table 2), the monetary financing of over one-third of the government deficit effectively implied that, on average, nine-tenths of the increase in the total monetary base was accounted for by the Treasury constraint[18], causing an expansion in high-powered money well in excess of that which would have been consistent with a reasonable stability in the value of the lira.

Moreover, in view of the constraints on long-term interest rates mentioned earlier, the redistributive effects of inflation were enormous, and of the same order of magnitude as those resulting from explicit taxation mechanisms[19]. Negative real yields on interest-bearing government debt, of course, implied that the government sector imposed a net inflation levy on private sector holdings of its bonds[20]. Also the sharp increase in the monetary base plus inflation meant that the public paid a growing part of taxes in the form of the (regressive) inflation tax on cash balances. Indeed, according to some rough estimates I have made, in the three years 1972–75 the yield from this tax turned out to be almost equal to that from income tax.

Monetary expansion, inflation, and negative real rates of interest, however, provided no lasting stimulus to real spending and no sustained increase in investment outlays[21]. Investment expenditure depends on the expected flows of total costs and revenues. If costs of labour and other material inputs are expected to increase at a rate no less fast than prices, even a negative rate of interest will not be sufficient to induce accumulation of productive capital. (This is especially true if one starts from initial positions of excess capacity.)

I shall not here go into the vexed question of whether increased costs of labour were the cause of inflation, or rather the response of social groups with strong bargaining power to an already established inflationary situation in a context which made negotiations on key issues, such as (after-tax) income distribution, practically impossible. It is, however, clear that there is an inverse relationship between the level of labour costs and that of sustainable employment. Within limits, changes in the real cost of capital can improve the trade-off in favour of employment; but when the disequilibrium is as severe and as protracted as it was in Italy the reverse becomes true, because the whole functioning of the economic system is impaired. Under these conditions an expansionary economic policy cannot be based on injections of base money, given the implicit constraints resulting from the open structure of the economy. The excess monetary balances, in the presence of already negative real rates of interest and low capacity utilization, largely led to direct pressures on the exchange rate and then on prices as a consequence of the attempts to re-establish equilibrium in the money market—which is intrinsically integrated in world financial markets.

4. Conclusions

On the basis of the considerations developed in this paper, I would regard the following policies as prerequisites for sound economic recovery in Italy:

(1)   Avoid automatic recourse to reserve money financing of the government deficit.

(2)   Let the market re-establish a structure of interest rates in real terms that is consistent with economic logic, taking into account international links[22], while explicit recourse to cost-benefit techniques should dictate departures from market-determined credit allocations to deal with externalities.

(3)   Give first priority to preparing an efficient fiscal system (and price policy for public services) in order to (i) avoid tax evasion and (ii) make taxation always manifest and able to cope with democratically agreed upon (i.e. approved by Parliament) targets for redistribution of national income.

(4)   Place wage adjustments in a framework consistent with the targets for domestic employment.

Not an easy package; but one which recent experience commands.

NOTES

1. I have examined these points in R. Masera, 'Floating exchange rates, international trade and domestic economic stability', in H. Fourier and J. Wadsworth (eds.), *Floating Exchange Rates—The Lessons of Recent Experience* (Leyden: A. Sifthoff, 1976).
2. The points have been elucidated in the 'monetary' approach to the balance of payments. See, for instance, H.G. Johnson, 'The monetary approach to the balance of payments', in *Further Essays in Monetary Economics* (London: Allen and Unwin, 1972).
3. The answer to this question is indeed a prerequisite for the formulation of overall economic policy, as indicated by the principle of effective market classification. See R. Mundell, 'The monetary dynamics of international adjustment under fixed and flexible exchange rates', *Quarterly Journal of Economics,* May, 1960.
4. For an analysis of these points see D. Patinkin, *On the Nature of the Monetary Mechanism* (Stockholm: Almquist and Wiksell, 1966).
5. On this see, for instance, P. Kouri, The Exchange Rate and the Balance of Payments in the Short and in the Long Run: A Monetary Approach, Paper presented to the Seminar on Flexible Exchange Rates and Stabilisation Policy, Institute for International Studies, University of Stockholm, 1975. Also R. Masera, 'Tassi di cambio, determinazione e contributo all'aggiustamento interno ed esterno: alcune considerazioni introduttive', preparatory paper for the Bank of Italy's *Annual Report* for 1975.
6. The reason for this will be explained later, see section 3. These considerations, in particular, make it difficult to cast the analytical framework in terms of the standard long-term models of portfolio balance, where the adjustment mechanism is related both to the changes in wealth implied by the current account balance and to the net foreign asset position of residents.
7. A useful survey of PPP theories is given by L. Officer, 'The purchasing-power-parity theory of exchange rates: a review article', International Monetary Fund, *Staff Papers,* March, 1976. On the specific point made here see R. Dornbush, The Theory of Flexible Rate Regimes and Macroeconomic Policy, Paper presented to the Seminar on Flexible Exchange Rates and Stabilisation Policy, Institute for International Studies, University of Stockholm, 1975. The usefulness, over relevant time periods, of PPP analyses to describe exchange rate movements since floating, particularly in the case of Italy, is explored in R. Masera, F. Papadia, and M. Villani, 'General statistical appendix', to their preparatory papers for the Bank of Italy's *Annual Report* for 1975; see also G. Tullio, Equilibrio di Portafoglio, Espansione Monetaria e Svalutazione della Moneta, Bank of Italy, June, 1976, mimeo.
8. For simplicity's sake the demand function is expressed on an aggregative basis rather than by attempting to separate demand of banks and non-banks.
9. Neglecting the random error term, the difference between the actual value of $\triangle NDA$ and that resulting from the econometric estimation might be interpreted as the outcome of independent monetary policy. On this point see S. Turnovsky and A. Kaspura, 'An analysis of imported inflation in a short-run macroeconomic model', *Canadian Journal of Economics,* August, 1974.
10. On these points see S. Turnovsky and A. Kaspura, *Ibid.,* and C. Goodhart, *Money, Information and Uncertainty* (London: Macmillan, 1975), chapter 14.

11.   It should be observed that the above formulation has the disadvantage of making it impossible to disentangle expectational influences on the rate of inflation, since expectations themselves are in all likelihood based on past experience. Experiments made by introducing the lagged value of the change in prices as a proxy for the expected rate (which would imply accepting an adaptive expectations hypothesis characterized by an adjustment coefficient of unity) gave results which were not considered satisfactory, in the sense that the expectational variable would explain too large a proportion of the total variance.

12.   Attempts to allow for price and real income variables as explanatory variables showed, if anything, procyclical behaviour. In general, however, the coefficients were not significant.

13.   For an explanation of the timing of the dummy, the reader is referred to the description of the working of the price control policies in the Bank of Italy's *Annual Report* for 1974 (Italian edition, pp. 148–9).

14.   On these points see R. Masera, F. Papadia, and M. Villani, 'General statistical appendix', to their preparatory papers for the Bank of Italy's *Annual Report* for 1975.

15.   The various administrative measures progressively adopted to this end are described in the Bank of Italy's *Annual Reports*.

16.   For a detailed analysis of these points see P. Baffi, 'Il risparmio in Italia, oggi', in F. Cotula and P. de Stefani (eds.), *Elementi per la Politica Monetaria* (Rome: Bulzoni, 1975). (The updating of the figures to 1975 was kindly made available by B. Bianchi.)

17.   The pace of inflation (and that of monetary aggregates) was very uneven during the period, owing to the relatively rapid alternation of stops and goes in economic policy. This enhanced the costs to the economy, also in view of the extra uncertainty imposed on the system. (On the latter point see H.G. Johnson, *Inflation and the Monetarist Controversy* (Amsterdam: North–Holland, 1972), p. 35.)

18.   The loss of sovereignty for the central bank caused by the budget constraint is stressed by P. Savona, *La Sovranità Monetaria* (Rome: Buffetti, 1975), part IV. See also M. T. Salvemini, *La Moneta nella Politica di Finanziamento del Disavanzo* (Milan: Giuffrè, 1974).

19.   See P. Baffi (note 16).

20.   For an analytical treatment of these issues see R. Masera, The Budget Restraint and the Tax Function: A Static and Dynamic Steady-State Analysis, Bank of England, 1976, mimeo.

21.   See P. Baffi, 'Italy's narrow path', *The Banker,* December, 1975.

22.   It should be observed that Italy has a relatively low capital/labour ratio. There is therefore a *prima facie* indication that an efficient full-employment policy should require a relatively high shadow price for capital.

Problems of Monetary Policy in Germany

Horst Bockelmann

Monetary policy in Germany has had its successes and failures, but on balance there is no reason for complacency. Economic developments during, say, the last five years, taken as a whole, have not been satisfactory when compared with previous performance or with the high ambitions of economic policy at the beginning of the 1970s. Monetary policy is, of course, only a part of economic policy, and economic developments, even if we confine ourselves to the domestic scene, are not fully controllable by economic policy. The economic well-being of a country depends first and foremost on the ingenuity, industry and cooperative spirit of its people. Economic policy has an important supporting role to play, but it is not the master of economic destiny. In addition, we have the external influences, which again are largely outside the control of economic policy. Thus there are plenty of excuses—even good ones—for monetary policy. But the fact remains that achievements have been meagre. Sufficient reason to ask what has gone wrong and why monetary policy has not been more successful.

Two outside factors will be high on the list of any observer who gives an opinion on the reasons for the deterioration of price performance in Germany and elsewhere:

(1) the speculative waves during the last phase of the Bretton Woods system; and
(2) the oil price hike.

The recession and the rise in unemployment are also partly linked to these disturbances, although more indirectly as a consequence of inflation and of the inevitable fight against inflation. I shall deal with these two aspects first, before I move on to the domestic issues.

Under the Bretton Woods system central banks were committed to stabilizing the exchange rates of their respective currencies *vis-à-vis* the U.S.

dollar. The question of how much room this left for an independent monetary policy had apparently not been foremost in the minds of the architects of the system. The assumption presumably was that before exchange-market intervention by central banks or other government agencies exceeded a tolerable level, the countries concerned would diagnose a fundamental disequilibrium in their balances of payments and hence adjust their exchange rates. Actually exchange rate adjustments have always been slow in coming. In Germany we had a protracted discussion in 1968/69 over the second revaluation, which even became an important issue in an election campaign. After the facts had become clear it took about a year in all before the necessary steps were taken. For other countries similar examples could be cited. This, of course, was an invitation to all those who recognized the inevitable and had at their disposal the means to engage in speculative buying of foreign exchange. The odds were all in their favour; the question was only whether and when an adjustment would occur, there was never any doubt as to the direction. In other words, they could only win. The speculative movements in the end destroyed the Bretton Woods system. They might never have assumed such dimensions had governments always acted swiftly in the appropriate circumstances. But then, could they be expected to do so, given the fact that a change in the exchange rate always implied a fair amount of redistribution of wealth and income within the economy?

The Federal Republic was one of the major targets of speculative attacks in the exchange markets and perhaps suffered more than most other countries from 'importing inflation'. But it had certainly no intention of opting out of the system as long as there was any hope of reform or of better coordination, or that somehow the problem might just disappear. By spring 1973, little more than a year after the 'realignment' under the Smithsonian Agreement (and with the additional experience of administrative controls on most foreign exchange transactions, which Germany had long hesitated to apply), there was general awareness that the system could not survive. Floating exchange rates had to take over. The sheer magnitude of the foreign exchange flows, in comparison with monetary developments up to 1973, may be seen from table 1.

The Bundesbank put up what could be called a gallant fight against the external domination of domestic money creation. It succeeded in one field: the effects on the liquidity of banks, but it failed in the other field, the one which matters most: the effects on the liquidity of non-banks. Bank liquidity is directly under the control of the central bank. Whatever the central bank has to give banks in the way of reserves through one channel (e.g. by purchasing foreign exchange), it can drain off through some other channel (e.g. by raising minimum reserve requirements). The money supply in the economy, on the other hand, can only be controlled indirectly by the central bank through its influence on domestic banks. If, as was the case in

Table 1.

	M_1	M_2	Net foreign assets of the banking system
		Increase (+) in DM billion	
1967	+ 8.3	+ 14.2	+ 6.3
1968	+ 5.5	+ 18.2	+ 10.9
1969	+ 6.0	+ 14.5	− 2.5
1970	+ 8.7	+ 16.4	+ 14.2
1971	+ 13.2	+ 25.0	+ 11.5
1972	+ 17.5	+ 33.5	+ 8.7
1973	+ 2.6	+ 31.9	+ 23.5

Germany, foreign funds flow predominantly to non-banks (which sell them to their banks and thus increase their bank balances), the ensuing monetary expansion can only be offset by correspondingly restricting domestic sources of monetary expansion, and that was quite impossible in the required magnitudes. It may not be necessary to elaborate on this. A few years ago, some people would try to prove that the Bundesbank could have controlled monetary developments after all, even under the regime of fixed exchange rates. To-day apparently the general belief is the reverse. Nowadays it is so obvious to most people that having an independent monetary policy was quite impossible in the circumstances that they even wonder why the Bundesbank ever tried.

The oil price hike, the other important outside factor affecting price performance in Germany, came at a most unfortunate time. With the external constraint greatly diminished under floating exchange rates, the Bundesbank succeeded in getting the money supply process under control. Monetary policy and fiscal policy operating jointly succeeded in containing demand; price increases both on the producer and the consumer level between August and October 1973 showed some signs of moderating. Whether others would have followed nobody can tell, because the oil price increase completely altered the situation. Its effect was twofold. Firstly, there was the initial change in the terms of trade, which was a cost-push effect, a real one (not simply a delayed demand-pull effect as many so-called cost-push effects are). Secondly, there was a boost to inflationary expectations, which had shown signs of weakening before. I am inclined to believe that the second effect was the more important of the two. The terms-of-trade effect, seen in isolation, meant a reduction in goods and services available for domestic use—in other words, a decline in real income—and hence would have called for a moderation in nominal wage demands. Because of the boost to inflationary expectations, however, the opposite happened: nominal wages went up as trade unions and employers alike expected prices to rise sharply. The inflationary effect was thus multiplied. On the other hand, as long as the oil producers did not claim their newly acquired share in the real product of the industrial countries, the oil price increase was deflationary as real demand was reduced. This peculiar mixture of inflationary and deflationary effects has confronted policymakers with difficult choices. Some countries have tried harder to avoid Scylla, others to avoid Charybdis. None have fully succeeded in avoiding either. In Germany fiscal policy switched to a neutral and soon to an expansionary stance, while monetary policy continued to resist stronger monetary expansion. The pressure monetary policy had to contain eased more and more, however, so that the counter-pressure it exerted (as indicated by the level of short-term interest rates) could also be reduced until, in the autumn of 1974, monetary policy likewise took a clearly expansionary stance. The problem was now no longer to avoid excessive monetary expansion, but to ensure sufficient monetary growth.

Considering the subsequent rather severe recession with a drop in real GNP and high unemployment, the question has, of course, to be asked whether, seen with the benefit of hindsight, monetary policy was not eased too slowly in 1974. We do not believe so. Countries which concentrated more on the deflationary dangers fared worse in respect of inflation, but no better in respect of unemployment and real output. This does not seem to be an accident. Inflation, unemployment, and growth are separately identifiable as statistical phenomena; as economic phenomena they are linked in a much more complex way than has generally been assumed until recently. Instead of seeing them as alternatives which can be traded off against each other, we have learned that inflation itself leads, not immediately but sooner or later, to recession. A policy which opts for more inflation in order to avoid recession will have to apply larger and larger inflationary stimuli and will still not avoid slump in the end. In the light of these experiences, there seemed to be no real alternative to continuing with the attempt to break the inflationary spiral and bring inflation rates down again. This, of course, takes time. As the inflationary pressures have, after all, built up progressively through stages of excess demand, higher prices for final products, higher wage demands, and higher costs, they will push up prices again as soon as demand has grown sufficiently to do so. If, however, wage settlements and costs in general have been moderated and the profitability of business has been restored before a new boom develops, inflation rates may continue to fall even at a time when demand is becoming more buoyant again.

We had reached this critical point in the Federal Republic in 1976. The rise in the consumer price index—calculated as the increase during the previous 12 months—had gradually slowed down to 5.0 per cent (against a peak of 7.8 per cent in December 1973). However, on past experience the beginning of an upswing is relatively the best moment in the cycle for price performance. Once an upswing has started the only question seems to be how quickly the situation will deteriorate again, which leaves little hope of further improvement. On the other hand, an upswing was certainly what was needed. Production was no higher than it had been two years before and the employment situation was far from satisfactory. The questions then were whether more could be achieved, or whether 5 per cent inflation was the best we could manage not because of imported inflation of one kind or another, but because of domestic factors? A hard question to answer, and yet clearly the outcome depended on the answer to be given. Should we resign ourselves to the assumption of living with at least this amount of inflation or should we, cautiously but steadily, continue to aim at a further lowering of inflation? A difficult dilemma to resolve, but the latter seemed more satisfactory in respect of all ecomomic goals.

I shall now turn to some more technical aspects of monetary policy in Germany. As already mentioned, monetary policy (together with fiscal policy) adopted a severely restrictive stance in spring 1973 immediately after the advent of floating exchange rates. One thing about this policy was quite new: the Bundesbank was prepared to let the so-called *free liquid reserves* of the banking system drop to an unprecedentedly low level; in fact, but for a small, purely technical margin no reserves of this kind were left at all. 'Free liquid reserves' of the banking system in this context mean the unutilized borrowing facilities of the banks with the Bundesbank plus their holdings of assets which the Bundesbank has undertaken to acquire virtually on demand. Up to 1970 the Bundesbank had been satisfied that the banks responded in their lending activities to changes in the total volume of free liquid reserves, as at least some of the important banks considered these assets to be the pivotal point of their liquidity arrangements. But since 1970 doubts had been growing as to whether the monetary policymakers could still count on such a response for restrictive purposes. It seemed that all banks were satisfied with substitutes for free liquid reserves, and hence did not hesitate to dispose of whatever free liquid reserves they had in order to get balances at the central bank whenever they needed them. The only possible conclusion for the Bundesbank was that it should rely not on control over something for which there were substitutes—free liquid reserves—but on control over the one thing which it clearly has a monopoly—central bank balances—and that it should block easy access to central bank balances through free liquid reserves. This change in policy had its counterpart in the Bundesbank's monetary analysis. Instead of demonstrating in its analysis how free liquid reserves had changed under the influence of 'market factors' and 'policy actions', the Bundesbank now concentrated on the amount of central bank balances it had supplied for monetary expansion. This the Bundesbank calls *central bank money,* a narrow, but, as we see it, quite useful definition that comprises of currency in circulation plus required minimum reserves for domestic liabilities (calculated at constant reserve ratios).

The step which the Bundesbank took in 1973—bringing free liquid reserves down to zero—gave a new quality to monetary policy, although the institutional arrangements under which it operates were not altered. In fact, banks have had free liquid reserves again since autumn 1974, i.e. since the Bundesbank started to stimulate monetary expansion. The mental hurdle which had to be overcome—and in fact was overcome in 1973—was to see that free liquid reserves are not essential to the proper functioning of the banking system and that they can be removed if this is necessary to get monetary expansion under control. Whether they may not be useful in other circumstances as a stimulus to the lending activities of banks is another question. Personally, I feel certain that they are unnecessary even for this purpose; I believe that monetary policy could achieve the same results in other ways, thus avoiding problems which are likely to arise later from a new accumulation of free liquid reserves. But while new ways are tried out after it has become evident that the old ways no longer lead to the promised land, there is hardly a case for trying new ways as long as the old ways lead in the desired direction. And nobody could argue that the old way—providing ample free liquid reserves—would not lead to a stimulation of monetary expansion.

The phase during which the banking system in Germany, for all practical purposes, operated without free liquid reserves (spring 1973–autumn 1974), gave us, however, a good opportunity to improve our understanding of how the monopoly of the central bank, as the only source of central bank money, can be utilized for controlling the money supply process. We found ourselves quite at variance with one feature of the monetarist position, which is basically that control can be exercised strictly by quantitative means. As there is, statistically, a close relationship between the monetary base (however defined) and monetary aggregates (however defined), apparently all the central bank has to do is to increase the monetary base at a rate equal to its desired rate of the increase in the money supply and the latter will follow in line. There are several flaws in this simple proposition in spite of its wide acceptance nowadays.

(1)   The money supply process is set in motion by many different stimuli; the monopoly of the central bank is not a monopoly of starting such processes.

(2)   The money supply process, once under way, generates a demand for additional central bank balances which is completely inelastic and which the central bank cannot help supplying in view of the implications. In other words, the monopoly of the central bank does not even give it the ability to approve or disapprove of money creation once it has started.

(3)   What the monopoly does give the central bank, however, is the

power to determine—ignoring for the moment whatever external constraints may exist—the conditions under which it will satisfy the demand of banks for additional central bank balances. These conditions determine short-term money market rates, to which most interest rates in the economy are linked in one way or the other. Through this indirect channel the central bank is quite capable of influencing monetary developments, although not with great precision and always with some delay. As I see it, this is true of virtually all institutional arangements. It is not a question of the instruments or the organization of the central bank but a question of the way the banking system operates, which in this respect is essentially the same in all Western economies.

However, the aspect of German monetary policy that made headlines was not so much these changes in strategy since 1973 as the announcement of a quantitative target. In December 1974 the Bundesbank announced that 'from the present perspective . . . a growth of about 8 per cent in the central bank money stock in the course of 1975 may be regarded as compatible with the aims of stabilisation policy'. The Bundesbank announced another target for central bank money in December 1975 not, however, for the growth in the course of the year, but for the difference between the average level in 1976 and the average level in 1975. Three beliefs of the central bank are a prerequisite for such an announcement:

(1)   that it knows how to come reasonably close to such a target;
(2)   that the growth of the aggregate in terms of which it formulates its target is the best way to describe what monetary policy is doing; and
(3)   that it is useful for everybody to know what monetary policy is aiming at.

As regards the first belief, the proof of the pudding is, needless to say, in the eating. In the course of 1975 the central bank money stock grew not by 8 per cent but by 10 per cent. This was due to exceptionally strong growth during the last few months of that year, which went far beyond the desired correction of the slow growth in the first part of 1975. The Bundesbank came to the conclusion that the way it had formulated its target for 1975 (which was generally interpreted as a strict comparison of the level of December 1975 as against that of December 1974) was too precise. From what I have said about the inevitably indirect control of monetary aggregates it is apparent that short-term fluctuations may not and need not be controlled. The switch to a formulation in terms of averages seeks to get around this problem. It must be mentioned also—although the question of which aggregate to choose comes up again when discussing the second belief—that the lack of confidence in coming reasonably close to a chosen target prevented either M_1 or M_2 from being selected as the relevant aggregate. Both these aggregates proved to be sensitive to interest rate changes—in opposite directions—to such an unpredictable extent that the Bundesbank would have felt quite unable to commit itself to a target for M_1 and M_2. Central bank money—rather like M_3—is broadly based (and therefore less sensitive to interest rate movements) as demand deposits, time deposits, and savings deposits are all subject to reserve requirements although with different reserve ratios (roughly twice as high for demand deposits as for savings deposits, while time deposits hold the mid-way position).

The second belief I have mentioned bears, of course, on the whole philosophy behind a quantitative target. I have tried to avoid the word 'indicator' as that seems to be a particularly ambiguous term. Those who introduced this concept into the discussion of monetary policy were looking for something to describe the stance of monetary policy as distinct from market influences on monetary developments, such as bank behaviour, non-bank portfolio decisions, credit demand, etc. They considered the 'monetary base' to be the best indicator in this sense as they understood it to be predominantly determined by the central bank. The monetary base is, however, a mixture of two quite distinct things:

(1) what we call 'central bank money', i.e. currency in circulation plus required reserves (the reserve ratio being held constant to eliminate the influence of changes in reserve ratios); and
(2) excess reserves.

As excess reserves are notoriously small—not only in economies where the banks are indebted to the central bank, so that this fact can be easily explained—it follows that the monetary base is not an indicator of monetary policy in the described sense but simply an indicator of monetary developments and also reflects all the other influences like bank behaviour, credit demand, etc. It is in this sense on an equal footing with other monetary aggregates. Our preference for central bank money is largely due to the fact that it is less prone to purely interest-rate-induced shifts and can be assumed to reflect more accurately the underlying trend of monetary developments. In addition, it highlights the responsibility of the central bank for monetary developments as it includes the elements of total money supply which are actually supplied by the central bank.

All these reasons would, of course, be of little significance if the linkage between central bank money and aggregate demand were weak, much weaker than, say, that between GNP and M_1 or M_2. But this is not so. As our econometric studies show, the long-term elasticity of the demand for central bank money with respect to nominal GNP is practically one; fluctuations being largely cyclical in nature, it is not surprising—in view of the cyclical movements of interest rates—that the money-demand relationship also shows a significantly negative interest rate elasticity. M_3 is a close rival to central bank money on all counts and might even be preferable should the unjustifiably high weight of currency in central bank money ever prove to be embarrassing. So far, this has not been the case. While the two components—currency and deposits as reflected in a fictitious reserve requirement (because reserve ratios are held constant)—have moved far apart at times, this has always corrected itself quickly; for 1975 there was virtually no difference at all in the growth rate of the two components.

One may perhaps wonder whether a monetary indicator which reflects not just the actions of the central bank but also activities in the economy is really suitable as a target for monetary policy. Would not a pure *policy* indicator be more appropriate? I do not think so. The only possible candidates for the role of a policy indicator I can think of (candidates which would meet the requirement of being solely or predominantly under the control of the central bank) are the interest rates of the central bank, short-term money market rates and a term for bank liquidity like our definition of free liquid reserves. I think these examples clearly show that they are quite meaningless looked at by themselves. They may describe a certain pressure exercised by the central bank, but one has to know the counter-pressure in order to know what this pressure will achieve. The same level of interest rates may be high in relation to a weak economy and low in relation to a strong economy.

The third belief I referred to is not confined to the Bundesbank but is widely shared in Germany by most public commentators, the Council of Economic Experts, and last but not least the Federal Government. The background was the experience of 1974, when trade unions and employers had been expecting an 'accommodating' monetary policy and found out that—apparently due to the moderate scale of the monetary expansion— actual price increases fell far short of their expectations. The inference was that, had they known in advance what the monetary expansion would be, they would not have pushed wages and prices up to an extent which led to a sharp increase in unemployment and business failures. This was sometimes simplified to the view that the target growth rate for central bank money was nothing but a kind of disguised wage guideline. The Bundesbank tried very hard to make clear that this was not the case, and even harder in respect of 1976 as it was hoped to keep wage settlements well below the 8 per cent increase envisaged, on the average, for central bank money.

Given all these prerequisites for announcing a quantitative target, the pertinent question is, of course, what the target should be. Sometimes this question is kept somewhat in the background in discussions of the issue, as if it were a matter of secondary importance compared with the fact of having a quantitative target at all and sticking to it as long as possible. But a quantitative target must fit into a central bank strategy designed to contribute to the economic well-being of the country, i.e. relatively high economic growth, high employment, a high degree of price stability. It must reflect policy intentions, not forecasts; not expected real growth, but potential real growth; not expected price rises, but a price rise which at present the authorities are prepared to tolerate. This explains largely why the target does not have to be revised with every revision of GNP estimates. In other words, it is not necessary to predict changes in velocity accurately in order to arrive at a meaningful quantitative target.

In concluding, two things should perhaps be stressed again. First, quantitative target or no quantitative target, monetary policy cannot be charged with any kind of exclusive responsibility for what happens in the economy, although there is a strong presumption that monetary policy has been remiss in its duties when price rises persist or even accelerate. Second, the way for a central bank to achieve a quantitative target is to operate through interest rates. There is no direct quantitative link between those quantities which the central bank can indeed easily control (like free liquid reserves) and those quantities which it wants to control, because it regards them as being of prime importance for economic developments.

Monetary Targets: Conceptual Antecedents and Recent Policies in the U.S., U.K. and West Germany[1]

Anthony S. Courakis

Socrates: Do you find that your monetary system works well?

Economist: Pretty well, thank you, Socrates, on the whole.

Socrates: That would be, I suppose not because of *the rather strange rules* of which you have told me, but because it is administered by men of ability and wisdom?

Economist: It would seem that that must be the reason rather than the rules themselves O Socrates.

Denis Robertson, 'British monetary policy',
Lloyds Bank Review, May, 1939.

1. Introduction

Over the last few years increasing attention has been devoted to explicit quantitative targets for growth of monetary aggregates. Early examples of such tendencies can be found in U.S. official statements[2] dating back to 1970. In October 1972 the E.E.C. Commission[3], with characteristic optimism, announced (and in 1973 the Council of Ministers agreed on) the objective that member nations pursue a policy of maintaining an annual rate of increase in their respective 'money supplies' equal to their respective rates of growth of output plus 4 per cent. Two years later the Bundesbank announced its decision to pursue a target rate of increase in a particular monetary aggregate[4]. At the beginning of 1975 the Swiss National Bank took pride in being 'one of the first central banks in the world to make public its target for the desired money supply growth'[5], and since spring of that year the monetary targets of the Federal Reserve have been made public[6]. For the Netherlands, a 'money supply' target was announced[7] in 1976, and in

France a quantitative objective pertaining to the rate of increase in wide money was included in the stabilization policy programme presented by the government in September of the same year[8]. In the United Kingdom, in July 1976 the Chancellor of the Exchequer declared a target[9] of 12 per cent for, as it was quoted in the press, 'monetary expansion' in the financial year 1976–77, while *The Times* ventured into a 'Programme for Economic Stability' that began with the objective

> Money supply growth . . . be kept to 9 per cent this year, 6 per cent next year, and 4 per cent thereafter, this commitment to be institutionally entrenched beyond doubt and pressure[10].

The major impetus for such tendencies and recommendations does of course derive from increasing acceptance of the view that control of inflationary processes requires control of monetary aggregates. It is less clear whether the connection perceived relates to acceleration of the rate of increase in the 'money supply' being seen as the primary *cause* of price changes, or whether it is felt that non-monetary explanations of inflation presuppose a particular *response* on the part of the monetary authorities[11] in the absence of which such pressures will be considerably reduced or disappear entirely. But to some extent these tendencies are also encouraged by a belief that such policies are conducive to greater stability of financial markets by eliminating the uncertainty implicit in a process of policy changes[12]. The latter is also pertinent to the smoother operation of foreign exchange markets, where it is felt that the basic objective of eliminating 'the sense of turbulence, uncertainty, and crisis that have been common in recent years . . . will be served as the domestic intentions of the monetary authorities become more predictable, and as confidence in the domestic monetary framework grows'[13].

At any rate the public has come to focus attention on official statements regarding monetary targets, and comparisons of current monetary statistics to the target values is an art to which much effort is now devoted. In short, as one author recently put it, 'the era of monetary policy by monetary targets has arrived'[14]. But what does this mean? An attempt to answer this question suggests the need to examine a variety of issues.

(1) Are 'targets' to be understood as '*Friedmanian rules*'?

(2) Are they to be understood as statements of acceptance that monetary aggregates comprise the best *intermediate variables* in determining economic activity?

(3) Are targets to be understood as *indicators of economic activity*?

(4) Are they to be understood as *policy indicators*?

(5) What criteria are employed in determining their values?

(6) In what sense do they imply a change in the behaviour of monetary authorities?

(7) What is the content of 'publicly announced' targets? and correspondingly,

(8) What are the commitments involved in such announcements?

It seems instructive, however, to begin with a preview of the "targets' that governments have come to set.

2. Monetary 'Targets': A Bird's Eye View of Prescriptions and Experience in Three Economies

THE UNITED STATES

Since March 1975, in response to a Joint Concurrent Resolution of the House of Representatives and Senate, the Federal Reserve Chairman is obliged *once a quarter* to report ranges for growth of monetary aggregates in the coming four quarters. These ranges themselves are defined in terms of upper and lower limits for growth rates in three definitions of the money supply and one of bank credit, as measured from the most recent *quarterly average* levels to their prospective levels four quarters hence. The three definitions of the money supply are currency plus demand deposits, M_1; the latter plus commercial bank time deposits, M_2; and the latter plus shares at mutual savings banks and savings and loan associations, M_3. The fourth aggregate, termed the adjusted credit proxy[15], is equal to total member bank deposits subject to reserve requirements plus non-deposit sources of funds, such as eurodollar borrowings and the proceeds of commercial paper issued by bank holding companies or other officiates. However lags in data availability have more recently resulted in the replacement of this fourth aggregate by bank credit which includes total bank loans and investments, measured on a monthly average basis, less interbank loans. Table 1 presents the annual growth ranges adopted and actual rates of growth of such aggregates realized in the period 1975 to 1978.

The precise ranges of the targets are decided by the Federal Open Market Committee (FOMC) in the light of econometric and qualitative projections of the consequences for the economy of alternative target ranges. From a long-run standpoint the acknowledged strategy is one of gradually reducing growth rates to levels that may prove compatible with price stability. From the 'one-year range' standpoint, however, it is stressed that '. . . inflation can lead a life of its own quite independent of current or past monetary development'[16] and hence the growth ranges adopted, take the 'underlying economic conditions' as given. Furthermore, personal judgement as to what comprises 'no more than accommodation' of such underlying economic conditions is allowed considerable free rein in view of the fact that the relationships between the four aggregates and GNP are subject to variations that preclude exclusive reliance on past statistical associations[17].

Table 1. *Annual growth targets and actual performance in the United States, 1975–78 (seasonally adjusted annual percentage rates).*

Period		Introduced	M_1		M_2		M_3	
			Range	Actual	Range	Actual	Range	Actual
March 1975	to March 1976	April 1975	5.0–7.5	5.0	8.5–10.5	9.6	10.0–12.0	12.3
June 1975	to June 1976	June 1975	5.0–7.5	4.2	8.5–10.5	8.7	10.0–12.0	11.2
1975:2	to 1976:3	July 1975	5.0–7.5	5.2	8.5–10.5	9.5	10.0–12.0	12.0
1975:3	to 1976:3	October 1975	5.0–7.5	4.6	7.5–10.5	9.3	9.0–12.0	11.5
1975:4	to 1976:4	January 1976	4.5–7.0	5.7	7.5–10.5	10.9	9.0–12.0	12.8
1976:1	to 1977:1	April 1976	4.5–7.0	6.3	7.5–10.0	10.9	9.0–12.0	12.8
1976:2	to 1977:2	July 1976	4.5–7.0	6.6	7.5– 9.5	10.7	9.0–11.0	12.4
1976:3	to 1977:3	November 1976	4.5–6.5	7.8	7.5–10.0	11.0	9.0–11.5	12.7
1976:4	to 1977:4	January 1977	4.5–6.5	7.8	7.0–10.0	9.8	9.0–11.5	11.7
1977:1	to 1978:1	April 1977	4.5–6.5	7.7	7.0–10.0	8.7	8.5–11.5	10.4
1977:2	to 1978:2	July 1977	4.0–6.5	8.2	7.0– 9.5	8.4	8.5–11.0	
1977:3	to 1978:3	October 1977	4.0–6.5	8.0	6.5– 9.0	8.2	8.5–10.5	

Source: Federal Reserve Bank of New York.

In pursuing its yearly targets the FOMC defines, in terms of one or both of the two narrower aggregates, short-run (current and next month) *tolerance ranges* at levels and spreads deemed consistent with *current developments* and with the adopted yearly targets. The Committee's instructions to the Manager of the System's Open Market Account accordingly provide for the accommodation of the public's demand for funds in the short-run while at the same time prescribing responses to be made when the growth of M_1 and/or M_2 (i.e. of the aggregate focused upon from a short-run operational standpoint) appears inconsistent with the Committee's longer-run objectives[18].

This is the principle at any rate[19]. In practice, however, the extent to which tolerance ranges have been observed has been limited. Examining, for example, actual experience during the first year of operation of the 'announced range scheme' one finds that, despite variations in the width of the tolerance ranges, the actual behaviour of the two aggregates deviated from the specified limits[20]. Nor was this pattern a manifestation of initial teething problems, for such over—or under—shooting has continued in the years since. On the yearly ranges, performance has varied as between aggregates. Interestingly, there was a greater tendency to 'achieve' all three targets in the earlier part of the period reviewed, a feature which corresponds to the pattern of declining growth ranges for M_1 coupled with increasing rates of growth of this aggregate during the period.

THE UNITED KINGDOM

In the British context, publicly announced monetary targets are a more recent phenomenon. In the Budget Statement of April 1976, the Chancellor indicated 'that after two years in which M_3 had increased at a rate less than GDP [he expected] their growth rates to come more into line in the financial year 1976/77 "though" it was still the government's objective that the growth of the money supply should remain moderate'[21]. A few months later, in July 1976, the Chancellor announced that M_3, i.e. the aggregate of currency with the public plus U.K. private and public sector sterling demand and time deposits plus U.K. resident deposits in other currencies, should grow by 12 per cent during the financial year 1976/77. In October this objective was reiterated; and though in December emphasis shifted to a target for domestic credit expansion (DCE) (as the Letter of Intent to the I.M.F. set limits on DCE for the financial years 1976/79), the authorities also announced corresponding objectives for the *sterling component* of M_3 in the form of a *range* of 9 to 13 per cent for the financial year 1976/77. This range was furthermore adopted in the Budget speech of 1977 as the joint objective, combined, that is, with a DCE ceiling of £7.7 billion set by the I.M.F. for the financial year 1977/78.

Unlike the United States, no precise information regarding short-run operational procedures is available. An address by the Governor of the Bank of England, however, does provide some insight into the *modus operandi* of pursuit of the M_3 objectives. Commenting on the 'Management of Monetary Aggregates', Mr Gordon Richardson summarized[22] the Bank of England's 'logic of operating' as seeking

> ... to manage the course of monetary aggregates by bringing about changes in interest rates. [However, the difficulty of predicting] ... the level and structure of interest rates at which the stock of money that the public wants to hold will be brought into equality with the stock the authorities would like to see being held [means that] in practice the authorities often try building up a forecast from, as it were, the 'supply' side. [This involves looking] ... separately at the main items which statistically speaking are the components of the money supply on a broad definition—such as the public sector borrowing require-ment, sales to the public of government debt, the volume of bank lending to the private sector and external flows to the private sector. What we are in effect doing in such an exercise is to attempt to predict what the rate of monetary expansion will be if we refrain from trying to change interest rates—as a preliminary to considering the need for intervention ... The essence of mone-tary management ... is to act to offset divergencies, in these sources of monetary expansion—difficult to predict and control—as soon as it becomes reasonably clear that inaction is likely to undermine achievement of the monetary target.

Whatever the precise operational context of policy[23], the record so far has not been in accordance with stated objectives. In the first year of operation, 1976/77, neither the original (July 1976, 12 per cent) target for M_3 nor the (December 1976, 9–13 per cent) target range for sterling M_3 were attained. The latter grew by 7.5 per cent and the former, as was the case in the previous two years, by 10 per cent only. Part of the reason for such under-shooting[24] was that the public sector borrowing requirement was some 25 per cent below the figure predicted even as late as December 1976. Further-more the demand for gilt edged was higher than anticipated, resulting in higher than forecast sales of securities to domestic investors despite the fact that the authorities refrained from selling gilt edged in the last two months of the financial year.

The performance in the financial year 1977/78 was not in accord with the target rate of increase postulated either. As table 2 reveals, in the first three quarters of the financial year sterling M_3 rose at an annual rate of almost 15 per cent. This was so despite continuing strong demand for gilt edged[25] and despite the authorities' eventual move to a more flexible exchange rate policy in late October 1977. Even this rate, however, was to be exceeded in the last quarter of the financial year, so that for the year as a whole the rate of growth of sterling M_3 was more than twice that of 1976/77.

Besides prompting the intriguing (?) comment in the Bank's *Quarterly Bulletin* that

Table 2. Target ranges and actual experience in the United Kingdom, 1976–78.

Target period	Target variable	Introduced	Target	yearly	Actual Experience[a] quarterly April-July	July-October	October-January	January-April
April 1976–April 1977	Sterling M_3 DCE (£m)	Dec. 1976	9.0 – 13.0% 9000	7.5 4944	3.1 2186	4.2 2918	−0.6 −140	1.4 380
April 1977–April 1978	Sterling M_3 DCE (£m)	April 1977	9.0 – 13.0% 7700	16.4 4448	2.6 749	3.2 −73	4.1 798	5.6 2989
April 1978–April 1979	Sterling M_3 DCE (£m)	April 1978	8.0 – 12.0% 6000		2.3 1531	1.3 956		

(a) Seasonably adjusted data; M_3 percentage changes; DCE £m.
Source: Bank of England Quarterly Bulletin.

with recovery in the real economy still very fragile, the authorities were naturally unwilling to see interest rates go higher than was essential[26].

this performance must have contributed to the move to six-monthly rolling targets, anticipated in the February 1978 lecture by the Governor of the Bank of England referred to earlier and announced in the Budget speech of April 1978—a '. . . minor but useful technical change to our continuing policy of having publicly announced monetary targets'[27] as the Governor saw it, but at any rate one which experience since has not challenged.

WEST GERMANY

While the movement to publicly announced targets in both the United States and United Kingdom followed a period during which monetary aggregates were accorded greater attention in policy design, the first publicly declared target for monetary aggregates was that of the Deutsche Bundesbank. In December 1974 this monetary authority 'broke new ground' in announcing a decision of the Central Bank Council stating that 'from the present viewpoint' it considered 'a growth rate of about 8 per cent in the Central Bank Money Stock during the year 1975 justifiable in the light of the aims of stabilization policy'[28]. The monetary aggregate chosen for this purpose is one that has featured in this central bank's policy statements[29] since early 1974. It is equal to currency in circulation plus banks' *compulsory* reserves against domestic liabilities of the private sector[30] adjusted for variations (over time) in reserve ratios. The exclusion of excess reserves and absence of offset for borrowed reserves does, of course, imply that this aggregate is conceptually different from what is sometimes defined as the adjusted monetary base[31]; and at least since 1976 the central bank money stock is increasingly presented as a weighted money stock aggregate[32].

In deciding on the precise figure of target rate of growth, the Bundesbank

. . . was mainly guided by the following variables: the growth of production potential, the change in the utilization of the production potential, the rate of 'unavoidable' price rises and the change in the 'velocity of circulation'[33].

Furthermore it was thought that

Of these four variables two—the utilization of the production potential and the velocity of circulation—are equally dependent on cyclical conditions. It can therefore be assumed that the utilization of the production potential and the 'velocity of circulation' both change in the same direction and that there is a relatively great probability of such changes continuing to run fairly parallel in future. Hence two components are particularly important in determining the target: the growth of the production potential and the rate of unavoidable price rises[34].

Granted such reasoning and projections suggesting an increase in nominal GNP of the order of 9–10 per cent, the target of 8 per cent increase in CBM between December 1974 and December 1975 was reached.

For the first few months of the year policy appeared to keep track of the objective. But by August the rate of increase of CBM was accelerating and, with an annual rate of increase of 13.6 per cent in the second half of the year, the December 1975 CBM was almost 10 per cent higher than a year earlier.

The experience of 1975 was thought to reveal that setting a precise quantitative target for monetary growth to be achieved in the course of precisely one year was too demanding a task for the monetary authority. Thus in defining its objectives for 1976 the Bundesbank set as its target not a figure to be achieved between *end*-1975 and *end*-1976, but rather a figure to be achieved *on average* during this time interval, *an average growth target*. But the criteria for target setting remained the same. In deciding on the precise figure, therefore, the principal, and publicly stated, assumptions were[35]

(1) a 2 per cent rate of growth of productive potential in 1976
(2) a 2.5 per cent rise in capacity utilization
(3) a virtually unavoidable rise in the price level of 4–5 per cent.

Altogether this amounted to an anticipated growth of nominal GNP of about 9 per cent. But granted the cyclical phase of the economy it was reasoned that this did not require an equal rate of expansion in CBM since

(4) a higher income velocity was to be expected.

Allowing for this last assumption the Bundesbank considered a rise of 8 per cent in CBM, comparing the average for 1976 with the average for 1975, to be appropriate.

While retaining any psychological benefit of continuity of an absolute figure for rate of growth of CBM, the new target, postulated on an average basis, meant of course a considerable reduction in the end-year to end-year growth objective. In the event the new target was also violated. Taking the average of all months the central bank money stock was 9.2 per cent higher in 1976 than in the previous year (though on an end-year to end-year basis the growth rate did decline to 8.4 per cent). Significantly this over-shooting was consistent with an actual increase in growth of real output in excess of that embodied in the assumptions on which the 8 per cent target was based, while the increase in prices was smaller than budgeted for. But the overall increase in nominal GNP was as originally projected so that, as the Bundesbank put it, 'the crux of the question was why the velocity of circulation did not increase, as had originally been assumed'[36].

Although no clear answer to the last question was forthcoming (see below) the Bundesbank persisted with its 8 per cent target for the year 1977 also. To preclude any misunderstandings regarding average as opposed to fixed inter-

Table 3. Monetary targets and actual experience in West Germany, 1975–78 (central bank money stock).

Period	Introduced	Actual experience					
		year[a]		'quarter'[b]			
		Dec.–Dec.	Av.–Av.	1	2	3	4
December 1974 to December 1975	Dec. 1974	10.0	*7.8*	8.8	7.3	7.7	12.5
Average of 1976 to average of 1975	Dec. 1975	*8.4*	9.2	8.3	5.0	11.7	9.4
Average of 1977 to average of 1976	Dec. 1976	*9.8*	9.0	7.6	6.4	12.2	11.0
Average of 1978 to average of 1977	Dec. 1977	—	11.4	13.8	9.5	10.8	13.1

(a) Figures in italics are provided for information only relating to performance had the regime not changed from an end year to an average target.
(b) Quarterly averages of seasonally adjusted data at annual rates.

val growth, the Bundesbank also announced that to meet this target it would strive to achieve a *steady* expansion in CBM of 6–7 per cent, comparing the average of the fourth quarter of 1977 with the corresponding quarter of 1976. Nominal GNP was, as in 1976, predicted to rise by 9 per cent, consistent with a 3 per cent increase in production potential, 2 per cent increase in capacity utilization and 4 per cent increase in prices. A change in velocity of circulation was expected (contrary to experience in 1976) to make up the difference between 8 per cent growth and 9 per cent increase in GNP.

At least as revealing as the Bundesbank's persistence to the magical figure of 8 per cent however, was the renewed emphasis, since late 1976, on the behaviour of banks' free liquid reserves as a focus for policy—an issue played down in the preceding three years[37]—and the unwillingness to resolve the dilemma that strong capital inflows posed by allowing the exchange rate to appreciate[38] rather than overshoot the 1976 target in the midst of a merry-go-round of sales of securities to absorb bank liquidity combined with a policy of stabilizing interest rates and total reluctance to raise the cost of Lombard credit in light of record recourse to such credit by commercial banks[39]. Thus while in December 1977 an 8 per cent growth target for CBM was once again adopted, in the light of predictions regarding the four key variables described above[40], we also find that its unequivocal pursuit was now much qualified. Indeed experience over the three preceding years culminates in the rationalization, found in the Bank's report for the year 1977 (published in April 1978), that

The Bundesbank had to assume from the outset [since targets were first announced that is] that there may be periods in which the pursuit of an 'intermediate target variable' as reflected in the announced rate of CBM cannot be given priority; it is then necessary to consider whether to tolerate the non-attainment of the original target or to revise the target. In 1977 as in 1976 the Bundesbank decided not to change the target but to explain the reasons for the divergence[41].

Whether such pronouncements suggest a shift in the Bundesbank's position will be discussed later. But from the standpoint of providing a broad record of events (as I have aimed to do in this section) we may note that the reasons given for the divergence in 1977 were that rises in interest rates such as would have been required to contain the growth of CBM would, on the one hand, have 'increased the risk of cyclical setback' and, on the other, 'would have been at variance with external requirements', placing that is more pressure on the Deutschemark to rise further. And since higher monetary growth in the short run was thought not to endanger price stability, the Bundesbank chose not only 'not to counteract accelerating monetary expansion' but indeed to initiate 'further monetary relaxations[42]'.

3. Conceptual Antecedents and the Interpretation of Policy

FRIEDMANIAN RULES?

There is much in the above that can be said to carry a Friedmanian tinge[43]. A yearning for a more stable economic environment after the vagaries of the first half of the 1970s is easily understood; and equally, when much else has failed, Friedman's vision may not tantalize all, but promises deliverance with seductive (apparent) simplicity. As he concluded in 1968:

> by adopting publicly the policy of achieving a steady rate of growth in a specified monetary total ... the monetary authority could make a major contribution to promoting economic stability. ... Other forces would still affect the economy, require change and adjustment and disturb the even tenor of our ways. But a steady monetary growth would provide a monetary climate favorable to the effective operation of those basic forces of enterprise, ingenuity, invention, hard work and thrift that are the springs of economic growth. That is the most that we can ask from monetary policy at our present stage of knowledge. But that much—and it is a great deal—is clearly within our reach[44].

This prescription, which appears to elevate the pursuit of a stable rate of growth of some monetary aggregate[45] to the status of a sole objective for monetary policy, derives we may remember from three premises, namely that

(1) the behaviour of the private sector is basically very stable;

(2) our ignorance of structural relationships precludes the use of monetary policy for fine tuning (so that the pursuit of such policy by the authorities is likely to result in instability in the sense of increasing the amplitude of the adjustment path that the private sector will generate in response to any given disturbance in the absence of policy);

(3) monetary policy, though it has important effects on real magnitudes, cannot peg real magnitudes at predetermined levels.

In principle these seem to be positive issues on which empirical investigation may be expected to adjudicate. In practice disagreement at the normative level, stemming from differences of opinion[46] regarding social order and time perspectives, has sustained, and will continue to sustain, some of the heat of the debate on 'rules versus discretion' in monetary or other policy. At the positive level, Friedman's rule comprises one of the alternatives open to the policymaker. At the normative level, it reflects his preference for limited government and, where government is essential, his preference for limiting government so far as possible by clearly specified rules rather than granting wide discretion to government officials[47]. To be sure, experience does affect normative judgements also. The performance of various countries in the last few years has induced considerable reflection on the extent to which governments can be expected to deliver such objectives as the market may (or does) fail to deliver. Furthermore the experience of the last few years has emphasized the trade-offs between short-run benefits and long-run losses[48]. Yet though the targets adopted do reveal increasing acceptance of the position that monetary acrobatics do not confer long-run benefits[49], and may indeed confer losses[50], while imperfect knowledge of the relevant parameters and lags in 'recognition', 'implementation' and 'effects' limits their short-run potential[51], it is also clear that the targets I have described in section 2 above, do not appear to qualify for the title of Friedmanian Rules[52]. The American ones are too frequently reviewed (and one perceives that they are revised to conform to what can be achieved when due regard is paid to other economic variables) to be consistent with Friedman's grand design and desire to deprive the monetary authority of discretion. The British ones have not been with us long; but as the move to 'rolling targets' à l'americaine *also* indicates in this respect they have much in common with those of the United States. And the Germans? They at least can claim to have kept to the same absolute yearly figure; though, as we have seen, granted revisions in measurement this has not really been the same all the time. More importantly, in Germany too the process whereby target values are derived is not one that abstracts from current conditions, resting on belief in the inherent stability of the economy[53], despite exhortations to the effect that in 'assessing the expansion of central bank money in a manner compatible with stability is . . .above all necessary to be guided by the somewhat *longer-term* possibilities of economic growth'[54].

THE NATURE AND CONDUCT OF ECONOMIC POLICY

Granted that the policies currently pursued cannot be accorded the status of Friedmanian rules, monetary targets could be seen in the context of resolutions to what, following Brunner and Meltzer, may be termed 'the policy problem'[55]. The latter[56] pertains to the conduct, and interpretation of the posture, of policy in an environment characterized by incomplete knowledge of the structural relationships intercalating instruments of policy and ultimate goal variables, and by imperfect information regarding current and even past values of the endogenous and exogenous variables in the system.

In Brunner's analysis[57], policy in such an environment is seen as comprising '. . . three major groups of problems: (i) *the information problem*; (ii) *the interpretation problem*; and (iii) *the determination problem*'[58]. The first of these relates to the assessment of the general movement of the economy, the pace of economic activity, the pressure on the price level and the trend in the balance of payments; in short to the identification of the current movement of the goal variables, whatever the cause of such movements may be. By contrast, *the interpretation problem* relates to the acquisition of 'information about the monetary thrust transmitted to economic activity'. Finally, *the determination problem* 'relates to the optimal strategy guiding the monetary authorities' behaviour in the context of prevailing institutional arrangements' as well as to the way in which alternative institutional arrangements impinge on the optimal strategy[59].

Although these problems are distinct *in some respects*, and in the work of Brunner and Meltzer, and others[60] considerable effort has been expended in separate discussions of the target and indicator problems, in recent years attention has focused primarily on the optimal choice of a short-run target governing the continuous adjustments of the policymakers control variables. In particular under conditions of *incomplete knowledge about the structure and information lags* policymakers have typically chosen to direct their policies to the attainment of specific values of endogenous variables that are observable with a lag shorter than that pertaining to the goal variables themselves and which, provided that they can be said to relate to the goal variables in a determinate fashion, serve as the 'proximate' or 'intermediate' targets for policy. Interest rates, monetary and credit aggregates are obvious candidates for this role and in this context the emphasis on 'monetary targets' may be interpreted to denote convergence of opinion to the view that (for the particular time interval to which policy choices relate) monetary aggregates comprise the 'best' intermediate variables in securing the attainment of desired values of the goal variables. While the latter may be true, we should note from the outset that both the theoretical models pertaining to this issue and the interpretations of current policies that claim (formally or informally) to depart from such models rest on a much more limited view of the problem than that explicit in Brunner's missionary discourses or indeed in descriptions of the deliberations of policymakers.

Intermediate Targets and Information Variables: the Variance Approach

At the expense of considerable simplification one may distinguish three aspects of incomplete knowledge, namely

(1) lags in information pertaining to the goal variables and other variables in the system;
(2) lack of knowledge of the structure, that is to say of the values of the parameters characterizing responses of economic actors in a particular economy at a particular interval of time; and
(3) random disturbances.

Recent analysis has focused entirely on the first and third of these aspects of experience[61] in notable disregard of the fact that, in view of the absence of precise information (consensus) regarding the structure and the increasing evidence that the desirability of particular strategies is intimately related to the precise nature of this structure, the questions pursued in such treatises bear a rather casual (or even remote) resemblance to those confronting the policymaker. Nevertheless one is impressed by the extent to which the authorities' behaviour in some countries can be said (or has been interpreted) to conform to the mould of the 'variance approach'.

In the context of this approach it is assumed that the policymaker in pursuing his goals seeks to minimize the expected value of a quadratic loss function[62] over a particular horizon. Besides the weights attaching to the goal variables in terms of preferences, the choice of strategy depends on the mean values of the parameters and stochastic properties of the model purporting to characterize the policymaker's perception of his environment, and also the flow of information about the exogenous and endogenous variables in the system.

Following Theil[63], the more popular variant of the approach, aptly described as 'certainty equivalence', assumes that the decision-taker perceives a linear structure and knows with certainty the constants and coefficients of this structure, so that stochastic variability is confined to additive disturbances[64]. The policy choice then reduces to a deterministic Tinbergen (instrument-goal) problem[65]. In particular, within the confines of the traditional Hicksian IS-LM structure (usually employed to illustrate the variance approach), the superiority of an interest rate policy over a money stock policy[66], measured by comparing the expected squared deviation of *the* goal variable (typically income) from its 'desired' value, depends on the variance-covariance structure of the additive disturbances attaching to the expenditure and monetary sectors and on the values of the parameters describing the response of expenditures to changes in *the* interest rate and of the demand for money to changes in *the* interest rate and income[67]. In such a model, furthermore, it can be easily deduced that if, as monetarists have often claimed, the demand for money is both more stable than the expenditure function and rather unresponsive to interest rate movements, a money stock policy is superior to an interest rate policy. Monetary growth targets therefore (it is inferred) can be interpreted to imply tacit acceptance of monetarist antecedents, reflecting, that is, prior information (or beliefs) that the underlying structure is such as for the variance in the goal variable under a money stock policy to be smaller than under an interest rate policy.

Whether the latter is an appropriate characterization of policymakers' current perception of their respective environments is an issue to which I will come in due course. For the moment let us delve further into what is to be understood by a money stock policy in such a frame. In an environment in which the money stock and the interest rate can be regarded as alternative instruments of policy[68] (in the sense that the authorities can set the value of either at the level consistent with minimizing the variance in the goal variable) and where decisions relate to an interval of time during which the authorities receive information neither about the value of the goal variable nor any other variable except that which they choose to control, the money stock policy relates to the choice of a single value of an instrument of policy to be maintained at the interval between policy reviews. Although therefore the setting of the money stock (in the hypothetical case in which M is an instrument) at the particular level consistent with minimizing the variance in the goal variable implies that the interest rate responds to movements in the demand for money and in the expenditure function, or correspondingly the setting of the interest rate—in a situation in which this alternative is deemed to minimize the variance in the goal variable between policy reviews—implies that the money stock varies, this variation is not (or cannot be) utilized by the authorities to effect revisions in their instrument that will reduce the variance in the goal variable further. On the other hand, if the authorities receive information on the behaviour of the variable whose value is not set as an instrument, with a regular frequency greater than that pertaining to the goal variable, they may choose to respond to such information by adjusting their instrument of policy[69].

In the latter case two kinds of response may be distinguished. The first is for the authorities to seek to infer, in the light of their prior knowledge about the structure and its stochastic characteristics, the likelihood that this deviation of the money stock (or interest rate) from its expected (and other things equal consistent with minimizing the variance in the goal variable) value is due to an IS disturbance and adjust their instruments of policy in accordance with the expectation of such a disturbance being reflected in the movement of the money stock or interest rate. The second is for the authorities to seek to adjust their instruments in such a way as to minimize the variance in the money stock[70], treating, that is, the money stock as the proximate policy objective—as the *intermediate target*. (A simple graphical representation of these alternatives is given in Appendix A below.)

Presented thus it is immediately obvious that such an *intermediate target strategy*, unless it can be maintained that the demand for money depends on income only[71], is inferior to '. . . the optimal policy . . . of first determining how much of the money surprise is likely to be due to a spending disturbance (thereby warranting an offsetting action) and then allowing for the LM curve slope in gauging the optimal policy'[72]. The optimal policy therefore requires that the money stock be treated as an 'information variable'[73] rather than a target. And even in this capacity there is no reason for exclusive attention on its path. For since the path of any other observable endogenous or exogenous variable also contains information that (in this scheme of things) can be interpreted through the structure, it will in general[74] be inefficient to abstain from exploiting fully[75] the information contained in observations of variables other than the money stock (or interest rate)[76].

Such an uncompromising verdict on the desirability of using any particular intermediate variable as a focus for policy (be it as an 'information variable' or an 'intermediate target'), however, cannot fail to raise the question of whether the particular characterization of the policy problem, encapsulated in what was termed the 'certainty equivalence' approach, bears any resemblance to that which confronts macroeconomic decision-takers and hence whether, in appraising current policy procedures, we are entitled to confine ourselves to such a mould. After all, if we accept '. . . at face value the proposition that central bankers are men and women of normal competence . . . who take decisions according to the advancement of the public weal . . .'[77] it seems hard, in the light of the above, to explain their alleged recurrent recourse to intermediate targets, unless of course by 'normal competence' we are to understand a level of intelligence below that required to comprehend that it is inefficient to disregard costlessly-provided and interpretable information that is *known* to be relevant to the pursuit of ultimate objectives.

Steeped in the variance mould it is tempting to seek an explanation in the nature of the disturbances[78]. For though policy simulations do in practice invariably rely on deterministic structures, the particular econometric model comprising the background to such simulations (the foundation of the prior beliefs) does, by definition, exhibit multiplicative disturbances and is thus 'at variance' with the popular 'certainty equivalence' variant of the variance approach. However, while multiplicative disturbances[79] result in optimal policies that imply a more conservative response on the part of policymakers to changes in the exogenous and/or endogenous variables in the system, and further still detract from the Tinbergen instrument-goal solution in that the policymaker will generally deploy as many instruments as are available irrespective of the number of goal variables he pursues (since such a course of action tends to reduce the risks associated with multiplicative disturbances), such a move towards reality—except perhaps in the, for our purposes, irrelevant case of infinite planning horizons—does not detract from the above conclusion that there exists an optimal policy, in the sense of a feedback rule that is superior to an intermediate target strategy.

All this however, it cannot be stressed enough, is *on the assumption that the decision-taker holds a particular prior belief about his environment, about the structure.*

Intermediate Targets under 'Uncertainty'

In contrast to the variance approach, the policy problem pursued in the Brunner-Meltzer writings (like Milton Friedman's) comprises as an essential ingredient:

> ... ignorance—or relatively incomplete information about the structure of the economy[80].

Ignorance of the structure relates to

> ... absence of quantitative estimates of the parameters of a general equilibrium macro-model, of the speeds of adjustment of many of the variables, and of the distribution of the effects of monetary policy through time[81].

> Both the values of the parameters and the distribution of the parameters are uncertain and in addition there is uncertainty about the form of the functions used to state hypotheses about the system and the variables admitted as arguments to these hypotheses[82].

A proper understanding (and appraisal) of policy and of intermediate targets, and indicators (see pages 280–86), cannot therefore depart from the assumption (criticized by Brunner and Meltzer) that 'A particular hypothesis relating monetary policy to [the goal variables] is well established', so that different policies (with or without feedback from information variables) can be uniquely ordered in terms of this hypothesis—but from recognition of the fact that

> ... the policy maker has many different competing hypotheses of the structure available to him[83].

That the conduct of policy in such an environment is a task distinct from that implied in the Poole–Kareken *et al.*–B. Friedman writings is blatantly obvious when we reflect on how sensitive the policy recommendations (the optimal policy that is) derived from any specific model are to the exact specification of the model[84], a fact which as Turnovsky has demonstrated 'is even more true when crucial parameters are subject to stochastic disturbances'[85].

Consider therefore a world, much as the real one, in which the decision-taker is confronted with an array of alternative theoretical structures and econometric estimates pertaining to various aspects of such structures. In principle of course all such structures can be explicitly defined and a systematic comparison be undertaken that yields some ordinal ranking and may render one or other of these structures as, statistically, the most acceptable characterization of the economy for a particular interval of time. Even if this were feasible in practice however (and if the will for such an undertaking existed which is doubtful in the face of current practice of '. . . econometric models mutating and multiplying at amazing speed . . .')[86], such a comparison would, at best, resolve the ambiguities regarding *the correct specification of the structure in the period to which our data sample pertains*. Although, therefore, it may strengthen the decision-taker's confidence in a particular paradigm, his awareness of: (a) the precariousness of the assumptions required to enable him to undertake the statistical comparison; (b) the protean nature of the economic system; (c) memories of how often other prior beliefs were shaken in the past; (d) the fact that any such verdict for the period as a whole need not imply the same verdict for all subperiods; as well as, possibly, (e) his unease with the performance of at least some of the equations of the model, will almost certainly prevent the convergence of his prior beliefs to a single paradigm[87].

Let us suppose that the above considerations result in the policymaker retaining a number of econometric models. In addition he may entertain a variety of beliefs regarding the path of the exogenous variables in the system that cannot be described by a mean value and some measure of dispersion. His policy problem then requires that he examines *how alternative policies perform under the assumptions/characteristics of the different models defined by the competing hypotheses about the structure and paths of the exogenous variables*. If, for example, we retain the assumption that his goal is a particular value of income, we may envisage a process of policy selection analogous to a pay-off matrix with different columns corresponding to different stochastic models and different rows corresponding to different policies to be examined, each element of the matrix (if we retain the quadratic loss function—'for simplicity') being the expected squared deviation of the goal variable from its desired value associated with a particular combination of model and policy[88]. The choice of policy could be determined '. . . by a Bayesian procedure. . .'[89], i.e. by attaching probabilities to the various models and proceeding to choose that strategy which minimizes the value of the (on these prior probabilities calculable) weighted sum of the elements as between rows[90]. More likely than not, however, the same considerations that contribute to the policymaker's reluctance to converge on a particular model will direct him to a maxi-min decision whereby '. . . the optimal strategy minimizes the worst variabilities over time attributable to . . . partial ignorance' of the structure and of the path of the exogenous variables in the system[91].

Notice that such a procedure suggests that *the policy adopted will not in general be 'optimal' when examined in the context of any of the competing models*. Like an intermediate target strategy (we may without commitment record) compared to the 'optimal policy' prescribed by a particular prior belief, the policy adopted on the maxi-min criterion will almost certainly be inferior when appraised in terms of any one of the alternative models; but it will, nonetheless, be a correct policy granted uncertainty over model selection. This does not of course establish that the intermediate target strategy is the same as the best maxi-min strategy. But it does reveal that, even if it could be shown that an intermediate target strategy is inferior to the 'optimal policy' embedded in each conceivable prior perception of our economic environment, we will not have secured a *sufficient* condition for dismissing intermediate targets as 'inefficient'.

This conclusion contrasts sharply with the dicta of the variance approach. Can it be also argued however that intermediate targets are, in a context of uncertainty over model selection, in some sense 'efficient'?

Tapping on the findings of the models that recognize multiplicative disturbances, we may conjecture that uncertainty over model selection (in addition to the presence of multiplicative disturbances for any given model) will in general provoke conservative adjustments in all instruments of policy. But this does not in itself constitute proof that the policy to be adopted is different from an intermediate target strategy since we are not operating in the instrument$\longrightarrow$(target)$\longrightarrow$goal-setting of the certainty equivalence mould. At the same time, since the maxi-min criterion for policy selection does not in itself provide any indication as to the kind or number of strategies (the number of rows of the pay-off matrix that is) which should be considered, there exists at the present state of our knowledge (and for both macroeconomic and microeconomic questions alike) no absolute criterion by which to establish whether the intermediate target strategy would be in some sense efficient. More precisely, in examining alternative policies, the policymaker will, of course, consider the maxi-min impli- cations of the optimal policies pertinent to each of the alternative models that he deems 'relevant'. But beyond this there is, in principle, an infinite number of other policies, of strategies 'governing the continuous adjust- ments of the policy maker's control variables'[92], of relations between changes in policy and conditions in the environment'[93], which are open to him. There does remain, therefore, the 'technical' (?) problem of: *by what reasoning is the policymaker to select the alternative strategies to be compared?*

In the latter context we can do no other but suppose that the *search procedure* will involve some 'rule of thumb', some *judgement*. Intuition may suggest a procedure that treats the optimal policies defined by each of the specific models as the limits of a range within which to search for superior maxi-min strategies. Yet this procedure, tempting though it is to the econometrician/statistician[94], does not appear simple (clear in its purpose) once we recognize that the 'optimal strategies' implied by each of the 'relevant' models involve different instruments and almost certainly more than one instrument in each case[95]. Similar feelings of *compromise* may encourage the identification of optimal policies implied in the (by defi- nition) irrelevant states of prior beliefs that assignment of equal or unequal probabilities to the relevant models will render, and the subsequent appraisal on a maxi-min basis of these policies in the context of the relevant models. *Compromise* may also suggest that we identify the strategy that derives from the *union* of the relevant alternatives, moving that is to a position of total ignorance of the behavioural characteristics of those aspects of our economy to which competing hypotheses of behaviour apply. The optimal strategy derived from a model that treats the values of magnitudes outside the union as given can then be examined in terms of its maxi-min implications within our relevant alternatives.

No doubt other such suggestions can be tendered. Formally the search procedure is *ad hoc*, though we ought at least to concede that the alternatives that spring to mind in the manner of those listed above stem from some process of reasoning, from some perception of 'order', from experience, that suggest 'compromise' as a reasonable 'rule of thumb'. On reflection, however, we may also remember that besides ignorance of the structure there are also data lags. But then would it be unreasonable to adopt a 'search procedure' in which we examine the maxi-min performance of strategies that minimize, for one or other of the relevant alternative models, the variance of one or other of the endogenous variables that are observable with a regular frequency greater than that pertaining to the goal variable—of strategies, that is, which relate to *intermediate/proximate targets*?

From this perspective the selection of a proximate target constitutes a choice from among the strategies that a *particular* search procedure renders. As such it need not be superior in a maxi-min sense to all other feasible strategies, but it cannot *a priori* be said to be no better than the superior strategy that emerges from comparison of the optimal strategies pertaining to each member of the group of models deemed by the decision-taker as relevant. Furthermore, it should be stressed that the choice of strategy is not (as indeed is true of the optimal strategy in the context of a particular prior belief) independent of the state/flow of information regarding the paths of other variables in the system since, even for strategies that derive from the particular search procedure of minimizing the variance of one or other of the 'irrelevant' endogenous variables, the policy vector is conditional on any information about the time path of the predetermined variables that is available[96].

Intermediate Targets and Policy Indicators

In the above I have interpreted *ignorance of the structure* to denote a situation in which the decision-taker is confronted with a number of alternatives each of which is 'equally likely'. In contradistinction to the rationale, to the apparatus of thought, on which the variance approach is based, I do not by this expression mean that the alternative hypotheses are 'equally probable' in the sense that 'equal numerical probabilities' can be attached to them, since with regard to the problem identified, as Shackle would put it

... it does not appear that numerical probability can express [the decision-taker's] state of mind when [he is] confronted with a number of alternative predicates between which [he] know[s] of no reason to discriminate[97].

This, I believe, is in the spirit of Brunner's analysis, though I should acknowledge that in what appears the most explicit of his statements of the problem, the role of numerical probabilities is quite ambiguous as we are told that '. . . the optimal strategy can be decided upon *either* by a Bayesian procedure in the case of incomplete stochastic information pertaining to the class of [alternative] hypotheses [about the structure and the path of the exogenous variables in the system] *or* in the absence of such knowledge by a suitable maxi-min decision'[98].

There are a number of reasons why 'numerical probabilities' and consequently the Bayesian procedure are, as I have already suggested, inappropriate. The first is that given a particular set of n alternative states of nature perceived by the decision-taker, the mean average of these states yields an irrelevant prior belief since in general it will not relate to a state of nature deemed by the decision-taker as equally likely as the alternatives initially perceived, or if by chance it averages out to being identical to one of these alternatives it must by definition be regarded as not more likely than the others. Secondly, if n is large the placement of a numerical probability equal to $1/n$ is a '. . . procedure which implies that we regard each [of the models and their outcomes] as *highly improbable.* But to say that each of them is highly improbable is to say more than we really mean when what we wish to express is "I have little relevant knowledge and so far as I am concerned any of the mutually exclusive contingencies $A, B . . . N$ could happen without seeming incongruous with what I do know of the circumstances". No one of these contingencies seems to me "improbable" in the sense that it calls for any stretch of the imagination to conceive it coming true'[99]. In the same vein consider the case in which we do attach equal probabilities to the alternative states. The mean average we have reasoned *cannot be considered more likely than the original states.* At best it may be regarded as equally likely, as it would be if we come to regard it as another possible state of nature. But 'The fundamental question which we are then led to ask is this: *Does an increase in the number of hypotheses (rivals to a given hypothesis), which we cannot reject as impossible, really reduce the degree of acceptance we accord to a given hypothesis?* Plainly . . . it does not. The mere recognition of a wider ignorance about what may happen does not alter or reduce the right of a given hypothesis to its place amongst those which our knowledge does not enable us to reject'[100].

In this scheme of things a maxi-min comparison of alternative strategies seems to me to comprise an approach consistent with the nature of the problem. This may, as Wallich has noted, '. . . seem to adopt a rather pessimistic slant'[101]; but the 'alternative procedures' suggested by him, namely '. . . to examine models for robustness of their policy advice under varying assumptions, or perhaps to look for a policy that is robust with respect to switches among models'[102] are (as I understand them) the same maxi-min decision.

From a taxonomic (classificatory) standpoint one may trace some overlaps between the two approaches. Thus in a sense the maxi-min approach to the 'determination (strategy, target) problem' comprises a general case within which the variants of the variance approach must in any given circumstance be nested. At the trivial level, for example, any particular prior belief about the structure and the path of the exogenous variables comprises one of the models, a limiting case, in the Brunner-Meltzer perspective. No less revealingly, Poole's analysis, it has been argued by Brunner, relates to '. . . an optimization procedure [which] minimizes the contemporaneous variance of the time path. The resolution of this problem assures us that the variability expected at any time point due to our incomplete information has been minimized by a suitable choice of policy adjustments. But we obtain no assurance from this procedure about the variability or instability of the process *over time*. Whatever the variability of the process over the *time profile*, variability due to stochastic structure has been minimized in the cross-section of time. The variance approach [in its Poole variant] provides thus only a very partial answer and applies probably to the pragmatically least important question'[103]. In contrast the approach emphasized here, though it permits the possibility that strategies focusing on intermediate targets are superior to the optimal strategies embedded in the alternative competing hypotheses, stresses the continuous adjustment elements of the problem, and will in general involve a feedback rule.

That this is so is clear once we recognize that an intermediate target strategy (unlike the framework defined by Poole) does not imply a particular set of values of the vector of instruments of policy (that is to say the intermediate target is an endogenous rather than a control variable) so that the pursuit of any particular value or path of the target variable is (as I have already noted) itself conditional on the information confronting the policymaker. But to recognize the need for feedback is to raise the question of on what the required adjustment in the vector of instruments of policy is to be based. In the framework of a particular prior belief about the structure and the path of the exogenous variables there is no such problem, since in that context the known structure renders a unique change in the vector of instruments of policy consistent with securing any particular outcome. But when competing hypotheses about the structure are acknowledged, a given change in instruments of policy is consistent with a number of responses of the endogenous variable that may serve as the target.

It is of course perfectly consistent with the maxi-min approach for the policymaker to adjust his instruments of policy in accordance with the parameter responses prescribed by one or other of the competing models comprising his prior beliefs, and hence to act *as if* all deviations of the target variable from its expected value defined by this model are due to exogenous factors calling for adjustment in the vector of instruments. Equally, however, the strategy adopted may, in conjunction with the endogenous variable selected as the target, rest on an *index* of the effect of policy changes that so far as possible is independent of the diversity of characteristics which the alternative hypotheses exhibit. In our discussion these comprise alternative solutions to the determination problem; and whether the latter is to be preferred to the former cannot, I believe, be decided independently of the characteristics of the environment in which the policymaker operates. Brunner and Meltzer, and Saving, however, attach considerable emphasis on a construct which, notwithstanding the competing hypotheses, '. . . yields reliable information about the monetary thrust transmitted to economic activity'[104]. Thus in discussions of policy under uncertainty, besides the target variable, there does appear another magnitude: *the policy indicator*. It is as though the diverse scenery of competing hypotheses requires more than one filter in tracing (in assessing, in appreciating) its contours so as to traverse to one's objective. But this has caused no small measure of confusion.

In Saving's discussion of the policy problem the policymaker, lacking complete knowledge of the structure and of the values of the non-policy determined arguments, is supposed to have enough information to determine the *direction* of the effect of policies on particular endogenous (including goal) variables[105]. If in addition, it is reasoned, he is '. . . reasonably certain of the relationship between some observable endogenous variable and the goal variables—even if he is very uncertain about the *exact* effect of his instrument on the goal variables—he may ... choose this observable endogenous variable as a target variable and adjust his instruments until this variable reaches its desired target level'[106].

Such a procedure, Saving claims, has two merits. First, the '. . . approach circumvents some of the uncertainties in the effect of policy on the goal variables [in that] if policy can be adjusted instantly to account for any random change between the policy and the target, then this part of the uncertainty can be removed'. Secondly, 'the use of the target variable can remove some of the uncertainty resulting from unobservable goal variables' in that, while, granted lags in observation of the goal variable, 'the effect of policy will only be seen after policy has been pursued for some time, [and] during this period exogenous changes may occur, making the effect of the policy chosen larger, or smaller, than it otherwise would have been; if a target variable is used then these exogenous changes may simply affect the magnitude of the operation necessary to make the target variable reach the level desired'[107].

In this context the policymaker does not, in order to adjust his instruments of policy, appear to require an index of the effect that changes in policy *will have* on the target and goal variables. On the other hand, it is recognized that

> the possibility that changes in the economy will occur during the implementa-
> tion of policy raises the need for an *indicator of the effect of the policy being
> pursued.* That is *if the policy-maker is to adjust his policy to changes in his
> environment occurring during the implementation of a particular policy,* he
> must have *an index of the effect of current policy.* Essentially the policy-maker
> requires *a separation of the change in his target variable into policy effect and
> an exogenous effect.* Since *observation of the changes in the target variable
> yields only the total effect,* some other variable or combination of variables is
> required to reflect the policy effect. This other variable or combination of
> variables, usually called '*a monetary policy indicator*', must be distinct from
> the target variable in the sense of being mathematically independent; that is,
> the indicator must not be a scalar multiple of the target variable. In addition,
> since the purpose of the indicator is to measure the policy effect, it must be
> chosen so that either (1) exogenous changes that affect the target variable do not
> affect the indicator, or (2) if these exogenous variables do affect the indicator,
> their effect must be swamped by the policy effect[108].

Thus for Saving the policy indicator serves to establish whether the specific value, or path, of the target variable pursued at any particular time is consistent with the goal, or whether changes in exogenous factors '. . . resulting in changes in the target variable'[109] call for revision in the target value in order to secure the attainment of the goal. Notice that this implies that, notwithstanding the competing hypotheses about the structure, the policymaker is assumed to be able to construct 'an index of the effect of current policy'. But a process in which the policymaker pursues a particular value (or path) of a 'target variable', so long as the 'policy indicator' takes a value (or sequence of values) deemed previously consistent with the attainment of the target and the goal, can equally well be *described* as a process in which the policymaker pursues a particular value or path of the 'indicator', so long as the 'target variable' takes a value or sequence of values deemed previously consistent with this value or path of the indicator and the attainment of the goal. From this viewpoint the assignment of the term 'target' to one or other of these two variables is a matter of semantics. Yet though this may perhaps account for a large part of the stupendous confusion that exists in the literature on the distinction between targets and policy indicators[110], we should not allow it to detract from the fact that the strategy advocated requires two variables or indices for its execution.

To emphasize the latter and also the confusion that has surrounded the issue, consider the following statement (echoing, and echoed, in a number of learned and/or official documents, I should add) from a paper '. . . mainly addressed to the problem of Targets and Indicators'

> In the real world, where knowledge is seriously incomplete and the effects of
> policy on ultimate goal variables are not precisely known in advance and

cannot be continuously monitored owing to delays in the collection of data and lags in the effectiveness of policy, it is usually thought useful to have *an indicator of policy which would also serve as the target for policy*[111].

To some extent the confusion stems, I believe, from too close identification with the static framework defined by Poole, in which no feedbacks are afforded and where both the money stock and interest rates can be regarded as alternative intruments of policy, while the choice of instrument to be made is tautologous with the choice of proximate target[112]. It also perhaps reflects the feeling that

> *... policy indicators should describe more than the effect of actions explicitly taken.* It is after all quite possible for lack of action to constitute a positive policy [since] for example a Central Bank contemplating open market sales could desist from taking action if it perceived that an increase in liquidity preference of economic units was about to arise, which would accomplish the increase in interest rates called for. A change in economic behaviour may thus be acquiesced in by a monetary authority to achieve its ends and it is desirable that [a policy] indicator should recognise this possibility and evaluate policy on the basis of any relevant changes in behaviour[113].

But though, with some qualifications[114], the latter is quite correct, *it does not follow* that

> An indicator of the kind described, if one can be found, cannot help but form an appropriate target variable for the monetary authorities. There is, apparently, no distinction between the two[115].

Indeed in the previous quotation the target is 'the increase in interest rates called for'. One may of course (when thinking of a cardinal scale and hence one that permits the possibility of assessing the change in policy instruments required to achieve any particular desired change in the target and goal variables) describe the policy objective as being the change in the policy indicator consistent with generating 'the increase in interest rates called for', thinking, that is, of the former as the target. But this does not alter the fact that an assessment of the effect of policy and of exogenous factors on the target variable is required in order to establish whether and what change in that variable to affect. In particular, suppose that the policymaker chooses an interest rate above the current level consistent with reducing aggregate demand, and manipulates his instruments until this target level of the interest rate is attained. If during this period expectations change, the policy actually undertaken may be one of *lowering* the interest rate to the previously defined target level, rather than raising it, thus increasing aggregate demand. In this context, as Saving notes, '... the use of an indicator can serve to separate the exogenous effect from the policy effect ...' so as to determine the desirable future course of policy.

But how is the policy indicator constructed? Here alas we are thrown back to the issue of knowledge or ignorance of the structure, for

> Since the task of the policy indicator [Saving explains] is to gauge the effect of monetary policy, *the choice of an indicator* requires *some hypothesis about the structure*. In addition [since the purpose of] the indicator is to measure [either directly or indirectly, i.e. through the target] . . . the effect of policy on the goal variables . . . the choice of indicator . . . involves the goal function. . . . the indicator must be (1) easily observable with little or no lag, (2) quickly affected by the policy undertaken, and (3) related to the target and goal variables. Because the indicator of policy gauges the effect of the immediate past policy and because the future course of policy will be influenced by the policy-maker's estimate of the effect of the policy, it is crucial that the indicator yields at least qualitatively correct results. Otherwise there is a danger that a policy will continue to be pursued that amplifies rather than moderates cyclical fluctuations in the goal variables[116].

Given that the problem defined arises from ignorance of the structure, it is perverse to be told that policy in such an environment 'requires some hypothesis about the structure'. And this confusion is further fostered by the Brunner-Meltzer ambiguities regarding the role of probabilities. For in presenting '. . . a formal analysis of the problem of choosing an indicator', they acknowledge as one possibility a procedure that '. . . postulates that our information can be expressed as probability statements about hypotheses and classes of hypotheses', a 'procedure', which they note, 'permits us to assign numbers to specific combinations of policy variables and thus provides a scale or indicator for policy'[117]. But this implies that we construct some specific new hypothesis from the alternatives perceived.

On a particular hypothesis about the structure, a policy indicator can be constructed as the weighted sum of the various instrument levels, with weights equal to the marginal multipliers of the corresponding instruments with respect to the target or (directly) the goal variable[118]. As the above quotation implies, the scale thus derived will depend (directly or indirectly[119]) on the goal function. Granted the hypothesis about the structure and the goal function, it conveys information about the 'known' (expected) thrust transmitted by policy onto the target variable. Observed movements in the target variable can thus be separated into policy-induced and exogenous components, causing policy adjustments aiming to offset undesirable impacts of unanticipated changes in exogenous variables on the goal variable.

On this interpretation, however, the combined target/policy indicator strategy is no different from the optimal policy derived in the context of the variance approach. And then, whatever the usefulness of the policy indicator as a shorthand expression of policy over any given interval of time, the construction of such an index does not seem to serve any real purpose in policy design. Furthermore, if prior beliefs pertain to a linear structure with additive disturbances and a single goal variable, the policy indicator is no other than the instrument chosen for this goal. On the other hand, if prior beliefs pertain to a non-linear structure (or a structure characterized by multiplicative disturbance) the construction of the scale is not feasible[120], and policy design on the basis of summary descriptions in terms of intermediate targets and policy indicators is nonsensical, since the weights attaching to the various instruments deployed to secure the desired objective(s) depend also on the values of the exogenous variables in the system.

Yet this interpretation (which, incidentally, is that characteristic of Ben Friedman's work on the indicator problem[121], and suggests that policy indicators are *at best* superfluous[122]) is *inappropriate*. That this is so one suspects not only because this interpretation detracts from that perception of ignorance, of uncertainty distinct from risk[123], which I have described above, but also from the fact that (save for the ambiguity mentioned above) neither for Saving nor Brunner and Meltzer is the policy indicator sought a fixed weight index of parametrically determined instruments of policy—such as the discount rate, bank reserve ratios, bid and ask prices (or quantities of securities offered for sale) announced by the manager of the government's/central bank's security portfolio. If it were, then it would (at least) be quite unnecessary to require, as a criterion for choice of policy indicator, that the effect of exogenous variables on the policy indicator must be swamped by the policy effect.

In part, of course, the latter requirement (which properly interpreted should not detract from the statement quoted earlier, namely that policy indicators should describe more than the effect of actions *explicitly* taken) may reflect the fact that both Brunner and Meltzer, and Saving seek to identify some *observable* magnitude that may itself be said to convey information about 'the thrust of monetary policy'; and the candidates considered (namely, money somehow defined, the interest rate, free reserves, 'the required rate of return on real capital', the monetary base and the adjusted monetary base)[124] are far from independent of the actions of market participants, though for some[125] it can be argued that they are policy-controlled variables. But their attempts to select an observable magnitude do reflect their conviction of the impracticality of constructing a policy indicator on the lines suggested above. The reason, of course, is ignorance or, if you prefer, the fact that

> . . . we do observe alternative and competing hypotheses [about the structure of monetary processes] with little evidence (as yet) to discriminate about their cognitive status[126],

combined with a suspicion, one must conjecture, for the Bayesian approach to the problem.

As in the case of strategy evaluation under uncertainty, a maxi-min procedure that minimizes the dependence of the index selected on the alternative hypotheses about the structure and the values of the exogenous variables comes to mind, and is indeed suggested by Brunner and Meltzer[127] as a means by which to select 'an optimal scale from those offered for systematic examination [that] assures us that [the] ordering of alternative actions by the monetary authority is closest to *the true but unknown and non-computable ordering*'[128]. In particular, the procedure suggested is that of finding first the lowest rank correlation between any given candidate and the alternative 'true' or 'ideal' indicators pertaining to the alternative states of nature comprised in our prior beliefs, and then selecting as the policy indicator that observable (or computable from observables) magnitude which has the maximum lowest rank correlation computed[129].

Clearly such a procedure enables the conversion of what, in the light of a number of competing hypotheses about the structure, is a non-ordered set of vectors of instruments of policy to be approximated by an ordinal scale. But besides the convenience implied in that alternative combinations of instruments may, when interpreted through this proxy, be ranked in a manner that enables the policymaker to compare their consequences, the purpose of such a construct, as Saving's discussion reveals, is to enable the policymaker to draw inferences regarding the effect of exogenous factors on the target and goal variable(s), and hence on the need for revision in the policy pursued. It is in this sense that the *indicator problem* is an *interpretation problem*[130] arising from the need for continuous adjustment to changes in the environment occurring during the implementation of a particular policy; a problem resulting from ignorance of the structure combined with information lags which cause an *endogenous* variable to serve as the proximate target.

The 'Two-Stage Procedure', 'Controllability' and 'Causality'

Ignorance of the structure and information lags commend (or result in) procedures in which policy actions utilize the information embodied in observable magnitudes to infer the impact of policy on the goal variables so as to adjust policy to conditions in the environment. But what insights does our discussion so far yield for the independent observer concerned in appraising the usefulness of any particular target and policy indicator which the authorities may employ in policy design?

In Ben Friedman's world, we have seen, the optimal policy requires the decision-taker to *infer*, on the basis of his prior knowledge of the structure and its stochastic characteristics, the likelihood that an observed deviation of the *information variable* from its expected (and other things equal consistent with minimizing the variance in the goal variable) value is due to an IS disturbance as opposed to a disturbance in the relationship between the information variable and the goal variable, and then to adjust his instruments of policy in accordance with the parameter responses defined by his prior beliefs. A policy aiming to minimize the deviations of any particular observable endogenous variable from its expected value will be optimal if, and only if, that relationship is independent of all eventualities whether due to policy or purely exogenous factors. Correspondingly, in appraising alternative magnitudes as appropriate target variables we find that, besides observability with a regular frequency greater than that of the goal variable, statistical association to the goal variable is the relevant criterion, since, curiously, in the words of Saving,

> All that is required is that the reduced form equations for the target variable
> and the goal variables be such that the policy vector that results in the target
> variable taking on its desired magnitude will, when substituted into the reduced
> form for the goal variables, result in their taking on certain values[131].

In the latter sense the optimal target is no more nor less *controllable* than the goal variable. Furthermore, the pursuit of policy objectives by means of targets does not imply any commitment to a prior belief that changes in the target variable *cause* changes in the goal variable. It is totally irrelevant whether *causality, in the sense that a theoretical structure can be identified which predicts that changes in X will result in changes in Z*, runs from the target variable to the goal variable or *vice versa*[132]. The term *proximate target* (rather than intermediate target) seems in this context more appropriate since it avoids any connotations of causal sequence. Indeed, *unless we are prepared to argue that all influences bear on the goal variable only through their effect on the target, we must conjecture that causation cannot run from the target variable to the goal variable*—certainly not, if in the context of the variance approach a proximate target strategy is not to be inferior to the optimal policy; and so perhaps a useful rule of thumb is to search for variables that are caused by the goal variable.

This view of proximate targets emanating from Ben Friedman's world must seem odd to the economist accustomed to thinking of *intermediate* targets, of *two-stage procedures* where the authorities *cause* changes in income, the goal variable, *by causing* changes in the money stock; to the economist, that is, accustomed to arguments that

> The rationale for introducing . . . 'proximate' or 'intermediate' targets *which lie
> between the instruments (or 'tools') of policy and the goals of policy* would seem
> to be the notion that a close and systematic relationship exists between proxi-
> mate targets and goals, the relationship holding over time and space, while the
> relationship between the tools and the proximate targets depends heavily on
> institutional factors which are stable neither over time nor over space[133].

and also to those for whom monetary targets stem from the fact, the opposite fact[134], that

The lag with which money *acts on* [the goal variable] is too long and too variable to make monetary policy an instrument of short run stabilization[135].

A proximate target that is no more controllable than the goal variable seems hardly consistent with orthodoxy which prescribes that

The first requirement [for monetary] policy is that the monetary authority should guide itself by magnitudes that it can control not by ones that it cannot control [and hence] a monetary total is the best guide or criterion for monetary policy[136].

Nor, therefore, does it square with empirical investigations that depart from the premise that

While a particular monetary aggregate might give very good projections of the likely pattern of economic activity, that information is not very useful to the monetary authorities for achieving a desired pattern if they have virtually no control over that aggregate[137].

Yet disregard of such issues is perfectly consistent with a circumstance in which, granted the absence of any doubts about the structure, we define, as in Ben Friedman, a problem that arises purely from information lags and hence as the sole scope of the inquiry—the identification of the best observable proxy of the goal variable[138].

Suppose, for example, as is consistent with (indeed compelling in the context of) the IS-LM model, that expenditure decisions are thought to depend on the stock of all 'fixed-in-nominal-terms-realizable-at-short-notice assets', FNRS[139]. Policy may then be directed towards securing a particular value (or rate of growth) of this aggregate. But unless we assume that: (1) the demand for this aggregate is known with certainty; (2) data on the stock of such assets are available on a continuous basis; (3) data on the determinants of demand for this aggregate (other than the goal variable) are available on a continuous basis, there can be room for selection of *another aggregate*, that for whatever reason is either found to bear a closer relationship to the goal variable, or observations on it are available on a more continuous basis than FNRS, to serve as the proximate target. Indeed, with nominal income as the goal variable, and in an IS-LM kind of world modified for anticipations and decision intervals, one may seek for this role an aggregate that corresponds to the *transactions demand for money*. Currency in circulation with the public or narrow money are candidates that easily come to mind, at least in demonstrating this point. For though no one can seriously suggest that changes in currency in circulation, or I contest— contrary to the impression one gets from some econometric studies resting on such models[140]—narrow money, *lead* to changes in aggregate expenditure[141], it may nonetheless be argued that for any given state of transactions technology (that is to say changes in the payments mechanism apart) this counterpart of Hicksian transactions demand[142] may serve as an index of aggregate expenditures; as the proximate target. Policy actions, to be sure, must still exploit the speculative/asset demand for money (defined as all safe assets), since the significance of such actions pertains to their implications for the determination of the opportunity cost of expenditures as defined by liquidity preference. But the need for such actions may be identifiable from the behaviour of narrow money; and if the relationship of the latter to the goal variable is proportional, policy may properly focus on minimizing the deviations of this variable from its expected value.

Such a variable may also serve as the target in a setting in which competing hypotheses about the structure are recognized. For though in that setting no unique expectation of this variable can be had, a strategy, which aims to minimize the deviations of this variable in accordance with one or other of the competing hypotheses about the structure, may nevertheless be superior to any strategy that minimizes the variance of some other endogenous variable including that which all of the alternative competing hypotheses suggest to be an important determinant of the goal variable. But the converse cannot in this case be precluded; and hence the correct strategy may be one where policy responses are geared towards achieving, or maintaining, some chosen path of the latter variable, although this path in no way mirrors the movement of the *indicator of economic activity* (as we may in the single goal variable, GNP, case call the optimal information variable), and does not therefore, in any regression analysis, render as close an association to the goal variable as the indicator of economic activity might.

In this case again no direct appeal to causality is made. But neither is any other criterion available that will secure the appraisal of the target in the absence of knowledge of the prior perception that has determined the policymaker's selection. The independent observer's appraisal of a particular target variable is thus confined to the examination of the validity of particular hypotheses that anecdotal or other material available from the policymaker reveal as essential ingredients in the perception of the environment that has conditioned his choice. And though the outcomes of such enquiries may result in revisions of the policymaker's beliefs, they would only afford the researcher the opportunity to suggest an alternative target variable when he is entitled to presume that he has simulated the decision-taker's imagination.

The latter is also true of the policy indicator, whether we perceive of it as an index of the effect that policy will have on the target variable, or as an index that conditions our interpretation of the effect of exogenous factors and hence as a means for assessing the extent to which revisions in the target are called for. At the same time, we should note that Saving's discussion of the target and indicator strategy resembles the example given above regarding strategy in the context of the variance approach. When emphasis is placed on Saving's particular examples and on Ben Friedman's reminder that the money stock is not a control variable[143], both cases can be described as denoting a circumstance in which an *intermediate* target (such as FNRS or the interest rate) is chosen as the *short-term objective* (one element of the overall strategy) to be revised in the light of new information about the movement of the exogenous variables. Of course the inferences drawn by Saving from the *policy indicator* need not (and in general would not) reflect those rendered by Ben Friedman's *indicator of economic activity*. But this does not detract from a description of decisions where

> The choice of monetary policy is determined by the view taken of the mechanisms through which money influences the economy. A target should play a key role in the transmission mechanism and policy can be effective if both the influence of the monetary policy on the target and the *impact* of the target on the authorities' objectives are understood[144].

Thus

> *For the monetarist* the money supply is the obvious target variable. The behaviour of the money supply can be *controlled* by operating on the monetary base and changes in the stock of money have predictable effects on economic activity . . .[145].

The selection of a *short-run target* (by which I mean an intermediate target revisable in the light of inferences regarding the impact of exogenous variables on the goal variable) then involves a causal relationship and thus implies identification with a particular subset of hypotheses pertaining to our economic environment.

Decision and Surprise

It should be stressed in both cases, whether, that is, we accept the framework of the variance approach or whether we opt for a characterization of the policymaker's perception of his environment that comprises a variety of competing hypotheses about the structure and paths of the exogenous variables in the system, that the discussion so far yields no insights regarding how the policymaker is to distinguish between changes that call for a revision in his perception of his environment and those that are consistent with his prior perception.

In the context of the variance approach for example, the feedback rule—being at the limit (when, that is, 'the money stock is continuously observable and the interest rate continuously adjustable'[146]), 'identical to Poole's combination policy'[147], whereby granted the interest sensitivity of the demand for money, policy aims at obtaining '. . . the optimal slope of the LM by making the supply of money interest sensitive'[148]—comprises a policy aiming to alter the *stochastic* properties of the model by interjecting a new element of (co)variation in the form of the policymaker's adjustment of control variables. *Nothing* is said about how the policymaker is to respond to *new data*, to what Keynes[149] called 'the news', or indeed how, in a stochastic environment, he is to distinguish between observations that comprise a change in the data and those which in respect of his prior beliefs are stochastic and thus leave the equilibrium of the system unaltered. It is heartening to be told, by Ben Friedman for example, that the policymaker should consider all information available to him to establish the nature of the disturbance; to use his puzzling phrase, to examine the information comprised in '. . . predictors of the stochastic elements of income'[150]. But this in no way answers the question of how the policymaker is to interpret any particular piece of news into a response, when this may constitute either an observation consistent with his prior beliefs or one that calls for a revision of such beliefs.

The issue should not be obscured by Ben Friedman's emotive term of 'surprise'. The intuitive appeal of the information-feedback rules derives from the fact that we are tempted to interpret deviations of the information variable from its expected value as signifying non-stochastic changes, rather than chance happenings which, by definition, may vanish before policy is implemented[151]. Yet the 'optimal policy' renders no insights on this when the prior perceived variance-covariance matrix of disturbances is employed to infer the response to any given deviation from the prior defined expectation. And though the recommendation that the authorities should exploit all available information makes some amends, it does so in a very partial way, never challenging, that is, the durability of the set of parameters characterizing the policymaker's prior beliefs regarding responses of economic actors.

The same is true in the framework of ignorance described above, so long as we insist on precise quantitative expression, on 'optimal strategies' capable of such expression, notwithstanding the acknowledgment of a variety of competing hypotheses about the structure and the paths of the exogenous variables in the system. Here again the continuous adjustment of the policymaker's control variables, the feedback rules, are then conditional on a prior perception of the environment which however varied renders no device for its replacement.

At best, therefore, in both worlds we are then faced with a Myrdalian sequence analysis, being told neither how the policymaker is to accommodate *the news*, nor what role must be assigned to '. . . uncertainty itself which must surely flow from any experience of falability of expectation . . .'[152]. For Ben Friedman, of course, (and all other variance approach exercises) there can by definition be no room for such 'niceties'(?). Probability which comprises the cornerstone of the variance approach leaves, as Shackle told us often enough, no room for '*novelty*'[153]. But in the Brunner-Meltzer framework, in which competing hypotheses about the structure and the paths of the goal variables in the system are recognized, in which, that is, the policy-maker recognizes the insufficiency of the information available in establish-ing either a particular prior belief about the structure or a particular path of the exogenous variables in the system, we must also conjecture that while policy may lay down rules of conduct for the range of 'no potential surprise', the policymaker's perception of his environment cannot be immune to fresh knowledge from the occurrence of events whose possibility was looked at and rejected or which were never even imagined.

Looking at policy as a process of decision, these considerations appear to raise awkward questions regarding the meaning to be attached to 'strategy' in a context of competing hypotheses about the structure. Can policy decisions, in a world characterized by ignorance, be adequately described and analysed as processes conditional on a number of alternatives between which we know of no reason to discriminate, without the need to enquire into the emergence and durability of such beliefs? Can the range of non-revision be 'objectively', 'universally' defined by appeal to statistical generalizations? Can isolated decisions be motivated or examined through schemes that rest on laws of sequences of trials? If we feel (and I suspect we may) that the answers to these questions are in the negative, then: what role must be accorded to judgment?

Yet on reflection we may feel that the analysis of policy under ignorance and uncertainty already described is not jeopardized by such conundrums; in that its purpose is not to render a precise formula, an algorithm, to replace the decision-taker but rather, as Keynes would have put it, to supply 'an apparatus of the mind, a technique of thinking, that helps its possessor to draw correct conclusions'. The search for an *ordinal* scale that permits *reliable* interpretations, *comparative statements*, *qualitatively* correct results, of the thrust transmitted by policy points in this direction. And so does Saving's discussion of a target which is revised in the light of such 'qualitative' information. Obviously such 'classificatory' statements do not render a sharp divide that permits a delineation of responses in accordance with a particular complex prior belief and a revision of such belief. 'There is a zone where the non-surprising outcome melts into the surprising, and a zone where the outcome which does not call for policy revision melts into the one that does'[154]. To be sure this vision lacks the elegance, and apparent precision of the paradigms that '... easily appeal to the sophisticated analytic instincts of economists'[155]. But then again the policymaker operates in a world in which 'things are too fluid, too complex, too mutually involved, too elusive, subjective, subtle, too much subject to learn-ing processes, too evolutionary, restless and fertile of surprise to yield a scheme of ascertainable, reliable and permanent parameter estimates'[156].

Monetary Targets in Pandora's World
Bearing in mind the remarks at the end of the last subsection, let us return to

the conduct of policy in the three countries considered. A quick glance at official statements (and papers produced by bodies influential in policy design) does reveal considerable eclecticism in the terms employed in connection with the chosen aggregates[157]. Intermediate target, proximate target, information variable, indicator of economic activity, policy indicator, monetary indicator, and even policy goal, are liberally bandied around, sometimes even in the same document, to describe the aggregate chosen. Correspondingly, causality, controllability, tightness of association with nominal income, stability and other characteristics of demand for money are offered to 'explain' the proffered policies and the choice of one aggregate over another.

Leaving aside the query that our preceding discussion poses regarding the meaning or significance which one should attach to any search for an aggregate that scores highly on all these counts[158], we may note that the advent of, and adherence to, proffered policies cannot be said to have rested, or to rest, on convincing evidence regarding the merits of the chosen aggregates on any of these counts.

The United States

In the United States, the second half of the 1960s was a period of radical reassessment of the role of monetary policy and of increasing scrutiny by Congress of the affairs of the Federal Reserve.

In 1968, the Committee on Standards for Guiding Monetary Policy[159], taking the view that the Federal Reserve can control the money stock, reasoned that while monetary policy has significant effects on expenditure, output and prices, *our knowledge is not such as to commend fine tuning policies*. Thus, while stressing the need for clearer indications of policy objectives by Congress to the monetary authorities (even entertaining the possibility that weights be attached to the various goals in order to define a goal function) it emphasized the need to avoid large swings in policy and noted '. . . that a steady rise in the money supply more or less consistent with the projected rate of economic growth—generally in the range of 3–5 per cent per year—would be a healthy long run ideal'[160]. It furthermore recommended that a report to Congress be tabled at the beginning of each year concerning monetary policies for the coming twelve months. Meanwhile some greater emphasis in policy design on credit and monetary aggregates began to be placed by the FOMC.

By the end of the 1960s, the FOMC had begun to distinguish between the *operating targets* (summarized in terms of money market conditions, and relating to the Federal Funds rate, member bank borrowings, net reserves and sometimes the Treasury Bill rate), which had comprised its entire concern previously and which were deemed to be under the short-run control of the Manager of the System's Open Market Account, and *intermediate targets* (initially bank credit and subsequently also monetary aggregates), which though not under its immediate control and subject to longer lags in data availability were deemed to bear a more determinate relationship to ultimate goal variables than interest rates. The new setting could be interpreted to imply a process running from money market conditions to monetary and/or credit aggregates, and thereby (perhaps through changes in relative yields) to ultimate goal variables; but a conception of monetary aggregates, at best, *as an indicator or economic activity rather than an intermediate target*[161] did not vanish. On the other hand, a longer-run outlook did emerge and with it more emphasis on systematic inferences of anticipated outcomes, through econometric forecasts (drawn from the Fed-MIT-Pen and other, smaller, models) combined with judgemental projections. Furthermore, a serious effort to examine questions relating to *controllability* of alternative aggregates[162], *the stability of demand for money* relationships[163], *the relationship of alternative aggregates to nominal GNP*[164], and also *the implications of alternative strategies* (placing different degrees of emphasis on monetary aggregates and interest rates)[165] was made.

The results of the investigations into the areas listed above did reinforce the belief that attention on monetary aggregates was not unwarranted. But neither the studies at the turn of the 1960s, nor those that followed, rendered an unequivocal verdict in favour of an intermediate target strategy in one or other of the aggregates, or on any feedback strategy based on observations of monetary aggregates alone. Significant doubts regarding the parameters of demand functions for some of the aggregates, short-run stability problems, relatively large errors in predictions based on monetary aggregates and such, combined with recognition of objectives more closely linked to interest rates (in particular, international movements and sectoral considerations—for example, housing) ensured that—except perhaps for a brief period—the shift in emphasis never went much beyond the point of directives for growth of bank credit and monetary aggregates to be achieved on average over the two months following the FOMC meeting subject to a clearly defined and rigidly adhered to Federal Funds rate proviso[166]. Only briefly in 1972 was something more akin to the policy indicator favoured in Brunner's writings, namely at first total reserves and shortly afterwards reserves against private deposits (i.e. a concept analogous to the reserve component of CBM), adopted as an 'operating target'.

Viewed from the standpoint of the beginning of 1975, the situation so far as knowledge of monetary processes is concerned looked no rosier than before. Certainly the more simple demand for money functions for M_1, the aggregate on which 'primary emphasis' at first continued to be placed in the FOMC's instructions to the Manager of the System's Open Market Account, as is well documented[167] and as tables 4(a) and 4(b) may serve to remind us, did exhibit considerable variation in parameter estimates depending on the sample period taken. The situation is better for M_2, which by 1976 came to command an equal weight in instructions pertaining to the monthly guidelines, but here again there is considerable variation suggested in quarterly estimates. Conversely, insofar as control of monetary aggregates is perceived in terms of '. . . sliding up and down the demand for money function'[168] by changing interest rates (treated as control variables), these functions render no precise solution to the control of monetary aggregates problem, while the same is true of results from approaches that focus on the relationship between the monetary base and the money supply[169]. In the same vein, relationships focusing on monetary aggregates as indicators of nominal income (revealing correlations in logarithmic first differences considerably below those secured by focusing on lagged values of the dependent variables) clearly suggest the rather limited value that one may have properly attached to them in this capacity when considering their merits as monetary targets. And whereas for a time, reduced form relationships did appear to provide support for fast, strong and predictable effects of money on nominal GNP[170], while statistical analyses supporting 'unidirectional causality' from the former to the latter[171] *may* have permitted the inference that such estimates could be relied upon in policy design without the risk that they would be shown to be specific to the policy regime (the institutional environment, the contingent circumstances) of the time interval from which they were drawn[172], even in St Louis the precise parameter estimates drawn from reduced form equations on different sample periods showed tremendous diversity. Furthermore, as M. Christ noted[173] in 1975, competing structural models of the U.S. economy (of which he examined eight) '. . . disagree so strongly about the effects of monetary and fiscal policies that they cannot be considered reliable guides to such policy effects'[174]. No less to the point, Christ stressed '. . . . that econometric model forecasts can be improved by the use of subjective judgement'[175], while he found that straight ' . . . use of actual values [in models not subjectively adjusted] does not help'[176].

On such an information set it seems hard to think of the announced targets and strategy as bearing any direct relationship to models couched in a particular prior belief about the structure. Nevertheless, the two-stage targeting procedure (i.e. quarterly revisions in the rate of growth of monetary aggregates and monthly guidelines to the Desk, see section 2 above) has been interpreted as a scheme where '. . . at least in principle the FOMC takes advantage once per quarter of the opportunity to reassess the money income relationship and determine what money stock is consistent with ultimate objectives'[177], but within the quarter 'pursues an operating strategy which makes the money stock the intermediate target for policy'[178]. A strict interpretation along mean variance lines furthermore has caused Ben Friedman to conclude that the abstinence of the FOMC from exploiting the within the quarter flow of new information—by determining how much of the money stock surprise is due to a spending disturbance and then allowing (granted that the demand for the relevant aggregates is certainly not independent of

Table 4(a). Some money demand estimates for the pre-target era.

Estimated relationship[a]: $M_t = a_0 + \sum_{j=0}^{j=1}(b_jY_{t-j}+c_jP_{t-j}+d_jR_{t-j})+\sum_{j=1}^{j=2}m_jM_{t-j}+u_t.$

Sample	a_0	Y_t	Y_{t-1}	P_t	P_{t-1}	R_t	R_{t-1}	M_{t-1}	M_{t-2}	S.E.	n_Y	n_P	n_r
U.S.A.; M_1; 1964:1–73:4	1.03 (1.98)	0.23 (1.56)	−0.04 (0.30)	0.63 (1.92)	−0.21 (0.67)	0.19 (1.29)	−0.43 (3.11)	0.79 (5.60)	−0.21 (1.24)	0.0050	0.39	0.97	−0.05
U.S.A.; M_1; 1964:1–74:4	0.16 (0.42)	0.23 (1.54)	−0.07 (0.53)	0.11 (0.42)	0.08 (0.26)	0.10 (0.76)	−0.35 (2.79)	0.83 (5.85)	−0.05 (0.33)	0.0052	0.68	0.85	−0.06
U.S.A.; M_2; 1964:1–73:4	0.20 (0.96)	0.31 (2.31)	−0.05 (0.40)	0.10 (0.36)	0.32 (1.19)	−0.32 (1.08)	−0.74 (2.33)	1.26 (10.00)	−0.56 (4.56)	0.0046	0.88	1.42	−0.18
U.S.A.; M_2; 1964:1–74:4	0.11 (0.68)	0.33 (2.92)	−0.05 (0.42)	0.02 (0.07)	0.41 (1.89)	−0.37 (1.35)	−0.72 (2.41)	1.27 (10.63)	−0.58 (5.03)	0.0044	0.92	1.38	−0.18
U.K.; M_1; 1964:1–73:4	0.85 (0.37)	0.03 (0.13)	0.14 (0.72)	−0.10 (0.44)	0.18 (0.72)	−0.97 (2.92)	0.39 (0.83)	0.65 (3.72)	0.27 (1.80)	0.0150	2.01	1.00	−0.32
U.K.; M_1; 1964:1–74:4	1.18 (1.04)	−0.06 (0.33)	0.12 (0.75)	−0.09 (0.39)	0.32 (1.39)	−0.88 (2.68)	0.17 (0.47)	0.60 (3.62)	0.23 (1.64)	0.0157	0.38	1.31	−0.26

											b	b	b
U.K.; M_3; 1964:1–73:4	-1.35	0.16	-0.04	0.17	-0.07	0.44	-2.16	0.87	0.17	0.0097			
	(1.04)	(1.22)	(0.35)	(1.11)	(0.44)	(0.71)	(3.18)	(6.07)	(1.05)				
U.K.; M_3; 1964:1–74:4	-1.38	0.15	0.03	0.13	0.02	0.75	-2.48	0.87	0.11	0.0097	9.00	7.5	-6.69
	(1.80)	(1.43)	(0.39)	(0.89)	(0.18)	(1.32)	(3.78)	(6.22)	(0.75)				
F.R.G.; M_1; 1964:1–73:4	0.50	0.76	-0.46	-0.32	0.83	0.03	-0.32	0.86	-0.31	0.0102	0.67	1.15	-0.03
	(1.90)	(4.73)	(2.78)	(0.91)	(2.24)	(0.41)	(4.27)	(7.25)	(2.52)				
F.R.G.; M_1; 1964:1–74:4	0.70	0.64	-0.43	0.26	0.25	-0.03	-0.32	0.84	-0.25	0.0109	0.53	1.29	-0.05
	(3.02)	(3.89)	(2.48)	(0.85)	(0.74)	(0.37)	(4.00)	(6.82)	(2.00)				
F.R.G.; CBM; 1964:1–73:4	0.05	0.04	0.08	0.29	-0.07	-0.23	-0.94	0.61	0.25	0.0055	0.87	1.60	-0.59
	(0.37)	(0.46)	(0.83)	(1.44)	(0.29)	(0.87)	(2.97)	(3.78)	(1.80)				
F.R.G.; CBM; 1964:1–74:4	0.03	0.03	0.09	0.32	-0.10	-0.32	-0.89	0.62	0.24	0.0053	0.90	1.55	-0.62
	(0.28)	(0.38)	(1.04)	(2.06)	(0.56)	(1.43)	(3.12)	(4.15)	(1.87)				

(a) All variables in natural logarithms; $R = (1 + r)$ where for 'narrow' money r is some short-term rate and for 'wide' money some long-term rate. For data sources and definitions of r, Y, and P see Appendix C.

(b) No long-run elasticities are calculated since $(1 - \sum m_j) < 0$.

Table 4(b). 'Conventional' money demand equations: estimates for the pre-target era.
Estimated relationship[a]: $M_t = \alpha(1-\rho) + \beta_1 Y_t + (1-\gamma)P_t + \beta_3 R_t + (\rho+\gamma) M_{t-1} - \rho\beta_1 Y_{t-1} - \rho\beta_3 R_{t-1} - \rho(1-\gamma) P_{t-1} - \rho\gamma M_{t-2} + \varepsilon$.

Sample	α	β_1	$(1-\gamma)$	β_3	γ	ρ	S.E.	χ^2_3	χ^2_4	χ^2_5	n_Y	n_r
U.S.A.; M_1; 1964:1–73:4	1.52 (1.68)	0.21 (2.21)	0.55 (1.92)	−0.02 (0.16)	0.45 (1.57)	0.43 (1.47)	0.0058	11.953	12.140	12.240	0.38	−0.00
U.S.A.; M_1; 1964:1–74:4	−0.24 (0.87)	0.03 (1.19)	−0.01 (0.07)	−0.23 (2.72)	1.01 (12.13)	−0.09 (0.54)	0.0059	9.047	11.664	16.466	b	b
U.S.A.; M_2; 1964:1–73:4	−0.34 (1.23)	0.15 (0.95)	0.10 (0.68)	−0.33 (0.92)	0.90 (6.04)	0.69 (3.83)	0.0059	22.787	20.105	20.907	1.50	−0.17
U.S.A.; M_2; 1964:1–74:4	−0.36 (1.37)	0.16 (1.18)	0.11 (0.86)	−0.43 (1.29)	0.89 (6.98)	0.68 (4.12)	0.0057	20.616	22.350	23.924	1.45	−0.20
U.K.; M_1; 1964:1–73:4	0.12 (0.17)	0.11 (4.64)	0.13 (1.86)	−0.56 (4.08)	0.87 (12.91)	−0.33 (2.17)	0.0155	2.096	2.773	15.317	0.85	−0.30
U.K.; M_1; 1964:1–74:4	0.84 (1.44)	0.12 (4.52)	0.20 (3.99)	−0.63 (5.08)	0.80 (15.69)	−0.29 (1.81)	0.0161	2.040	2.129	19.553	0.60	−0.39

U.K.; M_3; 1964:1–73:4	3.33 (7.49)	0.23 (3.63)	−0.11 (2.26)	−1.20 (4.01)	1.11 (23.72)	−0.06 (0.40)	0.0112	12.596	15.853	25.262	2.09	0.81
U.K.; M_3; 1964:1–74:4	−2.77 (7.42)	0.20 (3.88)	−0.07 (1.46)	−0.80 (4.42)	1.07 (21.61)	0.04 (0.26)	0.0117	28.401	16.854	25.937	b	b
F.R.G.; M_1; 1964:1–73:4	0.58 (1.49)	0.39 (2.38)	0.57 (2.25)	0.04 (0.45)	0.43 (1.72)	0.61 (2.77)	0.0142	25.280	26.295	28.432	0.68	0.00
F.R.G.; M_1; 1964:1–74:4	0.57 (2.95)	0.39 (2.43)	0.56 (2.35)	0.04 (0.37)	0.44 (1.83)	0.61 (2.95)	0.0140	22.282	22.093	22.190	0.69	0.00
F.R.G.; CBM; 1964:1–73:4	−0.22 (5.41)	0.16 (4.74)	0.12 (3.48)	−0.71 (5.09)	0.88 (24.80)	−0.19 (1.19)	0.0063	7.513	11.091	27.343	1.30	−0.42
F.R.G.; CBM; 1964:1–74:4	−0.22 (5.65)	0.16 (5.04)	0.12 (3.69)	−0.67 (6.28)	0.88 (26.28)	−0.21 (1.37)	0.0061	7.359	11.680	33.413	1.29	−0.40

(a) See note (a) of table 4(a).
(b) See note (b) of table 4(a).
Chi square ratios denote constraints on the parameters of the relationship shown in table 4(a), and subscripts indicate the number of degrees of freedom relative to that relationship.

χ^2_4 describes the constraints embodied in the relationships shown above;
χ^2_3 describes the same constraints as χ^2_4 except that of long-run homogeneity with respect to prices;
χ^2_5 describes the same constraints as χ^2_4 and in addition sets $\beta_3 = 0$.

Table 4(c). Some money demand estimates : to 1975:4 and 1976:4.
Estimated relationship: as for table 4(a).

Sample	a_0	Y_t	Y_{2-1}	P_t	P_{t-1}	R_t	R_{t-1}	M_{t-1}	M_{t-2}	S.E.	n_Y	n_P	n_r
U.S.A.; M_1; 1964:1–75:4	-0.40 (2.20)	0.10 (0.94)	-0.02 (0.14)	0.17 (0.65)	-0.17 (0.64)	0.09 (0.79)	-0.45 (3.47)	0.83 (6.15)	0.14 (0.99)	0.0054	2.67	0.00	-0.01
U.S.A.; M_1; 1964:1–76:4	-0.43 (2.60)	0.08 (0.82)	-0.01 (0.09)	0.22 (0.89)	-0.23 (1.02)	0.09 (0.73)	-0.45 (3.65)	0.85 (6.90)	0.14 (1.03)	0.0053	7.00	-1.00	-1.79
U.S.A.; M_2; 1964:1–75:4	-0.12 (0.87)	0.20 (1.89)	0.07 (0.67)	0.01 (0.04)	0.33 (1.49)	-0.58 (2.09)	-0.55 (1.74)	1.28 (10.13)	-0.54 (4.44)	0.0049	1.04	1.31	-0.23
U.S.A.; M_2; 1964:1–76:4	-0.10 (0.71)	0.20 (1.91)	0.03 (0.26)	0.16 (0.67)	0.12 (0.61)	-0.53 (1.94)	-0.40 (1.28)	1.35 (11.13)	-0.57 (4.69)	0.0050	1.05	1.27	-0.23
U.K.; M_1; 1964:1–75:4	0.10 (0.15)	0.03 (0.21)	0.18 (1.12)	-0.05 (0.23)	0.25 (1.13)	-0.75 (2.49)	0.05 (0.15)	0.56 (3.80)	0.21 (1.67)	0.0157	0.91	0.87	-0.23
U.K.; M_1; 1964:1–76:4	-0.16 (0.28)	0.05 (0.34)	0.20 (1.30)	0.03 (0.13)	0.17 (0.82)	-0.74 (3.07)	0.03 (0.10)	0.55 (3.91)	0.20 (1.66)	0.0156	1.00	0.80	-0.22

U.K.; M_3; 1964:1–75:4	−2.48 (4.98)	0.14 (1.26)	0.07 (0.62)	0.06 (0.38)	−0.05 (0.36)	−0.27 (0.68)	−1.12 (2.68)	0.95 (7.07)	0.10 (0.66)	0.0108	a	a	a
U.K.; M_3; 1964:1–76:4	−2.83 (6.14)	0.14 (1.23)	0.07 (0.63)	0.06 (0.37)	−0.09 (0.63)	−0.45 (1.27)	−0.98 (2.57)	0.92 (6.95)	0.16 (1.07)	0.0111	a	a	a
F.R.G.; M_1; 1964:1–75:4	0.74 (3.79)	0.63 (4.20)	−0.44 (2.92)	0.27 (0.90)	0.25 (0.76)	−0.03 (0.43)	−0.31 (4.12)	0.86 (7.47)	−0.25 (2.15)	0.0107	0.50	1.33	−0.04
F.R.G.; M_1; 1964:1–76:4	0.78 (3.40)	0.64 (3.70)	−0.40 (2.31)	0.45 (1.29)	0.12 (0.32)	−0.08 (0.86)	−0.32 (3.61)	0.73 (5.88)	−0.18 (1.50)	0.0126	0.54	1.27	−0.04
F.R.G.; CBM; 1964:1–75:4	−0.13 (1.36)	0.11 (1.21)	0.06 (0.72)	0.21 (1.22)	−0.02 (0.08)	−0.29 (1.21)	−0.68 (2.36)	0.67 (4.30)	0.17 (1.30)	0.0060	1.09	1.20	−0.44
F.R.G.; CBM; 1964:1–76:4	−0.15 (1.46)	0.10 (1.10)	0.06 (0.61)	0.32 (1.82)	−0.17 (0.87)	−0.20 (0.80)	−0.58 (1.46)	0.72 (4.99)	0.14 (1.14)	0.0065	1.14	1.07	−0.41

(a) See note (b) of table 4(a).

Table 4(d). 'Conventional' money demand equations: to 1975:4 and 1976:4.
Estimated relationship: as for table 4(b).

	α	β_1	$(1-\gamma)$	β_3	γ	ρ	S.E.	$\chi^2_3{}^a$	$\chi^2_4{}^a$	$\chi^2_5{}^a$	n_Y	n_r
U.S.A.; M_1; 1964:1–75:4	5.46 (2.39)	0.39 (3.93)	0.82 (5.79)	0.20 (1.53)	0.18 (1.30)	1.07 (19.30)	0.0070	11.639	24.162	26.505	0.48	0.01
U.S.A.; M_1; 1964:1–76:4	1.52 (2.16)	0.36 (3.27)	0.72 (5.29)	0.20 (1.47)	0.28 (2.05)	1.00 (29.30)	0.0070	12.526	29.351	31.517	0.50	0.01
U.S.A.; M_2; 1964:1–75:4	−0.35 (1.39)	0.12 (0.98)	0.07 (0.61)	−0.41 (1.29)	0.93 (8.66)	0.65 (4.58)	0.0059	15.191	17.978	19.585	1.78	−0.33
U.S.A.; M_2; 1964:1–76:4	−0.45 (2.02)	0.12 (1.07)	0.05 (0.52)	−0.52 (1.79)	0.95 (10.02)	0.63 (4.89)	0.0058	11.362	15.931	18.991	2.43	−0.58
U.K.; M_1; 1964:1–75:4	0.26 (0.58)	0.12 (4.48)	0.14 (4.42)	−0.58 (4.91)	0.86 (26.66)	−0.31 (2.25)	0.0162	1.356	2.677	21.198	0.82	−0.31
U.K.; M_1; 1964:1–76:4	2.94 (0.46)	0.03 (0.16)	0.13 (0.81)	−1.31 (3.47)	0.87 (0.75)	1.23 (5.10)	0.0320	1.309	75.057	24.972	0.24	−0.81

											b	b
U.K.; M_3; 1964:1–75:4	−2.78 (8.48)	0.22 (4.30)	−0.06 (1.49)	−0.80 (6.02)	1.06 (25.06)	−0.00 (0.03)	0.0118	6.813	9.299	25.612	b	b
U.K.; M_3; 1964:1–76:4	−2.80 (8.51)	0.23 (5.07)	−0.05 (1.47)	−0.80 (6.37)	1.05 (31.48)	−0.01 (0.08)	0.0121	5.796	8.450	30.118	b	b
F.R.G.; M_1; 1964:1–75:4	0.06 (0.34)	0.17 (1.48)	0.20 (1.29)	−0.01 (0.12)	0.80 (5.00)	−0.38 (1.92)	0.0149	28.023	31.343	31.345	0.85	−0.00
F.R.G.; M_1; 1964:1–76:4	0.04 (0.38)	0.17 (2.46)	0.20 (2.27)	−0.15 (1.37)	0.80 (9.30)	0.09 (0.56)	0.0160	21.657	24.750	25.913	0.88	−0.04
F.R.G.; CBM; 1964:1–75:4	−0.22 (5.62)	0.16 (4.92)	0.13 (3.56)	−0.69 (6.08)	0.87 (25.20)	−0.19 (1.23)	0.0064	4.130	5.696	27.416	1.29	−0.39
F.R.G.; CBM; 1964:1–76:4	−0.18 (4.84)	0.17 (4.83)	0.14 (4.02)	−0.58 (5.29)	0.86 (24.07)	−0.21 (1.47)	0.0068	4.072	4.104	22.054	1.17	−0.29

(a) See table 4(b) for note on chi square ratios.
(b) See note (b) of table 4(a).

opportunity costs, see tables 4(a) to 4(d) and the discussion in Appendix B) for the LM curve slope in gauging the optimal policy—is lamentable.

The descriptive account of section 2 does reveal that in the United States the quarterly policy reviews comprise occasions in which the FOMC utilizes whatever information is available to decide whether and what revisions are required to its projected growth ranges for the various aggregates. But although announcements regarding the yearly growth ranges are only made on such occasions, it is at best a gross simplification to argue that the Committee pursues in the intervals between the quarterly policy reviews an intermediate target strategy of the kind described on pages 272–3 above. True enough the setting of tolerance ranges, and the granting of specific instructions regarding responses if such ranges are violated, does bear a *resemblance* to a strategy in which, within specified limits, the short-run objective is to minimize the expectation of the square of the deviation of M_1 or M_2 (i.e. the aggregate chosen as the focus from the short-run operational standpoint) from the path considered at the last policy review as consistent with the attainment of the desired value of the goal variables. But the resemblance (at least to the certainty equivalence variant of the variance approach) wanes when we remember that: (a) tolerance ranges are set not only for monetary aggregates but also for the Federal Funds rate; (b) the percentage point spreads embodied in the two months monetary aggregate ranges have generally been set considerably wider than the spreads announced in the quarterly/one year target ranges; (c) the *monthly* instructions to the Manager of the System's Open Market Account have varied considerably in emphasis as between monetary aggregates and interest ranges—so much so in fact as to have directives labelled 'aggregates' directive and 'money market' directive—and often recorded considerable changes in the width of the range for the Federal Funds rate[179]; (d) tolerance ranges for both monetary aggregates and interest rates are thus often varied within the quarter; and even so (e) whereas deviations of the Federal Funds rate from the specified ranges have been rare, they have not been so for monetary aggregates nor have they regularly provoked responses that will bring the aggregates within 'tolerance'[180].

Obviously the Federal Funds rate proviso sets a limit to the freedom afforded to the Desk to pursue an intermediate target strategy. 'So long as the funds rate remains within its specified range the Manager does have leeway to respond to evidence that the weighted growth rates for M_1 and M_2 are approaching or moving outside the limits of their ranges'[181]; but 'if growth rates for M_1 and M_2 . . . appear to be remaining outside the Committee's desired ranges and the Manager's actions to counter this deviation have moved the funds rate to the upper or lower limits of its range, he must request new instructions from the Committee'[182], which in turn, as is abundantly clear from its monthly directives, utilizes whatever information is available to it to identify the source of the disturbance so as to respond

according to its 'judgement' of the situation and hence in apparent conformity with what in Ben Friedman's analysis comprises the 'optimal strategy'.
Two features should be noted however. The first is that the objectives
implicit in the monthly revisions do not coincide with those conditioning
longer-term choices. From a short-run standpoint, external considerations
and concern with conditions in financial markets continue to play a more
major role than what may be considered longer-run ultimate objectives.
Secondly (though not quite unrelated to the former), the width of the tolerance ranges highlights the fact that, in contrast to the simple variance
models, the absence of precise information about the structure, at least over
shorter intervals of time, in general precludes any systematic inferences from
deviations in the growth of monetary aggregates on the gains to be had from
offsetting any part of such deviations. As Davis has noted, there is 'no really
good way to detect when short-run deviations in monetary growth from
longer run targets are truly temporary and when they reflect more fundamental developments . . . [and hence] to avoid over-reacting to short-term
developments the Federal Reserve has in practice . . . to tolerate short-run
swings over fairly wide ranges'[183]. Consequently short-run variations in the
money stock comprise, if at all, a very limited source of information on the
basis of which the FOMC may alter its policy instruments either 'efficiently'
or 'inefficiently'—and correspondingly short-run deviations of the aggregates from their 'desired' path are not in general a source of concern since
'there seems to be little or no evidence that short-run fluctuations in
monetary growth rates even over periods of up to six months have major
impacts on the economy'[184]. On the contrary, '. . . the Committee's belief [is]
that the short-run volatility in market interest rates likely to result from . . . a
policy [seeking to attain closer short-run control of monetary aggregates]
would risk greater disruption to the economy than the short-run instability
in money growth rates the policy was seeking to avoid'[185].

In this environment where precise relationships seem ephemeral and, as
Burns has noted, 'the relationship between monthly or even yearly rates of
monetary expansion and the performance of the economy is subject to
considerable uncertainty under the best of circumstances'[186], where even for
the narrower aggregates there are questions of coverage and errors in
measurement[187], where lags in effect of instruments of policy on monetary
aggregates are long relative to forecasting ability[188], where 'the demands of
the public are subject to rather wide short-term variations'[189], the question of
yielding to fixed formulae hardly arises. In this environment, as Volcker put
it, '. . . the Federal Reserve has pointed out now and again that it is neither
possible nor desirable to attempt close control over the growth of monetary
aggregates during short periods of time of say a few weeks or even
months'[190]. In this environment, 'confronted with an unexpected overshoot
or undershoot of its money growth targets the FOMC has taken moderate
action neither fully responding nor fully ignoring the rises until the under-

lying growth tendency can be differentiated from the noise of short-term aberrations in the data'[191] while it continuously taps on all sources of information available to it to gauge the movements in its goal variable. In this environment

> ... monetary policy represents [the Fed's] best *judgement* of what is appropriate in the light of evolving economic and financial developments[192].

Monetary aggregates serve neither as an intermediate target nor as a unique source of information[193]; and so also the recommendation that the FOMC 'abandons its operating strategy which makes the money stock the intermediate target for policy'[194] is quite superfluous.

The United Kingdom

A similar picture emerges in the context of the United Kingdom. Here again the late 1960s did witness a shift towards greater attention on monetary aggregates. To some extent this shift in emphasis—away from interest rates and credit conditions towards domestic credit expansion and the 'money supply'—was 'encouraged' by the requirements which the International Monetary Fund placed in extending its support to the United Kingdom. But the advent of Competition and Credit Control, allegedly heralding the era of money stock control, of emphasis on 'quantities' rather than 'prices', also reflected the optimism that the early (and rather few) studies on the demand for money fostered[195]. Indeed, at least in retrospect, the extravagance of the claims that hinged on them is quite staggering. For in one clean sweep they appeared, and were interpreted, it seems, to afford a revision of long cherished beliefs regarding not only the *ability to control monetary aggregates*, but also, in a more vague sense, the *desirability of so doing*, and the *information value* of such aggregates.

In 1969 the authorities' concern to exercise greater control of domestic credit expansion was still subdued by long-standing doubts[196] regarding the effect of more aggressive operations on the gilt-edged market. Reflecting views expressed since the late 1950s, and eloquently presented in the Bank of England's 1966 description of 'Official Transactions in the Gilt-Edged Market'[197], the official position was that

> Because the market response to a moderate price change for gilt-edged has been found to be unstable and often perverse in the short-term, the movement of interest rates required to achieve adequate liquidity absorption through debt operations may be so large that a rapid or seemingly arbitrary adjustment could permanently damage the willingness of investors to hold gilt-edged, compounding the difficulties of monetary management in the future . . .[Thus] official operations in gilt-edged continue to be constrained both by the underlying market situation and by long-term concern for the maintenance of a broad market[198].

In 1970, the Bank in its evidence to the Select Committee examining its activities continued to refer to the '. . . difficulty'. . . [of] reconciling the pedestrian day to day desire for an orderly gilt-edged market with the policy of restraining the money supply'[199]. But by 1971 the Competition and Credit Control announcements seemed to suggest no conflict of this kind any more. As Charles Goodhart put it

> The early studies on demand for money functions [within the Bank] which appeared to show a fairly stable relationship between money holdings and current and previous income and interest rates helped to dissipate the previous pessimism that financial markets are so fickle and susceptible in the short term to the wayward play of extrapolative expectations, that control of the monetary aggregates through normal market mechanisms would be impracticable . . . Insofar as the demand for money has a stable and predictable inverse relationship with interest rates it would seem to imply that an increase in rates by the authorities would have a determinate effect on the money stock . . . Furthermore by concentrating on the relationship between the aggregate money stock, incomes and interest rates, the thrust of this research pointed towards a policy of controlling monetary aggregates through market mechanisms and away from the previous policy of controlling a component of domestic credit through physical rationing'[200].

To be sure the gains to be had from such control were far from clear as ignorance (evident no less in the total absence of monetary variables from forecasting models[201]) surrounded the effects of changes in the money stock on the composition of expenditures and even reduced-form relationships, replicating investigations of U.S. experience, seemed to render much more equivocal an answer for 'the importance of money' than believers might have hoped[202]. But then again there was evidence of sorts in the Bank's own research[203] that such correlation as there was between money and income ran from the former to the latter, while also (and one may add, curiously) since under fixed exchange rates '. . . the level of interest rates was largely determined by external considerations, the demand for money equation seemed to allow one to read off what rate of monetary growth would be consistent (or more restrictive or more expansionary) than the government's domestic objectives'[204].

Paying little attention to the considerable differences in parameter estimates rendered by different formulations of demand for money functions and by even small variations in the time period employed, it was furthermore reasoned that the estimated relationships could serve to infer the movement in income. 'In practice', Lionel Price argued, 'the authorities do not know the current level of incomes in the economy as a whole; a reasonably comprehensive and reliable picture emerges only some months after the event. Meanwhile they must grasp at straws in the wind. As interest rates are known from day to day and monthly data on the money stock are received quite quickly, the demand for money equation could be applied to discover what level of income would be consistent with the observed interest rates and money stock; this provides an early if approximate indicator of movements in income besides those already available'[205].

Whether such perceptions amounted to monetary aggregates being seen as information variables, whether they commended the pursuit of a policy aiming to minimize the deviations of monetary aggregates from their expected path, or whether a feedback rule seemed in the circumstances preferable, is hard for the outsider to decipher. Most likely no clear view had emerged as even looking back Charles Goodhart conflated these issues when suggesting that one could '. . . indeed go further [than Price] by adding that by taking steps to counteract the divergences of monetary aggregates from their expected path—when such divergences were not held to be due to money market disturbances—one could hope to use [the] information [about income rendered by the demand for money function] to stabilize the path of incomes'[206]. But at any rate targets did not come then; and by the time they came nothing of the confidence of the turn of the 1970s remained.

The precise experience in the post-Competition and Credit Control, pre-targets era is conveyed too clearly elsewhere in this volume[207] to permit that I venture into a detailed description, which at any rate would be beyond the scope of this paper. But whatever the reasons, the ground on which targets sprouted has a more ragged appearance, resembling more in some respects the 1960s and the view of the United States described above, than the 'brave new world' that Competition and Credit Control envisaged. Indeed, looking back, Competition and Credit Control, as alas one could have predicted[208], seems to have been the last and most short-lived of the manifestations of 'the permissive society'. By mid-1972 the emphasis on control of quantities through variation in prices seemed a delusion, or at least something to be interpreted much more cautiously than some had a year earlier been encouraged to surmise, as the discomfort provoked by anticipations of unloading of gilts by the banks was relieved by the authorities' provision of a 'special loan facility' to the banks, alleviating the squeeze on their reserves at a time of unprecedented increases in bank lending to the private sector and in the money supply. Informal requests to the banks regarding lending, a ceiling on savings deposits rates, and last but not least the supplementary deposits scheme, suggested that neither sectoral effects were beyond the concern of the authorities, nor was control of deposits through variation in interest rates as straightforward an exercise as it seemed only shortly before.

Whether by 1976 anything remained that could still be said 'to dissipate the previous pessimism that financial markets are so fickle and susceptible in the short term to the wayward play of extrapolative expectations, that control of the monetary aggregates through normal market mechanisms would be impractical', is on the evidence very doubtful. But the experience also rendered awareness that the choice between quantity and price is conditional on the time interval considered, and hence the compromise: 'In the short run financial markets can be notably volatile while expenditures and output roll forward with stolid inertia . . .; so during short intervals, e.g. day by day and week by week, the random variance in money markets will probably be large relative to that in the goods markets with the implication that the shorter the time period the greater the emphasis the monetary authority should place on stabilizing interest rates in the money market'[209].

Equally to the point however, even over longer intervals of, say, a quarter or more, the confidence that could be placed on any prior beliefs and consequently the information to be had from movements of monetary aggregates was increasingly (and, as the results of tables 4(a) and 4(b) reveal, justifiably) questioned. The bitter disappointment of this experience is eloquently conveyed in Charles Goodhart's conclusion on post-1970 evidence: 'The monetarist edifice' he commented, 'rests largely on the stability and predictability of the demand for money function. Econometric study of the data in the 1960s had suggested that in the U.K. we too could build part of our monetary policy on this basis. Subsequent experience has revealed weaknesses in this foundation'[210].

In fact to this day no demand for money function for M_3 or sterling M_3 has been traced that exhibits even 'sensible' let alone 'stable' responses and which may therefore be said to provide 'a reliable foundation for policy design'. Reflecting on the estimates presented above and those of table 5 one may suggest that it is hardly a coincidence that the Bank of England has been reluctant to present *anything* regarding the performance of demand for sterling M_3, or for M_3 for the period beyond 1973. But even its recent excursion[211] into M_1 (clutching at whatever reed seems less slippery, one may say) rendering as it does a range of long-run elasticities of -0.045 to 1.741 for real income, 0.098 to 1.791 for the price level, and -0.096 to 0.548 for the short-term rate[212], suggests that the evidence available to the U.K. authorities from their attempts at estimation of demand for money functions presents a serious challenge to the contention that adherence to 'quantity' oriented targets can be justified or explained (as official appeals to intellectual antecedents encourage us to believe[213]) by reference to Poole's contribution to the policy problems. To be sure, predictions of behaviour of the real sector leave much to be desired. But bearing in mind also the rather infant stage of incorporation of monetary variables into the authorities' econometric models[214], it seems pertinent to conclude that a justification for intermediate targets in terms of the variance approach must provoke as a minimal comment that made by Lionel Price, namely that: 'At present instability—in the sense of economists' failure to predict events, or even to explain them satisfactorily with the benefit of hindsight—is rife both in goods markets and financial markets . . . It is, therefore, difficult to judge the strength of Poole-type arguments in the U.K. at the present time'[215].

Granted this it is not surprising that the U.K. monetary authorities, like

Table 5. *Some results on demand for £M_3.*

Estimated relationship: as tables 4(a) and 4(c)

Sample	a_0	b_0	b_1	c_0	c_1	d_0	d_1	m_1	m_2	S.E.	n_Y	n_p	n_r
U.K.; £M_3; 1964:1–73:4	1.39 (1.03)	0.13 (0.95)	0.02 (0.14)	0.17 (1.04)	−0.04 (0.25)	0.16 (0.25)	−1.91 (2.63)	0.90 (5.88)	0.11 (0.68)	0.0100	b	b	a
U.K.; £M_3; 1964:1–74:4	−1.06 (1.30)	0.09 (0.79)	0.11 (0.93)	0.11 (0.70)	0.10 (0.65)	0.66 (1.09)	−2.41 (3.28)	0.89 (5.87)	0.05 (0.30)	0.0105	2.97	3.18	−2.10
U.K.; £M_3; 1964:1–75:4	−2.27 (4.44)	0.09 (0.81)	0.14 (1.14)	0.03 (0.16)	0.02 (0.11)	−0.31 (0.75)	−0.93 (2.16)	1.02 (7.42)	−0.02 (0.11)	0.0113	b	b	b
U.K.; £M_3; 1964:1–76:4	−2.62 (5.53)	0.09 (0.79)	0.14 (1.16)	0.02 (0.13)	−0.03 (0.16)	−0.49 (1.38)	−0.72 (1.93)	1.02 (7.64)	0.02 (0.14)	0.0115	b	b	b

Estimated relationships: as tables 4(b) and 4(d)

Sample	α	β_1	$(1-\gamma)$	β_3	γ	ρ	S.E.	χ_3^2	χ_4^2	χ_5^2	n_Y	n_r
U.K.; £M_3; 1964:1–73:4	−3.34 (7.05)	0.26 (3.96)	−0.08 (1.69)	−1.20 (3.79)	1.08 (22.79)	0.01 (0.06)	0.0113	6.236	10.015	18.689	b	b
U.K.; £M_3; 1964:1–74:4	−2.60 (5.90)	0.23 (3.83)	−0.03 (0.44)	−0.73 (3.60)	−1.03 (17.52)	0.15 (17.52)	0.0125	11.154	15.410	21.360	b	b
U.K.; £M_3; 1964:1–75:4	−2.69 (7.35)	0.24 (4.40)	−0.03 (0.67)	−0.78 (5.43)	1.03 (23.05)	0.07 (0.53)	0.0122	5.742	7.351	22.010	b	b
U.K.; £M_3; 1964:1–76:4	−2.72 (7.67)	0.24 (5.12)	−0.03 (0.90)	−0.80 (5.82)	1.03 (31.51)	0.06 (0.44)	0.0123	5.134	6.308	25.269	b	b

(a) See note (a) of table 4(a)

their U.S. counterparts, neither regard any monetary aggregate as the (short-run?) intermediate target nor as a unique source of information on the basis of which to judge the adjustment to their policy instruments required to minimize implicit deviations of the goal variables from their desired values. Indeed the view that in the 'short-run financial markets are notably volatile', characterized (as Bank of England commentaries sometimes stress) by sharp swings in confidence, is conducive to emphasis being placed on stabilizing interest rates. External considerations and other sectoral effects, such as those pertaining to the behaviour of building societies and the housing market also play a role in this context[216]. In addition, however, the failure of the U.K. authorities to secure any reliable information regarding the parameters of the demand for money function implies that the confidence placed on any forecast rate of growth of the chosen aggregate is severely circumscribed[217], and hence also the failure to attain any such target strongly discounted (as 'in the United Kingdom', the Governor of the Bank of England remarked, 'we have not recently been able to observe a continuing stable relationship between money and incomes'[218]) *except insofar as the model employed by other economic units in interpreting such deviations is not subject to the same uncertainty.* With policymakers perusing (after the hopes of the turn of the decade) an environment that brings to mind passages from the Radcliffe Report[219], the pursuit of a proximate target is both half-hearted[220] and also subject to no obvious strategy in which to commit such instruments of policy as are available[221]. Besides, one may add, policy-makers now know that even if the demand functions for monetary aggregates were better behaved, delays in statistical information make it difficult to '. . . act to offset . . . divergences from forecast'[222], while there is also the caveat that '. . . stable and steady monetary growth carries with it the risk of instrument instability in that interest rates will need to fluctuate increasingly widely'[223].

West Germany

At first sight at least the situation in West Germany appears to have been rather different. From a longer-run perspective, the high priority accorded to price stability throughout the postwar period, and the relative emphasis on monetary, rather than fiscal, policy for much of this period, are features that distinguish West Germany from the other two countries considered[224]. Unlike the United States and the United Kingdom, the role accorded to monetary policy was never deemed to be that of accommodating fiscal policy. Indeed until 1967 the Bundesbank's actions (revealing marked differences in objective functions between it and the various tiers of government regarding the pursuit of *price stability, employment and growth*) invariably aimed to counteract not only the influence of purely exogenous factors but also the procyclical responses of the various tiers of government. And when in 1967 a move towards limiting discretion occurred, it was to constrain fiscal freedom, as the Stability and Growth Act sought to ensure greater coordination of Federal and Länder government policies and defined precisely the adjustments in government budgets (through so-called 'cyclical reserve funds') deemed to constitute the appropriate fiscal countercyclical action in the face of fluctuations in economic activity.

Yet the significance that has traditionally attached to Central Bank Policy should not, I believe, be interpreted to have implied, in the 1960s at least, emphasis on control of the money supply (however defined) as a means by which ultimate objectives could be achieved. References to the money stock are in fact rather scarce before the turn of the 1970s. Instruments of policy are deployed to effect 'bank-free liquidity' (i.e. bank holdings of central bank money and other short-term assets that can be used to increase such holdings, *minus* compulsory reserves) and thereby interest rates, credit and the demand for money. The influence of policy on ultimate goal variables is not perceived to operate through changes in the stock of money balance, but rather through changes in the asset composition of bank portfolios that cause changes in expenditures through changes in *availability and cost of credit*. In this respect the emphasis is on *flows* rather than *stocks*, and the money stock is conceived as a consequence of the effect of policy on other intermediate targets and of their effect on the goal variables.

By the beginning of the 1970s there are sounds of regard for money as a determinant of expenditures. Changes in bank credit are referred to as factors to which '. . . the Bundesbank . . . pays special attention, not only because, simply in quantitative terms, bank loans are normally the most important factor affecting monetary conditions, but also because this is a field in which the Bundesbank can exercise the strongest influence, by means of its instruments of monetary policy, on changes in the money stock'[225]. Yet, significantly, it is noted that the fact that its '. . . instruments have not enabled the Bundesbank to exercise strict control over the money creation of the banking system, despite the great effectiveness of liquidity policy in many respects . . . need not be considered a disadvantage insofar as *control of money creation as such is not the sole important factor in the control of aggregate demand in the economy; equally essential, and perhaps more so, is control of interest rates for this influences the calculations of borrowers* [who, it is explained, compare 'the nominal interest rate with the expected yield and with expectations as to the future course of the value of money'] *and hence the demand for credit*'[226]. Indeed, although some homage is paid to money stock control, at least until 1973, one feels it to be incidental. 'Monetary policy in Germany' we are told in 1972, 'is guided by the basic concept of controlling the bank's supply of credit, and the resultant increase in the money stock via bank liquidity, and in addition, of influencing non-banks' demand for credit by changing the interest rate level'[227]. But the analysis that follows such statements focuses *entirely* on free liquid reserves and credit conditions, while the impression continues that, with regard to expenditures and hence ultimate goal variables, the time lag between policy action and effect is that perceived to attach to changes in free liquid reserves and effect on bank credit to the private sector[228].

Interestingly the latter is so notwithstanding awareness '. . . that the size of the money stock [equal to private-resident-non-bank holdings of currency and sight deposits] is closely related to the course of economic activity as reflected by, say, the gross national product'[229] and the finding '. . . that divergences in the movement of the two aggregates, that is, fluctuations in the velocity of circulation, follow a regular pattern that may be linked both with the level of interest rates and with the cyclical situation'[230]. For, while noting that regressions '. . . suggest that fluctuations observed in the velocity of circulation are more a symptom of cyclical movements than a reaction to interest rates'[231] (notice the similarity to more recent utterances regarding the cyclical behaviour of CBM), it was stressed that 'By their very nature regression computations do not indicate the cause of the statistical correlation between the aggregates mentioned—whether, that is, monetary movements determine economic movements or whether the course of economic activity, dictated by other influences results in fluctuations in the monetary sphere'[232].

Nor is there any evidence later invoked to resolve this quandary. Rather the increasing emphasis on monetary aggregates in official statements coincides (and is often referred to in connection) with the advent of floating rates and with a break in the stylized facts previously invoked to describe the empirical relationship between free liquid reserves and credit expansion[233]. Insofar as floating rates do permit greater freedom in adjusting short-term rates to domestic conditions, a shift in emphasis from bank liquidity to the monetary liabilities of the government/central bank seems consistent. But the shift was induced no less by the fact that 'From Spring 1970 onwards [the] basic premise of liquidity policy became increasingly questionable . . . as even when the free liquid reserves had been reduced to a level which previous experience had shown to be "critical", credit expansion continued unabated or even accelerated. It [thus] became evident that the basic condition for liquidity policy [namely that 'there is in general a typical time lag of about a year observed in every phase of the cycle between the change in the liquidity position of banks and hence their credit creation potential on the one hand and the actual use of this potential on the other'[234]] in the form hitherto pursued was no longer assured'[235]. It is in this context that the stock of central bank money emerged as a *policy indicator*[236], as the index performing the task of '. . . measure of the expansive or restrictive effect of monetary policy'[237] that free liquid reserves were previously deemed to perform. And yet a year later, without relinquishing, it seems, in the eyes of the authorities its role as a policy indicator[238], it comes to serve as the *target*.

In this context although no allusions to the variance approach[239] are, to my knowledge, to be found in any official statements, certain aspects of the Bundesbank's policy conception and design seem more consistent with proximate (intermediate) targets than policy in either of the two countries so far examined. In particular, as the choice of single-value yearly targets may suggest, the degree of error attaching in the Bundesbank's opinion to the function describing the demand for CBM was at least initially thought to be small. And though in first announcing a monetary target the Bundesbank pointed out 'that in the short run there is no close relationship between the movement of the national product and that of central bank money'[240], the extent to which such remarks referred even to random fluctuations in demand for this aggregate is somewhat unclear, granted the tendency to augment such statements by referring to a systematic pattern of behaviour, that is that 'the relationship of central bank money ... to the nominal gross national product is subject to procyclical fluctuations [so that] ... during an upswing the national product rises faster than the money stock and the opposite occurs in a downswing'[241]. Otherwise the central bank money stock, it was claimed, shows a course which is substantially free from special influences[242]. Thus, insofar as the relationship of this aggregate to nominal GDP was thought to be not responsive to changes in interest rates, this being a major reason for the choice of this aggregate in preference to M_1 or M_2 in the first place[243], the behaviour of CBM could be said to possess by 'divine ordinance' or careful selection, the characteristics traced above as necessary in the context of the variance approach for the treatment of a monetary aggregate as a proximate target to be efficient.

Tables 4(a) to 4(d), and Appendix B, do reveal a contrast between experience in West Germany and the other two countries considered. As in the case of the United States and the United Kingdom the precise parameters recorded do depend on the nature of the estimated relationships. On the other hand, unlike the other two countries, the pattern of responses and temporal stability of the functions purporting to describe demand for CBM seem more satisfactory. In this respect the question of selection of '... the best available demand for money function'[244] and of a particular prior belief about the structure may for West Germany be thought more compatible with experience. But the results also reveal that from a variance approach standpoint a proximate target strategy in CBM is by the Kareken *et al.*-Ben Friedman reasoning, likely to have been inferior to a feedback rule that allows for the comparatively strong and certainly significant (see also χ_4^2 and χ_5^2 in tables 4(b) and 4(d)) interest elasticity of demand for CBM.

Yet it is doubtful whether the Bundesbank's strategy was (and/or is) perceived from a variance approach perspective. Certainly appeals to intellectual antecedents reveal closer kinship to our discussion of policy under uncertainty.

The relationship between what monetary policy does and what it ultimately causes to happen [H. Bockelmann notes] is so hard to fathom, according to a widely accepted view that the actions of a central bank cannot be directly guided by it. Hence *the Bundesbank*, like other central banks, *is following a two stage procedure*. The real objectives of economic policy, as set out, for example, in the German 'Act to Promote Economic Stability and Growth' of 1967 with regard to price stability, employment, external equilibrium, and steady and appropriate economic growth, are transformed into a monetary growth target. Monetary policy uses its instruments to come as closely as it can to this target. We fully realise that in theory serious objections can be raised against this two-stage procedure of monetary policy: ... the two stages of the monetary policy process are in fact not totally independent in the presence of uncertainty[245]. In the case of the intermediate target 'money stock' for instance, interest rates play a part at both stages, not only in the relationship between instruments and money stock but also in the relationship between the money stock and the real objectives of monetary policy[246]. In spite of these difficulties a case can be made for formulation of an intermediate target that covers the effects of policy in the *financial field*. In principle the central bank is in a strong position here because the banks' money creation cannot function without its support. On the other hand it cannot achieve very much on its own; the banks and their customers must go along with it. Even limiting monetary expansion is not as easy as may be supposed on the basis of the dictum that nothing can be done without the central bank. It costs the central bank a great deal of effort to make the relationships approximate to its ideas, and hence it is important to know how far it has been successful in so doing. An intermediate target appears to be the best means to this end[247].

And in discussing 'which variable best reflects the impact of monetary policy in the financial field?', he continues[248]

In the debate on monetary theory during the last few years central banks who have chosen an interest rate target have often been charged as trusting a highly unreliable compass. It is argued that a fall or a rise in interest rates on the credit market cannot be interpreted as indicating an easing or tightening of monetary policy as they may only be due to changes in demand for credit. A central bank which is guided by monetary developments it is claimed cannot be guilty of such misinterpretation. If interest rates rise in an economic upswing, the argument runs, the central bank will not be able to construe this as implying a restrictive policy if monetary growth increases further at the same time. Conversely falling interest rates are not indicative of a successful expansionary policy as long as the growth rates of the money stock continue to decline[249].

One can hardly fail to be struck by the similarity to Saving's approach to the policy problem in a world characterized by lack of complete knowledge of the structure and information lags discussed on pages 281–90 above. The emphasis on *intermediate target* and *two-stage procedures* springing from ignorance of the precise effects of policy on ultimate goal variables is unmistakable. Momentary reflection however also unveils the statement as one that conflates intermediate targets and policy indicators[250]. In the first half the discussion focuses firmly on intermediate targets; but when we come to 'In spite of . . .' we are moving to policy indicators, and in the quotation that follows we are clearly there.

From a narrow standpoint one may lend more emphasis to the former (that is to intermediate targets rather than to policy indicators) by noting the concern expressed in Bundesbank statements regarding the need to distinguish CBM from the concept of the monetary base[251]. Yet acknowledging the fact that (as our discussion of policy indicators reveals) one is not bound to accept for all institutional structures the Brunner-Meltzer identification of 'the base' with 'the ideal policy indicator', this is clearly not sufficient to resolve the issue. More revealing perhaps are utterances regarding 'the second stage' of the 'two-stage procedure'. Here statements stress a close connection between CBM and ultimate goal variables (or more precisely the gross national product)[252], and invariably even permit the inference of a causal sequence from the former to the latter; the choice of 'CBM as a target' being on several occasions presented as an attempt to identify *not only* an aggregate the demand for which, unlike M_1 and M_2, is not subject to shifts induced by interest rate movements (a feature for which M_3, i.e. the simple summation of currency plus sight plus time plus saving deposits, could have served just as well), but *also* an aggregate so structured as to reflect the '*moneyness*' of different kinds of deposits[253].

Since no detailed account exists of what the expected configuration of output and price developments *during the year* has been at the point of each yearly policy review, the extent to which the authorities have sought to pursue a proximate or intermediate target strategy cannot be ascertained simply by looking at the actual path of CBM. On the other hand, the descriptive accounts of the conduct of policy since 1975, the tendency to overshoot the target in the light of errors in prediction regarding velocity or output, the periodic emphasis on external considerations, and the occasional concern with stabilizing bond rates and securing orderly conditions in security markets[254], do reveal that the announced objectives for CBM have not comprised a target to be pursued in disregard of other objectives or of the information forthcoming in the course of the year.

Acknowledging such features of behaviour in the years since the introduction of CBM targets one cannot dismiss the possibility that this reflects the challenge to prior beliefs which experience since 1974 has posed. For not only have short-run deviations from the targeted rate of growth of CBM been stressed not to bear any relationship to movements in nominal income (and further 'that the trend of a few months must not be overrated'[255]) but also even over longer intervals (over the cycle) experience has not conformed to the relationship originally perceived by the Bundesbank to hold between real and nominal income and the stock of CBM. As the President of the Bundesbank remarked in late 1977, 'what has proved difficult is to correctly forecast the velocity of money or its rate of turnover. Our present economic recovery is not following a normal cyclical pattern and this probably explains why the velocity of money has not quite conformed to historic cyclical patterns'[256].

As the results presented above and in Appendix B suggest, the lack of conformity to historic cyclical patterns must to some extent be due to lack of conformity of nominal interest rates to historic cyclical patterns and the tendency of the Bundesbank to underplay the influence of such variables on the relationship of money to income[257]. Yet besides such systematic influences there have also been, it appears, other factors effecting the relationship in specific periods. Certainly in deciding on policy at any given point the Bundesbank has continuously sought to establish the nature of the disturbance, thus listing over the years a wide menu of factors accounting for unanticipated decreases (or more precisely, for the failure of anticipated increases to materialize) in the ratio of nominal GNP to CBM; explanations that have ranged from 'errors in seasonal adjustments'[258], to 'precautionary motives' increasing the currency component[259], to 'growing holdings of Deutsche Mark notes outside the Federal Republic [plus] the disproportionately steep increase in income of pensioners who traditionally hold more cash, and the increase in cash payments in the "grey areas" of business activity'[260], to lags in response of expansionary policy[261]. Correspondingly one notes increasing emphasis on 'explaining the reasons for divergencies from the target', a feature that reflects a flexibility in operating procedures analogous to that traced *de facto* for the United States and the United Kingdom, as well as the abandonment in December 1978 of the single-valued, year-on-year average target in favour on average of last-quarter to last-quarter target *range* of 6–9 per cent for the growth of CBM launched with acknowledgements both to the effect that '. . . when setting the target it proved particularly difficult to gauge the extent to which the available money stock could be used'[262] and that '. . . the target range attests that policy has to adapt itself to changing conditions both at home . . . and vis à vis the rest of the world'[263].

IN FULL PUBLICITY AND COMMON KNOWLEDGE

While permitting the inference of greater attention on monetary aggregates and of greater awareness of longer-run aspects of policy in conceptions of the responsibilities of the monetary authorities, our preceding discussion does not suggest that these derive from perceptions of relative stability of real and financial markets or from clearer evidence on characteristics of behaviour. Furthermore, it will appear that in none of the three countries has the behaviour of the authorities been of a kind that fits a description of policy-makers who *periodically* decide on the growth of monetary aggregates deemed (on the information available at that point in time) consistent with the attainment of ultimate objectives, and then proceed to pursue the particular path of these aggregates so derived in disregard of the information rendered *continuously* by the environment, except insofar as such information furthers the attainment of the monetary aggregate objectives already set and declared. Rather experience, since the introduction of publicly announced monetary targets, suggests a setting in which the policymaker seeks to infer the implications of current developments for ultimate goal variables and hence perceptions of policy that (provided we recognize the rather impressionistic nature of the policymaker's knowledge of his environment and, correspondingly, the grey area in which the outcome that does not call for policy revision melts into the one that does) can be said to be consistent with the *spirit* of information feedback strategies and intermediate target/policy indicator settings, but as such do not detract from a position where ' . . . *judicious assessment* of the complexities of actual conjuncture [is deemed to] allow a better selection of policy than sticking to any *predetermined posture*'[264].

Why then 'monetary targets'? What is the nature of the pledge?

Policy Anticipations and the Choice of Policy

Nothing has so far been said of the public's perception of the environment and of the 'publicly announced' aspect of recent policies. The policy problem described was seen to depend on information lags, on random disturbances, on lack of knowledge of the structure, but not, *explicitly* at least[265], on private agents' perception of policy and on the way policy may impinge on the structure. Yet publicly announced targets, emerging as they do in a period of inflation and uncertainty, owe much of their existence to such considerations.

That policy outcomes would not in general be independent of the public's perception of the aims of policy, of the policy regime, of anticipations of how the policymaker will respond to shocks, is a relatively old position[266] that, though many often forget[267], few would deny. What is a matter of current dispute is the implications of such behaviour for the choice of strategy to be followed by the authorities.

Starting from the ' . . . presumably unobjectionable idea that people fully exploit whatever information they have'[268], it is pertinent I believe to distinguish between two circumstances. The first relates to a situation in which private agents hold a particular (stochastic) perception of the environment. The second, as in our discussion of policy under uncertainty, affords no such unique (and exhaustive) prior belief.

In the former case the assumption of a particular prior perception about the structure entitles us to reason, following Muth, 'that expectations, since they are informed predictions of future events, are essentially the same as the predictions of the relevant economic theory'[269] and hence, *provided that we stress the durability of a particular prior belief*, envisage a situation in 'which people's expectations are identical to the corresponding expectations conditional on the process generating those outcomes'[270]. The latter of course incorporates the response functions of the authorities. And when the authorities are assumed to hold a particular prior belief about the structure and to be endowed with the same information as the public about the path of the exogenous variables in the system, their precise response to any given eventuality can be accurately inferred by the public so that any action by them is fully anticipated. If, furthermore, we assume that 'the relevant economic theory' reveals that monetary policy cannot affect (peg) real magnitudes, it follows that monetary policy—being perfectly predictable and, as all other phenomena, rationally processed in its implications— cannot effect the probability distribution of real output[271]. The 'distribution of output does not depend on the parameters of the feedback rule for the money supply'[272]; 'a definite rule emerges only [when we assume that the authority's goal function] incorporates a target *value* for the price level'[273].

In terms of output (and employment) therefore, the monetary authorities' actions matter only to the extent that (a) they embody non-systematic elements, 'surprise', or (if they embody no such elements), (b) when over the 'relevant horizon'[274] money is not neutral. Furthermore as '. . . there is no way that the monetary authority can base a countercyclical monetary policy on . . . [surprise], since there is no way [it] can regularly choose [the random term that constitutes the surprise] in response to the state of economic affairs in order to offset other disturbances in the system'[275], no output gains are to be had from discretionary (surprise) policy. Conversely since 'an increased variance [as distinct from systematic feedback] of money reduces the information content of observed prices and therefore makes it more difficult for individuals to respond 'appropriately' to changing patterns of relative supplies and demands . . . there is an efficiency argument for making money as predictable as possible'[276].

It should be noted that this analysis does not lead directly to the conclusion that has been appended to it, namely that '. . . following Friedman's X percent growth rule . . . can be defended as the best the authority can do'[277]. There is many 'a slip twixt cup and lip'. For it is certainly not enough to have reached the conclusions of the previous paragraph, nor the result that '. . . a unique equilibrium price level does not exist [when] the monetary authority pegs the rate of interest period by period regardless of how its value varies from period to period'[278]. Indeed in a world of the kind defined by Sargent and Wallace it seems hard to comprehend why the monetary authority's goal function incorporates among its arguments the price level. And though we can readily accept the argument against an increased variance of money, we should be less disposed to readily accept the yet unproven appendage namely: *that the costs of systematic feedback rules designed to ensure a steady rate of growth of the money stock are smaller than those of any other of the feedback rules between which the models constructed strictly suggest that we should be indifferent.*

At any rate one may (and many have) challenge(d) the assumptions leading to the conclusion that with regard to output and employment there is nothing to choose between feedback rules. Objections to neutrality—ranging from effects of expected inflation on the demand for money[279] and other assets, to Franco Modigliani's contrasts between inside and outside money[280], to sticky prices, with wages as a prime example[281]—spring easily to mind. No less digestible seems the assumption that people's subjective expectations are identical to the corresponding objective expectations conditional on the process generating those outcomes. For even if we are willing (as our discussion of pp. 272–4 above suggests authors to be) to endow the policymaker with such a perspective, the fact that the acquisition and processing of information is not costless suggests that we should be reluctant to afford the same knowledge to (all) private agents and thus reluctant to accept the contention that these agents too '. . form their expectations "as if" they know the true model of the economy'[282].

Either of these departures from the macro-rational expectations assumptions provides us with a role for monetary policy. As Barro and Fischer note, if '. . . the policy maker has superior information about the economy—for example he obtains information more rapidly than the public about aggregate prices and output [—then] . . . countercyclical monetary policy . . . can work to move the economy toward the level of output that would be chosen under full current information [since] policy can be designed that induces individuals to act as though they were aware of the extra information possessed by the policy maker'[283]. Even in the absence of such informational asymmetries, a systematic '. . . active monetary policy can effect the behaviour of output if there are long term contracts'[284], since by responding to shocks that occur after wages contracts have been concluded by *part* of the labour force it can influence the variation in output[285].

From a more embracing standpoint however, we may note that non-neutralities are the counterpart of costly to acquire and process or indeed incomplete information. Whether in our conception of the monetary economy we emphasize an 'uneven distribution of information' with money resulting '. . . from economic agents' innovational responses to the operation of information and adjustment costs'[286], or we stress '. . . the indissoluble link between money and unknowledge'[287], non-neutralities have to be recognized. The existence of contracts denominated in money terms—a 'corollary' of which in Keynes is liquidity preference[288], and in Hayek reflects '. . . the existence of a generally used medium of exchange'[289]—signifies *at least* the fact that the costs of collecting and processing information will result in contracts that are conditional on particular information subsets. Such reasoning does imply that the policymaker will always be able to 'exploit' some non-neutralities. It also admits that the information sets upon which contracts (or more generally decisions) are made contingent will not in general be independent of the characteristics of the economy including the policy of the authorities.

On the other hand, this feature (which even with regard to anticipated price movements implies a change in the opportunity set of the social group) has as its counterpart a perception of the environment in which decisions of private agents cannot be said to rest on exhaustive enumerations of all possible alternatives. We cannot suppose the economic agent '. . . to have looked at every value in the logically possible range of the variable and assigned to it a degree of standing as a hypothesis in answer to his question: What will the measurement prove to be? . . . a sweep of thought that can scarcely be supposed to miss out or neglect any contingency which another mind could point to or which the course of events will be able to provide'[290]. Correspondingly, our mode of thought and our conception of the role of policy must acknowledge that economic agents base their decisions on 'fragmentary evidence'[291].

Whether we still choose to describe private agents' decisions in terms of probabilities which are 'subjective'[292], whether we append to them Bayesian perceptions, degrees of 'confidence'[293], or whether we choose to opt for a mode of thought that seeks to recognize 'uncertainty over model selection'[294], incomplete information admits that situations can arise such as run counter to judgement duly passed upon their claims to conform to the capacities of the world or even such as have never entered the economic agents' mind; situations that suggest '. . . that the nature of things has been fallaciously conceived [that] make it seem that the prevailing picture of the world is wrong in some more or less essential and radical respect'[295]. When so, we may accord to policy the role of seeking to ensure that economic agents' perceptions of the nature of things are preserved—and perhaps, at times when circumstances command, that they are orderly revised. This obviously implies that other things equal, policy itself should not be the source of the unexpected. But unless we assume that nothing else can challenge prior beliefs, policy has a role to play. It is a rather delicate role since, unless the intent is clear, it may itself cause people to think that the nature of things is fallaciously conceived. If the event has not been accounted for in other economic agents' perceptions, neither has the policy response required to meet it. One senses that policy should receive, to use Myrdal's phrase, '. . . full publicity and common knowledge'[296], and that the policymaker should explain such divergencies as may in the course of time arise. Of course to do so reduces, we may say, the costs to the public of inferring what policy may be; it also implies that fewer resources '. . . have to be devoted by private agents to contingency planning, to adjusting schedules and designing for flexibility'[297], this being after all a counterpart of an economic organization that delegates some of the responsibilities to a common body. Again, since in the absence of a unique prior belief we must presume that, even with regard to prospects of common interest, economic agents will interpret policy actions differently, publicly announced targets can contribute to consistency of plans.

Yet it will be noticed that inherent in this process of reasoning is the belief that the authorities have a positive role to play and that they can and do play this role. But what if circumstances prove that the role previously ascribed to them is misconceived in that either objectives previously perceived to fall within their province are beyond their control, or that the pursuit of such objectives causes changes that challenge prior beliefs in other ways? Then private agents cannot rely on the authorities' action to ensure the particular picture of the world previously envisaged. The result may be a different assignment, more consistent you might say with the capabilities of the body in question. But except perhaps in the transition, when that is economic agents seek to ascertain what has been due to errors in policy and what may otherwise be the nature of things, it seems unlikely that the assignment of the policymaker will be to ensure that policy itself is not the source of the unexpected.

The Nature of Public Announcements

As mentioned earlier, the experience of the late 1960s and the first half of the 1970s has, in general, induced considerable reflection on the extent to which governments can be expected to deliver some of the objectives (and in particular 'full employment' in the sense of a 'sociopolitically' desirable level of employment) previously thought to fall within their province. Furthermore inflation (now more prominent among ultimate objectives) whether in fact the outcome of the authorities' earlier misconceptions regarding the implications of changes in monetary aggregates, or of rational responses by them to pressures for monetary accomodation[298], has been increasingly perceived *by the public* as a monetary phenomenon—a belief which, however subject to qualification by the specialist, cannot be treated as 'of no consequence' by the policymaker.

From this standpoint publicly announced monetary targets denote changes in objective functions, statements of the nature of the unexpected against which policy undertakes to provide in a language that accords with (but in the process also reinforces) what the Governor of the Bank of England described as ' . . .the layman's apparently intuitive perception of the broad relationship between monetary growth and inflation—clearer perhaps to him than to the professional who knows all the necessary qualifications'[299].

As Paul Volcker noted

Monetary targeting is first of all a useful tool of communication to the public. The relationship between money and inflation in its broader terms is readily understood. So long as the monetary authority's expression of intent has a degree of credibility (and maintenace of credibility will be crucially important over time) the announcement of the so-called growth ranges *at a minimum* sets a general framework for expectations of inflation, defining at least the upside potential. There is no doubt that control of inflation ... depends importantly on containing price expectations. Any public action that can dampen fears of new inflationary outbursts improves our chances of satisfactory economic results including prospects of reducing inflation[300].

Even more revealing perhaps is the Bundesbank's view that

the primary aim ... of specifying a monetary growth target is to give those involved in economic activity ... especially those who have to make far reaching decisions on costs and prices ... an indication of the monetary course they can expect in the coming year[301].

a position echoed in the Bank of England's *Bulletin*, which notes

In publicly specifying these monetary objectives the intention is to give those responsible for economic decisions throughout the economy—including decisions affecting costs and prices—a clear indication of the course the authorities intend to pursue in the years ahead[302].

In short one may say

Publicly announced monetary targets ... [reflect] an effort to adopt in the world today a sensible and comprehensible *symbol of policy*[303].

Such statements, however, raise a number of questions and permit a number of interpretations regarding the nature and significance of the pledge. In the first instance, and as our previous discussion reveals policy-makers recognize, monetary targets in no way define over the horizon pertinent to most contracts 'the upside potential' for inflation. Correspondingly, from the standpoint of those making 'far reaching decisions on costs and prices' monetary targets contribute little or no indication of what they can expect 'in the coming year', as both inflation and demand are subject to longer (and variable) lags in response to variations in monetary growth, while announced desired growth rates of the money supply are interpretable into statements regarding interest rates and loan availability only when taken in conjunction with (and hence seen as conditional upon) a rather wide set of other informational inputs. Conversely if monetary targeting aims at consistency of plans, and granted our earlier discussion suggesting policy responses that are conditional (or at least refer) to ultimate goals, the question arises as to whether the announcements reveal commitments to monetary targets or descriptions of conditions during the coming year that combine intentions to employ policy instruments in such a fashion as to achieve the verification of predictions regarding specific variables deemed to enter *directly* in decisions of economic agents.

Focusing on West Germany for example, our discussion in section 2 above reveals that policy announcements contain *explicit* inflation forecasts.

Furthermore an appraisal of performance since the introduction of publicly announced targets reveals for the period 1975 to 1978 (inclusive) a much smaller mean error in the actual rate of inflation to that forecast a year earlier than in the actual to 'targeted' central bank money stock[304]. This is true in all four years and on average describes errors in the former of less than one-third of those in the latter. While this in no way implies that the announcement of monetary targets is irrelevant to the attainment of the forecast rate of inflation, or that the emphasis[305] put on announcements of *single valued* targets, rather than ranges, was in any way misplaced, it does suggest that, other things equal, anticipations of inflation based on inflation forecasts are more accurate than anticipations based on announcements of the rate of growth of CBM. This is the more so when we acknowledge the errors in forecasting real GNP over the period. Correspondingly one cannot on this evidence dismiss the possibility that public announcements, aiming to ensure convergence of expectations of inflation, not only provide *direct* information regarding expected inflation but are also interpreted to denote a pledge regarding inflation rather than the pursuit of a monetary target beyond the stage at which the authorities believe that violation of the announced target for CBM may threaten the public's confidence in the intent of policy regarding prices.

On such reasoning, and in conjunction with our earlier discussion of actual policy, one may suggest the following description of German policy. At the point of decision of target rate of growth the authorities resolve that a particular rate of inflation is implicit in contracts concluded for the coming year. Publicly announced targets combined with explicit inflation forecasts—that unavoidable rate of price changes continuously stressed in their calculation—aim to provide information for such sectors as have not yet entered in fixed contracts as to what the aggregate price level expectations embodied in such contracts ought to be, so that (as in Myrdal's *'Monetary Equilibrium'*) '... flexible prices can be made to adapt to the level of the sticky ones'[306]. Policy then aims (subject to all the qualifications raised in our earlier discussion regarding policy effects) to ensure validation of such price expectations, and if successful in so doing would, *other things equal* (if, that is, output and velocity forecasts prove to have been correct), also result in the attainment of the 'targeted' rate of growth of CBM. The attainment of the 'target' comprises a manifestation that expectations are verified and not the absence of discretionary policy aiming at ultimate goal variables. The attainment of the 'target' constitutes an objective in itself only to the extent that continuous divergencies from forecast may (notwithstanding explanations of the reasons for the divergence) undermine the credibility of the simple (quantity theory) model that the Bundesbank employs in public announcements to 'reinforce' people's confidence in the inflation forecasts presented by it.

If so, the central bank money stock serves neither as a policy indicator nor as a target in the sense that these have been defined in our earlier discussion. The unitary long-run elasticity to nominal GNP it is claimed to exhibit is of consequence not in the context 'control theory policy-hydraulics', but in answer to the question of how best to convince the public that such inflation objectives as the autorites regard feasible are indeed feasible. The search for an aggregate whose relationship to nominal GNP is not subject to interest induced shifts—however irrational the composition of that aggregate may be—and the choice of single value targets are part and parcel of the same confidence 'experiment'. So are (perhaps—for one may not preclude the possibility that policymakers fall victims of their own ploys) the claims for more accurate reflection of 'moneyness' described in the weights of CBM.

Insofar as 'the overriding aim is . . . to co-ordinate the decisions of economic groups more effectively' the publicity stand of ' . . .monetary growth [targets] acting as a signpost. . . '[307] has not in Germany been unsuccessful. For as H. Schlesinger notes '. . . experience. . . permits [the inference] that the formulation of this target helped to bring about a 'social consensus' among all groups, even though other factors may have contributed to this consensus'[308]. But what of the other two countries?

In the United Kingdom even more than in Germany one observes a change in the policymakers' goals and objective functions. Furthermore, again, if we treat target ranges as denoting a 'mean of the range' objective, we find that over the period of publicly announced monetary targets the error in the actual to forecast rate of inflation has each year been less than the equivalent for $£M_3$ and over the three years of targets a ratio of the average of the former (as derived from the OECD forecasts) to that of the latter of less than one-third. On the other hand, while the authorities' derivation of monetary targets combines inflation forecasts, monetary target announcements do not; and insofar as attempts through incomes policies over the period 1976 to 1978 may be said to articulate an inflation commitment, one should note that these have not sought to present a consensus view between such rates of inflation as the 'layman' is encouraged (in Bank of England statements of the relationship between money and prices) to infer from publicly announced targets and the wage agreements he is asked to engage in. Such discrepancies are hardly conducive to convergence of expectations of inflation, to consistency of plans, to clarifying the role of policy. But they reflect not merely inconsistencies in overall policy design, as they also denote the fact that in the United Kingdom monetary targets combine with other economic policies in an aim to effect a revision of aspirations regarding real income and of earlier perceptions and trends regarding income distribution, to a greater extent than may be said to be true of West Germany and certainly, since 1977, with lesser success than in that and some other similar economies.

As regards expectations and consistency of plans however, one must also note the difference between the German single valued targets and the (wide) ranges opted for in the United Kingdom; ranges that—in the absence of the qualifications regarding the relationship between money and prices known to the specialist, and, depending on the interpretation one places on the aims of policy, even for the specialist—permit a wide dispersion of forecasts of the magnitudes that impinge directly on the decisions of economic units. In this connection one perceives also differences between the United Kingdom and West Germany regarding how in the light of *past experience and institutional characteristics* one may best nurse the required confidence in the intent of policy pursued.

Such contrasts also become any attempt to generalize German perceptions regarding monetary targets to United States targeting and experience. If American targets are to be interpreted to comprise a device whereby 'social consensus' regarding inflation can be achieved, one cannot but marvel at the conclusions to be drawn regarding economic man in different countries when reflecting on

The Americans find it necessary (desirable) to announce (stress) *four, quarterly revisable* target *ranges.*

The Germans have been particularly anxious to adhere to a *single valued yearly* target.

One may of course rationalize the contrast by noting the possibility that, in the eyes of American policymakers, economic units focusing on the same variables (e.g. prices) hold different perceptions of the nature of things and thus rely on different models and require different inputs regarding monetary aggregates. Similarly it may be argued that any given economic unit may draw more accurate inferences regarding a *wider* range of variables (or regarding the time path of variables) that impinge directly on its actions from announcements that convey information of the *relative* paths of a number of aggregates. But in either event monetary targets in the United States and West Germany seem amenable to treatment as creatures of the same species only for purposes that permit a very wide (and otherwise vacuous) definition of the species. Interestingly this also appears to reflect on attitudes of U.K. and U.S. market participants compared to those in West Germany. Monetary targets seem to comprise a vital statistic for participants in financial markets in the United States and the United Kingdom and relatively less so for participants in labour markets, whereas the converse may be said to apply to West Germany. For both the United States and the United Kingdom one may note the thunder and smoke that deviations of actual growth rates from their ranges (particularly upper bounds) have often created; and correspondingly one may wonder whether greater stability of financial markets has ensued from monetary targets. But on another plane the United States also contrasts with the United Kingdom, as inflation, one finds, has carried there a much lower priority among ultimate goals than in the other two (or indeed in all other major industrial) countries. For the

United States the errors in inflation forecasts have been larger than the corresponding errors for M_1. For the United States the focus with regard to ultimate objectives has been, with considerable success, on output and employment rather than prices. Of course there is nothing in the dicta relating to monetary targets that compels a particular goal function. Yet all in all our discussion suggests that few genalizations other than of a kind that may have been drawn for policy in yesteryears can be drawn from cross-country comparisons during the (first phase (?) of the) 'era of monetary targets'.

4. The Last Curtain with Ghosts of the Past

Almost a century and three-quarters ago, the Bullion Committee (of 1810) concluded that:

> The most detailed knowledge of the actual trade of the Country combined with the profound science in all the Principles of Money and Circulation would not enable any man or set of men to adjust and keep always adjusted the right proportion of circulating medium in a country to the wants of trade[309].

In 1927 Governor Strong and other witnesses testifying before the Committee of the United States Congress on Stabilization appointed to examine the wisdom of a proposed amendment to the Federal Reserve Act, the effect of which would have been to lay upon the Federal Reserve the duty of using all the powers at its disposal to 'promote a stable price level for commodities in general'[310], expressed considerable doubts towards the idea that 'the Federal Reserve System has the power to raise or lower the price-level by some automatic method, by some magic mathematical formula'[311]. Strong's position is summed up in the following excerpt:

> I believe that administration of credit such as is afforded by the Federal Reserve System, is capable of exerting an influence upon the volume of credit employed by the country and upon the cost of that credit. Within the limitation which the volume and the cost of credit exert an influence upon the price-level, and only within that limitation, can the operations of the Federal Reserve System influence prices. But there will be times when even the power to somewhat regulate the volume of credit and its cost will fail to achieve complete or anything like complete regulation of the price-level because there are many other things far beyond the influence of the volume and cost of credit, such as the mood of the people. Therefore if any expression is contained in the Federal Reserve Act which appears to represent to the people that the Federal Reserve System can do more in stabilizing the price-level than the limited control of credit is capable of performing, I am afraid that disappointment will come when there are fluctuations of prices which cannot be controlled within the strict limitations that I have described[312].

Commenting on this position in 1930 Keynes found himself to 'have more sympathy' 'with some of the doubts' than he had had a few years before. But he reasoned:

> I think that in one fundamental respect they have mistaken the character of the problem and underestimated the possibilities of control. . . . if the inability to sell current output at the current cost of production is *general* . . . this is an indication of a maladjustment on the side of demand rather than of supply, [and] the only way of influencing demand is by increasing investment relatively to saving . . . To refrain from lowering the rate of interest during a slump. . . could only have the effect of accentuating the violence of the Credit Cycle; . . .
>
> According to my own definition 'sound credit conditions' would of course be those in which the market rate of interest was equal to the natural-rate, and both the value and the cost of new investment were equal to the volume of current savings. If we take this as our criterion, many of Governor Strong's perplexities will become much less formidable. We could, I think, in each case tell him in general terms what he ought to do to preserve stability[313].

And though in the paragraphs following (as perhaps in the parenthetical reference to 'in general terms' quoted above), 'certain limitations' were recognized by Keynes on '. . . whether in practice it does always lie within the power of the banking system to control the rate of investment', as, for example, when 'non-monetary causes of instability . . . arise so suddenly that it is impossible to counteract them in time [and hence] . . . an interval should elapse before stability is restored'[314]—the era of stabilization policy had clearly begun.

The shift in ethos was eloquently presented in the 1931 Macmillan Report[315].

> Between liberty and government [the Committee noted] there is an age-long conflict. It is of vital importance that the new policy, while truly promoting liberty by securing better conditions of life for the people of this country, should not, in its zeal for interference, deprive them of their initiative and independence which are the nation's most valuable assets.
>
> The lesson [of experience] . . . is that in the case of our political and social institutions we may well have reached a stage when an *era of conscious and deliberate management must succeed the era of undirected natural evolution* . . . We must now choose our path deliberately and consciously. In other words we stand in need as never before of a definite national policy in our financial dispositions[316].

In the latter vein the report stressed the importance of economic research[317] but did not expect it to deliver the philosopher's stone. Thus it was reasoned:

> . . . if [economic fluctuations] are even partly under human control [as indeed the disturbances due to monetary factors are], it is of the utmost importance for

the betterment of humanity and the stability of society that such methods of control as may exist should be worked out and put into practice, even if as is and will remain true, there exist no simple scientific rules by the mere application of which such control can be exercised. The management of currency and credit is essentially an art and not a science[318].

By 1936 Keynes' position on the role of monetary policy had, as we well know, shifted to one in which the ability of the monetary authorities to influence the level of demand was thought to be very limited. And so he reasoned that:

'. . . it seems unlikely that the influence of banking policy on the rate of interest will be sufficient by itself to maintain an optimum rate of investment'[319].

Others, however, did not share Keynes' views on the limitations of monetary instruments; and wary of the capacity of mortal men to wield such power for the common weal, sought to devise rules to limit the exercise of discretionary power by the monetary authority. Thus in the same year as *The General Theory* there appeared Henry Simons' *Rules versus discretion in monetary policy*[320]. A rule to deliver the objective sought by the 1927 Committee of the United States Congress mentioned above was favoured by Simons and Mintz. Significantly, for it pre-empts more recent feedback rules, the rule proposed was that the central bank be required to engage in open market purchases and sales of securities whenever a broad index of prices moved outside a specified narrow range.

Simons and Mintz[321], however, did consider other rules. Simons, to quote Friedman, 'vacillated between favoring a rule expressed in terms of the quantity of money . . . and a rule expressed in terms of a price index'[322]. And, just as, for some Keynesians, orthodoxy hardened to a position in which demand management was the answer to all evils but within that frame the role ascribed to monetary policy was that of accommodating fiscal policy, so also, at the opposite end of the spectrum, those disposed to interpret the evidence on the ability of the market to disseminate information and on the significance of monetary changes differently, sought to harness the discretion allowed to the monetary authorities. Thus, in 1959, Friedman noted:

The granting of wide and important responsibilities that are neither limited by clearly defined rules for guiding policy, nor subject to test by external criteria of performance, is a serious defect of our present monetary arrangements. It renders monetary policy a potential source of uncertainty and instability. It also gives greater power to the men in charge for good or ill, greater 'flexibility' to meet the problems as they arise, to use the phrase that the Reserve System likes to emphasize. [Yet]. . . experience suggests that eliminating the dangers of instability and uncertainty in policy is far more urgent than preserving flexibility[323].

Hence the recommendation to:

> Instruct the System to use its open market powers to produce a 4 per cent per year rate of growth in . . . [currency and commercial bank deposits of the public] . . ., to keep the rate of growth as steady as it can week by week and month by month and to introduce no seasonal adjustment movement of the money stock[324].

Yet Friedman's rule has not had the impact that his teachings on the importance of money have had. The Simons-Mintz favourite is in some ways *conceptually* more akin to the experience described in this paper; in that although the objectives of the monetary authorities have encompassed other goals besides a reduction in the variance of prices or the rate of change in prices, the emphasis on the latter and the element of feedback from currently available information are unmistakably contemporary. But then again when a range of objectives replaces a single objective, when differences in time perspectives are recognized, when revisions of proximate targets are the rule, when in each particular circumstance judgement is, and has to be, exercised so as to distinguish a particular manifestation from other apparently similar events recorded in the past, no less when our appraisal of any particular recommendation is so subject to uncertainty regarding the characteristics of our economy, the brave new-world of (feed-back) rules affords a great deal of room to (and policy resembles much of) yesterday's Art of Central Banking.

To be sure policymakers have not been immune to experience nor to the strides that economic analysis has made. Looking back they may not object to the view of the Radcliffe Committee[325]:

> That the authorities . . . have to regard the *structure* of interest rates rather than the money supply as the centrepiece of the monetary mechanism, [which] does not mean that the money supply is unimportant but that its control is incidental to interest rate policy[326].

But they will also take heed, when in yesteryears others failed, of the Committee's view that:

> The authorities should not aim at complete stability of interest rates, but should take a view as to what the long-term economic situation demands and be prepared by all the means in their power to influence markets in the required direction[327].

As we have seen, this has not implied that they are oblivious to the short-run; for they '. . . pay attention to the short-term as well as to the long-term situation'[328]. But whatever the perception of trade-offs, there is now emphasis on the need to provide information of the content of policy; there is strong awareness that, in the words of the Macmillan Committee:

... a change of no great significance which is likely to be merely temporary or seasonal may cause undue alarm and may have a seriously unfavourable psychological reaction on business confidence[329].

a fact for which, as that same Committee reasoned,

... the only remedy ... is to be found ... in [readiness on the part of the authorities to ensure] *a diffusion of knowledge* as to the relevant facts[330].

In a world where 'failure to predict events or even to explain them satisfactorily with benefit of hindsight' is not the exception, even this is quite a tall order. But though in so doing economic analysis is invaluable, we may also bear in mind Edgeworth's remarks of long ago:

The theorist must not pretend to wisdom, if he knows so little what he is about as to mistake his abstract formulae for rules immediately applicable to practice[331].

Appendix A: Intermediate Targets and Information Variables: A Graphical Representation

Consider a case in which the demand for money is known while the IS is stochastic. An intermediate target strategy, maintaining the money stock constant is the policy which (in the absence of information feedbacks) minimizes the variance in the goal variable, Y.

When at the point of decision, however, with an expectation of the IS of $\hat{IS}$, the money stock is set at M^*, consistent with Y^*, then with the IS being subject to random disturbances the interest rate will vary between R_1 and R_2 as the unobservable goal variable takes values Y_1 or Y_2. In this case the interest rate can serve as the information variable in that the policymaker observing a deviation of the interest rate from its expected, R^*, value, can infer, in the light of his prior beliefs about the structure and its stochastic characteristics, the implicit deviation of the goal variable from its desired value and the adjustment in the money stock required to offset this deviation in the goal variable. Such a process is described by the induced shifts in the LM shown in figure 1.

With the money stock at M^* an observation of the interest rate at R_2 provokes a reduction in the money supply to M_2, raising the interest rate to $\bar{R}_2$ and reducing income from Y_2 to Y^*. Alternatively an observation of the interest rate at R_1 provokes an increase in the money to M^*, reducing the interest rate to R_1 and raising income from Y_1 to Y^*.

As is apparent this information feedback process generates a set of points (A, B, C) analogous to a vertical LM, and correspondingly, as Ben Friedman notes, the alternative intermediate target strategy will be as efficient as the

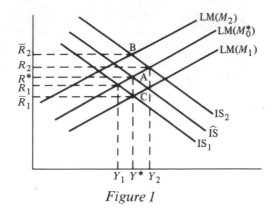

Figure 1

optimal policy if the demand for money is a function of income only.

It should be noted that in the above example I have employed the money stock as the instrument and the interest rate as the information variable. Ben Friedman on the other hand describes, as I have already discussed in the main part of this paper, a case where the interest rate is the instrument and the money stock the information variable. Figure 2 depicts such a case.

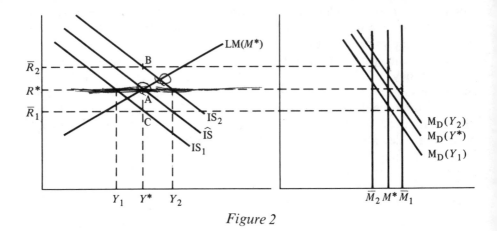

Figure 2

Suppose that the rate of interest is set at R^*. An observation of the money stock at $M_2 > M^*$ provokes an increase in the rate of interest to $\bar{R}_2$, corresponding to a decrease in the money stock to $\bar{M}_2 < M^*$, reducing income from Y_2 to Y^*. Similarly an observation of the money stock at M_1, implies that the unobservable goal variable has taken the value $Y_1 < Y^*$, and provokes a reduction in the rate of interest to $\bar{R}_1$, inducing a rise in income to Y^* and in the information variable to $\bar{M}_1$.

Appendix B: On the 'Demand for Money Functions'

Lest the few estimates I have presented in this paper are misinterpreted, I should stress that the relationships and estimates described in tables 4(a) to 4(d) and table 5 do not purport to comprise the outcome of a search for the 'best' demand for money function pertaining to each of the various aggregates considered. Indeed whether 'best' is to be understood in terms of statistical performance in sample or post-sample 'goodness of fit' comparisons (beyond the level in which the statistics presented reveal) or, on a criterion I prefer, namely, in terms of examination of comparative performance of precisely defined structural/behavioural hypotheses, no such systematic assessment do I wish to claim in the present context. On the contrary, the functions rest on slender conceptual antecedents and encompass a variety of implicit assumptions, a fact which limits their contribution to our understanding of our environment but also in general affords to them a rather precarious existence.

Nevertheless these are *the kind* of relationships that invariably appear in empirical studies of the demand for money and are incorporated in forecasting models (in the latter perhaps with more justification, given lags in availability of data on arguments such as wealth which one may regard as also important—though even in forecasting one may lament the lack of systematic treatment that characterizes such approximations[332]). Furthermore, the *precise* functions here presented do not, in comparison to more general distributed lags structures, fare any worse than particular relationships that have appeared in recent official publications[333].

Table 6. Actual and predicted rates of growth^a for 1976:4

Monetary aggregate	Actual	Predicted from sample period ending:			
		1973:4	1974:4	1975:4	1976:4
U.S.A.; M_1	1.98	6.41	3.56	1.67	1.67
U.S.A.; M_2	3.52	5.21	4.72	4.27	4.08
U.K.; M_1	−0.20	−1.93	5.22	0.92	2.25
U.K.; M_2	0.47	6.68	9.26	2.69	3.42
U.K.; $£M_3$	0.67	8.10	10.06	3.34	3.78
F.R.G.; M_1	−1.06	0.38	1.41	2.12	0.81
F.R.G.; CBM	2.13	2.43	3.42	2.75	2.86

(a) Predicted values rest on the estimates presented in tables 4(a) and 4(c) and employ actual values of *all* explanatory variables. Rates of growth are calculated relative to the actual levels recorded for the end of 1976:3.

Granted this, the estimates of table 6 suggesting (for some of the aggregates) rather wide ranges in predictions derived from relationships based on different sample periods, may serve as an indication of the problems that attach to projections of rates of growth of the money stock, to inferences drawn from such projections, and also to the short-run attainment of announced targets.

Appendix C: Data Description and Sources

All data employed in estimation, other than that pertaining to interest rates, are seasonally adjusted. Furthermore, some of the interest rate series are averages of the actual figures recorded during the observation interval. Granted the pitfalls in such prior adjustment of economic series, one must stress the general undesirability of employing such data. But (besides the fact that policy decisions generally rest on data so adjusted, and that this was in some cases the only data available to me) as the purpose of the estimates presented is primarily to reveal the fuzziness that confronts the policy-maker, rather than supply a precise explanation of demand characteristics for the various aggregates, it seems sufficient to rely on such data.

DESCRIPTION OF VARIABLES

United States
(Sources: OECD Economic Indicators and Bank of England Overseas Department.)

M_1 = currency of the public plus sight deposits;
M_2 = M_1 plus commercial bank time deposits;
Y = GNP at constant prices;
P = implicit GNP deflator;
RL = $(1 + r)$ where r is the yield on long-term government bonds, end of quarter;
RS = $(1 + r)$ where r is the three-month Treasury Bill rate, end of quarter.

United Kingdom
(Source: Bank of England Economic Intelligence Department.)

M_1 = currency of the public plus sight deposits;
M_3 = as defined on p. 263;
$£M_3$ = the sterling component of M_3;
Y = total final expenditure at constant prices;
P = total final expenditure deflator;
RL = $(1 + r)$ where r is the running yield on 20-year gilt edged, average of quarter;

RS = $(1 + r)$ where r is the local authority short rate,
average of quarter.

West Germany
(Source: Statistical supplements to *Deutsche Bundesbank Monthly Reports*
and OECD Economic Indicators.)

M_1 = currency of the public plus sight deposits;
CBM = as defined on p. 266 above;
Y = GNP at constant prices;
P = implicit GNP deflator;
RL = $(1 + r)$ where r is the yield on long-term bonds, end
of quarter;
RS = $(1 + r)$ where r is the call money rate, end of
quarter.

NOTES

1. I wish to acknowledge the financial support of the Houblon Norman Foundation in connection with some of the inputs to this paper.
2. See the discussion in 'Monetary aggregates and money market conditions in open market policy', *Federal Reserve Bulletin,* **57** (2), 1977, pp. 79–103, e.g. pp. 82–3.
3. R.I. McKinnon, 'On securing a common monetary policy for Europe', *Banca Nazionale del Lavoro Quarterly Review,* No. 104, 1973, pp. 3–21.
4. See *Deutsche Bundesbank Monthly Report,* **26** (December), 1974.
5. K. Schiltknecht, 'The Swiss National Bank's experience with monetary targets', Paper presented to the SUERF Colloquium, Wiesbaden, 29 September to 1 October, 1977.
6. *Federal Reserve Bulletin,* **55** (April), 1975.
7. *De Nederlandsche Bank NV Annual Report for the Year 1976,* pp. 20–1.
8. Bank of International Settlements, *Forty-Seventh Annual Report* (Basle: Bank of International Settlements, 1977), p. 66.
9. *Bank of England Quarterly Bulletin,* **15** (September), 1975.
10. *The Times,* 20 September, 1976, p. 13.
11. See R.J. Gordon, 'The demand for and supply of inflation', *Journal of Law and Economics,* **18** (December), 1975, pp. 807–36; and pp. 1–63 in this volume.
12. See, for example, *Bank of England Quarterly Bulletin,* **17** (June), 1977, p. 151; and P.A. Volcker, 'A broader role for monetary targets', *Federal Reserve Bank of New York Quarterly Review,* **2** (Spring), 1977, pp. 23–8, and 'The role of monetary targets in an age of inflation', Paper presented to the Annual Meeting of the American Economic Association, New York, 30 December, 1977.
13. P.A. Volcker, 'The role of monetary targets in an age of inflation', p. 28 (see note 12).

14.   B. Friedman, 'The inefficiency of short-run monetary targets for monetary policy', *Brookings Papers on Economic Activity*, **8** (2), 1977.

15.   In passing we may note that bank credit has figured in policy design since 1966, and was contained in the so-called 'proviso' whereby, as in the FOMC Directive of 16 December 1969, the Manager of the System Open Market Account was instructed to pursue a specific money market objective provided that no 'unusual liquidity pressures' developed and that doing so did not cause bank credit to deviate from a specified range ('Monetary aggregates and money market conditions in an open market economy', p. 82 (see note 2)); but see also T. Mayer, 'The Federal Reserve's policy procedures', *Journal of Money, Credit and Banking*, **4** (3), 1972, p. 531, reporting Axilrod's argument that 'this proviso [was] much less important than [was] widely believed'.

16.   R.G. Davis, 'Monetary objectives and monetary policy', *Federal Reserve Bank of New York Quarterly Review*, **2** (Spring), 1977, pp. 29–36. See also G. Richardson, 'Reflections on the conduct of monetary policy', Bank of England, mimeo, 1978.

17.   R.G. Davis, 'Monetary objectives and monetary policy', p. 38 (see note 16).

18.   See, for example, H.C. Wallich and P.M. Keir, 'The role of operating guides in US monetary policy: a historical review', *Kredit und Kapital*, **11** (1), 1978, pp. 30–51. See also pp. 293–305 below.

19.   *Ibid.*

20.   'For 1975 as a whole', it was commented in the Federal Reserve Bank of St Louis study, '. . . the Manager of the System Open Market Account was much more successful in achieving the interest rate targets than the monetary growth targets'; N. Jianakoplos, 'the FOMC in 1975: announcing monetary targets', *Federal Reserve Bank of St. Louis Monthly Review*, March, 1979, pp. 11–12. See also note 180.

21.   *Bank of England Quarterly Bulletin*, **16** (September), 1976, p. 296.

22.   G. Richardson, 'Reflections on the conduct of monetary policy', pp. 10–11 (see note 16).

23.   See L.A. Dicks-Mireaux, 'British monetary experience 1973–1977', Paper presented to the Eighth Konstanz Seminar on Monetary Theory and Monetary Policy, 8–10 June, 1977, p. 20. See also Bank of England Economic Intelligence Department, 'Monetary targets in the United Kingdom', Paper presented to the SUERF Colloquium, Wiesbaden, 29 September to 1 October, 1977, p. 6; and L.D.D. Price, 'Monetary objectives and instruments in the United Kingdom', Bank of England, mimeo, 1977.

24.   See the commentaries in the *Bank of England Quarterly Bulletins*.

25.   *Ibid.*

26.   *Bank of England Quarterly Bulletin*, **18** (2), 1978, p. 166.

27.   G. Richardson, 'Reflections on the conduct of monetary policy', p. 37 (see note 16).

28.   See *Deutsche Bundesbank Annual Report for the Year 1975*, p. 5.

29.   A.S. Courakis, 'Monetary thought and stabilization policy in the Federal Republic of Germany', in S.F. Frowen, A.S. Courakis, and M.H. Miller (eds.), *Monetary Policy and Economic Activity in West Germany* (London: Surrey University Press, 1977), pp. 13–47.

30.   Contrast this with the U.K. definitions in which monetary aggregates include public sector deposits.

31.   See, for example, M. Willms, 'Monetary indicators in the Federal Republic of

Germany', in S.F. Frowen, A.S. Courakis, and M.H. Miller (eds.) *Monetary Policy and Economic Activity in West Germany* (London: Surrey University Press, 1977), pp. 49–69; and M.J.M. Neumann, 'A theoretical and empirical analysis of the German money supply process', in S.F. Frowen, A.S. Courakis, and M.H. Miller (eds.), *ibid.*, pp. 73–127.

32.   See A.S. Courakis, 'Monetary thought and stabilization policy in the Federal Republic of Germany' (see note 29); and 'A note on the Bundesbank's monetary target', Brasenose College, Oxford, 1976, mimeo; also H. Bockelmann, 'Experience of the Deutsche Bundesbank with monetary targets', Paper presented to the SUERF Colloquium, Wiesbaden, 29 September to 1 October, 1977.

33.   *Deutsche Bundesbank Annual Report for the Year 1975*, p. 10.

34.   *Ibid.*

35.   *Deutsche Bundesbank Annual Report for the Year 1976*, p. 13.

36.   *Ibid.*, p. 20.

37.   A.S. Courakis, 'Monetary thought and stabilization policy in the Federal Republic of Germany' (see note 29).

38.   J.M. Parkin, 'The transition from fixed exchange rates to money supply targets', *Journal of Money, Credit and Banking*, 9 (February), 1977.

39.   *Deutsche Bundesbank Annual Report for the Year 1976*, pp. 16–18.

40.   *Deutsche Bundesbank Monthly Report*, 38 (January), 1978, p. 6.

41.   *Deutsche Bundesbank Annual Report for the Year 1977*, p. 22.

42.   *Ibid.*, pp. 20–2.

43.   See, for example, M. Friedman, 'A monetary and fiscal framework for economic stability', *American Economic Review*, 38 (June), 1948, pp. 245–64; *A Program for Monetary Stability* (New York: Fordham University Press, 1959); 'Should there be an independent monetary authority', in L.B. Yeager (ed.), *In Search of a Monetary Constitution* (Harvard: Harvard University Press, 1962); *Capitalism and Freedom* (Chicago: Chicago University Press, 1962); *Dollars and Deficits* (Englewood Cliffs, N.J.: Prentice Hall, 1968); 'The role of monetary policy', *American Economic Review*, 58 (1), 1968, reprinted in *The Optimum Quantity of Money and Other Essays* (Chicago: Aldine, 1969), chapter 5; and M. Friedman and W.W. Heller, *Fiscal vs. Monetary Policy* (New York: Norton, 1968).

44.   M. Friedman, 'The role of monetary policy', p. 110 (see note 43).

45.   Neither the precise choice of monetary aggregate nor the particular rate of growth are in Friedman's opinion of primary importance. As he commented in 1968, '. . . I believe that it matters much less which particular aggregate is chosen than that one is chosen', M. Friedman, 'The role of monetary policy', p. 109 (see note 43). And further, '. . . in presenting the 5 per cent rule I have always emphasized that a *steady* and known rate of increase in the quantity of money is more important than the precise numerical value of the rate of increase. . . Either a 5 per cent rule or a 2 per cent rule [consistent with the attainment of an Optimum Quantity of Money] will be far superior to the policy we have actually followed. The gain from shifting to the 5 per cent rule would, I believe, dwarf the further gain from going to the 2 per cent rule even though that gain may well be substantial enough to be worth pursuing'. As we will see the latter is a more acceptable contention than the former.

46.   To quote, 'A scholar's basic values undoubtedly affect the way he resolves the inevitable uncertainties of his scientific judgements when he comes to recommend policies—and it is proper that they should. A person . . . who regards freedom as the

major objective in relations between individuals and who believes that the preservation of freedom requires limiting narrowly the role of government and placing primary reliance on private property, free markets and voluntary arrangements—such a person will resolve his doubts about the precise effect of any measure in favor of policies relying on the market. By contrast a person who regards welfare or security as the major objective in social relations and who believes that this objective can best be attained by governmental measures controlling and regulating private activity—such a person will resolve his doubts in favor of policies relying on government. Each will place the burden of proof differently—one on the proponent of government intervention, the other on the proponent of *laissez-faire*'. (M. Friedman, *Dollars and Deficits,* chapter 1, p. 7 (see note 43).) Friedman also notes 'that basic values' enter into policy choices through differences in time perspectives. In particular, given the same scientific judgements, the choice among policies will often depend on the importance attached to short-term versus long-term consequences of policy. Furthermore, there is 'a close connection between beliefs about the role of government and time perspectives. Those who are adverse to government intervention would tend to take a long-run view, putting major emphasis on the ultimate consequences of policies while the opposite is true of those who believe in greater governmental control'. (*Ibid.,* pp. 8–9). See also M. Friedman, *Capitalism and Freedom* (see note 43).

47.   See, for example, M. Friedman, *A Program for Monetary Stability*; *Capitalism and Freedom*; and *Dollars and Deficits*, chapters 1 and 6 (see note 43).

48.   Notice, for example, the attention that the Bacon and Eltis thesis has received in comparison to other, and in some respects similar, writings of one, two and three decades ago (R. Bacon and W. Eltis, *Britain's Economic Problem: Too Few Producers* (London: Macmillan, 1976).

49.   M. Friedman, 'The role of monetary policy', pp. 99–107 (see note 43); and R.A. Volcker, 'A broader role for monetary targets', p. 24 (see note 12).

50.   Besides those resulting from an anticipated rate of change in prices that is inconsistent with the attainment of Friedman's 1969 optimum quantity of money; see, for example, M. Friedman, 'Nobel lecture: inflation and unemployment', *Journal of Political Economy,* **85** (3), 1977.

51.   For example, M. Friedman, 'The effects of full-employment policy on economic stability: a formal analysis', retranslated from the French with slight revisions (*Economie Appliquée,* July-December, 1951) and reprinted in M. Friedman, *Essays in Positive Economics* (Chicago: Chicago University Press, 1953); and 'The lag in effect of monetary policy', *Journal of Political Economy* ,**69** (October), 1961, pp. 447–66.

52.   In passing we may note that *The Times,* 'A Programme for Monetary Stability' (see note 10) is more in line with this.

53.   See, for example, K. Brunner, 'The monetarist revolution in monetary theory', *Weltwirtschaftliches Archiv,* **105** (1), 1970, pp. 5–6, for a summary statement of monetarist beliefs in this context.

54.   *Deutsche Bundesbank Monthly Report,* **28** (1), 1976, p. 6, emphasis added.

55.   K. Brunner and A.H. Meltzer, 'The meaning of monetary indicators', in G. Horwich (ed.), *Monetary Process and Policy* (Homewood, Illinois: Irwin, 1967), pp. 187–217; 'The nature of the policy problem', in K. Brunner (ed.), *Targets and Indicators of Monetary Policy* (San Francisco: Chandler, 1969); and K. Brunner, 'A

false. For although, as Mayer notes, Poole writes that: 'The crucial issue for deciding
Zeitschrift für Volkswirtschaft und Statistik, **106**, 1970, pp. 110–29.
56.   Important facets of which are examined in Friedman's seminal paper, 'The
effects of full-employment policy on economic stability: a formal analysis' (see note
51).
57.   K. Brunner, 'A survey of major issues in monetary theory and monetary
policy', pp. 110–27 (see note 55).
58.   *Ibid.*, pp. 110–1.
59.   *Ibid.*
60.   See, for example, T.R. Saving, 'Monetary targets and indicators', *Journal of
Political Economy*, **75**, 1967, supplement, pp. 446–59.
61.   See, for example, W. Poole, 'Optimal choice of monetary policy instruments in
a simple macro model', *Quarterly Journal of Economics*, **84** (May), 1970; and B.
Friedman, 'The inefficiency of short-run monetary targets for monetary policy' (see
note 14).
62.   In this and in some other respects the analysis is antedated by that of M.
Friedman, 'The effects of full-employment policy on economic stability: a formal
analysis' (see note 51).
63.   H. Thiel, 'A note on certainty equivalence in dynamic planning', *Econometrica*, **25**, 1957, pp. 346–9; *Economic Forecasts and Policy* (Amsterdam: North
Holland, 1958); *Optimal Decision Rules for Government and Industry* (Amsterdam:
North Holland, 1964); H.A. Simon, 'Dynamic programming under uncertainty with
a quadratic criterion function', *Econometrica*, **24**, 1956, pp. 78–81; G. Chow,
'Optimal stochastic control of linear economic systems', *Journal of Money, Credit
and Banking*, **2** (3), 1970; S.J. Turnovsky, *Macroeconomic Analysis and Stabilisation Policy* (Cambridge: Cambridge University Press, 1977).
64.   See, for example, W. Poole, 'Optimal choice of monetary policy instruments in
a simple macro model' (see note 61); J.H. Kareken, T. Muench, and N. Wallace,
'Optimal open market strategy: the use of information variables', *American Economic Review*, **63** (1), 1973, pp. 156–72; and B. Friedman, 'The inefficiency of short-
run monetary targets for monetary policy' (see note 14).
65.   J. Tinbergen, *On the Theory of Economic Policy* (Amsterdam: North Holland,
1952). See also S. Turnovsky, *Macroeconomic Analysis and Stabilisation Policy*,
chapters 13 and 14 (see note 63). I have changed here the standard terminology of
'instrument-targets' to 'instrument-goals' so as to avoid confusion between proximate
and ultimate objectives.
66.   And a monetary base policy when, as is sometimes the case, a money supply
function in terms of the monetary base is also defined; see R. Holbrook and H.
Shapiro, 'The choice of optimal intermediate targets', *American Economic Review*,
60, papers and proceedings, 1970, pp. 40–6.
67.   We may note that there appears to be considerable confusion on this point in
the literature. Mayer, for example notes that a '. . . way of seeing the distinction
between the ratist-stockist dispute on the one hand and the Keynesian-quantity
theory dispute on the other is to note that in the Poole model the choice between a
ratist and a stockist policy depends on the unpredictable *shifts* of the IS-LM curves,
whereas in Tobin's [1955] celebrated framework the difference between the
Keynesian and quantity theories depends upon the *slopes* of the *curves*' (T. Mayer,
'The Federal Reserve's policy procedures', pp. 541–2 (see note 15). *This is certainly*

survey of major issues in monetary theory and monetary policy', *Schweizerische* upon whether an interest rate policy or a money stock policy should be followed is the relative size of the disturbances in the expenditure and monetary sectors. . . . the issue is not whether the interest elasticity of the demand for money is relatively low or whether fiscal policy is more or less powerful than monetary policy', the relationships presented in W. Poole, 'Optimal choice of monetary policy instruments in a simple macro model' (see note 61) clearly exhibit that the choice of money stock versus interest rate depends on *both the shifts and the slopes.* Nor, it should be stressed, is it the case that prior to Poole the dispute was one about *slopes* alone. On the contrary, in his celebrated 'Restatement', Friedman lists differences of opinion on the 'stability . . . of the demand function for money' as one of the three issues lying at the root of differences in importance attaching to money; the other two issues being '. . . the independence of factors affecting demand and supply; and . . . the form of the demand for money function' (M. Friedman, 'The quantity theory of money: a restatement' in M. Friedman (ed.), *Studies in Quantity Theory of Money* (Chicago: Chicago University Press, 1956) reprinted in M. Friedman, *The Optimum Quantity of Money and Other Essays,* p. 62 (see note 43)). Indeed Friedman stresses that 'The quantity theorist accepts the empirical hypothesis that the demand for money is highly stable—more stable than functions such as the consumption function that are offered as alternative key relations' (*Ibid.*). Furthermore, it is to the empirical verification of this proposition that (however debatable in its insights it may have been) his enquiry on 'The relative stability of the investment multiplier and monetary velocity in the United States 1897–1958' was devoted. (See M. Friedman and D. Meiselman, paper of same title in Commission on Money and Credit, volume on Stabilization Policies (Englewood Cliffs, N.J.: Prentice Hall, 1963). The issue of *stability* has moreover been recognized as at the centre of the dispute also in the emphasis placed on the speculative motive by Keynes disciples (as distinct from a portfolio approach to the demand for money), in the dicta of the Radcliffe Report (*Report of the Committee on the Workings of the Monetary System,* Cmnd. 827 (London: HMSO, 1959)) and in numerous writings and empirical studies echoing Harry Johnson's famous survey that listed as one of the three substantive issues outstanding, the question of '. . . whether the demand for money is sufficiently stable to provide, in conjunction with the quantity of money a better explanation of observed movements of money-income and other aggregates than is provided by models built around income-expenditure relationships' (H.G. Johnson, 'Monetary theory and policy', *Economic Journal,* **70,** 1962, reprinted in The American Economic Association and Royal Economic Society (eds.) *Surveys of Economic Theory; Volume 1, Money, Interest, Welfare* (London: Macmillan, 1968), pp. 9–10.

68.   This is the context in which W. Poole's contribution 'Optimal choice of monetary policy instruments in a simple macro model' (see note 61) is staged.

69.   J.H. Kareken, T. Muench, and N. Wallace, 'Optimal open market strategy: the use of information variables' (see note 64); and B. Friedman, 'The inefficiency of short-run monetary targets for monetary policy' (see note 14). In control terms we have used a closed-loop feedback solution to the strategy problem.

70.   I am here relaxing the assumption of M being an instrument and treating (as Ben Friedman does) revisions in the rate of interest as the means by which deviations in M from its initially expected (and consistent with the desired value of the goal variable) path can be ensured.

71.   That is to say unless *prior beliefs* are such as to regard the demand for money as a function of income only, in which case the very discussion of monetary policy within an IS-LM context seems superfluous.

72.   B. Friedman, 'The inefficiency of short-run monetary targets for monetary policy', p. 29 (see note 14). The same kind of conclusion is reached in J.H. Kareken, T. Muench, and N. Wallace, 'Optimal open market strategy: the use of information variables', p. 167 (see note 64).

73.   In the context of this analysis the term 'information variable' is attributable to J.H. Kareken, T. Muench, and N. Wallace, 'Optimal open market strategy: the use of information variables', p. 157 (see note 64).

74.   So long as the demand for money is not a deterministic function of instruments and the goal variable only.

75.   That is to say 'interpreting through the model'.

76.   B. Friedman, 'The inefficiency of short-run monetary targets for monetary policy', p. 36 (see note 14).

77.   *Ibid.,* p. 3.

78.   Poole, for example, draws attention to the fact that his results are conditional on the assumption of known parameters and only suggestive of what may be '. . . if the parameters are not known exactly . . .'. (W. Poole, 'Optimal choice of monetary policy instruments in a simple macro model', p. 214 (see note 61); but both he and others, for example S. Turnovsky ('Optimal choice of monetary instrument in a linear model with stochastic coefficients', *Journal of Money, Credit and Banking,* 7 (1), 1975, pp. 51–80; and *Macroeconomic Analysis and Stabilisation Policy* (see note 63)) think entirely in the context of multiplicative disturbances, rather than on the lines discussed in the next section of this paper, to conclude that feedback rules will, in general, be preferable to proximate targets.

79.   See, for example, S. Turnovsky, 'Optimal choice of monetary instrument in a linear model with stochastic coefficients' (see note 78); and *Macroeconomic Analysis and Stabilisation Policy* (see note 63); W. Brainard, 'Uncertainty and the effectiveness of monetary policy', *American Economic Review,* **57,** papers and proceedings, 1967, pp. 411–25; and J. Kareken, 'The optimum monetary instrument variable', *Journal of Money Credit and Banking,* 2 (August), pp. 385–90.

80.   See K. Brunner and A.H. Meltzer, 'The meaning of monetary indicators', p. 187 (see note 55).

81.   *Ibid.*

82.   K. Brunner and A.H. Meltzer 'The nature of the policy problem', p. 9 (see note 55).

83.   T.R. Saving, 'Monetary targets and indicators', p. 448 (see note 60).

84.   See, for example, T.J. Sargent, 'The optimum instrument variable in a linear macro model', *Canadian Journal of Economics,* 4 (February), 1971, pp. 50–60.

85.   S. Turnovsky, 'Optimal choice of monetary instrument in a linear model with stochastic coefficients', p. 74 (see note 78).

86.   K. Brunner, 'A survey of major issues in monetary theory and monetary policy', p. 120 (see note 55).

87.   Having expended a considerable amount of effort on econometric comparisons of alternative hypotheses (see, for example, A.S. Courakis, 'Clearing bank asset choice behaviour: a mean variance treatment', *Oxford University Bulletin of Economics and Statistics,* **36** (3), 1974, pp. 273–301; 'In search of an explanation of clearing bank portfolio selection', Paper presented to the MSG-Oxford Conference in

Honour of G.L.S. Shackle, 15–17 September, 1975; 'Serial correlation and a Bank of England study of the demand for money: an exercise in measurement without theory', *The Economic Journal,* **88** (October), 1978), I would not wish to be interpreted as suggesting that such comparisons are futile. But although I regard them an essential part of the process of securing a better understanding of our economic environment, not to mention an essential duty to our audience to systematize empirical evidence on the myriads of paradigms that we devise, their findings do not, and should not be interpreted to, constitute more than that.

88.   See G. Chow, 'Control methods for macroeconomic policy analysis', *American Economic Review,* **66,** papers and proceedings, 1976, pp. 340–5; and K. Brunner, 'A survey of major issues in monetary theory and monetary policy', pp. 122–5 (see note 55).

89.   K. Brunner, *ibid.,* p. 125.

90.   G. Chow, 'Control methods for macroeconomic policy analysis', p. 345 (see note 88).

91.   K. Brunner, 'A survey of major issues in monetary theory and monetary policy', p. 125 (see note 55). I should perhaps note that Brunner appears to view the Bayesian and maxi-min strategies as alternatives. If so, I should like to record my dissent from this view. The Bayesian case constitutes a process whereby a new prior belief is constructed from the variety of prior beliefs existing at a particular point in time. The policy content in this case is then identical to that of the variance approach. But the maxi-min strategy is conceptually very different since, to illustrate, it by definition assumes that, at least with regard to some of the parameters of the structure, no single mean value can be assumed.

92.   K. Brunner, 'A survey of major issues in monetary theory and monetary policy', p. 122 (see note 55).

93.   K. Brunner and A.H. Meltzer, 'The nature of the policy problem', p. 22 (see note 55).

94.   Resembling as it does exercises in which, for example, serial correlation coefficients are sought by trial and error or more generally diagnostic procedures that do not rest on a particular prior belief about the underlying structure, i.e. by a prior belief that defines a precise relationship between the explanatory variables and the process generating non-independent disturbances.

95.   K. Brunner and A.H. Meltzer, 'The nature of the policy problem', pp. 23–5 (see note 55).

96.   This as we shall see also reflects on the indicator problem.

97.   G.L.S. Shackle, *Expectations in Economics* (Cambridge: Cambridge University Press, 1949), p. 113.

98.   K. Brunner, 'A survey of major issues in monetary theory and monetary policy', p. 125, emphasis added (see note 55). This kind of ambiguity characterizes also Saving's discussion. For although, in his discussion of the target problem, we are told that '. . . since the structure is unknown the exact effect of policy cannot be obtained from the structure (in the stochastic specification of the structure, take "exact" to mean "expected effect")' (T.R. Saving, 'Monetary targets and indicators; p. 448 (see note 60)), and therefore we are invited to conceive of a situation in which the policymaker does not know the 'expected effect' of his policies (as will be true in a situation of competing stochastic or non-stochastic hypotheses about the environment) in the footnote to this very statement we are told: 'If the problem were

considered in the Bayesian framework, then we could construct a measure over the class of all structural hypotheses and calculate expected values. In this sense the problem of lack of knowledge is similar to introducing a stochastic element into a known structure' (*Ibid.,* footnote 4).

99.   G.L.S. Shackle, *Expectations in Economics*, p. 109 (see note 97).

100.   *Ibid.,* pp. 113–4, emphasis added.

101.   H.C. Wallich, 'Discussion of application of optimal control to problems of economic stabilization', *American Economic Review,* **66** (Papers and Proceedings), 1976, pp. 357–8. It smacks perhaps of 'too little, too late'.

102.   *Ibid.,* p. 358.

103.   K. Brunner, 'A survey of major issues of monetary theory and monetary policy', p. 124, emphasis added (see note 55).

104.   *Ibid.,* p. 112.

105.   In this respect the various paradigms perceived by him converge at least in terms of the qualitative effects they assign to particular policy actions.

106.   T.R. Saving, 'Monetary targets and indicators', p. 448 (see note 60).

107.   *Ibid.,* pp. 448–9.

108.   *Ibid.,* p. 450.

109.   *Ibid.,* p. 449.

110.   See, for example, W.G. Dewald, 'A review of the conference on targets and indicators of monetary policy', in K. Brunner (ed.), *Targets and Indicators of Monetary Policy,* pp. 321ff (see note 55); and M.J. Artis, 'Monetary policy in the 1970s', in H.G. Johnson and A.R. Nobay (eds.), *Issues in Monetary Economics* (Oxford: Oxford University Press, 1974), pp. 518–47.

111.   M.J. Artis, *ibid.,* p. 519, emphasis added.

112.   '. . . if as assumed. . . the money stock can be set at exactly the desired level, then the money stock may as well be called an instrument of monetary policy rather than a proximate target' (W. Poole, 'Optimal choice of monetary policy instruments in a simple macro model', p. 198 (see note 61)).

113.   M.J. Artis, 'Monetary policy in the 1970s', pp. 519–20, emphasis added (see note 110).

114.   In an IS-LM context the policy indicator should then allow for the expansionary (contractionary) effects of decreases (increases) in the speculative/asset demand for money, but should not respond to changes in the demand for money resulting from changes in the goal variable caused by factors other than the policy itself.

115.   M.J. Artis, 'Monetary policy in the 1970s', p. 520 (see note 110).

116.   T.R. Saving, 'Monetary targets and indicators', p. 450 (see note 60).

117.   K. Brunner and A.H. Meltzer, 'The nature of the policy problem', p. 16 (see note 55).

118.   See J. Niehans, *The Theory of Money* (Baltimore: John Hopkins University Press, 1978), pp. 267–8; and K. Brunner and A.H. Meltzer, 'The meaning of monetary indicators'; and 'The nature of the policy problem' (see note 55) for their discussion of the 'ideal' indicator.

119.   That is, through the target variable.

120.   Brunner and Meltzer, we may note, assume linearity, but claim that '. . . the results can be easily generalized to piece-wise linear systems' (K. Brunner and A.H. Meltzer, 'The nature of the policy problem', p. 17, footnote 11 (see note 55). They do

not, however, offer any indication as to how this generalization is to be achieved.

121.   See B. Friedman, 'Targets, instruments and indicators of monetary policy', in K. Brunner and M.J.M. Neumann (eds.), Inflation, Unemployment and Monetary Control, supplement to Kredit und Kapital, 12 (5), 1979, particularly pp. 277ff.

122.   A position shared by Niehans (J. Niehans, The Theory of Money (see note 118)).

123.   See F. Knight, Risk and Uncertainty (Boston: Houghton Mifflin, 1921) for an early distinction between risk and uncertainty. The full flavour and implications of this distinction (see, for example pp. 20 and 226) is eloquently conveyed in Shackle's numerous and careful writings, which use 'potential surprise' as the index on which to order the varying outcomes perceived by a decision-taker as attaching to his actions under uncertainty.

124.   See, for example, K. Brunner and A.H. Meltzer, 'The meaning of monetary indicators', pp. 196–203; and 'The nature of the policy problem', pp. 10–16; K. Brunner, 'A survey of major issues in monetary theory and monetary policy', pp. 114–8 (see note 55); also T.R. Saving, 'Monetary targets and indicators', pp. 449–51 (see note 60); and W.G. Dewald, 'A review of the conference on targets and indicators of monetary policy', pp. 318–9 (see note 110).

125.   Such as the adjusted monetary base in the writing of Brunner and Meltzer and their disciples, see, for example, M.J.M. Neumann, 'A theoretical and empirical analysis of the German money supply process' (see note 31). Indeed in their 1967 paper, 'The meaning of monetary indicators' (see note 55), Brunner and Meltzer discuss the monetary base in a section entitled 'The true or ideal indicator', whereas other candidates are discussed under the heading 'A comparison of some proposed endogenous indicators'.

126.   K. Brunner, 'A survey of major issues in monetary theory and monetary policy', p. 118 (see note 55).

127.   See K. Brunner and A.H. Meltzer, 'The meaning of monetary indicators', p. 203; 'The nature of the policy problem', pp. 16–22; and K. Brunner, ibid., pp. 118–21 (see note 55).

128.   K. Brunner, ibid., p. 121, emphasis added (see note 55).

129.   See K. Brunner and A.H. Meltzer, 'The nature of the policy problem', pp. 19–22 (see note 55). We may note that this procedure for identifying a variable to serve as the policy indicator is, as the authors remark, an improvement on their earlier suggestion of identifying that observable magnitude which minimizes, over all relevant states of nature and feasible policy actions, the maximum absolute difference between the particular indicator considered and the true or ideal indicators corresponding to each of these states of nature (see K. Brunner and A.H. Meltzer, 'The meaning of monetary indicators', pp. 203 and 210–11 (see note 55)). As they put it in the later paper: 'The indicator computed in this way provides no measure of its own reality' (K. Brunner and A.H. Meltzer, 'The nature of the policy problem', p.20).

130.   In passing, however, I should not disguise my bewilderment on at least one of Brunner's remarks on this issue (K. Brunner, 'A survey of the major issues in monetary theory and monetary policy' (see note 55)). The indicator problem, we are told, relates to the question of 'how to interpret policy' (p. 112); to '. . .a measure which yields reliable information about the monetary thrust transmitted to economic activity' (p. 112); to '. . . the determination of an optimal scale permitting the measurement in at least an ordinal sense of the thrust applied by the behaviour of the

monetary authorities. Policy actions depend on reliable interpretations of these actions with respect to their consequences, and most particularly with respect to their effects on economic activity' (p. 118). But following his 'General Description of the Indicator Problem', we are told 'One last caution should be added. The optimal scale *gauging* monetary policy and the scale for *interpreting* monetary impulses are in general quite distinct and involve separate issues. The general formulation of the problem in the paragraphs above is constrained to the optimal selection of a scale *gauging* monetary policy' (p. 121).

131.   T.R. Saving, 'Monetary targets and indicators', p. 449, footnote 6 (see note 60).

132.   My definition of causality, I should stress, bears no resemblance to what lamentably has been defined as such in recent investigations of relationships between time series, such as the so-called causality exercises of the relationships between money and income performed by Sims for the United States (C.A. Sims, 'Money, income and causality', *American Economic Review,* **62,** 1972, pp. 540–552), and mimicked by Williams, Goodhart and Gowland for the United Kingdom (D. Williams, C.A.E. Goodhart and D.H. Gowland, 'Money, income and causality: the UK experience', *American Economic Review,* **66,** 1976, pp. 417–23). Except in their possible usefulness in documenting associations, these exercises, it must be stressed, contain no insights about behaviour, or more specifically about the role of money in the economies for which they have been performed. To use the phrase I borrowed from T. Koopman on another occasion (A.S. Courakis, 'Serial correlation and a Bank of England study of the demand for money: an exercise in measurement without theory' (see note 87)) to refer to statistical *ad hockery* in the use of distributed lag structures, such investigations comprise 'an exercise in measurement without theory'. It is indeed a sad reflection of the turn that economic research(?) has taken in the last decade, that whereas Friedman felt compelled to explain his claims for causality running from money to income by arguments other than mere statistical associations (that span from contrasts with 'pin theories' to the invariance of the money-income relationship over periods that had witnessed substantial changes in institutional arrangements regarding the supply of money, to the emphasis placed on historical episodes associated with autonomous changes in the supply of money, etc. (see M. Friedman and A.J. Schwartz, 'Money and business cycles', *Review of Economics and Statistics,* **45** (Supplement, February), 1963, reprinted in M. Friedman, *The Optimal Quantity of Money and Other Essays,* chapter 10 (see note 43); and *A Monetary History of the United States 1867–1960* (Princeton, NJ: Princeton University Press, 1963); M. Friedman, *A Program for Monetary Stability* (see note 43); 'The lag effect of monetary policy' (see note 51); and 'The monetary studies of the National Bureau', in Friedman, *The Optimum Quantity of Money and Other Essays,* chapter 12 (see note 43), reprinted from *The National Bureau enters its 45th Year, 44 Annual Report, 1964)*) and even then his last defence was that '. . . it is not easy to rationalize positive conformity [in the money-income relationship] as reflecting a supply response (M. Friedman, 'The monetary studies of the National Bureau', p. 270) the Bank of England Group noted that 'Insofar as the authorities primarily aim to regulate the structure of interest rates, movements in the money stock can be expected to respond to movements in income' (D. Williams, C.A.E. Goodhart and D.H. Gowland, *ibid.,* p. 417) but in no way felt obliged to enter into what has been standard Bank of England response in the gilt-edged market, or even to

refer to Tobin's demonstration of the vacuity of timing relationships in the context of establishing causality (J. Tobin, 'Money and income, post hoc ergo propter hoc', *Quarterly Journal of Economics,* **84** (2), 1970, pp. 302–24). In this context see also K. Brunner, 'A survey of major issues in monetary theory and monetary policy', pp. 98–9 (see note 55).

133.   W. Poole, 'Optimal choice of monetary policy instruments in a simple macro model', p. 198 (see note 61). Similarly Saving, in explaining the usefulness of inter-mediate targets, notes '. . . part of the variance in the goal variable is due to uncertainty between the target variable and the policy. If the policy can be adjusted instantly to account for any random change between the policy and the target, then this part of the uncertainty can be removed' (T.R. Saving, 'Monetary targets and indicators', p. 448, note 5 (see note 60)).

134.   By which I do not mean that the relationship between tools and proximate targets does not depend heavily on institutional factors which are stable neither over time nor over space; but rather that the target goal relationship is not generally accepted to hold over time and space either. We are perhaps more aware of the latter today. But Friedman's argument, which even Poole describes (see W. Poole, 'Optimal choice of monetary policy instruments in a simple macro model', pp. 210–11 (see note 61)) was never conducive to a view of 'a close and systematic relationship between proximate targets and goals'.

135.   J. Niehans, *The Theory of Money,* p. 284, emphasis added (see note 118). This of course summarizes Friedman's position as expressed in M. Friedman, *A Program for Monetary Stability* (see note 43); 'The lag effect of monetary policy' (see note 51); 'The role of monetary policy' (see note 43); and M. Friedman and W.W. Heller, *Fiscal vs. Monetary Policy,* pp. 48–50 (see note 43).

136.   M. Friedman, 'The role of monetary policy', p. 108 (see note 43).

137.   L.C. Andersen and D.S. Karnovsky, 'Some considerations in the use of mone-tary aggregates for the implementation of monetary policy', *Federal Reserve Bank of St. Louis Monthly Review,* **59** (9), 1977, p. 2. See also S.H. Axilrod *et al.,* 'A proposal for redefining the monetary aggregates', *Federal Reserve Bulletin,* **59,** 1979, pp. 30–31.

138.   This is not to suggest that the effort expended in debates between monetarists and Keynesians on the issues of controllability and causality has not had a purpose, but rather that from this standpoint we must distinguish between the importance of such issues in interpreting past experience and enhancing our understanding of our environment, in defining our prior beliefs, and their lack of significance as an essential ingredient in the selection of proximate targets.

139.   See A.S. Courakis, The Definition of Money, Nuffield College, Oxford, 1970, mimeo; and Unit of Account, Medium of Exchange, Store Value: on the Essential Ingredient of the Monetary Economy, Brasenose College, Oxford, 1978, mimeo.

140.   See, for example, J.R. Moroney and J.M. Mason, 'The dynamic impacts of autonomous expenditures and the monetary base on aggregate income', *Journal of Money, Credit and Banking,* **3** (4), pp. 793–814.

141.   Unless we are prepared to argue that wealth effects alone comprise the means by which 'money' bears on economic activity and that, as in Pessek and Saving, besides non-interest bearing liabilities of the government and the banking sector, no other financial asset comprises net wealth (B. Pessek and T. Saving, *Money, Wealth and Economic Theory* (New York: Macmillan, 1968)). The alternative characteristic

of these assets, namely fixity of own rate, which in Tobin's general equilibrium approach to monetary theory '. . . is the secret of the special role of money' (J. Tobin, 'A general equilibrium approach to monetary theory', *Journal of Money, Credit and Banking,* **1,** 1969, p. 26) will not in general suffice as a justification for using M_1, since '. . . it is a secret that would be shared with any other asset with a fixed interest rate' (*Ibid.*).

142.   J.R. Hicks, *Critical Essays in Monetary Theory* (Oxford: Oxford University Press, 1967), p. 17.

143.   B. Friedman, 'The inefficiency of short-run monetary targets for monetary policy' (see note 14).

144.   A.D. Bain, *The Control of the Money Supply,* 2nd ed. (Harmondsworth: Penguin, 1976), p. 150, emphasis added.

145.   *Ibid.,* p. 151, emphasis added.

146.   B. Friedman, 'The inefficiency of short-run monetary targets for monetary policy', footnote 36 (see note 14).

147.   *Ibid.*

148.   W. Poole, 'Optimal choice of monetary policy instruments in a simple macro model', p. 208 (see note 61).

149.   J.M. Keynes, *The Treatise on Money* (London: Macmillan, 1931).

150.   B. Friedman, 'The inefficiency of short-run monetary targets for monetary policy', p. 58 (see note 14).

151.   This does not, of course, apply to the case of serially-correlated disturbances.

152.   G.L.S. Shackle, *Decision Order and Time in Human Affairs* (Cambridge: Cambridge University Press, 1969), p. ix.

153.   For '. . . the character of probability is its additiveness. When we speak of probability we have implicitly in mind a complete set of all the things that can happen, and we accordingly suppose it to be certain that one or other of these things will happen. Thus probability is a unity to be divided out amongst the constituent contingencies of the set. When each contingency has been assigned its probability these probabilities *add up* to one. If, then, we are to discard the notion of a known set of contingencies, it seems that we must exclude any additive character of our chosen uncertainty language. A language is required to assign *standing*, that is seriousness or realism, to any hypothesis, in terms which do not have to add up to a total representing certainty' (*Ibid.,* pp. 279–80).

154.   *Ibid.,* p. 296.

155.   K. Brunner, 'A survey of major issues in monetary theory and monetary policy', p. 124 (see note 55).

156.   G.L.S. Shackle, *Decision Order and Time in Human Affairs,* p. 292 (see note 150).

157.   See the official documents referred to in this subsection.

158.   S. Axilrod *et al.* ('A proposal for redefining monetary aggregates', pp. 24–32 (see note 137)) examine, for the various aggregates currently figuring in (or tendered as improvements for) U.S. policy design: (a) 'the properties of demand equations'; (b) 'reduced form equations that relate the annualized percentage change in GNP measured in current dollars, to current and lagged annualized percentage change in monetary growth . . .'; (c) 'indicator properties'; and (d) 'controllability'.

159.   See U.S. Congress Joint Committee on Standards for Guiding Monetary Policy, Monetary Policy: Hearings and Report, June, 1968. A summary of this and

other related reports can be found in R. Zecher, 'Money and Congress: a review of Congressional activity relating to monetary policy', *Journal of Money, Credit and Banking,* **3** (3), 1971, pp. 680–92. The period immediately preceding monetary targets is discussed in C.F. Christ, 'An evaluation of economic policy proposals of the Joint Economic Committee of the 92nd and 93rd Congress', in K. Brunner and A.H. Meltzer (eds.), *Institutions, Policies and Economic Performance,* The Carnegie-Rochester Conference Series on Public Policy, Vol. 4 (Amsterdam: North Holland, 1976).

160.   U.S. Congress Joint Committee on Standards for Guiding Monetary Policy: Hearings and Report, June, 1968.

161.   See, for example, S. Axilrod, 'The FOMC Directive as structured in the late 1960s: theory and appraisal', in Board of Governors of the Federal Reserve System, *Open Market Policies and Operating Procedures,* Staff Studies (Washington DC: Federal Reserve System, 1971), pp. 1–36. See also T. Mayer, 'The Federal Reserve's policy procedures', pp. 530–1 (see note 14).

162.   See, for example, R. Davis, 'Short-run targets for OMO's', and L. Andersen, 'Selection of a monetary aggregate and use in the FOMC directive', both in Board of Governors of the Federal Reserve System, *Open Market Policies and Operating Procedures* (see note 159). See also A.E. Burger, 'Money stock control'; and J.L. Pierce and T.D. Thomson, 'Some issues in controlling the stock of money', both in Federal Reserve Banks of Boston, *Controlling Monetary Aggregates II: The Implementation* (Boston: Federal Reserve Bank of Boston, 1972), pp. 33–55.

163.   W. Poole, 'Whither money demand', *Brookings Papers on Economic Activity,* **2**, pp. 485–500; and M.B. Slovin and M.E. Sushka, *A Financial Markets Approach to the Demand for Money and Implications for Monetary Policy* (Washington DC: Federal Reserve System, 1972).

164.   See L. Andersen, 'Selection of a monetary aggregate and use in FOMC directive' (see note 162).

165.   See J. Pierce, 'Some rules for the conduct of monetary policy', in Federal Reserve Bank of Boston, *Controlling Monetary Aggregates* (Boston: Federal Reserve Bank of Boston, 1969); and 'The trade-off between short-term and long-term policy goals', in Board of Governors of the Federal Reserve System, *Open Market Policies and Operating Procedures* (see note 161). See also W. Poole, 'Rules of thumb for guiding monetary policies', in Board of Governors of the Federal Reserve System, *ibid.*

166.   See, for example, H. Wallich and P.M. Keir, 'The role of operating guides in U.S. monetary policy: a historical review', pp. 30–51 (see note 18).

167.   See, for example, S.M. Goldfeld, 'The demand for money revisited', *Brookings Papers on Economic Activity,* **4** (3), 1973, pp. 577–638, and 'The case of missing money', *Brookings Papers on Economic Activity,* **7** (3), pp. 683–730.

168.   W.R. White, 'The demand for money in Canada and the control of monetary aggregates. Evidence from monthly data', *Bank of Canada Staff Research Studies,* **12,** 1976, p. 98.

169.   See P. Frost, 'Short-run fluctuations in the money multiplier and monetary control', Journal of Money, Credit and Banking, **9** (1), 1977, pp. 165–81.

170.   See the various Federal Reserve Bank of St. Louis studies.

171.   C.A. Sims, 'Money, income and causality' (see note 132).

172.   In this context see also R.E. Lucas, 'Econometric policy evaluation: a

critique', in K. Brunner and A.H. Meltzer (eds.), *The Phillips Curve and Labor Markets* (Amsterdam: North Holland, 1976), pp. 19–46; and T. Muench *et al.*, 'Tests for structural change and prediction intervals for reduced forms of two structural models of the US: the FRB-MIT and the Michigan quarterly models', *Annals of Economic and Social Measurement,* **3** (July), 1974, pp. 491–519.

173.   C.F. Christ, 'Judging the performance of econometric models of the US economy', *International Economic Review,* **16** (1), 1975, pp. 54–74.

174.   *Ibid.,* p. 54.   Christ goes further to argue that such models cannot be considered reliable guides to policy effects 'until it can be determined which of them are wrong in this respect and which if any are right'. Although this is quite correct, we may, nevertheless, note that this does not mean that these competing models cannot or should not be employed in policy design in a maxi-min setting of the kind described earlier in this paper.

175.   *Ibid.,* p. 59.

176.   *Ibid.*

177.   B. Friedman, 'The inefficiency of short-run monetary targets for monetary policy', p. 32 (see note 14).

178.   *Ibid.,* p. 67.

179.   See, for example, A.R. Holmes and P.D. Sternlight, 'The implementation of monetary policy in 1976', *Federal Reserve Bank of New York, Quarterly Review,* **2** (Spring), 1977, particularly pp. 41–9.

180.   In 1976, for example, the actual rate of growth of M_1 was outside the specified two month tolerance range in seven of the twelve overlapping periods and that of M_2 in six, while the Federal Funds rate was always within range. Indeed, in the three years since March 1975 the growth of M_1 was outside range about half the time whereas the Federal Funds rate hardly ever.

181   H.C. Wallich and P.M. Keir, 'The role of operating guides in US monetary policy', p. 44 (see note 18).

182.   *Ibid.*

183   R.G. Davis, 'Monetary objectives and monetary policy', p. 35 (see note 16).

184.   *Ibid.,* p. 36. Or as put by a member of the Board of Governors of the Federal Reserve: We '. . . continue to believe that the [appropriate] course is to limit the speed with which money market conditions are adjusted to changing monetary growth rates. We believe this partly because the monetary aggregates—particularly M_1— have proved to be inherently unstable in the short-run. Bulges of a month or two in duration are often reversed subsequently . . . Prudence in our actions is dictated also by the fact that the relationship between the various measures of monetary growth and the performance of the economy is loose and unreliable, since it is subject to rather abrupt shifts as a result of changing financial practices and economic conditions'. (C. Partee, Statement before the Subcommittee on Domestic Monetary Policy of the Committee on Banking Finance and Urban Affairs, U.S. House of Representatives, 27 September, 1977', *Federal Reserve Bulletin,* **57** (October), 1977).

185.   H.C. Wallich and P.M. Keir, 'The role of operating guides in US monetary policy', p. 47 (see note 18).

186.   A. Burns, Statement before the Committee on Banking, Finance and Urban Affairs, U.S. House of Representatives, 29 July, 1977; reprinted in the *Sixty-Fourth Report of the Board of Governors of the Federal Reserve System,* p. 98, emphasis added.

187.   See, for example, H.C. Wallich and P.M. Keir, 'The role of operating guides in US monetary policy', pp. 45–6 and 48–9 (see note 18); and S. Axilrod *et al.,* 'A proposal for redefining the monetary aggregates' (see note 137).
188.   See, for example, H.C. Wallich and P.M. Keir, 'The role of operating guides in US monetary policy', p. 44 (see note 18).
189.   A. Burns, *Federal Reserve Bulletin,* **55** (October), 1975, p. 627.
190.   P. Volcker, 'A broader role for monetary targets', p. 25 (see note 12).
191.   H.C. Wallich and P.M. Keir, 'The role of operating guides in US monetary policy', p. 47 (see note 18).
192.   A. Burns, Statement before the Committee on Banking, Finance and Urban Affairs (emphasis added) (see note 186).
193.   As Chairman G.W. Miller put it, 'While monetary aggregates are useful indicators of financial conditions, the continuing change in the institutional environment and in the public's preferences for different deposits indicates that any single monetary measure, or even a set of several measures, can by no means be the sole focus for policy. Thus a broad range of financial indicators—including nominal and real interest rates, credit flows and liquidity conditions—necessarily must be considered in assessing the stance of monetary policy' (Statement before the Committee on Banking, Finance and Urban Affairs, U.S. House of Representatives, 16 November, 1978; reprinted in *Federal Reserve Bulletin,* **58** (November), 1978, p. 847).
194.   B. Friedman, 'The inefficiency of short-run monetary targets for monetary policy' (see note 14).
195.   See D.W. Laidler and J.M. Parkin, 'The demand for money in the United Kingdom 1955–1967: preliminary estimates', *The Manchester School of Economic and Social Studies,* **38** (3), 1970, pp. 187–208; C.A.E. Goodhart and A.D. Crocket, 'The importance of money', *Bank of England Quarterly Bulletin,* **10** (2), 1970; and L.L.D. Price, 'The demand for money in the United Kingdom: a further investigation', *Bank of England Quarterly Bulletin,* **12** (1), 1972, pp. 43–55.
196.   One can find clear traces of this position in Keynes' *General Theory.*
197.   *Bank of England Quarterly Bulletin,* **6,** 1966, pp. 140–8. See also C.A.E. Goodhart, 'The gilt-edged market', in H.G. Johnson *et al.* (eds.), *Readings in British Monetary Economics* (Oxford: Clarendon Press, 1972); and A.S. Courakis, 'Monetary policy: old wisdom behind a new facade', *Economica,* **40** (157), 1973, pp. 73–86.
198.   Bank of England, 'The operation of monetary policy since Radcliffe', in D.R. Croome and H.G. Johnson (eds.), *Money in Britain 1959–1969* (Oxford: Oxford University Press, 1970), pp. 212–230. See also L.A. Dicks-Mireaux, 'Discussion paper', in *ibid.,* pp. 69–74.
199.   Select Committee on Nationalised Industries, *First Report on the Bank of England* (London: HMSO, 1970), p. xviii.
200.   C.A.E. Goodhart, 'Bank of England studies of demand for money function', in F. Masera *et al.* (eds.), *Econometric Research in European Central Banks* (Rome: Banca d'Italia, 1975), pp. 508 and 514.
201.   See, for example, G.A. Renton (ed.), *Modelling the Economy* (London: Heinemann, 1975); and M. Posner (ed.), *Demand Management* (London: Heinemann, 1978).
202.   See M.J. Artis and A.R. Nobay, 'Two aspects of the monetary debate', *National Institute Economic Review,* No. 49, August, 1969.

203.   A.D. Crockett, 'Timing relationships between movements of monetary and national income variables', *Bank of England Quarterly Bulletin*, **10** (4), 1970.
204.   C.A.E. Goodhart, 'Problems of monetary management: the UK experience', this volume, pp. 111–44.
205.   L.L.D. Price, 'The demand for money in the United Kingdom: a further investigation' (see note 195).
206.   C.A.E. Goodhart, 'Bank of England studies of demand for money function', p. 520 (see note 200).
207.   C.A.E. Goodhart, 'Problems of monetary management: the U.K. experience', this volume, pp. 111–44.
208.   See A.S. Courakis, 'Monetary policy: old wisdom behind a new facade' (see note 197).
209.   C.A.E. Goodhart, *Money Information and Uncertainty* (London: Macmillan, 1975), p. 235.
210.   C.A.E. Goodhart, 'Problems of monetary management: the U.K. experience', this volume, p. 132.
211.   R. Coghlan, 'A transactions demand for money', *Bank of England Quarterly Bulletin*, **18**, 1978, pp. 48–70.
212.   *Ibid.*, tables A and B.
213.   See, for example, G. Richardson, 'Reflections on the conduct of monetary policy' (see note 16), and Bank of England Economic Intelligence Department, 'Monetary targets in the United Kingdom' (see note 23).
214.   As mentioned earlier, the development of monetary sectors for the various British models is a rather recent phenomenon. Indeed it is only very recently that a monetary sector has been grafted onto the Treasury model (see P. Spencer and C. Mowl, 'The model of the domestic monetary system', in H.M. Treasury, A Financial Sector for the Treasury Model, Government Economic Service Working Paper No. 17, December, 1978). At the same time, British econometric models apparently exhibit a smaller degree of disagreement in simulation exercises of the impact of alternative (primarily fiscal) policies than that recorded by Carl Christ (see note 173) for the United States. Examining the effects of specific fiscal changes under alternative assumptions regarding interest rates (fixed vs. endogenous) J. Laury, G. Lewis and P. Ormerod conclude that their comparisons of the Treasury, National Institute and London Business School models encourages a 'less pessimistic' view than that recorded by Christ, since '. . . as far as the pattern of fiscal policy impacts is concerned, the British models are telling much the same story' ('Properties of Macroeconomic Models of the UK economy: a comparatie study', *National Institute Economic Review*, No. 83, February, 1978, pp. 52–65). One must, however, stress that agreement on *pattern* is hardly enough to ensure a successful stabilization policy based on a particular prior belief about the structure.
215.   L.D.D. Price, 'Monetary objectives and instruments of policy in the United Kingdom', p. 13 (see note 23). Or, as L.A. Dicks-Mireaux remarked, 'operating with monetary aggregate objectives implicitly assumes greater stability in the behaviour of financial markets than of goods markets. But to judge from the experience of the last three years, it would be difficult to assert with confidence which of the two markets had, in fact, exhibited the greater stability. Certainly as far as the available evidence about the working of the economic system is concerned, predictions of the course of the money stock have possibly been no more successful than predictions of the real

variables in the economy' (L.A. Dicks-Mireaux, 'British Monetary experience 1973–1977' (see note 23)).

216.   See, for example, L.D.D. Price, 'Monetary objectives and instruments of policy in the United Kingdom', pp. 14–15 (see note 23); and L.A. Dicks-Mireaux, 'British monetary experience 1973–1977', pp. 11–15 (see note 23).

217.   As L.A. Dicks-Mireaux (*ibid.*) notes 'in the absence of stable estimated demand for money functions the quantification and appropriateness of monetary targets has inevitably been in doubt'.

218.   G.A. Richardson, *Bank of England Quarterly Bulletin,* **17** (March), 1977, p. 50. See also Bank of England Economic Intelligence Department, 'Monetary targets in the United Kingdom', p. 5 (see note 23); and C.A.E. Goodhart, 'Bank of England studies of the demand for money function', pp. 509 and 517–58 (see note 200). And see also L.D.D. Price, 'Monetary objectives and instruments of policy in the United Kingdom', p. 9 (see note 23); L.A. Dicks-Mireaux, 'British monetary experience 1973–1977' (see note 23), both of whom proceed in subsequent pages to describe also the difficulties encountered in identifying the effects of monetary changes on other magnitudes such as investment and the price level. An informative survey of the effects of changes in monetary variables on various components of expenditure is presented in D. Savage, 'The channels of monetary influence: a survey of the empirical evidence', *National Institute Economic Review,* No. 83, 1978, pp. 73–89.

219.   See *Report of the Committee on the Workings of the Monetary System,* Cmnd. 827 (London: HMSO, 1959) for example para 39.

220.   See, for example, the section on adherence to targets in the Bank of England Economic Intelligence Department's 'Monetary targets in the United Kingdom' (see note 23).

221.   '. . . the authorities cannot always be sure as to how the expectations of agents [active in financial markets] will be affected by policy action' (L.A. Dicks-Mireaux, 'British monetary experience 1973–1977', p. 16 (see note 23)).

222.   G. Richardson, 'Reflections on the conduct of monetary policy', p. 11 (see note 16).

223.   L.A. Dicks-Mireaux, 'British monetary experience 1973–1977', p. 20 (see note 23).

224.   For a relevant bibliography, see S.F. Frowen, A.S. Courakis and M.H. Miller (eds.), *Monetary Policy and Economic Activity in West Germany* (London: Surrey University Press, 1977).

225.   'Longer-term movement of the money stock', *Deutsche Bundesbank Monthly Report,* **23** (7), 1971, p. 16.

226.   *Ibid.,* p. 18, emphasis added.

227.   *Deutsche Bundesbank Annual Report for the Year 1972,* p. 25.

228.   This is consistent, we may note, with the Bundesbank's 1970 finding that '. . . almost without exception the results of calculations in which variables [i.e. money and nominal income] of the same period were compared were better than results of calculations in which time-lags were assumed' (see 'Longer-term movement of the money stock', p. 15 (see note 225)).

229.   'Longer-term movement of the money stock', p. 14 (see note 225).

230.   *Ibid.*

231.   *Ibid.* In passing we may note that this conclusion rests on regressions that do

not jointly employ changes in income and interest rates so that the two appear to be seen as *alternatives*.

232.   *Ibid.,* pp. 14–15.

233.   See, for example, H. Schlesinger, 'Recent developments in West German monetary policy', in S.F. Frowen, A.S. Courakis and M.H. Miller (eds.), *Monetary Policy and Economic Activity in West Germany* (London: Surrey University Press, 1977), pp. 1–12.

234.   *Deutsche Bundesbank Annual Report for the Year 1966,* p. 40.

235.   *Deutsche Bundesbank Monthly Report,* **26** (July), 1974, p. 14. See also H. Bockelmann, 'Current problems of monetary policy in Germany', this volume, pp. 249–58.

236.   See, for example, H. Schlesinger, 'Recent developments in West German monetary policy', p. 3 (see note 233).

237.   *Ibid.,* p. 4. I should note, however, that there is some dissent from this view at least as regards terminology, see H. Bockelmann, 'Current problems of monetary policy in Germany', this volume.

238.   This seems to be more than terminological confusion since, as Schlesinger put it, '. . . the concept of central bank money is in this respect Janus-faced—serving both as a target and as indicator of policy—. . .' (H. Schlesinger, 'Recent experiences with monetary policy in the Federal Republic of Germany', *Kredit und Kapital,* **12,** 1979, p. 314).

239.   As opposed to references to the relationships between CBM and GNP and to the demand for CBM and other aggregates.

240.   *Deutsche Bundesbank Monthly Report,* **26** (12), 1974. This statement was repeated in the *Report of the Deutsche Bundesbank for the Year 1975* (published Spring, 1976), p. 9.

241.   *Report of the Deutsche Bundesbank for the Year 1975,* pp. 9–10. See also H. Bockelmann, 'Experience of the Deutsche Bundesbank with monetary targets', p. 8 (see note 32) and 'Current problems in monetary policy in Germany', this volume; *Deutsche Bundesbank Monthly Report,* **28** (1), 1976, p. 2; *Report of the Deutsche Bundesbank for the Year 1976,* p. 13; *Deutsche Bundesbank Monthly Report,* **29** (1), 1977.

242.   *Deutsche Bundesbank Monthly Report,* **28** (1), 1976, p. 6.

243.   See, for example, H. Bockelmann, 'Experience of the Deutsche Bundesbank with monetary targets', p. 2 (see note 32); and *Report of the Deutsche Bundesbank for the Year 1975,* p. 11.

244.   M. J. Parkin, 'A comparison of alternative techniques of monetary control under rational expectations', *The Manchester School of Economic and Social Studies,* **45** (December), 1978.

245.   Bockelmann is here quoting Ben Friedman (see note 121) and correspondingly the reference to uncertainty must be read to refer to stochastic disturbances, to 'risk' rather than 'uncertainty' that is.

246.   Notice that a connection between interest rates and the relationship of money to ultimate goal variables is recognized in this context. This may be interpreted to imply recognition that the ratio of money to nominal income depends on interest rates. But whether this carries over to the relationship between CBM and nominal GDP over and above cyclical correspondence between real GNP and interest rates or whether this is an 'in general' statement is unclear.

247.   H. Bockelmann, 'Quantitative targets for monetary policy in Germany', *Banque de France, Cahiers economiques et monetaires,* **6,** 1977, p. 12, emphasis in the original.

248.   Before discussing quantitative targets versus interest rate targets Bockelmann examines money versus credit. Curiously, given our discussion of earlier beliefs, he comments that 'Lending [to domestic non-banks] is . . . rarely proposed as an intermediate target' (*ibid.* p. 12).

249.   *Ibid.* pp. 12–13.

250.   In passing I should, however, draw the reader's attention to Bockelmann's remarks on the 'indicator' concept on p. 256 of this volume.

251.   See for example H. Bockelmann, 'Quantitative targets for monetary policy in Germany', p. 15 (see note 247).

252.   *Ibid.,* p. 16 for example.

253.   *Ibid.,* p. 14; H. Bockelmann, 'Experience of the Deutsche Bundesbank with monetary targets', p. 3 (see note 32); *Report of the Deutsche Bundesbank for the Year 1975,* p. 11. As Schlesinger put it: 'With a broad definition of the money stock, such as M3, it would be possible to eliminate interest-induced shifts between sight deposits and time deposits or between savings deposits and time deposits. But the more broadly the money stock is defined, the further away one moves from the assumed relationship between the expansion of the money stock and the increase in demand for goods and services. On the other hand the shifts cannot be ignored altogether. It has to be acknowledged that there is no clear-cut dividing line between money and other financial assets but only areas of declining "degrees of moneyness". This fact seemed to us to be adequately taken into account by the concept of central-bank money in which the relative "weights" of sight, time and savings deposits are 4 : 3 : 2. This weighting results from differing sizes of the minimum reserve ratios, which are graduated in the manner stated, in accordance with the degree of liquidity of deposits. This presumably makes better allowance from the "moneyness" of the deposits—at least in trend—than would a simple addition, as in M3, where the weighting is 1 : 1 : 1 (although here savings deposits for fixed periods are not included at all)'. H. Schlesinger, 'Recent experiences with monetary policy in the Federal Republic of Germany', p. 313 (see note 238).

254.   As was the case in the autumn of 1975 and more recently in the summer of 1978.

255.   See *Deutsche Bundesbank Monthly Report,* **27** (December), 1975, p. 12.

256.   O. Emminger, 'An "Interview" ', *The Banker,* **128** (October), 1977, pp. 97–8.

257.   See also A.S. Courakis, 'On unicorns and other such creatures: the case of the German central bank money stock', paper presented at the Seventh Money Study Group Conference, Oxford, September, 1978.

258.   *Deutsche Bundesbank Monthly Report,* **27** (February), 1975, p. 12; **29** (June), 1977, p. 9.

259.   *Deutsche Bundesbank Monthly Report,* **27** (September), 1975, p. 9.

260.   *Deutsche Bundesbank Monthly Report,* **30** (June) 1978, p. 17.

261.   *Deutsche Bundesbank Monthly Report,* **29** (January), 1977, p. 6.

262.   *Deutsche Bundesbank Monthly Report,* **31** (January), 1979, p. 6.

263.   *Ibid.*

264.   C.A.E. Goodhart, *Money, Information and Uncertainty,* p. 238 (see note 209).

265.   For implicitly there is, of course, no reason why the menu of alternative struc-

tures perceived by the policymaker should not include variants of models that recognize such responses.

266. One can instance A.C. Pigou's *A Study of Public Finance* (London: Macmillan, 1928), *announcement effect*, and certainly R.G. Hawtrey's *A Century of Bank Rate* (London: Longmans Green, 1939), *psychological effect*, in the context of the effect that policy acts have in changing the *prospect* which people think they have before them. See also J.R. Hicks, 'Automatists, Hawtreans and Keynesians', *Journal of Money, Credit and Banking*, 1 (3), 1969, pp. 307–17.

267. Econometric studies being prime examples, as R.E. Lucas, 'Econometric policy evaluation: A critique' (see note 172), forcefully reminded us.

268. B. Friedman, 'Comments and discussion on M.N. Baily's "Stabilization policy and private economic behavior" ', *Brookings Papers on Economic Activity*, 9 (1), 1978, p. 54.

269. J. Muth, 'Rational expectations and the theory of price movements', *Econometrica*, 29 (July), 1961, p. 316.

270. B. Friedman, 'Comments and discussion', p. 54 (see note 268).

271. See T.J. Sargent and N. Wallace, 'Rational expectations the optimal monetary instrument and the optimal money supply rule', *Journal of Political Economy*, 23, 1975, pp. 241–54.

272. *Ibid.*, p. 247.

273. *Ibid.*, p. 249; emphasis added to denote that, as Sargent and Wallace also show, if the goal function depends 'only on the variance of the price level then one deterministic rule is as good as any other'.

274. I chose to stress 'relevant horizon' since agreement on long-run neutrality is clearly not sufficient to secure consensus over the usefulness of monetary management. Keynes' reminder that 'in the long run we are all dead' renders a useful perspective in this context. But so does M. Friedman's view of the existence of 'a close connection between the role of government and time perspectives' mentioned in note 46 above.

275. T.S. Sargent and N. Wallace, 'Rational expectations the optimal monetary instrument and the optimal money supply rule', p. 249 (see note 271).

276. R.J. Barro and S. Fisher, 'Recent developments in monetary theory', *Journal of Monetary Economics*, 2, 1976, p. 162.

277. T.J. Sargent and N. Wallace, 'Rational expectations the optimal monetary instrument and the optimal money supply rule', p. 242 (see note 271).

278. *Ibid.*

279. To which one may add M. Friedman's optimum quantity of money option '. . . to hold the absolute quantity of money constant'; see *The Optimum Quantity of Money and Other Essays*, p. 46 (see note 44). See also K. Brunner, 'A survey of selected issues in monetary theory', pp. 20–5 (see note 55).

280. F. Modigliani, 'The monetary mechanism and its interaction with real phenomena', *Review of Economics and Statistics*, 45 (February), 1963, pp. 79–107.

281. S. Fisher, 'Long-term contracts, rational expectations and the optimal money supply rule', *Journal of Political Economy*, 85 (February), 1977, pp. 191–205.

282. B. Friedman, 'Comments and discussion', p. 55 (see note 276).

283. R.J. Barro and S. Fisher, 'Recent developments in monetary theory', p. 162 (see note 271).

284. S. Fisher, 'Long-term contracts, rational expectations and the optimal money

supply rule', p. 204 (see note 281).

285.   This is of course in close conformity with the traditional Keynesian analysis of stabilization policy in the context of sticky wages.

286.   See in particular K. Brunner, 'A survey of selected issues in monetary theory', pp. 2–19 (see note 55); K. Brunner and A. Meltzer, 'The uses of money: money in the theory of an exchange economy', *American Economic Review,* **61,** (5), 1971, pp. 785–805.

287.   G.L.S. Shackle, *Keynesian Kaleidics* (Edinburgh: Edinburgh University Press, 1974), p. 8.

288.   J.M. Keynes, *The General Theory of Employment Interest and Money,* (London: Macmillan, 1936), p. 238.

289.   F. A. Hayek, *Prices and Production* (London: George Routledge & Sons Ltd, 1934), p. 131.

290.   G.L.S. Shackle, 'Decision, order and time in human affairs', p. 283 (see note 150).

291.   G.L.S. Shackle, *Keynesian Kaleidics* (see note 287).

292.   See R.E. Lucas, 'Understanding business cycles', in K. Brunner and A.H. Meltzer (eds.), *Stabilization of the Domestic and International Economies,* Carnegie-Rochester Conference Series on Public Policy, Volume 5, 1977, particularly pp. 14–15.

293.   J.M. Keynes, *General Theory,* the discussion on the state of long-term expectations (see note 288); and G.L.S. Shackle, *Keynesian Kaleidics* (see note 287).

294.   G.L.S. Shackle, 'Decision, order and time in human affairs' (see note 150).

295.   *Ibid.,* p. 284.

296.   G. Myrdal, *Monetary Equilibrium* (London: William Hodge and Co., 1939), p. 148.

297.   M.N. Baily, 'Stabilization policy and private economic behavior', p. 13 (see note 268).

298.   See R.J. Gordon, 'International monetarism, wage push and monetary accommodation', this volume; also Maurice Scott, *Can We get back to Full Employment?* (London: Macmillan, 1978), particularly p. 36.

299.   G. Richardson, 'Reflections on the conduct of monetary policy', p. 7 (see note 16).

300.   P.A. Volcker, 'A broader role for monetary targets', pp. 8–9 (see note 12).

301.   *Deutsche Bundesbank Monthly Report,* **29** (January), 1977.

302.   *Bank of England Quarterly Bulletin,* **17**(3), 1977, p. 297.

303.   P.A. Volcker, 'A broader role for monetary targets', p. 9 (see note 12).

304.   This is true whether we compare actual performance to the rate of inflation embodied in the official announcements describing the choice of target value for CBM or whether we employ as our basis of comparison the *OECD Economic Outlook* forecasts for the implicit GNP deflator, or those for consumer prices, as presented in December of the year in which the yearly target is announced.

305.   See for example, H. Bockelmann, 'Quantitative targets for monetary policy in Germany', p. 17 (see note 247) and H. Schlesinger, 'Recent experiences with monetary policy in the Federal Republic of Germany', p. 312 (see note 238).

306.   G. Myrdal, *Monetary Equilibrium,* p. 135 (see note 296).

307.   H. Schlesinger, 'Recent experiences with monetary policy in the Federal Republic of Germany', p. 308 (see note 238).

308. *Ibid.*

309. E. Cannan, *The Paper Pound of 1797–1821* (London, 1919), p. 52; as quoted in E.V. Morgan, 'The Radcliffe report in the tradition of official British documents', in D.R. Croome and H.G. Johnson (eds.), *Money in Britain 1959–1969* (Oxford: Oxford University Press, 1970).

310. As quoted in J.M. Keynes, *The Treatise on Money,* Vol. II (London: Macmillan, 1930), p. 340.

311. *Ibid.*

312. *Ibid.,* pp. 341–2.

313. *Ibid.,* pp. 349–50.

314. *Ibid.,* pp. 350–1.

315. Committee on Finance and Industry, *Report,* Cmd 3897 (London: HMSO, 1931).

316. *Ibid.,* p. 5, emphasis added.

317. *Ibid.,* p. 129.

318. *Ibid.*

319. J.M. Keynes, *The General Theory of Employment, Interest and Money,* p. 378 (see note 288).

320. H.C. Simons, 'Rules versus discretion in monetary policy', *Journal of Political Economy,* **44,** 1936, pp. 1–30.

321. L.W. Mintz, *Monetary Policy for a Competitive Society* (New York: McGraw-Hill, 1950) pp. 224–5; and H.C. Simons, *Economic Policy for a Free Society* (Chicago: University of Chicago Press) pp. 174–5.

322. M. Friedman, 'The monetary theory and policy of Henry Simons', *Journal of Law and Economics,* **10** (October), 1967; reprinted in M. Friedman (ed.), *The Optimum Quantity of Money and Other Essays,* p. 83 (see note 43).

323. M. Friedman, *A Programme for Monetary Stability,* p. 86 (see note 43).

324. *Ibid.,* p. 100.

325. Committee on the Working of the Monetary System, *Report,* Cmnd. 827 (London: HMSO, 1959).

326. *Ibid.,* p. 132, paragraph 389, emphasis added.

327. *Ibid.,* p. 175, paragraph 490.

328. *Ibid.*

329. Committee on Finance and Industry, *Report,* p. 97 (see note 315).

330. *Ibid.*

331. F.T. Edgeworth, 'The mathematical theory of banking', *Journal of the Royal Statistical Society,* **51,** Part I (March), 1888, p. 127.

332. See also A.S. Courakis, 'Theories of consumption and consumption behaviour in the short-run', forthcoming.

333. See, for example, R. Coghlan, 'The transactions demand for money' (see note 211).

Aspects of the Oil Supply Problem

Robert Mabro

1. Introduction

The main themes of this paper are, first, that the energy crisis of 1973–74 was related to the existence of imbalances in the long-term structure of energy supplies; secondly, that neither politics nor the economics of mono-polies and cartels provide a sufficient explanation of the energy crisis; and, thirdly, that the imbalances may persist over the next ten or fifteen years with detrimental effects on the prospects of any sustained and significant world economic recovery. Further, the possibility of a second energy crisis in 1985 or soon after cannot be easily discounted.

The existence of structural imbalances suggests that neither market forces—even when allowed to operate in an unhindered fashion—nor tinkering with the usual instruments of fiscal and commercial policy can produce the rapid and significant adjustments needed to reconcile economic growth with a reasonable measure of price stability. Co-operation between major oil-consuming countries (say, OECD) and large oil-producing econo-mies (say, OPEC) may be one of the conditions needed to ensure economic recovery and to avoid a second energy crisis. Co-operation may involve a difficult international agreement on such matters as prices, rates of oil depletion, investment programmes for new sources of energy as well as special provisions relating to the economic development of producer coun-tries and to the international placement of 'surplus funds'.

There are all too many obstacles in the way of international co-operation in the field of energy. The probability attached to the successful conclusion of an agreement between oil producers and consumers may not be very high. The incentive to work out such an agreement or to arrive at a meaningful and effective understanding may not be very strong because consuming country governments are at present more concerned with price stability and balance-of-payments equilibrium than with economic growth. In addition there are, of course, a host of political factors and conflicts of interests which could inhibit significant attempts at co-operation. Yet the task is both urgent and important. To stress this simple truth, again and yet again may sharpen perceptions and contribute to some modest increase in the probability of success.

2. Alternative Concepts of an Energy Crisis

The oil events of late 1973 which are now being referred to as the 'energy crisis of 1973-74' by oil consuming countries and as 'the oil revolution' by OPEC members were preceeded by much talk and predictions about impending crises. The views expressed in 1972 and 1973 were so varied as to make one wonder whether the actual events fulfilled any particular prediction and if so which? Yet these various views have survived the events and the conventional wisdom of today seems to incorporate them all. A critical review may be called for from the outset.

One conception of the energy crisis relates to the fact that oil is a depletable resource and that rapid economic growth, given the very high levels of *per capita* consumption of non-reproducible resources in the advanced countries, will lead to exhaustion. Specific predictions about the world running out of oil were made at a time when attention was being drawn by the Club of Rome to the more general issues of the *Limits to Growth*. All that was, and still is, the subject of controversy. The view that economic growth is 'bad' is contentious; the relationship between such views and those of various movements for the protection of the environment, and finally the almost explicit reference to Doomsday arouse certain suspicions.

It remains true, however, that natural resources are finite and that rapid economic growth sustained over long periods may involve significant social diseconomies which should be weighed against the benefits. Some economists would argue that the exhaustion of a natural resource will be signalled well ahead of time by rising prices, and these in turn will induce wide-ranging adjustments and stimulate technical progress. But there are serious qualifications. Firstly, prices do not always reflect market forces as they may be interfered with by, say, governments (as indeed for oil in the United States and elsewhere). Secondly, future markets do not fulfil their theoretical function of arbitrators between the present and all future points of time because they only deal in the real world with short contracts. Thirdly, technical progress often involves long 'lead-in times' and, of course, much uncertainty. In short, I do not share the 'eschatological' concept of the energy crisis, nor do I believe in dire predictions about catastrophes conveniently set for the end of a century which happens to coincide with the end of a millenium. The truth is less spectacular. Yet, important and valid points about resource supplies constraining growth, problems of conservation, and,

concerned with the science of the 4 last things —

Table 1. U.S. annual production, consumption and imports of oil 1965–75 (million tonnes).

Year	1965	1966	1967	1968	1969	1970	1971	1972	1973	1974	1975
Production	431.2	458.0	487.9	506.7	515.1	537.5	530.0	532.2	519.0	496.7	473.2
Consumption	548.9	575.6	595.8	635.5	667.8	694.6	719.3	775.8	818.0	782.6	764.2
Imports	127	133	131	147	163	176	201	242	316	315	300

Source: BP Statistical Review of the World Oil Industry 1975.

perhaps, the need to plan replacement in sufficient time, should not be lost in the controversy.

There also were political conceptions of the energy crisis. They emanated mainly from the United States. Various lobbies and centres of powers began to worry in the early 1970s about the growing gap between domestic production of hydrocarbons and their consumption in the United States. In fact oil production began to decline steadily after 1970, the year during which output reached its peak, while consumption, always at a higher level, continued to rise until the events of 1973. Growing dependence on oil imports was perceived as a dangerous strategic weakness for a super-power. Furthermore, new imports were expected to come increasingly from the Middle East and Africa, that is from areas judged politically unstable. Disruptions were possible and, because of the United States involvement as ally of one of the parties to the Arab–Israeli conflict, there were fears that the United States would lose some degrees of freedom in foreign policy. It seems that somebody succeeded in extrapolating the U.S. energy problem to the world at large; the strategic U.S. problem of import dependence was transposed as a world energy crisis. Some commentators have suggested that the transposition was deliberate. Some powerful American lobbies worried by increased dependency for oil on imports might have actively sought significant rises in world oil prices in order to encourage the development of domestic oil and gas production and to induce investment in oil substitutes. They might have found it useful to create an atmosphere of world crisis in order to remove objections to investment in nuclear power stations and in the Alaska pipeline, and in order to induce a momentum in favour of 'energy independence'. There is no need to discuss here the merits of conspiratorial theories.

Oilmen had different perceptions. They announced the crisis, thus incurring the wrath of those who believed that they were making money out of self-fulfilling prophecies. The oilmen's argument consisted of two main elements: firstly a linear projection of demand for OPEC oil (which, by the way, was growing at an accelerating rate in the late 1960s and early 1970s, while aggregate demand for oil was rising at a high but steady rate), and secondly an analysis of the alleged behaviour of Arab oil-producing countries. The linear projection of demand for OPEC oil showed that Saudi Arabia would have to produce some 20 million barrels per day by 1980 in order to satisfy world requirements. The demand projection, when set against supply forecast and data on expected discovery, also revealed a dramatic fall in the reserve to production ratios during the 1980s. Arab oil-producing countries were expected to react to the situation by choosing to keep oil in the ground. To sell the quantities demanded from them, even at relatively moderate prices, would lead to the accumulation of unwanted surplus funds. The assumption, of course, was that the absorptive capacity of desert economies was low. The oil companies thought until June or July 1973 that the posted price of crude would be set a U.S. $5 a barrel in 1975 at the expiration of the Tehran agreement. It was set at U.S. $5.119 on 16 October 1973 and at U.S. $11.651 on 1 January 1974! The producer government revenue per barrel (marker crude) rose from U.S. $1.82 to U.S. $3.45 in October 1973 and to U.S. $9.31 in January 1974.

The oil companies' predictions provided the arguments which some U.S. interests needed to proclaim the imminence of an energy crisis. Some of the arguments were distorted by other interests who interpreted the energy crisis in terms of a political bogey, the Arabs. The Arabs were going to hold the world at ransom not only through the control of oil supplies, but also through the control of huge liquid assets placed with international private banks in major financial centres. The impending energy crisis was seen as an act of political aggression involving two weapons: oil and money. Pro-Zionist lobbies promoted at first the political bogey, and then changed their minds lest the United States and other Western powers took the danger too seriously and made political concessions which would weaken Israel. Hence their campaign suggested at times that the oil companies had invented the energy crisis, and on other occasions that OEPC is a cartel which would have behaved as a cartel whether the Arab–Israeli conflict existed or not. The message is abundantly clear: if the Arab–Israeli conflict is irrelevant to the issue of oil supplies, no change in the foreign policy of the powers *vis-à-vis* the Middle East is required for a solution of the energy crisis.

The various sets of perceptions which led different observers to expect a 'political' energy crisis in or after 1975 and a 'geo-physical' crisis some time between 1990 and 2000 contain, of course, elements of truth. The growing import dependence of the United States is a fact; whether this dependence makes the country vulnerable to pressures which it could not resist by other means is a matter of opinion. A continual, one should say an exponential, increase in world demand for oil would have led to a very significant fall in the reserve/production ratios—the signal that physical scarcities will soon set limits to supply, but why should anyone expect the price of oil to remain invariant in conditions of rapid demand growth or, alternatively, think that the rate-of-demand increases will not be adversely affected by price increases? The problems of absorptive capacity are real; but recent experience has revealed that governments do not find it difficult to spend. The difficulty, rather, is to invest profitably. Finally, the temptation to 'keep oil in the ground' may be strong, but the ability to withstand the political pressures of big oil-consuming countries (prone to discern threats of economic strangulation even when reasonable oil conservation measures are applied by producers) should not be taken for granted.

3. The Economics of the Oil Crisis

Crude oil is a natural resource. Ultimate availabilities are unknown. But at any point of time there are known reserves—the ready-shelf inventory of the industry in Adelman's terminology[1]. Production draws from reserves. Productive capacity can be increased in the short-term through development expenditures, which enable a higher rate of output from proven reserves and which may lead, up to a point, to some additional reserves being proven from known fields. Exploration is a different process whose aim is to discover new fields, hence to make substantial additions to reserves. Development of existing fields may involve surprises but the results, in general, are not too uncertain. Exploration entails greater uncertainties. The rate of new discoveries, that is the rate of additions to reserves, in conjunction with the rate of growth of demand is a critical variable for the oil industry.

Because of a strong element of chance in the timing and size of new discoveries, the total supply curve of the industry is liable to move to the right at an erratic pace. One possible pattern is slow movement over a relatively long period of time followed by a sudden and very significant shift. The latter occurrence may cause a temporary upheaval in the market, forcing prices down to the point where oil would be wasted in a variety of ways. Such a situation invites some form of regulation. The discovery of East Texas in 1930, which added enormous amounts to availabilities at a time when the Great Depression was causing a severe reduction in demand, is an important illustration of these dramatic shifts in supply which lead to regulation. In the United States supplies were then administered by the Texas Railroad Commission and similar organisations.

Gluts are followed by fears of shortages almost as surely as night follows day. Demand continues to grow in an inexorable way while the supply curve moves ahead in its erratic fashion. There is glut when a significant discovery takes place, fears of shortages when supplies seem to expand sluggishly in relation to demand. The oil industry is always in need of some regulation.

Consider the broad features of the supply equation during the past 30 years. Significant discoveries took place in the 1940s in Kuwait and Saudi Arabia. The total availability curve moved far out to the right. A long supply wave starting at around 1945 and ending some time ahead, in the 1980s perhaps, characterizes the recent history of the oil industry.

The advent of massive sources of supply just after World War II transferred the centre of gravity of the world oil industry from the Gulf of Mexico to that other Gulf in the Middle East. It stimulated until the early 1970s, through low prices, the growth of oil demand and the substitution of oil for coal and other solid fuels. The availability of a cheap energy input must have contributed to economic growth, to the unprecedented achievement of high and sustained rates over some 25 years (late 1940s to early 1970s) in industrialized countries. Of course, there was regulation by the Seven Sisters—orderly markets and, initially at least, prices higher than might have obtained had the new supplies been allowed to exercise their full disruptive effects. History will later judge whether the major oil companies in pursuing their own interest gave the world a good turn.

New suppliers entered the scene in the 1960s, some 15 or 20 years after Kuwait and Saudi Arabia—first Libya and then Nigeria and Abu Dhabi. But these shifts in the total availability curve (which, at the time, created an impression of glut, led to an erosion of the real price of crude oil, and gave rise to Adelman's famous predictions about 'one-dollar' oil) were not very significant compared to the growth in demand. Libya, the largest of these new producers, peaked sooner than expected; Nigeria's development was interrupted by the Civil War; and Abu Dhabi, immediately successful because it provided a sweet and clean crude[2], could not be compared in quantitative size to either Kuwait or Saudi Arabia. The point is that these new suppliers emerged at a time when both levels and annual increments of world demand were manifoldly larger than in the late 1940s and early 1950s. Their contribution to total availabilities was smaller both in absolute terms and relative to the state of demand than the earlier additions provided by the big Middle Eastern fields.

Hence the sudden change in perceptions: all observers were talking of glut until 1970 and 1971 and then began to look ahead and realized that the rate of discovery was not sufficient to sustain growth in the two decades ahead. Any observer with eyes fixed on the present and the immediate future could legitimately argue that availabilities were more than adequate—the proven and probable reserves are very large especially in the Middle East. But the medium and long-term are also extremely important because of the time lags involved in changing the structure of both energy supplies and energy uses.

The total availability curve could shift once again in a very significant manner[3] at some future date. Nobody at present expects such a phenomenon for the next ten years, save perhaps in Iraq. A new supply epoch would be inaugurated by a very major discovery. The implications for the world petroleum market will depend, among other things on where the discovery takes place—Iraq, or the United States, the Soviet Union or China? And the fascinating questions for futurologists are: which country or group would then succeed in regulating the market, and what would be the mode of control?

If none of that happens the supply epoch begun after World War II would end some years ahead. This does not mean that the world will soon run out of oil. In fact the 'oil mountain' may not peak before 1990 on present demand and supply forecasts. The end of an epoch is defined in dynamic terms with reference to the rate of discoveries.

The situation today is that we can see the end of a supply epoch and not yet the beginning of the next one[4]. These perceptions provide an important background to the understanding of the 'oil crisis' though they do not explain by themselves why prices should have risen in the manner they did.

4. The Emergence of OPEC

Oil is a primary commodity exported by a small number of developing countries. It is a depletable material resource. Historically, the processes of discovery, development, production and exports were in the hands of a few major Western companies. They were seen by their apologists as agents of development and by their detractors as agents of imperialism. The truth is that they did the work and appropriated that share of the returns which reflected the current balance of power. Their operations in Third World countries began during the colonial period and continued well beyond the decolonization era which followed World War II. The other important feature of oil is that its production in OPEC countries involves very small amounts of domestic factors. In fact the total contribution of labour and capital equipment to crude oil production is small. Oil production tends to generate a rent which reflects at different times a varying combination of monopolistic elements and an implicit 'depletion' allowance. As there were always two agents with claims on the rent (the government representing the national ownership of the resource and the companies, the necessary inter-mediaries between the ultimate seller and the ultimate buyers) bargaining became inherent to the relationship between the oil-exporting countries and companies holding concessions.

The implications of all that are obvious. The developing country which has entered into agreement about a share of the mineral rent with a foreign company in the context of colonial relationships is bound to resent the agreement and will attempt to claim full sovereignty rights over the natural resource. Mexico nationalized oil before World War II. Mossadeg of Iran made an attempt in 1950 and although he failed for all practical purposes, the principle of national ownership was upheld in the ensuing settlement. Saudi Arabia—hailed as the most moderate country in OPEC—was the driving force, in the late 1960s, behind the demand for equity participation by the state in the concessions. The desire to exercise full sovereignty is a very powerful force.

The frustrations associated with the struggle to fulfil that desire, and the perception that solidarity between agents on one side could increase their bargaining power in negotiations with agents on the other side explain why an organization like OPEC should be established. But it is interesting to note that the organization could not have been founded at the beginning of the supply epoch described above. It is perhaps no accident that the idea of an association of oil-exporting countries, propagated by Venezuela in the late 1940s and early 1950s, did not materialize until 1960. At the end of World War II, Venezuela was an 'old producer' already established in the world market. Kuwait and Saudi Arabia were 'new producers' who had not yet acquired an adequate share of the market. In 1960, Venezuela, Iraq, Iran, Saudi Arabia and Kuwait were all established producers. They could now join together to protect their economic interests threatened by unilateral reductions in the posted price of oil decreed by the companies without having to worry too much about their market shares. And they did. Libya, the newcomer of the time, joined OPEC in 1962 but did not toe the line immediately. To secure a place on the market, Libya at first breached the OPEC fiscal rule[5] and allowed independent oil companies to pay taxes on the basis of *realized* rather than of the then higher *posted* prices. It revoked that concession a few years later having quickly established itself as a major producer in the buoyant market of the 1960s.

OPEC did not achieve spectacular results in the 1960s. Its existence was something like a signal to the companies that producers could get together and show symbolically some psychological solidarity. OPEC was not yet an effective force. But small and inconspicuous achievements—halting the fall in posted prices, securing minor tax advantages, establishing the principle of similar treatment for all members, etc.—built its confidence and strength.

Major sucesses were scored in 1970 and 1971 through the Tripoli and Tehran agreements. But these were not the result of concerted OPEC action. Paradoxically, all was then achieved by Libya who, on joining the organization, breached the rules. But Libya benefited in 1970 from a very strong position in its own market, produced by the expanding demand for oil which was clean at a time when environmental awareness was heightened, and close to Europe when (and this is the more significant factor) there was a temporary bottleneck in tanker transportation. OPEC was truly born in 1973. A story to which we now turn.

5. The Economic Mechanism of Price Increases

The events of late 1973 are now better understood with the benefit of hindsight. As mentioned earlier, the main feature of the petroleum market before October 1973 was a steady growth of the demand for oil and accelerated growth of exports from OPEC. By the summer of 1973 most OPEC members were operating either close to capacity or close to a ceiling determined by long-term conservation objectives[6]. As seen in table 2, Saudi Arabia, despite its huge reserves and possibilities of rapid development in productive capacity, was temporarily stretched. The world economy was booming at the time. The expected expansion in demand for oil during the winter of 1973/4 could only be supplied by OPEC (as there were no significant amounts of idle capacity outside OPEC and, even worse, prospects of declining production in the United States). In fact, Saudi Arabia was expected to supply on its own a large proportion of world incremental demand.

The medium-term outlook was not much different. If growth continued, even at a moderate rate, every OPEC country would have found itself

Table 2. Oil production compared to installed capacity in OPEC— September 1973 (million barrels per day).

Countries	Installed capacity	Production
Venezuela	3.5	3.4
Ecuador	0.2	0.2
Algeria	1.1	1.0
Libya	2.8	2.3
Nigeria	2.1	2.1
Iraq	2.2	2.2
Kuwait	3.5	3.2
Saudi Arabia	9.0	8.3
Neutral Zone	0.5	0.5
Abu Dhabi	1.6	1.4
Qatar	0.6	0.6
Dubai	0.3	0.3
Iran	6.0	5.8
Indonesia	1.3	1.3
Total	34.7	32.6

Note: Though installed capacity is estimated at 2.8 mbd in Libya and 3.5 mbd in Kuwait, the relevant concept for these countries is the conservation ceiling. It is worth noting that both Libya and Kuwait were operating in September 1973 above their preferred ceilings (2.0 mbd and 2.5 mbd respectively).

Source: Petroleum Intelligence Weekly. Also data from a major oil company.

operating close to capacity and Saudi Arabia willy-nilly would have been engaged in a race between production and development of capacity. No relief from the North Sea could be expected before the end of the 1970s. Alaskan oil then appeared to be a remote proposition since the construction of the pipeline was effectively blocked. And it is doubtful whether the pre-October 1973 price of oil would have induced much investment in petroleum substitutes.

In such a situation prices are bound to rise. When the powerful economic forces described above are in operation, politics need not intervene for prices to increase. As it happened, political factors and events appeared to occupy the front of the stage in late 1973. They were much in evidence and nobody should be blamed for thinking that they did all the work. My belief is that they helped in some ways. The Arab–Israeli War provided a convenient timing. The short-lived embargo enabled producers to discover that some buyers in a market subjected to minor supply restrictions were willing to seek oil for seven or eight times the going price. But the political factors were not the cause of the price rise. The increase would not have been possible if the market were slack, and had it obtained fortuitously nothing would have made it stick. The conspicuous presence of political actors on the scene concealed the operation of economic forces which alone explain why prices were subject to strong upward pressures. Politics may be necessary, but it is the market which ultimately provides the determining conditions.

The mechanism through which economic forces indicate to OPEC members that the time for an upward revision of their adminstered price has come is fairly simple. Pressures on productive capacity in some countries signal the existence of excess demand for certain varieties of crude. Rises in the spot price for these varieties in Rotterdam and other markets accompany the emergence of excess demand, a concomitant signal. Producing countries are strongly induced to consider an upward adjustment whenever the market starts pushing consistently the *spot* above the *official* price. All that happened in 1973 and it happened again in the second half of 1976 with a difference. In the latter instance, stock building in anticipation of a price rise (that buyers associated with strong expectations of an *economic* recovery) was a significant component of the growth in demand which, thus, appeared to be transitory.

The argument is often made that Saudi Arabia could always satisfy excess demand when a boom takes place and that prices need not rise if Aramco is then allowed to increase output. But that argument if correct simply reinforces the economic explanation. In a supply structure where small producers hit capacity, and a single large producer has control over incremental supplies prices will naturally tend to rise. When the expansion of demand begins to stretch the small exporting countries, all the monopoly power becomes vested with the incremental supplier. Yet, two further elements must be considered. First, Saudi Arabia does not always have much idle capacity available for *immediate* expansion of export during a boom. The bottlenecks tend to arise in offtake rather than production facilities. Saudi Arabia, of course, can always develop these facilities and remove the bottlenecks soon after they arise. The point, already mentioned, is that Saudi Arabia in a boom could find itself engaged in a race in which expanding production and offtake continually hit against a shifting capacity constraint.

Secondly, Saudi Arabia faces a long-term conservation problem. The country has a long temporal horizon for economic development. There is a deep awareness in government of the difficulties in effecting a rapid transition from underdevelopment to modern industrialization. Oil will be needed later as much as (if not more than) it is needed now. To respond passively to the demands of a thirsty consuming world and agree to supply 12, 15 or 20 million barrels a day just when this suits importing countries, at the risk of depleting the reserves too soon is not a very attractive proposition. Economically, the financial assets received in exchange for oil are difficult to place in inflation-proof havens. Politically and socially, high rates of output would be resented as waste by the country almost in the same way as the flaring of associated gas. This would not surprise the reader familiar with the early history of the petroleum industry in the United States and the strong emotional connotations attached to the concepts of waste and conservation. In any case, the issue is not purely emotional. It reflects legitimate social views about time preferences and risks.

The Saudi reluctance to rush and develop productive capacity to the point necessary to flood the market and break the OPEC price is not vulgar monopolistic practice. A monopoly restricts output in order to raise prices. The Saudis want to produce within a ceiling related to long-term objectives. What is at issue, primarily, is the changing composition of their portfolio of assets—oil, foreign financial papers, productive and infrastructural equipment at home—over time. The movable ouput ceiling naturally influences the level of oil prices. But it is important to realize, for a proper understanding of OPEC and of Saudi behaviour, that the general production policy seems more related to broad long-term objectives than to short-run profit maximization through restrictive practices.

6. Critical Limits of Oil Supplies

OPEC strength partially depends on a peculiar supply structure. When demand for OPEC oil collapsed in 1975 following the world economic recession, the organization was able to hold the price line. The argument often made is that OPEC is a cartel and that cartels if they are effective will, indeed, hold the price line. It is also said that cartels do not retain their power for very long, they tend to collapse fairly quickly. The informed reader knows however that OPEC has never succeeded in devising or implementing a pro-rationing system. The Organization does not control the allocation of output between members and does not have a say in the output ceilings which individual countries may choose to set for a variety of technical, economic, or political reasons. OPEC held the line in the very depressed market of 1975 without attempting to fix output. Saudi Arabia kept the reference price—the price of Arabian light 34° API—fixed and implicitly allowed other members to find, by a process of trial and error, the correct price differentials for their own varieties of crude petroleum[7]. This means that Saudi Arabia absorbed from month to month all the fluctuations transmitted through the actions of other OPEC members—now under-pricing, now overpricing their oil, in search of the right level. Saudi Arabia acted as a bufferstock in the depression. It could afford to play that role because of certain characteristics of its productive capacity, which is both large and flexible, and because its average oil revenues are much higher than the level of expenditures. Paradoxically, Saudi Arabia did not lose in terms of its relative share of the market in that game. On the contrary, the average percentage loss in its output during the depression was smaller than the percentage drop in total OPEC output. In short, OPEC can hold the price line in a depression largely because the supply system is endowed with a natural (hence, costless) bufferstock. It is generally agreed, however, that a persistent decline of offtake around or below 22–24 million barrels a day could strain, but may not break, the solidarity of OPEC. In 1975 offtake remained slightly above this *critical lower limit.*

There is a *critical upper limit* to the offtake from OPEC which is bound to trigger significant price rises if producers feel that demand will continue to press on that supply constraint. This limit was approached in the third and fourth quarter of 1976. I tend to put it, for 1976, at around 32–33 million barrels per day. This figure is easily justified. Total installed capacity in OPEC was estimated at 38.8 million barrels per day in that year by *Petro-Leum Intelligence Weekly.* The breakdown is shown in table 3. The capacity level attributed to Nigeria is notional as it has never been approached even during the strongest boom in favour of Nigerian crude. A level of 2.3 mbd seems to be more realistic. Kuwait and Libya have explicit conservation limits at 2.5 and 2.0 mbd respectively. Relevant capacity in OPEC (excluding Saudi Arabia) was probably closer to 25 mbd than to the 27.2 mbd shown by the table. Now, I very much doubt whether Saudi Arabia had export facilities consistent with an output level of 11.5 mbd. The relevant capacity was probably of the order of 9.5 mbd and the aggregate capacity figure for OPEC, 34/34.5 mbd. When actual production approaches such a limit within a margin of say 5 per cent—say 32–33 mbd in 1976—the supply system begins to lose its flexibility. Excess demand for this or that variety of crude may begin to appear and small technical accidents can frustrate *ex ante* offtake plans. This upper critical limit, defined at around 32–34 mbd in

Table 3. Estimated installed capacity, 1976 (million barrels per day).

Country	Capacity	Country	Capacity
Saudi Arabia	11.50	Venezuela	2.75
Iran	6.60	Nigeria	2.70
Kuwait	3.00	Libya	2.50
Neutral Zone	0.50	Indonesia	1.75
Iraq	2.80	Algeria	1.10
Abu Dhabi	2.00	Gabon	6.25
Dubai	0.33	Ecuador	0.22
Sharjah	0.05	Total	11.27
Qata	0.65		
Total	27.43	Grand Total	38.80

Source: *Petroleum Intelligence Weekly,* **15** (44), 1976, p. 11.

1976, shifts forward from year to year. The rate of expansion may well be in the order of 1 mbd a year (on odd occasions 1.5 mbd).

The years 1975 and 1976 may well have been unusual. But the remarkable feature of OPEC offtake is that during a short period of 12 months it approached once the lower (October 1975, output 25.2 mbd) and once the upper limit (October 1976, output 32.8 mbd). There was some economic recovery in between, but not much. There was a stock building cycle. The 1976/7 winter was not expected to be very cold. The message is simple. Any combination of say two out of these three factors—accelerated rate of activity, stock building, cold weather—could well bring OPEC output up against the upper limit. Alternatively, depressions, mild winters and running down of stock could bring output down by several million barrels a day in a fairly short period of time.

7. Conclusions

Looking at the future is a risky exercise. To predict what may happen to OPEC and the price of oil depends crucially on two unknowns: the rate and the timing of world economic recovery. In the last years of the 1970s and early 1980s the oil supply system will have to absorb a net increment of some 5–6 million barrels a day from non-OPEC countries. New energy sources—nuclear, coal etc.—will not make a strong impact on total supplies and it is doubtful whether economies in use will be very significant unless governments supplement the price effect by quantitative regulations. A moderate growth of world demand (outside the USSR, East Europe and China) of say 3 per cent per annum, would very quickly absorb the extra 6 million barrels (3 to 3.5 years between say 1978 and 1981). OPEC may find itself pushed down towards the critical lower limit if an economic depression coincides with the emergence of new oil supplies at the end of the decade. But OPEC would be easily in a strong position in any of these years if they witness a boom. The question, of course, is 'could a boom really gather momentum?' And the answer is 'probably not'. Not necessarily because OPEC would rush prematurely with a price increase but because the spot market will force price rises, inducing OPEC to ratify the market verdict, as soon as the supply system begins to feel the strain. The best timing for an economic boom, from the consuming country point of view, is 1979/80, the worst 1977/78. A depression in 1979–80 would subject OPEC to stresses. Ironically this may not serve the long-term interests of the consuming world. A significant fall in the real price of oil at the end of this decade may kill any incentive to go ahead with investment plans in substitutes. And the final sobering thought is that whatever happens at the end 1970s and in early 1980s, a second energy crisis would be looming on the horizon. The normal growth in demand would soon absorb the new supplies of 1979–80. Significant new sources are not in sight until the late 1980s. The world economy may well go through a difficult impasse in or around 1985.

The emphasis in this paper has been on structural problems. The essence of structural problems is that they cannot be removed by adjustments at the margin. A good international agreement between producers and consumers could help the smooth, but long passage of the world economy from a situation of structural imbalances to a stage characterized by new structures of energy supplies and use. But governments are too short-sighted and the immediate conflict of interests are too sharp to warrant much optimism.

NOTES

1. M.A. Adelman, *The World Petroleum Market* (Baltimore: John Hopkins University Press, 1972).
2. A low sulphur content crude much in demand at the time when environmental conciousness was at its height in Japan and the United States.
3. Alaska and the North Sea resemble more the Libyan addition of the 1960s than the Saudi Arabian.
4. The next supply epoch could involve either oil or substitutes, or both. That nothing much is in sight at present does not mean that nothing will ever emerge on the horizon.
5. E.T. Penrose, *The Large International Firm in Developing Countries* (London: Allen and Unwin, 1968), p. 205.
6. Kuwait and Libya had imposed conservation ceilings considerably earlier.
7. Crude petroleum is not a homogeneous product. Variations can be measured in terms of gravity and sulphur content. As petroleum is a tightly traded commodity, location becomes an important characteristic of the product.

Index